Political Risk and the Institutional Environment for
Foreign Direct Investment in Latin America

T0316442

Göttinger Studien zur Entwicklungsökonomik
Göttingen Studies in Development Economics

Herausgegeben von/Edited by Hermann Sautter

Bd./Vol. 15

PETER LANG

Frankfurt am Main · Berlin · Bern · Bruxelles · New York · Oxford · Wien

Jörg Stosberg

Political Risk
and the Institutional
Environment for Foreign
Direct Investment
in Latin America

An Empirical Analysis
with a Case Study on Mexico

PETER LANG
Europäischer Verlag der Wissenschaften

Bibliographic Information published by Die Deutsche Bibliothek
Die Deutsche Bibliothek lists this publication in the Deutsche
Nationalbibliografie; detailed bibliographic data is available in
the internet at <http://dnb.ddb.de>.

Zugl.: Göttingen, Univ., Diss., 2004

D 7
ISSN 1439-3395
ISBN 3-631-53346-2
US-ISBN 0-8204-7659-5

© Peter Lang GmbH
Europäischer Verlag der Wissenschaften
Frankfurt am Main 2005
All rights reserved.

All parts of this publication are protected by copyright. Any
utilisation outside the strict limits of the copyright law, without
the permission of the publisher, is forbidden and liable to
prosecution. This applies in particular to reproductions,
translations, microfilming, and storage and processing in
electronic retrieval systems.

Printed in Germany 1 2 3 4   6 7

www.peterlang.de

Editor's Preface

One of the most important aspects of globalization is the intensification of international capital flows. The rapid development of information technology and decreasing transaction costs created an international environment characterized by an increasing volatility of financial transactions. For developing countries, which are in urgent need of external financing, capital volatility poses problems, as the probability of financial crisis rises. It has been shown that Foreign Direct Investment is a less volatile source of external financing. Therefore, the attraction of Foreign Direct Investment is a viable option for developing countries that want to ensure external capital flows. Moreover, this kind of financing is connected with the transfer of technology, with an improved acces to foreign markets and (possibly) with positive external effects on the domestic economy. Foreign Direct Investment decisions, in turn, depend to a large extent on the decisions of multinational enterprises. Besides other factors political risks like expropriation, political instabilities, riots and so on influence these decisions to a large degree.

This volume empirically analyzes the impact of political risk on Foreign Direct Investment flows to Latin America. Additional evidence is given by an in-depth case study on Mexico. As a theoretical basis the author presents a macroeconomic model with microecomic foundations that explains the reaction of investors to the emergence of political risk. Furthermore, the book offers a theoretical foundation and classification of political risk factors. The empirical analysis shows that governance is the most important political risk while catastrophic risk factors as the risk of turmoil are of lesser importance. These results highlight the importance of good governance in developing countries which are eager to actively participate in the process of globalization. The author shows that political institutions "matter" for economic outcomes and highlights the importance of institutional reform to further strenghten the attractiveness of Latin America for foreign investors. With these theoretical and empirical results, Dr. Stosberg provides a valuable contribution to the literature on political risks of Latin America.

Hermann Sautter

Göttingen, September 2004

Acknowledgements

Writing a PhD thesis often is an autistic project leaving the author alone with his thoughts, his ideas, his frustrations and his problems. Nevertheless, the publication of this work would not have been possible without the support and the help of many other people. First of all I have to thank my academic teacher and supervisor Professor Dr. Sautter for his ability to give me freedom for my research while still being there with his support when it was needed. I am also very grateful to Professor Dr. König for co-supervising the thesis and to Prof. Dr. Betz for the kind participation in the final examination. Furthermore, I am grateful for the help and support of my colleagues at the Ibero-Amerika Institute in Goettingen and in particular to Dr. Felicitas Nowak-Lehmann whose knowledge in empirical research methods and willingness to comment on my early drafts was a great help to me. Furthermore, I have to thank Dr. Matthias Blum and Dierk Herzer for many interesting conversations and the open atmosphere at our institute that was very helpful in the completion of this work. Dr. Rolf Schinke was very helpful in commenting on my work during our doctoral colloquium and in helping with the organization of my research in Mexico City. Moreover, I have to thank all the other PhD students of Prof. Sautter for reading early drafts of my work and commenting on the contents. I am particular grateful to Silke Woltermann for providing the right incentives for regular jogging that helped conserving my physical fitness and to Dirk Holzhey for providing regular intellectual divertissements during my time in Goettingen. Aynur Scholz provided invaluable help in preparing my stay in Mexico City and Adriana Cardozo offered valuable research assistance. On the other side of the Atlantic Ocean I am deeply indebted to all members of the CEI at the Colegio de México and the Institute of Economic studies at UNAM who supported my research in too many ways to list here. Moreover, I would like to thank all my friends there and in particular Dr. Fikrat Abdullaev as well as Sabina Osorno and her family who received me openly and provided many insights into Mexican life and culture. I would also like to thank my parents and my family for supporting my academic studies and the realization of my PhD thesis. This book would not have been possible without them. Last but not least I am highly indebted to Laura whose love, care and continuos supply of fine Italian cooking helped me to finish this project.

Table of Contents

List of Figures

List of Tables

List of Abbreviations

BERI ....Business Environment Risk Intelligence
BIT ....Bilateral Investment Treaty
BRS ....Business Risk Service
CEN ....Confiscation, expropriation,
....nationalization insurance capacity
CNIE ....Comision Nacional de Inversiones Extranjeras
CRS ....Country Risk Service
EPR ....Ejército Popular Revolucionario
EZLN ....Ejército Zapatista de Liberación Nacional
FDI......................................Foreign Direct Investment
FI ....Fractionalization Index
FTA......................................Free Trade Agreement
ICRG...................................International Country Risk Guide
IFC.......................................International Finance Corporation
MAI ....Multilateral Agreement on Investment
MIGA ....Multilateral Investment Guarantee Agency
MNE....................................Multinational Enterprise
NIE.......................................New Institutional Economics
NPV ....Net Present Value
OPIC....................................Overseas Private Investment Corporation
ORI ....Operation Risk Index
PAN ....Partido de Ación Nacional
POLCON ....Political Constraints Index
PRI.......................................Political Risk Index
PRI.......................................Partido de la Revolución Institucionalisada
PRS Group ....Political Risk Services Group

List of Variables

c	User Cost of Capital
CF	Periodical Cashflows
F	Value of the Investment Opportunity
I	Investment
i	Current interest rate
K	Capital stock
K*	Profit maximizing capital stock
NP	A Firm´s net profit
p	price of a given good
PM	Current Value of a firm´s capital stock
PR	Replacement value of a firm´s capital stock
rK	Price for the rental of capital
q	Tobin q
Q	Net worth
t	Time index
V	Value of the Investment Project
V*	Critical value of the Investment Project
w	Wage Rate
C	Adjustment Costs
c	User cost of capital
σA	Aggregate Project Risk
σPR	Political Risk Multiplier
κ	Variation of the Capital Stock
π	Firm Profit
φ	Value of the Portfolio

But 'tis the very point in question, whether every thing must
have a cause or not; and therefore, according to all just
reasoning, it ought never to be taken for granted.
David Hume, A Treatise of Human Nature

1 Introduction

1.1 The problem

Most of the day-to-day activities of people deal with the planning of future developments. As dealing with the future by definition generates uncertainty decisions makers are almost everywhere confronted with this phenomenon. If you enrol in university to study engineering because you are convinced that this will offer you the possibility of earning your living you can never be sure that you will really succeed in doing so. Maybe you will face an economic downturn at the end of your studies so that you cannot find a suitable job. Maybe you will not succeed in the necessary exams to enter the labor market as an engineer. All you can do ex ante is to make an analysis of possible future developments based on the current available information about your personal capabilities and the environment.

Firms planning investments are essentially in the same situation. They will engage in a project when they have the opportunity to make an investment which is expected to be profitable. However, as most of the earnings that are generated by the project will be received in the future, investors can never be sure that their profits are really evolving as it was planned before. Instead they have to face the possibility that the expected revenue stream of the investment is altered. Reasons for these alteration are various. It can be a general economic downturn that renders the investment disadvantageous or it may be technical progress that changes the competitivity of the product or a major change in consumer taste that unfolds its negative impact on the profitability of the project. For firms engaged in cross-border activities the problem is usually more severe. They are not familiar with the institutional structure and the political environment of the host country and their information and understanding of the history and the culture of the host country often remains limited.

Hence, for international corporations or those that are intending to go abroad the topic of international risk management is essential. It is straightforward to see that the scope of possible risks for foreign investors is wide. The wish to offer a complete assessment of all possible risks for foreign investors would therefore be too ambitious. Instead, this volume focuses on risks that are caused by the political and institutional environment of a host country. In other words, this volume deals with a phenomenon that is referred to as *Political Risk* or *Country Risk* in publications on international finance and investment. Thinking of expropriations by host governments all over the world one can easily understand how national politics influence the business environment for international investors in a given country. Although outright expropriations of multinational corporations or catastrophic events like wars and revolutions are most likely the events that cause the biggest attention among observers and analysts, more often the actions of governments influence the revenue stream of investors in a more subtle way. Discriminatory taxation or regulation, extensive labor protection, massive corruption or bureaucratic inefficiencies are real world examples for national policies that may adversely affect the profits of foreign investors. Although no outright expropriation these national policies affect the political and economic conditions of every day firm operations implying a direct influence on their profits. In addition to direct governmental action, revolutions, strikes, riots or other forms of civil unrest may endanger the assets of foreign firms or bring production to a halt.

Only citing these few examples it is straightforward to see that national politics establish a basic framework for the business activities of investors. The existing political system and current politics as well as their likely evolution in the future influence the expected profits of investors and affect their incentives to invest in foreign markets. If investors cannot be sure of reaping the full benefits of their projects, incentives to invest are decreasing despite of potentially high future returns. This is in particular the case for investments with long pay-off periods, as it is hardly surprising that investors in those sectors are more severely affected by uncertainty over future developments than investors in footloose industries. Governments that cannot credibly commit not to opportunistically interfere in the investor´s business are shaping incentive structures that are not favorable for investment. The same holds for governments that do not succeed in properly providing basic public goods that are essential for successful business operations as for example public security, property rights protection or legal certainty.

Political risk however, is not a topic that is only relevant for a few multinational corporations. Instead it becomes one of the most relevant problems for developing countries that are eagerly seeking to ensure the external financing of their economic development. As figure 1.1 impressively highlights public capital transfers to developing countries, such as development aid and other transfers, are stagnating while private capital flows approximately increased by factor six during the 90s indicating that relying on public capital transfers is by no means sufficient for developing countries.

The dynamic evolution of private international capital movements rather suggests that the future development perspectives of developing nations will to an enormous extent depend on their ability to attract private foreign investors. However, more than their public counterparts private foreign investors are averse to risks that may endanger their future profits. Despite of the vast increase of international capital flows to developing countries several emerging market crises during the 90s impressively underlined the volatility of international capital flows. International investors quickly react to potential political risks as for example unstable macroeconomic environments or risks of expropriation as wells as riots or other forms of social unrest by quickly pulling out their capital. In turn, investors that have been seriously hit by losses due to political risk will hesitate the next time to engage in investment projects in the developing world.

Figure 1.1: Evolution of Public and Private Capital Transfers to Developing Countries (in billions of US$)

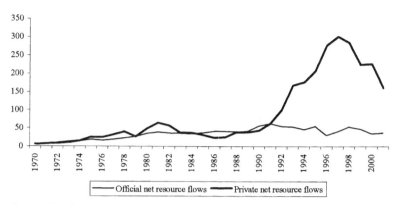

Source: Own figure, public capital transfers contain Official Development Assistance (ODA) and other public inflows. Private capital transfers contain FDI flows, portfolio flows and bank loans and other flows. Source: World Bank (2002): Global Development Finance.

Therefore high levels of political risks may seriously endanger successful economic development as current investors may pull out and future investments are deterred.[1] Hence, poor policies and weak institutional frameworks are extremely costly in terms of foregone FDI flows. Consequently developing countries which are in urgent need of foreign investments should make political risk prevention and management one of the priorities of national economic policy.

Despite of many economic problems during the last two decades the countries of Latin America are still interesting markets with a large potential for future growth. During the 90s liberal economic policies increased investor confidence and stimulated private capital flows to the region. However, while writing these lines it seems as if many countries of the region experience serious fallbacks into the past. Recent events in Argentina, that abandoned the dollar parity and witnessed violent social unrest following a severe economic crisis, indicate the importance of political risk analysis for foreign investment projects. Economic and political crisis in Venezuela resulting in large upheavals of opposition groups against the rule of president Chavez paralyzing the entire economy and the continuing presence of large guerilla groups in Colombia are other examples for the need of careful and detailed political risk evaluations. However, it is not always clear what international investors are looking for and what in turn should be the domestic policy preconditions to encourage FDI. Of particular importance are the following questions. Is political risk a major determinant of investment decision by foreign investors? And if yes, to what extent and which political risk factors are decisive for the decisions of

---

[1] Diamonte/Liew/Stevens (1998) show that changes in political risk have a higher impact on returns in emerging markets than in developed countries indicating that emerging market investors are more risk averse.

multinational companies? How do political risks emerge ? How can political risks be measured and quantified ? And eventually, how can political risks be successfully and efficiently mitigated ? The following chapters analyze all these questions by quantitative research on a sample of Latin American countries and a qualitative case study on Mexico .

Concerning the analysis of political risks, Mexico is a country of particular interest in the region. The moratorium on international debt in 1982 followed by the deep economic crisis of the 80s resulted in extremely high levels of country risk. However, in a quick economic transformation Mexico managed to become a country with low to moderate country risk ratings during the second half of the 90s. This comparatively rapid gain in investor confidence makes Mexico an interesting and challenging case for studying the extent and the determinants of political risks. The process of radical change from an economy based on import substitution and high protection with low investor confidence to an open economy that successfully attracts large amounts of FDI makes Mexico a fascinating case study to determine the political risk variables that matter the most for foreign investors. Although considered as a raw model for successful economic reform in the beginning of the 90s, the "Tequila-Crisis" in late 1994 preceded by the armed uprising in Chiapas and the assassination of the presidential candidate Colossio are good examples to illustrate that the climate for foreign investors in Mexico still is far from being ideal. But there is more than just that to the Mexican case. Simultaneously to its economic reform program the country embarked on an ambitious political reform program. The dismantling of the semi-authoritarian system established by the ruling revolutionary party and the continuing process of democratization coincide with the economic reform program. It is interesting to analyze if the process of democratization that culminated in the election of Vincente Fox, the first president since 71 years that is not a member of the PRI, affects the level of political risk and the attractiveness for foreign investors. The case study in Chapter 5 pictures the evolution of political risks for foreign investors in Mexico for the period between 1982 and 2003 and identifies the major risks that inter-national investors presently face in the country. It furthermore analyzes how Mexico succeeded in quickly mitigating high levels of risks and regaining the confidence of international investors.

1.2   Concept and Methodology

The second chapter starts with a brief overview of basic concepts in investment theory. Then a brief overview over the modeling of investment decisions under certainty and uncertainty is given where the main focus is on models where investment projects are assumed to be irreversible and firms have the possibility to delay investment decisions. The chapter continues with a brief review of the theory of international capital flows. This part provides definitions and a brief review of the theoretical and empirical evidence on potential determinants of FDI. Furthermore the chapter reviews existing models of political risk and draws conclusion from the models of investment under uncertainty. It closes with a synthesis of the presented models and a summary of the main hypotheses. Chapter 3 turns to an analysis of the factors that create political risks in host countries and discusses the determinants of risk for foreign investors. At the same time it offers a basic theoretical framework for the analysis of political risk by referring to the theoretical contributions of New Institutional Economics. The second part of Chapter 3 deals with the problem of empirical measurement of political risk and analyzes different potential risk mitigating strategies for host countries. Chapter 4 presents an econometric analysis of FDI flows to Latin American countries. The influence of different political risk factors on FDI is assessed by using a panel of Latin American countries for the period 1982-1997. Chapter 5 analyzes political risk in Mexico for the period between 1984 and 2003 and gives additional qualitative evidence on the relevance of political risk for Latin American countries. Chapter 6 summarizes the main findings of the study, and presents a conclusion as well as an outlook for Latin American countries.

2. Risk in the Theory of Investment
2.1 General Theory of Investment
2.1.1 Basic Theory of Investment
2.1.1.1 Definition and Categories of Investment

As economic actors make investments practically every day investing is a core economic activity. Firms build new production facilities, acquire better machines or try to enhance the capabilities of their staff by paying for seminars. In doing so they try to achieve future goals of the company by spending money or resources at present. Investment decisions deeply influence the profitability of firms in the future because they are a decisive determinant of the future competitive position. Therefore, staying in the market and making profits requires a careful planning of the investment program. Although the term investment is ubiquitously used in economic theory, its precise meaning often remains unclear. The etymological root of the word "Investment" lies in the Latin word "investire" which means to dress up. Modern economic theory offers various definitions of the term investment which cannot be completely discussed here.[1] In microeconomics one can refer to an action as an investment when an economic actor spends money at present with the expectation to receive future returns which are supposed to be higher than the amount that has originally been spent. Investments usually imply the purchase of material or immaterial assets serving the interest of the investor. Economic theory claims that rational investors only invest in projects that help to attain the goals of the investor implying that investments will only be made, if they increase the profits of private firms.

Usually the price of an investment is known to the investor when planning a project. The benefits of investment projects, however, are normally uncertain. Investors may plan the expected cash flows from a given project but can never be sure that unforeseen events in the future will not alter this expected revenue stream. Essentially investments are a bet on returns that depend on uncertain future developments that cannot be completely foreseen ex ante. This is of particular importance, if the investment has a long pay off period. For example, an investment in a power plant requires huge payments for construction and operation. The benefits that are generated every year by the consumers' payments are rather small compared to the initial cost implying that the break even point of the investor lies in the far future. It is straightforward to see that when investors plan future revenues for a long period, the risk that unforeseen events occur is higher. Corporate planning and strategic management of enterprises, however, involve many situations where the plans of the deciding actors extent to many periods. These characteristics imply that investment decisions are complex processes being the result of individual decisions based on current expectations about the future. Therefore, economic theory suggests that investment behavior is not only influenced by the volatility of the environment but also by the personal characteristics of the deciding actors. In sum, their information, their attitude towards risk and their personal

---

[1] For an overview see Perridon/Steiner (1995), p.25.

expectations about the future all become decisive determinants of investment behavior.

Macroeconomics defines investments as payments that augment the physical capital stock of the economy. Aggregate investment and capital accumulation are decisive determinants of the economic performance of countries. In the neoclassical growth model the accumulation of physical capital can explain differences in per capita income. More recent contributions in growth theory consider investments in human capital and technological progress as decisive determinants of growth.[2] Therefore, investment decisions of firms and private actors are highly relevant for national growth. Moreover, aggregate investment is a decisive component of the demand side in national economies implying that modeling in macroeconomics requires the study of the determinants of aggregate investment.

Economic theory identifies different categories or classes of investments. Although they cannot be completely discussed here, figure 2.1 depicts some basic classifications that are useful for a better understanding of the characteristics of investment projects.[3] Financial investments may be made in stocks or bonds or other financial products. One can distinguish financial investments with fixed rates of return as for example government bonds from investments where investors mainly have speculative objectives.

Figure 2.1: Categories of Investments by Object

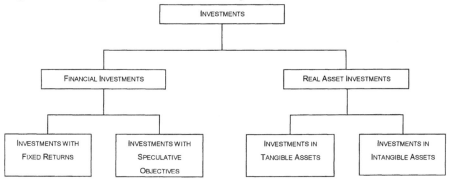

Source: Own figure with reference to Götze/Bloech (1993).

The latter motive is relevant for investments in stocks or financial derivatives. Investments in non-financial assets in turn, can be either tangible or intangible. If a physical economic good is purchased one could speak of an investment in a tangible asset. If, in turn, a firm invests in the further qualification of the staff one may speak of an investment in intangible assets.

---

[2] For an overview of growth theory see Barro/Sala-I-Martin (1995).
[3] For an overview see Adam (1994).

2.1.1.2 Opportunity Costs, Time Preference and Net Present Value Approach

The previous paragraph showed that investments entail a payment for the acquisition of an asset, may it be tangible or intangible. Therefore, investing means a loss of liquidity, as financial capital of the investor is bound in acquired assets reducing the possible returns that economic actors could obtain by simply depositing their money in a bank. Hence, every individual has to consider these opportunity costs of investing by integrating foregone interest payments into his calculus since to be advantageous an investment has to offer higher returns than these opportunity costs. Moreover, as future profits do not have the same value as present payments, future cash flows have to be discounted with the current interest rate in order to make payments in different periods comparable and to allow for the calculation of a measure indicating the profitability of an investment. Assuming that firms can raise and deposit capital at the same level of interest, the interest rate becomes the best indicator for the opportunity costs of investment. In this framework the interest rate does not only cover the opportunity cost but also time preference. The so-called Net Present Value (NPV) is a measure capable of deciding whether investments should be undertaken or not. In economic models opportunity costs are usually modeled by using this approach. The NPV, however, assumes the existence of a perfect capital market meaning that financial capital is always available and that shortages in the supply of capital as credit rationing are absent. Moreover, a perfect capital market has a unique interest rate which is supposed to be valid for both investing and raising capital. These assumptions allow to analyze the profitability of investments apart from their financing as it is proposed in the Fisher-Separation-Theorem.[4] Using these assumptions one can apply the following formula to calculate the profitability of a project:

(2.1) $\qquad NPV = -I_0 + \sum_{i=1}^{t} CF_t (1+i)^{-t}$

where I is the initial payment for an investment and the second term on the right hand side the sum of the expected periodical cash flows CF discounted with the assumed interest rate i. If the NPV exceeds 0, the investor should make the investment because its profitability is higher than the opportunity cost, that is, by investing in this project the actor is better off than by investing money at the current interest rate i. If, in turn, the NPV is below 0, investing at the current interest rate i leaves the investor better off than realizing the project.

In addition to assuming a perfect capital market the NPV approach makes two more subtle assumptions. First, investments are supposed to be reversible, that is, acquired assets can be sold at any given point in time without additional cost. In other words, if the revenue stream changes in a way that the investment will become non-profitable, the investor has the possibility to disinvest without additional cost. The model assumes that investors can

---

[4] See Fisher (1997).

completely skip the project without facing "lock-ins" or sunk costs. It is obvious that many real world investment projects violate this assumption. Second, a possibility of waiting is absent in this approach. The NPV rule neglects the investor's possibility to postpone the decision which would be rational if the deciding actor can generate further useful information about the project. The NPV model, in turn, assumes that a firm has the possibility to invest right now or never again. Examining real world investment decisions one finds that post-ponement is at least a feasible option. If the strategy of waiting reduces un-certainty over future prices, costs or market developments, it is rational for the decision maker to wait. In this case a rational investor would weight the costs of waiting against the benefits of new information. Costs of waiting are twofold: foregone future cash flows and advantages potential competitors might gain during the period of delay. If the benefits of waiting exceed the cost, rational investors would postpone the investment and preserve an option to invest in the future.[5] The discussion shows that although widely used the NPV rule only has limited explanatory power for the analysis of investment projects.

2.1.2 Models of Investment under Certainty
2.1.2.1 Overview
This paragraph reviews some theoretical models of investment under certainty that have been influential in the literature.[6] The accelerator approach based on pioneering work by CLARK models aggregate demand as the decisive determinant of the capital stock. Variations of demand imply variations of the capital stock via investment implying that the main determinant of investment is the variation of demand.[7] KEYNES focuses on the role of private expectations to explain investment. He points out that the decision to invest depends on the expected future profits of investment projects. KEYNES uses the marginal efficiency of capital as a measure on which firms base their investment decisions.[8] If the NPV approach is applied, marginal efficiency is obtained by setting equation (2.1) equal to 0 and solving for i:

$$(2.2) \qquad NPV = -I_0 + \sum_{i=1}^{t} CF_t (1+i)^{-t} = 0$$

The marginal efficiency of capital is the rate of return of an investment. If the investment yields a higher return than the market rate, it is profitable and will be realized. The opposite holds if the current market rate exceeds the marginal efficiency. The marginal efficiency of capital is sensitive to changes of expectations. If economic actors expect a general economic downturn in the future, they will also expect lower cash flows. Therefore, a change in the investors' perception of the future can depress the level of investment without

---

[5] I will extend this critique of the NPV approach in paragraph 2.1.2.3 Paragraph 2.1.3 introduces two models that capture the effects of irreversibilities and the option of waiting.

[6] Although many of these models have the drawbacks that have been exposed in the preceding paragraph, they are briefly exposed here because they are widely used in the literature.

[7] See Clark (1917).

[8] See Keynes (1989).

a change of fundamental economic variations. Uncertainty, however, is only mentioned verbally in the work of KEYNES but not explicitly modeled.[9]

One of the most frequently used specifications for the analysis of investment behavior is the neoclassical model based on pioneering work by JORGENSON.[10] In this model the firm maximizes the discounted flow of profits over time by choosing the corresponding optimal capital stock. Investment is induced by the difference between the current capital stock and the profit maximizing capital stock K*. The basic idea of the model can be illustrated by using a simple example. Assume that firms can rent capital at a price of r_k and the profit of a firm p depends besides other factors characterized by $A_1,...A_N$ on the amount of capital that is employed. The net profit of the firm at a given point in time becomes:

(2.3) $$NP = \pi(K, A_1,.., A_n) - r_k K$$

The profit maximizing choice of capital is given by the first order condition where $\partial p/\partial K$ is the first partial derivative of NP with respect to K:

(2.4) $$\frac{\partial p}{\partial K}(K, A_1,..., A_n) = r_K$$

Equation (2.4) states that the firm will rent capital up to the point where its marginal revenue equals its rental price r_K which implicitly defines the capital stock maximizing net profit. Investment is then determined by the difference between the current capital stock and the desired stock of capital.

JORGENSON makes use of this basic thought in his neoclassical model.[11] The demand for the capital stock is determined to maximize net worth which is defined as current revenue less expenditure including taxes. Maximizing net worth subject to a standard neoclassical production function with the constraint that the rate of growth of K is net investment (gross investment less replacement) JORGENSON obtains the following first order conditions:

(2.5) $$\frac{\partial Q}{\partial L} = \frac{w}{p}$$

(2.6) $$\frac{\partial Q}{\partial K} = \frac{c}{p}$$

Equation (2.5) states that in the optimum the marginal productivity of labor $\partial Q/\partial L$ has to equal the real wage w/p. Equation (2.6) shows that the marginal

---

[9] The reason why the model of Keynes is placed under the heading models under certainty may seem puzzling. But as argued above his treatment of uncertainty remains verbal and is not formally modeled. Therefore, the author decided to leave the theory in this paragraph.
[10] See Jorgenson (1963) and (1971).
[11] See Jorgenson (1963).

productivity of capital $\partial Q/\partial K$ has to equal its cost. The difference between (2.4) and (2.6) lies in the interpretation of the cost term. As firms usually do not rent capital, the numerator of the second ratio of equation (2.6) can be interpreted as the price of capital which JORGENSON called the user cost of capital c which depends on a set of variables that vary with the national tax system.

JORGENSON assumes that output, employment and capital stock are determined by an iterative process. Each period, production and employment are set to the levels corresponding to the first marginality condition with capital stock fixed. Under the described assumptions the process converges to the desired maximum of net worth where the optimal capital stock K* depends on the planned output and a set of price variables which appear in the user cost of capital. As the firms do not face adjustment costs or delivery lags, they can achieve any K* instantaneously implying that the current capital stock immediately adjusts via investment to the desired capital stock that maximizes net worth. Investment is thus determined by variations of the optimal capital stock ΔK*.

There are many critical remarks concerning the neoclassical investment model which cannot be listed here completely.[12] For our purpose it is enough to underline two shortcomings of the reviewed models. Since both models use the NPV approach, they are subject to the same criticism that has already been exposed above, that is, they assume that investments are reversible and that there is no option to wait. Unlike the Keynesian model, the neoclassical model does not incorporate uncertainty or expectations of actors. Instead, firms choose their optimal capital stock by equating the user cost of capital with the marginal revenue of capital. Investment decisions are taken without regard to what costs or marginal revenue of capital are to be assumed for the future.

2.1.2.2 The q-theory of Tobin
2.1.2.2.1 The Basic Model
The basis for the q theory of investment pioneered by TOBIN is the theory of portfolio selection that analyzes how investors structure investment portfolios considering risks and returns of assets they currently hold or intend to hold.[13] Rational investors choose a utility maximizing portfolio by considering return, risk, transaction cost for acquisition and liquidity of assets. Portfolio diversification allows for the reduction of the aggregate risk, if acquired assets are not completely and positively correlated. TOBIN'S q is defined as the market value of a marginal unit of capital divided by its replacement cost and can be written as:

$$(2.7) \qquad q_t = \frac{P_M}{P_R}$$

---

[12] An overview is given by Chirinko (1993) p.1879.
[13] See Tobin (1969).

where P_M is the current market value and P_R the replacement cost. TOBIN argues that a firm increases its capital stock by investing, if the value of this ratio is greater than unity because in this case additional capital is value increasing for the firm. Values of q smaller than unity imply that the firm has an incentive to reduce the capital stock either by disinvestment or decreasing replacement spending. It has to be underlined that the results are only valid for marginal variations of the capital stock and not average q. In economic models q is used to model private incentives to increase or decrease the capital stock via investment. A value of q exceeding unity triggers additional investment because the current market value of capital is higher than its replacement cost. In turn, values of q less than unity mean that the market value of additional capital is lower than the replacement costs which implies a reduction of the capital stock. The equilibrium value of q is unity because firms neither have an incentive to invest nor to reduce the capital stock.

2.1.2.2.2 The Romer Model
2.1.2.2.2.1 The Model

In the ROMER Model q is interpreted in a different way.[14] Assume the presence of N identical firms, a purchase price of capital goods that is constant and equal to unity. Further assume a firm that maximizes its profits facing costs of adjusting its capital stock taking account of the fact that it is costly for a firm to increase or decrease its physical capital stock. The marginal adjustment costs are assumed to be increasing in the size of the adjustment, that is, the bigger the desired change, the higher the cost of changing the capital stock. Finally, assume for simplicity that the rate of depreciation is 0. In the discrete time model the firm's maximization problem can be formally described with the following Lagrangian:

$$(2.8) \qquad L = \sum_{t=0}^{\infty} \frac{1}{(1+r)^t} \left[\pi(K_t) - I_t - C(I_t) + q_t (K_t + I_t - K_{t+1}) \right]$$

where $\pi(K_t)$ are the firm's profits, I_t its investment and $C(I_t)$ the adjustment costs that depend on I, and the last term describes the condition that the capital stock in the next period equals the sum of the current capital stock plus investments in the current period. Calculating the first order condition and rearranging terms one obtains equation (2.9):

$$(2.9) \qquad 1 + C'(I_t) = q_t$$

The equation implies that a firm will invest up to the point where the cost of acquiring capital equal the value of the capital. The cost of capital consists of the purchase price that was assumed to be fixed at unity and the marginal adjustment costs C'. q can be interpreted as the shadow price of capital

---

[14] If not cited otherwise the following explanations are based on Romer (2001). Only the necessary formal components of the model will be presented. For a detailed formal formulation of the model see Romer (2001) p. 370.

because it shows how an additional unit of money invested in the capital stock changes the present value of the firms' profit. In other words, q measures the impact on profits if the capital constraint is loosened marginally. If q is high, the firm has a high incentive to invest, if q is low the opposite holds. q can also be interpreted according to the definition of TOBIN as the ratio of the capital's market value to its replacement costs. If q exceeds unity, (2.9) implies additional investment and vice versa.

To show how q evolves over time one can use a current-value Hamiltonien function to solve the maximization problem of the firm.[15] In analogy to the discrete time case one obtains the following first order condition characterizing the optimum:

(2.10) $1 + C'(I_t) = q(t)$

Like in the discrete time case the firm invests up to the point where the cost of acquiring new capital equals the value of capital. One can derive a second condition which characterizes the optimum in the continuous time case:

(2.11) $\pi(K(t)) = rq(t) - q_c(t)$

This condition states that the marginal revenue product of capital equals its user cost where q_c is the derivative of q with respect to time. Rewriting this as an equation for q yields:

(2.12) $q_c(t) = rq(t) - \pi(K(t))$

This implies that q is constant when rq= π (K$_t$), or q=π(Kt)/r. From (2.12) equation (2.13) can be derived stating that the value of a unit of capital at a given time equals the discounted value of its future marginal revenue products.

(2.13) $q(t) = \int_{T=t}^{\infty} e^{-r(T-t)}\pi(K(T))dT$

Having derived the characteristic conditions in the optimum one can now analyze the dynamics of the model in a phase diagram. If the rate of change of the capital stock is denoted with κ, one can show that the variation of K depends on the value of q. Equation (2.10) states that each firm invests up to the point where the purchase price of capital plus the marginal adjustment costs equal the value of capital q. Since C'(I) is increasing in I, it follows that I is increasing in q. The fact that C'(0) is zero implies that I is zero when q equals unity. Therefore it can be derived that κ is 0 when q is one and that κ is increasing when q>1. On the other hand when q<1 I becomes negative. Economically this means that if q equals unity, the firms do not have an incentive to invest as the market value of the marginal unit of capital equals its replacement costs. Consequently the capital stock remains unchanged and it

---

[15] For the formal solution see Romer (2001).

follows κ=0. However, if q has a value which exceeds unity, it becomes advantageous to invest since the market value of the marginal unit of capital exceeds its replacement costs. Thus, κ>0 and the capital stock will grow which is shown by the bold arrow in the upper part of Figure 2.2. Finally, if the value of q is smaller than unity, the firm has an incentive to disinvest and the growth rate of the capital stock will be negative as it is shown by the bold arrow in the lower part of figure 2.2. Thus, for all points above the q=1 line κ is positive implying a growing capital stock while for every point below the q=1 line κ is negative which implies that the capital stock is decreasing.

Figure 2.2: Dynamics of the capital stock

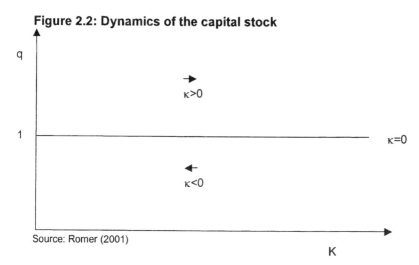

Source: Romer (2001)

The dynamics of q_c can be derived from equation (2.12) and its implications.

Figure 2.3: Dynamics of q

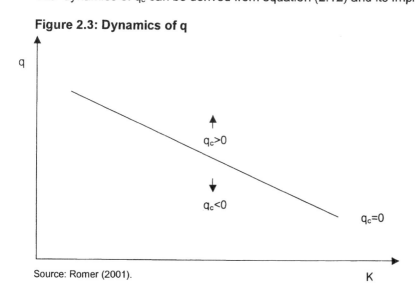

Source: Romer (2001).

Since π (K) is assumed to be decreasing in K, the set of points that satisfy equation (2.12) is downward-sloping in the (K,q) space which is shown in figure 2.3. The fact that q_c is increasing in K implies that q_c is positive to the right of the $q_c=0$ line and negative to the left.

The phase diagram in figure 2.4 combines the information of the two previous figures in one graph by showing how K and q must behave to satisfy the conditions that describe the derived optimum.

Figure 2.4: The Phase Diagram

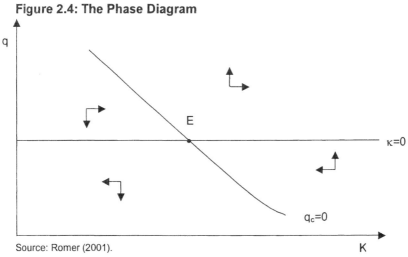

Source: Romer (2001).

In point E the system reaches its stable long term equilibrium. When the initial value of the capital stock is given while the market value of capital is free to adjust, all initial levels of the capital stock that lie above the $\kappa=0$ and right to the $q_c=0$ as well as all that below the $\kappa=0$ line and left of the $q_c=0$ will not converge to a stable equilibrium. However, it can be shown that these paths violate the transversality condition that must hold in the optimum implying that all these paths can be ruled out.[16] For all other initial levels of K the dynamics of q and κ bring the system to the saddle path and finally to the long-run-equilibrium in point E.

The saddle path is shown as a bold line in figure 2.5. The economic intuition behind this path is straightforward. Assume the systems starts at a given point on the saddle path to the left of E. As the corresponding value of q is greater than unity, additional investment is induced and the capital stock is growing. Decreasing returns to scale imply that the market value of capital is decreasing with further accumulation of capital. Hence, additional capital accumulation is falling over time. As prices are assumed to be constant, the value of q is constantly falling until again unity is reached bringing the system to the long run equilibrium E where q is equal to unity which implies that $\kappa=0$ and q=0.

---

[16] See Romer (2001).

Economically this means that the firms have no further incentive to decrease or increase their capital stock. For all initial levels of K that lie to the right of the relevant saddle path the line of argumentation is analogous.

Figure 2.5: The Saddle Path

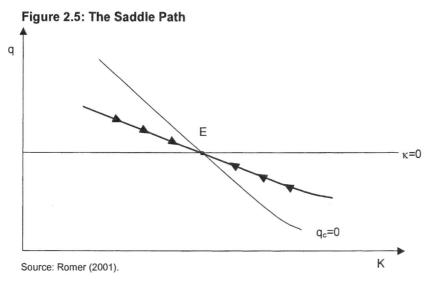

Source: Romer (2001).

The phase diagram allows for the analysis of the impact of exogenous shocks on investment behavior and the evolution of the capital stock.

2.1.2.2.2.2 Analyzing the Model
This paragraph analyzes the impact of exogenous shocks on investment behavior and the long run equilibrium by using the example of a change in national tax policy. Assume that the tax takes the form of a direct payment which applies to the purchase price of the capital.[17]

Figure 2.6 illustrates the effects of a tax reduction on the variation of the capital stock. Assume that the economy starts in the long run equilibrium E_1. One can see from equations (2.11) and (2.12) that a higher tax would reduce the firm's profits for a given level of K while a lower tax would have the inverse effect. Changing the tax code would therefore shift the $q_c=0$ locus up or down since profits are now higher or lower for any given capital stock. If firms are optimizing, q_c will jump up immediately to the point A on the new saddle path where q exceeds its equilibrium value of unity which implies additional investment. The dynamics of K and q will then gradually move down to the new long run equilibrium in E_2.

---

[17] In reality the effects of taxing on investment are much more difficult to measure because they alter the financing structure of firms as credit or bond financing has a tax shield effect. For reasons of simplicity these effects will be neglected.

Figure 2.6: Effects of Tax Reduction

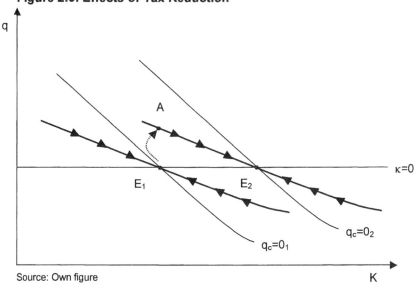

Source: Own figure

The economic logic behind this process is straightforward. In the initial equilibrium E_1 the new tax code increases the market value of capital. As replacement costs were assumed to be fixed at unity, q jumps up to a value greater than unity implying new investment. Facing decreasing returns to capital the additional profits of capital accumulation are falling with additional investment. Thus, over time the accumulation of capital reduces the value of q until the system reaches the new equilibrium in E_2 where q=1. In other words, a permanent tax cut produces a temporary boom in investment that leads to a higher capital stock corresponding to E_2.

2.1.2.3 Critical Evaluation of the Models

The review of commonly applied investment models already showed some of their common characteristics. With the exception of verbal arguments by KEYNES all reviewed models do not include uncertainty about future developments. As real world investors constantly deal with problems of uncertainty, the explanatory value of investment models remains limited unless uncertainty is explicitly modeled. The previous analysis also highlights that most of the orthodox models are explicitly or implicitly based on the NPV-approach. As already pointed out, this relies on two basic assumptions: the reversibility of investments and the absence of a waiting option. In real world investment projects these assumptions are often violated. First, real world investors are usually confronted with asset specificity meaning that acquired capital goods cannot or only at high costs be utilized for other purposes. WILLIAMSON identifies several forms of asset specificity, namely physical aspects, brand name specificity and human capital specificity.[18] The basic idea of asset

---

[18] See Williamson (1991).

specificity can be illustrated by the concept of fundamental transformation. If a contract between two economic actors results in an investment that is specific for the contracting parties free choice of contracting is lessened by the resulting mutual dependence of the contracting parties because of the irreversible characteristics of the investment.[19]

While in transaction cost theory asset specificity explains vertical integration, here it is enough to conclude that asset specificity leads to sunk costs. Sunk costs are defined as the share of investment projects that cannot be recovered if the project is skipped. A good example is an investment in a power plant. Machines that are used for power generation can hardly be used for other purposes. The workforce is solely trained to work in power generation implying high additional costs of schooling when people have to be employed elsewhere. The costs for marketing campaigns cannot be recovered at all when the project is skipped. The fraction of an investment that can be considered as sunk varies considerably with the characteristics of the analyzed object. In general, industrial investments should theoretically imply a high degree of sunk cost because the acquired capital goods are specifically designed to produce a certain product or a group of products. Consequently their use for other purposes is limited and canceling a project implies a loss of the money invested in those specific capital goods. In particular investments in infrastructure are characterized by high irreversibility as the provision of services normally requires huge networks or large specific production facilities. Although one may plausibly argue that the degree of irreversibility is lower in the service sector, even certain investments in this sector require high specific investments for human capital formation or specific information technology. To sum up, the degree of reversibility depends on the individual characteristics of the project and the sector that is invested in.

When examining the reversibility of non-specific capital goods such as computers, one has to take into account the "lemons problem".[20] As the quality of used durable goods cannot be exactly estimated by potential customers, they are not willing to pay high prices. A demand favoring low prices however leads to an offer of reduced quality. These imperfections of the market are finally leading to adverse selection. For investors this means that even theoretically reversible investments yield lower returns when they are sold on the market for other purposes. Eventually, also existing regulations and institutional settings can reduce the reversibility of invested capital. An example are national laws protecting workers and restricting layoffs. All these real world characteristics of investment projects lead to the conclusion that the neo-classical assumption of full reversibility of capital is too restrictive.

A second fundamental assumption of the NPV-approach is the absence of a waiting option. Since the NPV assumes that firms have the possibility to invest right now or never, the model neglects the possibility to postpone a decision, which would be rational if the deciding actor can generate further useful

---

[19] See Williamson (1985).
[20] See Akerlof (1970).

information about the project. Summing up, the reviewed orthodox models are not suitable for the analysis of investment problems because they neglect waiting options and asset irreversibility.

2.1.3 Investment under Uncertainty
2.1.3.1 Overview
All models that have been analyzed up to the point were based on the assumption of complete information. Investors are perfectly informed about their future revenue streams and do not face uncertainty about these payments. If not perfectly informed about the future, investors face the risk of unforeseen events that may decrease the planned profit of investment projects. Unforeseen events may even be influential enough to make investments unprofitable that have ex-ante been considered as advantageous. Therefore, it may be assumed that introducing uncertainty into models of investment should have a considerable impact on the investment decisions of firms. Furthermore, the orthodox models assumed implicitly that investments are completely reversible meaning that investors can sell their capital goods at any given point in time without additional cost. It has been argued above that this assumption is strong and usually not in line with the characteristics of real world investments. Problems of asset specificity and adverse selection imply that investment projects contain a considerable fraction of sunk costs. As firms are faced with the irreversibility problem ex ante, they will be aware of it when making a decision. Moreover, it was argued that orthodox models of investment do not include a waiting option although a strategy of waiting may be profitable if waiting generates new valuable information. The models which are presented in the following paragraphs release the assumption of complete certainty, full reversibility and no waiting option.

2.1.3.2 Characteristics of Uncertainty and Risk
Using the terms uncertainty and risk requires a precise definition of their meaning. Orthodox models assume that investors know a project's revenue stream ex ante implying that the decision of the investor is made under certainty. Formally this means that the future outcome of the investment has only one value or revenue stream x_1 that is realized with the probability of $p(x)=1$:

(2.14) $x_1, p(x) = 1$

Uncertainty occurs when the revenue stream of the investor is not secure, that is, ex ante the investor does not know future outcomes. Usually all real world investment decisions are made under complete uncertainty which is characterized by two facts. First, the investor does not know the number of possible scenarios that may occur in the future. Second, the probabilities for the occurrence of possible future scenarios are unknown to the decision maker. These two properties of complete uncertainty render the decision problem even more complex. To keep the decision problem simple and analytically tractable it will henceforth be assumed that uncertainty only means choosing between different possible data situations in the future. That is, the number of possible data situations and their corresponding payoffs are assumed to be known by the deciding agent. Formally this means, that there is now more than one outcome or revenue stream that may be generated in the future, say x_1, x_2,....., x_n. Thus, one can write the possible outcomes as

(2.15) $x_1, x_2, ... x_n, with\ 0 < p(x_i) < 1$

If the probabilities of the x_i are known to the investor, the literature speaks of risk. If, on the contrary, they are unknown the situation is classified as uncertainty.[21] Despite of this fixed terminology the author prefers to define the situation with known probabilities as uncertainty while the case of unknown probabilities may be denominated complete uncertainty. This distinct definition is useful because classifying a situation as risky requires another important property that will be described later. To sum up, uncertainty and risk occur in situations where future returns vary about an expected amount. The greater this variability of expected future returns, the greater the uncertainty or the risk for the investor.

Faced with uncertainty a carefully planning firm can structure the decision problem with the use of two criteria. First, the frequency with which a decision problem occurs, and second, the availability of probabilities for the possible future outcomes x_i. The combination of these two criteria leads to three possible classes of uncertainty that are depicted in figure 2.7.

Figure 2.7: Classes of Uncertainty

		AVAILABILITY OF PROBABILITIES	
		Yes	No
FREQUENCY OF DECISION	Unique	Informational Shortcomings	Complete Uncertainty
	Often	Uncertainty	Informational Shortcomings

Source: Own figure based on Adam (1996).

In the literature on decision making under uncertainty only the case of complete uncertainty and uncertainty are covered. However, it is obvious that in both cases of informational shortcomings the investor has the possibility to increase his level of information by generating probabilities for future data scenarios. If a decision problem occurs frequently, investors can use statistical methods to generate a probability distribution. Hence, over time they dispose of probabilities for the different future scenarios and the decision problem may be classified as uncertainty. For the case that the decision problem is unique, but probabilities are known the actor faces an informational asymmetry, as he does not dispose about information that is available on the market. That may be the case if the wanted probabilities are known by insurance companies that

---

[21] See Levy (1998) p.5-8 or Farrar (1963).

will base their decision on them but not by firms that sign insurance contracts. However, if markets were perfect the actor could base the decision on the information. That is to say, if markets are assumed to be efficient the decision maker faces the problem of uncertainty. Therefore, one can argue that if markets are perfect and decision makers use all available information, uncertainty and complete uncertainty remain the only relevant cases for analysis. The existing decision rules for the case of complete uncertainty however, only offer poor results because the problem becomes formally untreatable. Therefore, the analysis will henceforward be restricted to the case where the number of future scenarios and their corresponding probabilities are known to the investor.

Although the literature speaks of risk in this case, it is important to stress that introducing uncertainty to an investment problem does not necessarily imply the emergence of a risk for the decision maker. Thinking of a firm which has to choose between two strategies leading to different future payoffs in different data situations, uncertainty does not imply a risk for the company, given the possibility that it can adjust its strategy afterwards without facing additional cost. Only if the company has to make an ex ante decision which is not or only at high cost reversible, it has to deal with risk as the current decision affects future profits of the company.[22] Therefore, risk can be defined as uncertainty over future developments affecting the investor's future returns because a chosen strategy is irreversible. Uncertainty, on the contrary, only refers to situations where the evolution of future payoffs is not known to decision makers but where an adjustment of strategy is possible without additional cost.

2.1.3.3 Uncertainty in the Romer Model
2.1.3.3.1 Modification of the Model
If uncertainty about the future profitability of investment is assumed, the model of paragraph 2.1.2.2.2.1 has to be modified. As uncertainty can have various reasons that will not be further discussed here, the example of uncertainty about changing tax policy will be analyzed. If uncertainty is introduced into the model, equation (2.13) which states that the value of a unit of capital at a given time equals the discounted value of its future marginal profits has to be modified. With uncertainty about future profitability the firm will now base its decision on the expected value of profits. Thus, equation (2.13) will modify to:

$$(2.16) \qquad q(t) = \int_{T=t}^{\infty} e^{-r(T-t)} E_t \left[\pi(K(T)) \right] dT$$

According to (2.16) as before firms invest up to the point where the cost of acquiring new capital equal the expected market value of capital. From this one can derive:[23]

---

[22] See Adam (1996) p.215-305.
[23] See Romer (2001).

(2.17) $E_t\left[\dot{q}_c(t)\right] = rq(t) - \pi(K(t))$

This expression is analogous to equation (2.12) with the expectations term for q_c being the only difference to the model with certainty meaning that the market value of capital depends on expected payoffs instead of certain cash flows.

2.1.3.3.2 Effects of Uncertainty on Reversible Investments
If investments are assumed to be reversible, investors can disinvest at any given point in time without additional cost. It was pointed out verbally in paragraph 2.1.3.2 that uncertainty only causes risks for investors when irreversibility of assets exists. If, in turn, investments are completely reversible uncertainty does not imply a risk because strategies can still be adapted to changing circumstances. Integrating this flexibility into the model means that adjustment costs are symmetric for increasing and decreasing a firm's capital stock.

To show the effects of uncertainty the example of the tax cut will be modified for the case of uncertainty. Consider that the government is planning a reduction of taxes at a given time in the future and that the proposal for the tax cut will be voted on after a time interval T. Let us further assume that the probability that the proposal will pass is 0.5 and that there is no other source of uncertainty. Figure 2.8 illustrates the evolution of the capital stock in the phase diagram.

Figure 2.8: Tax Reduction with Uncertainty and Reversible Investment

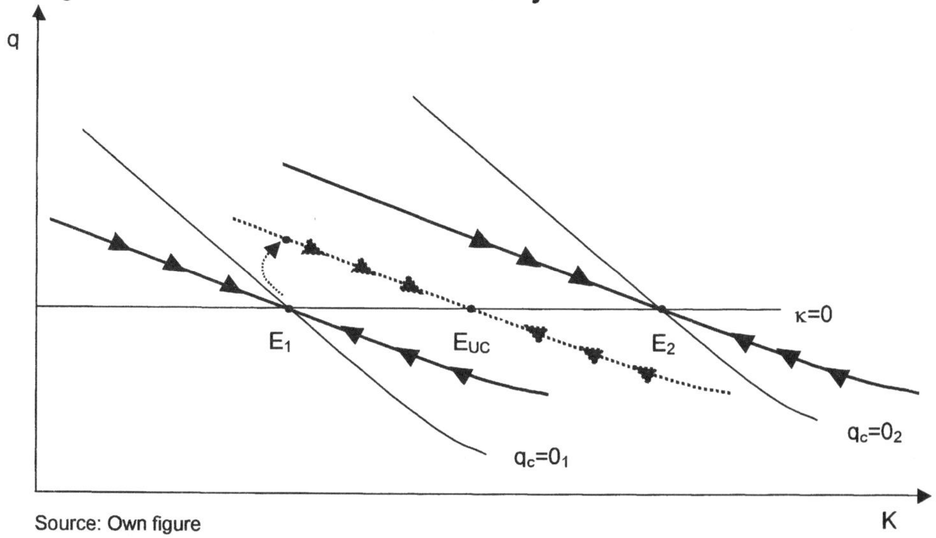

Source: Own figure   K

In the case of certainty an acceptance of the proposal would shift the $q_c=0$ line to the position of the $q=0_2$ line with the new intercept of the $\kappa=0$ and the $q_c=0$ line marking the new long run equilibrium E_2. If the proposal was rejected the $q_c=0$ line would remain unchanged with the old intercept marking the old long run equilibrium. Hence, after the proposal is voted on in T the system will converge to either E_1 or E_2.

If the proposal is already discussed but not voted on, the resulting uncertainty changes the outcomes. Since the probability of a successful vote is 0.5, the expected $q_c=0$ line must be midway between $q_c=0_1$ and $q_c=0_2$. The saddle path corresponding to the case of uncertainty is shown as a dotted line in figure 2.8. Before the vote the dynamics of q of K would converge to the point E_{UC} marking the intercept of this line with the $\kappa=0$ line. If the vote takes place, q will jump up or down corresponding to the outcome of the vote implying that as long as uncertainty persists the system is on a different saddle path than without uncertainty. Compared to the saddle path of the long run equilibrium E_2 under certainty investment is lower when uncertainty exists.

Assume that the proposal will be passed after a certain time of uncertainty. As argued above for the time of uncertainty the dotted saddle path becomes relevant. Remember that κ is increasing in q which means that the jump of q induces additional investment. Let us assume that the proposal is accepted implying that the long term equilibrium is E_2. The lower jump of q compared to the case of certainty acts to reduce the value of capital before the vote, and thus reduces investment. Compared to points on the saddle path corresponding to E_2 as final outcome one can identify an investment gap which is shown by the bold arrow in figure 2.9.

Figure 2.9: Effects of Uncertainty with Reversible Investment

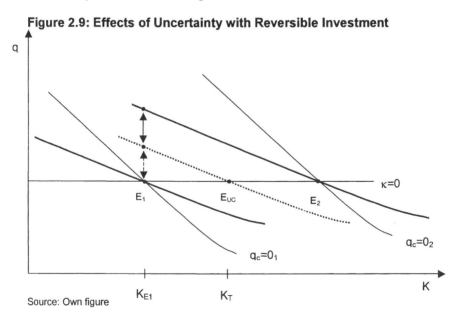

Source: Own figure

Specifying the interval of uncertainty $[K_{E1}, K_T]$ it is obvious that the jump of q and the corresponding level of investment is lower than in the certain case for every possible level of K. If the proposal is rejected, the investment gap turns to an investment surplus depicted by the dotted arrow in figure 2.9. For a given interval of uncertainty q implies higher investment for every possible level of K than in the case of certainty. Thus, one can conclude that uncertainty over future economic policy measures with an expansive impact reduces invest-ment. On the other hand, uncertainty can also imply additional investment when there is uncertainty over restrictive policy measures. Therefore, the model does not permit to derive a clear cut result concerning the effect of un-certainty on investment spending. This result is consistent with the analysis in paragraph 2.1.3.2 which concluded that in the case of fully reversible assets uncertainty does not imply a risk for investors and should not have an effect on investment behavior.

2.1.3.3.3 Effects of Uncertainty on Irreversible Investments
In this paragraph it is assumed that investment projects are irreversible. Irreversibility can be modeled by assuming that the adjustment costs for variations of the capital stock are asymmetric meaning that reducing the capital stock is more costly than augmenting it. In the phase diagram a saddle path with irreversibility becomes concave because if K exceeds its long run equilibrium value, it will fall only slowly because disinvestment is costly. On the other hand, if K is less than the long–run equilibrium, K grows very fast as upward adjustments are less costly. This new slope of the saddle-path is depicted in figure 2.10.

Figure 2.10: Effects of Tax Reduction with Uncertainty and Irreversible Investment

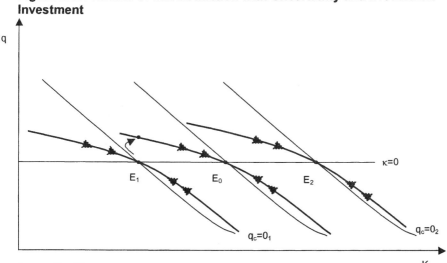

Source: Own Figure

Consider again the example of a planned tax cut. As before, uncertainty causes the saddle path to be midway between the two saddle paths that represent the two long-term equilibria under certainty. With uncertainty about the proposal q still jumps up but less than in the case of reversible investments indicated by the bold arrow in figure 2.10. As higher values of q imply higher investment spending the introduction of irreversibility causes the amount of induced investment to be smaller.

The economic logic behind this result is straightforward. Knowing that they cannot reduce their capital stock without additional cost in the future firms hesitate to invest more unless they have a clear picture of the future. This decreases the market value of capital before the vote and reduces investment. Obviously there is a value of waiting that reduces the additional amount of investment.[24]

Figure 2.11 compares the different effects of introducing uncertainty when investment is assumed to be either reversible or irreversible. The model starts from the initial long run equilibrium corresponding to point E_0. The saddle paths under certainty are represented by SP_1 and SP_2. Assuming that the proposal is finally passed permits an analysis of the effects of uncertainty on investment. The two saddle paths in between characterize the situation of uncertainty if again a 50% chance of the proposal for being passed is assumed. The concave saddle path represents the situation where investment is irreversible while the straight line represents the saddle path for reversible investments. In the case of certainty the tax cut would shift the saddle path to SP_2 corresponding to the long run equilibrium in E_2 and q jumps up to point A. Then the dynamics of q and K will bring the economy to its new long run equilibrium.[25]

In a situation of uncertainty the two saddle paths which are located midway between SP_1 and SP_2 become relevant. When investment is reversible, the saddle path is a straight line and thus q jumps up to the point B. For the interval of uncertainty the system will converge along the saddle path to the uncertain equilibrium E_{UC}. During the time of uncertainty investment is therefore lower than in the certain case. The arrow AB in figure 2.11 shows the lower level of q that implies foregone investment for one given level of K. This amount is again depicted in the lower part of figure 2.11 showing the relation between q and investment spending where I is assumed to be a linear function of q . In the following analysis this amount will be referred to as the "Uncertainty Gap".

---

[24] Paragraph 2.1.3.4 offers a detailed analysis of the Dixit/Pindyck model which assumes that there is an option value of waiting which reduces the amount of investment.

[25] Note that in the case of certainty the saddle path cannot be curved. As future events are clear to foresee for investors they can always choose the corresponding optimal capital stock without the risk to overinvest. Thus, the benchmark curve for the saddle path of irreversible investment is a straight line.

Figure 2.11: Effects of Uncertainty with Irreversible and Reversible Investment

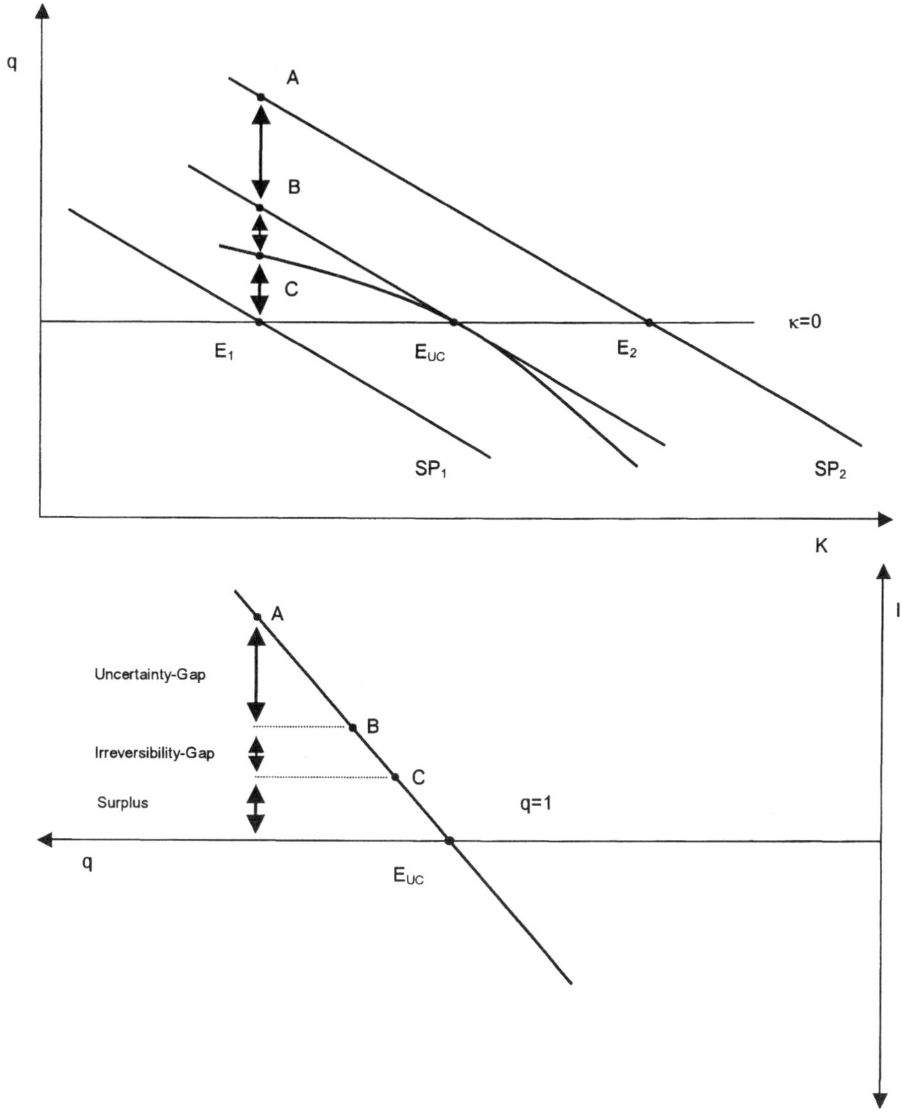

Source: Own figure

When investment is irreversible the relevant saddle path is concave implying that at the time the proposal is considered q jumps up to point C. Due to the slope of the saddle path the resulting jump of q is smaller than in the case of certainty. During the interval of uncertainty the system will converge along the new saddle path to the uncertain equilibrium E_{UC}. Knowing that the uncertain equilibrium E_{UC} can only be reached for an infinite interval of uncertainty it may be concluded that investment in this case is lower than in the case of reversibility for every possible level of K. Thus, for any given level of K there is an amount of investment that is foregone due to the existence of irreversibility. This gap that will henceforth be called "Irreversibility Gap", is depicted with the arrow BC in the upper and the lower part of figure 2.11.

In contrast to the results of the previous paragraph the investment surplus in case of a rejection of the proposal (line E_1C) is smaller than the investment gap (line AC). Hence, the existence of the irreversibility gap permits the conclusion that uncertainty reduces investment spending when investments are irreversible. Knowing that a higher degree of irreversibility causes the saddle path to become more concave and the "Irreversibility Gap" larger one can further conclude that the amount of forgone investment is growing in the degree of irreversibility.

The economic reasoning leading to this result is intuitive. As firms know that building up higher capacities in times of uncertainty could imply an undesirable "lock-in" when the ex-post environment turns out to be less favorable, their investment will all other things equal be lower than under certainty. In this case there seems to be a value of waiting for the firm that keeps it from investing at present.

2.1.3.4 The Dixit/Pindyck Model
2.1.3.4.1 Overview
The macroeconomic model in the previous paragraph was not capable to explain the value of waiting that implied the reduced investment spending in the presence of irreversible investments. Recent developments in investment theory offer new tools for the analysis of investment problems that may serve as microeconomic foundation for this value of waiting. PINDYCK and DIXIT/PINDYCK offer a new perspective for the analysis of investment problems by using the analogy to option pricing and introducing irreversible investments and waiting options.[26] The basic idea is that opportunities to invest are comparable to common stock options. Investment opportunities are characterized by a firm's ability to make an investment in the future based on its individual technical knowledge, experience, market position, patents, the ownership of land or other possible resources. Economic theory postulates that the value of a company depends on its discounted future cash flows that in turn depend on its capacity to generate investment opportunities for the future. With an investment opportunity the firm holds an option that is comparable to a financial call option on a common stock. It offers the right but not the obligation to buy an asset at some future time for a fixed price, the value of which is unknown ex ante. Likewise, a real option allows the firm to invest in a project the future value of which is unknown today. Making the investment is analogue to exercising the option because it means loosing the

---

[26] In the literature this approach is referred to as a real option approach. See Dixit/Pindyck (1994) and Pindyck (1991). See also the review by Hubbard (1994).

flexibility to invest in the future if projects are irreversible since in a world with sunk cost resources are bound. Making the investment also implies not having the possibility to wait for new useful information about the future. As loosing these future options implies opportunity costs for the firm every decision rule that ignores the destroyed option value has to be in error.

As already argued above all orthodox models of investment do not consider this option value.[27] This implies that the decision rule changes to NPV>F(V) where the expression on the right side represents the value of the option which measures the opportunity costs of investing at present that are caused by the elimination of the option for a future investment. Introducing this basic idea into an investment model DIXIT/PINDYCK find that higher uncertainty over future developments increases the value of the option to invest but decreases investment spending. Confronted with increasing uncertainty over future developments it becomes advantageous to keep the option to invest because the value of future information is increasing.

2.1.3.4.2 The Model

This paragraph presents a basic version of the DIXIT/PINDYCK model illustrating the general idea and allowing for a better understanding of the argument.[28] Assume that a firm which is considering an irreversible investment faces uncertainty about its future product prices. In the next period the price of the product will either rise with the probability of p to a known level P_1 or fall with the probability of (1-p) to a known level P_2 and then stay forever at this level. If the price falls, the investment generates a negative NPV which means that a rational investor would not engage in the project. For simplicity further assume that the firm produces one product per year without operating cost. To decide if it is better for the investor to wait one year or to invest now one can compare the NPV at both times. Assuming that the facility can be used forever and produces one product per year the NPV now is given by:

$$(2.18) \qquad NPV_0 = -I + \sum_{t=0}^{\infty} E(P)/(1+r)^t$$

where I is the price of the facility and E(P) the expected value of the cash-flow equal to the expected price of the product. Postponing the investment one period the NPV becomes:

$$(2.19) \qquad NPV_1 = p\left(-I/(1+r) + \sum_{t=1}^{\infty} P_1/(1+r)^t\right)$$

---

[27] This may explain why many empirical studies of investment behavior do not offer satisfying results. Firm level studies have shown that the internal hurdle rates of firms are usually higher than orthodox models would predict. This may be explained by the option value that is implicitly considered by the enterprises. See Dixit/Pindyck (1994) p.7.

[28] If not indicated otherwise the following is based on Dixit/Pindyck (1994) and Pindyck (1991).

Note that in period 0 there is no expenditure and no revenue. In period 1 the firm will only invest if the price goes up to P_1, which happens with a probability of p. As the price of the product is known in one year, the firm may discount its certain future cash-flow P_1 to the period 0. By comparing both values the investor can decide if it is advantageous to invest now or to wait a year and make the investment decision subject to the new information about the product price. If the value of NPV_1 exceeds the value of NPV_0 waiting will be a better strategy for the firm. To better illustrate the implications of this approach I use a simple numerical example.[29] Consider that a firm is planning to invest irreversibly in a ship building facility that can be constructed instantly at a price I. For simplicity assume that the facility can produce one ship per year at operating costs of zero. Currently the price of ships is 200 €. With a probability p the price of ships will go up to 300 € and with the probability of (1-p) the price will fall to 100 € and then remain forever at the newly fixed level as it is shown in figure 2.12.

Figure 2.12: Evolution of the Ship Price

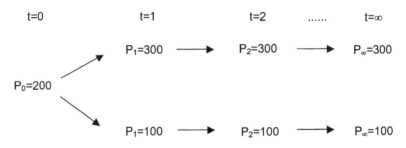

Source: Dixit,/Pindyck (1994) p.27

Assume that I=1600, the discount rate is 0.10 and that p=0.5. Now the NPVs of the project can be calculated to decide if it is better to invest now or to wait one year for the new information about the evolution of ship prices. Investing now would generate the following present value:

$$(2.20) \qquad NPV_0 = -1600 + \sum_{t=0}^{\infty} 200/(1,1)^t = -1600 + 2200 = 600$$

The current value of the ship building facility 2200 € exceeds its initial cost of 1600 € entailing that the NPV is positive. According to the orthodox NPV rule the investment is profitable and investors should go ahead with the investment. Let us now assume that the investor waits one year and invests only if the price for ships goes up to 300 €. The NPV of investing in one year is:

$$(2.21) \qquad NPV_1 = 0,5(-1600/1,1 + \sum_{t=1}^{\infty} 300/(1,1)^t) = 773$$

---

[29] See Dixit/Pindyck (1994).

Since the NPV is higher if the firm waits a year, waiting is the better decision. If the investment is made today, the investor pays 1600 € for a project that is worth 2200 €. In turn, if he waits a year, he will pay 1600 € for a project that is then worth 3300 €. With a falling price he would pay the same amount but receive an asset that is just worth 1100 € implying that in this case he will not make the investment and keep the option to invest. The flexibility to make the investment decision next year is exactly worth the difference of the two NPV: 173 €. In other words, the investor should be willing to pay 173 € for an investment opportunity that is flexible. An investment decision just based on equation (2.20) neglects the opportunity costs of investing now, disabling an investment in one year. It is important to stress that this result only holds, if the investment is irreversible and if there is a possibility to wait. If another firm is considering the same investment and a first mover advantage only allows the first mover to operate the business profitably, there is no waiting option and no opportunity cost of investing now. In this case the traditional NPV-rule is valid and the investment should made today. The same result is obtained when the project is reversible, that is when the initial payment of 1600 can be fully recovered if the price of ships should fall. Therefore, the opportunity costs of investing today (losing the opportunity to invest in one year) only needs to be considered if the investment is irreversible and a waiting option exists.

An analogy to financial call options on common stocks is useful for a better understanding of this result. A stock option gives the right to make an investment expenditure (the exercise price of the stock) the value of which varies stochastically. An investment problem has essentially the same characteristics. The investor has the option to invest in a project at a price I, the value of which varies with the evolution of the price of ships in the next period. The option will only be exercised when the price of ships goes up to 300 €. If the price falls, a rational investor will not exercise the option because the NPV becomes negative. This analogy to stock option permits to calculate the value of the investment opportunity with methods of option pricing.[30]

Let F_0 be the value of the investment opportunity today and F_1 the value next year. F_1 is a random variable that depends on the ship price next year. The two possible values of F_1 are known. If the price goes up, the value of F_1 is 1700 ($\sum 300/(1.1)^t$ -1600), if the price goes down the investor will not exercise the option because the NPV becomes negative making the value of the option 0. The problem is to find the value of the investment opportunity today F_0. To do so one can create a portfolio containing the investment opportunity and a number of ships that makes the portfolio risk free, that is, independent of the evolution of the ship price. A given risk free rate that is assumed to be 10% permits to calculate the option value by simply setting the portfolio's return equal to that rate.[31] Let us assume a portfolio in which the investor holds the

---

[30] For an introduction to option pricing see Perridon/Steiner (1995).

[31] This equation must hold because otherwise there would be the possibility of arbitrage for investors. The construction of the portfolio requires the existence of a "spanning possibility" that is there has to be a future market for ships. See Pindyck (1991) p.1116.

investment opportunity and sells short the number n of ships for hedging it. The value of this portfolio today is:

$$(2.22) \qquad \Phi_0 = F_0 - nP_0 = F_0 - 200\,n$$

The value of the portfolio in one year is given by:

$$(2.23) \qquad \Phi_1 = F_1 - nP_1$$

depending on the future value of P_1. With $P_1=300$ one obtains $\phi_1=1700-300n$, with $P_1=100$ $\phi_1= -100n$. To be independent of the evolution of P, n must have a value that solves 1700-300n = -100n. Solving this equation one obtains n=8,5. The return from holding the portfolio over the year is given by equation (2.24) where the term $0.1P_0$ has to be included because the expected value of P_1 is 200. With an expected price change of 0 however, no rational investor would be willing to hold the long position unless he receives a payment which at least equals the risk free rate that was assumed to be 10%.

$$(2.24) \qquad \Phi_1 - \Phi_0 - 0.1nP_0 = 680 - F_0$$

As the portfolio is risk free, its return equals 10% of the initial value of the portfolio because otherwise rational investors had the possibility of arbitrage. Hence, one can write:

$$(2.25) \qquad 680 - F_0 = 0.1(F_0 - 1700)$$

From equation (2.25) one can easily see that F_0 is 773 €, which is exactly the same value that is obtained by calculating the NPV under the assumption of waiting a year. The value of the investment opportunity, that is, the option to invest in a given project in the future is 773 €. Recall that the payoff from investing today in equation (2.20) was 600 €. Loosing the option to invest in the future implied an opportunity cost of 773 € that exceeds the expected pay-off from the investment (600 €) The full cost of the investment are therefore I+F(V), in our example they amount to 1600+773. One can easily see that 1600+773>2200, which means that the full cost of the project exceeds its benefits and the firm should keep alive the option to invest. If the firm based its decision on the simple NPV rule it would make a sub-optimal choice.

Figure 2.13 illustrates this graphically. The thin line in figure 2.13 shows the value of V-I while the bold line represents the value of the option F(V) depending on the value of the project V. For all values of V<I/1,5 the value of the option is 0 because the firm will never invest because even if the ship-price goes up by 50% the value of V will be less than the initial cost of the project. If the firm never invests the option value has to be zero because in any case

there will be no investment in the future. For values of V>I/1,5 the value of the option becomes positive. The V-I line shows the net benefits of the project. In absence of the opportunity cost of the option value every present value of future payments that exceeds the cost of investment I would make the project profitable. One can see that the critical value for the profitability of the project V^C is identified by the intersection of the V-I-locus and the abscissa. If the firm considers the full cost of the investment, profitability requires a discounted value of future payments that exceeds the sum of initial cost and opportunity cost.

Figure 2.13: Cost and Benefits of the Project with Option Value

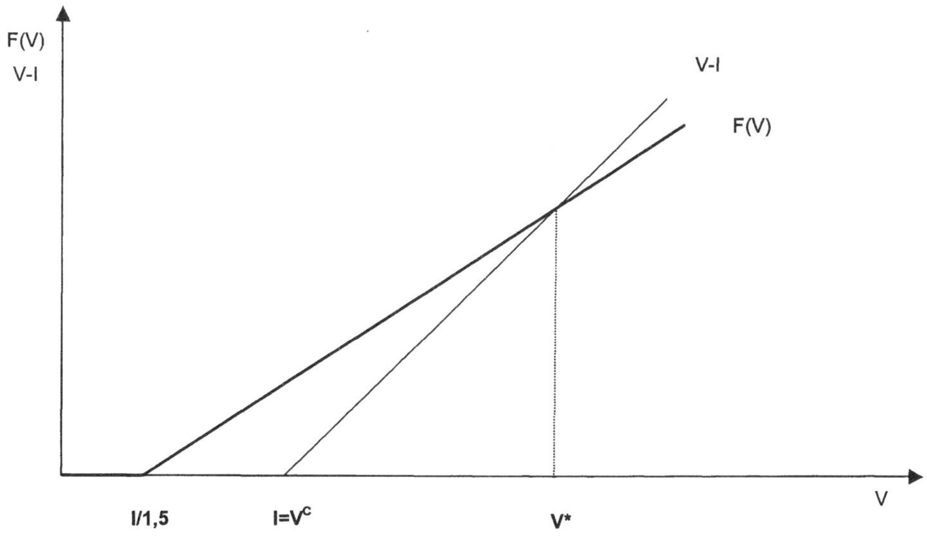

Source: Own figure

V* marks the new critical value where V=I+F(V) implying that for values of V which exceed this critical value the project's return is higher than its full cost. In our example this would imply that V>1600 + 773.

It can be concluded that the presence of the option value can make the analyzed project unfavorable in the current period. Hence, with uncertainty fewer investment projects will be profitable compared to the case of certainty. Therefore, in the presence of uncertainty investment spending in the current period is, all other things equal, lower. The value of the option drives a wedge between the traditional NPV rule and the new profitability criterion the size of which is determined by the value of the option to invest in the future. The DIXIT/PINDYCK model permits to derive the result that in the presence of irreversible investments uncertainty implies a value of waiting that reduces investment spending in the current period. However, as uncertainty is only modeled for two periods, it is interesting to extend the analysis to more periods.[32]

In a complexer model DIXIT/PINDYCK show the effects of uncertainty when the value of the project varies continuously over time. In this model the level of uncertainty is measured with the parameter σ that is defined as the variance of the project's value over time. As figure 2.14 indicates the graphical solution is analogous to the previously analyzed model and its characteristics are essentially the same. The value of the option follows a curved line when it depends on a V that varies continually over time. V* characterizes the critical value at which it is optimal for the firm to invest when there is a positive option value. For the case of certainty V-I shows the net return of the project. In this case F(V)=0 and the investment is favorable if V-I>0. V-I is represented by the straight line in figure 2.14. V^C is the critical value for V in the case of the certainty.

Figure 2.14: Characteristics of the Solution in the Continuous Time Case

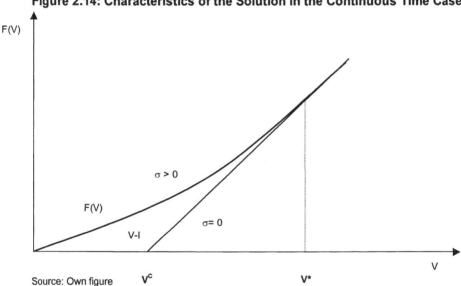

Source: Own figure

Including the opportunity cost of investing today the critical value of V is given by V*. which is the tangency point of the F(V) line and the V-I-locus. In this point F(V)=V-I, that is, the opportunity costs of investing today equal the net value of the project. In other words, the value of the project V equals its full costs I+F(V) consisting of its direct cost I plus the opportunity costs of investing F(V). For the investment to be profitable V has to exceed V* at least at an infinitesimal small amount. For every V below V* one can see that V<I+F(V) implying that investing is not favorable because the project's value is lower

---

[32] The analysis can be extended to 3 or more periods with the same approach. See Dixit/Pindyck (1994) p.41.

than the full cost of the project. As in the two period model the positive option value (F(V)>0) in the case of uncertainty implies that fewer investment projects may be considered as profitable. In the case of uncertainty the critical value of V exceeds the critical value in the case of certainty by $V^* - V^C$. Therefore, the occurrence of uncertainty depresses investment because the opportunity costs of investing render fewer projects profitable. While uncertainty about future evolutions of the product market increases the value of V, it decreases current investment spending.

2.1.3.4.3 Analyzing the Model

This paragraph analyzes the effects of a variation in the model's parameters which permits to model the effects of increasing uncertainty. In the DIXIT/PIDYCK model growing uncertainty can be modeled by increasing σ. Recall the example of the ship building facility in the two periods framework. Assume that due to higher volatility on the market for ships the variation of the ship price in period 1 increases. With the same probability of 0.5 the price will now either rise to 350 € or fall to 50 €. This new situation is depicted in figure 2.15.

Figure 2.15: Evolution of Ship Prices

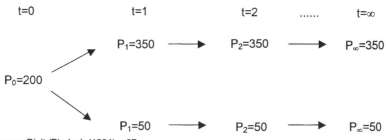

Source: Dixit,/Pindyck (1994) p.27

With increasing up and down changes the variance of P_1 rises which reflects the higher uncertainty on the ship market while the price change is mean preserving, that is, the expected value of P_1 is still 200 €. Calculating the value of the investment as above with the new value of P_1 entails that F_0=1023 €. Hence, higher uncertainty increases the value of the option to invest. As a higher value of the option means higher opportunity cost of investing today, fewer projects will become profitable. Thus, all other things equal, higher uncertainty reduces investment (because the investors will rather wait) but increases the value of the investment opportunity. The reason for the increase of the option value is straightforward. The mean preserving spread of the ship price in period 1 increases the upside potential pay-off from the option because if the price goes up to 350 the value of the investment opportunity grows. At the same time the downside pay-off remains unchanged because if the price goes down to 50 the value of the project is less than in the case where the price changed to 100. Since the investor will not invest in this case (he will not exercise the option), the value of the option remains zero.

However, when potential profits increase while potential losses remain unchanged, the value of the option necessarily has to increase. Higher
uncertainty, in turn, means a greater incentive to wait because the option value
increases. Figure 2.16 depicts the graphical solution of the continuous model
which is analogue to the two periods model.

Figure 2.16: Effects of Higher Uncertainty

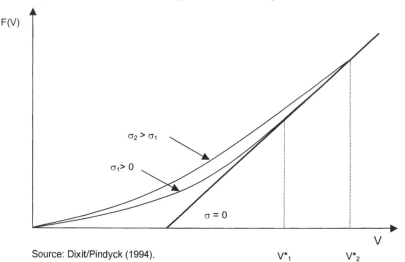

Source: Dixit/Pindyck (1994).

As the variance of the expected returns grows, the possible positive variation
of the value of the firm's investment increases. Like in the two-periods model
potential loss is limited to 0 because the option to invest will only be exercised
if the value of V goes up. Therefore, the tangency point of the F(V) line and V-I
has to be at a higher value of F(V) and the F(V)-line shifts to the left. As figure
2.16 highlights the new tangency point V^*_2 indeed corresponds to a higher
level of F(V). A higher value of F(V) in turn implies higher opportunity costs
which renders fewer projects profitable.

An increase in uncertainty therefore means a reduction of investment, as it
becomes more profitable to keep the option to invest instead of making the
investment. This reduction of investment is accompanied by a rising value of
the investment opportunity. Measuring the value of the firm as the sum of all
investment opportunities this result implies that the value of the firm is rising
with higher uncertainty although it invests and produces less.[33] Summing up,
the model shows that an increase of σ further reduces investment spending of
firms permitting two final conclusions. First, the occurrence of uncertainty

---

[33] Pindyck (1991) uses this implication of the model to explain the behavior of oil companies
in the 80s. While prices were falling, uncertainty over future prices rose. In response, oil
companies paid more and more for oil-bearing lands while their development expenditures
and their production were falling.

decreases investment spending. Second, investment spending is falling, when uncertainty increases as current investment flows are falling in σ.

2.1.3.5 Critical Evaluation of the Models

The previous paragraphs reviewed two models analyzing the effects of uncertainty on investment behavior. The ROMER model with reversible investment offered ambiguous results. In contrast, when investments were assumed to be irreversible, the model shows that uncertainty reduces investment spending and this reduction is growing in the degree of irreversibility. The DIXIT/PINDYCK model confirms these findings and provides an intuitive microeconomic foundation for the results of the ROMER-Model. Moreover, the model permits to show that rising uncertainty depresses investment spending, that is, higher uncertainty means less investment.

ABEL/EBERLY argue that these findings are only valid for firms starting with a capital stock of zero because irreversibility also has a so called hangover-effect which prevents the firms from reducing their capital stock in economic downturns. As disinvestments, which would be economically desirable, are not possible due to the irreversibility firms keep the existing capital stock. Therefore, the net effect of uncertainty on the capital stock is in the long-run unclear.[34] Although this criticism is valid for the evolution of investment stocks, the effects on periodical investment flows are not affected by a hangover effect. If firms are aware of the fact that over-investment may be hard to reduce in future periods, periodical investment spending will be lower implying that the hang-over effect is irrelevant for investment flows in a given period. Therefore, despite of the hang-over effect, the conclusion that uncertainty combined with asset irreversibility reduces investment flows remains valid.

A more severe drawback of the DIXIT/PINDYCK model is that it neglects first mover advantages since firms are assumed to have a waiting option. The observation of real world markets shows that this is not the case in many industries. In particular investments in high technology sectors as microprocessors are characterized by enormous first mover advantages. Therefore, the neglect of first mover advantages limits the explanatory power of the model. Nevertheless, it is possible to identify many real world situations where the delay of an investment project is a feasible option.

2.1.4 Summary of Propositions

This paragraph summarizes the main propositions of the investment models that have been reviewed on the previous pages. It was found that uncertainty theoretically has a depressing effect on investment spending, if investments are irreversible. Furthermore, increases in uncertainty further depress investment spending, that is, periodical investments are decreasing in the level of uncertainty. Therefore, all exogenous influences that imply further uncertainty for firms will all other things equal result in less investment spending. Moreover, it can be concluded that reductions of investment spending are

---

[34] See Abel/Eberly (1994).

growing in the degree of irreversibility confirming the intuitive economic logic that investment projects with a high share of sunk costs are more sensitive to rising uncertainty. Apart from these direct results the investment models also have important implications for the dynamics of investments behavior. As uncertainty only implies risk for investing firms if investment is not reversible an economy with long lasting high levels of risk will not only observe a reduction of investment but most likely also a change in the structure of investment. The reason for this dynamic effect is straightforward. Perceiving long lasting levels of high uncertainty economic actors prefer investments with low levels of irreversibility and short pay-off periods. However, many investments that are crucial for economic development are characterized by the opposite characteristics. For example infrastructure projects usually imply a high degree of irreversibility and long pay-off periods. Therefore, high uncertainty over long periods of time can result in systematic under-investment in sectors with low reversibility.

> *Whether one likes this or not, the multinational corporation is probably*
> *a tendency that cannot be stopped. Through its propensity to nestle everywhere, settle*
> *everywhere, and establish connections everywhere, the multinational corporation*
> *destroys the possibility of national seclusion and self-sufficiency and creates a universal*
> *interdependence.* [35]

2.2 Theory of International Investment
2.2.1 Overview
The economic literature on the theory of international investment is far too large to cover it completely in this volume.[36] Nevertheless, the author considers it useful to offer a brief overview of the most important theoretical contributions in this field to allow for a better understanding of the following arguments. Although international capital flows may be divided into foreign direct investments (FDI), portfolio investments, loans and grants, this analysis entirely focuses on FDI.[37] The following paragraph starts with a brief definition of FDI and sums up its main characteristics. It is argued that studying the theory of FDI eventually means studying the determinants that drive the decisions of international corporations because international capital flows are closely related to the behavior of multinational enterprises (MNEs). Thus, understanding the underlying logic of FDI flows requires basic knowledge about the theory of MNEs. Thereafter, follows a closer analysis of the determinants of FDI and the influence of uncertainty and risk on incoming flows. Although the current theory does not provide clear recommendations about the determinants of aggregate FDI, potential determinants and their theoretical plausibility are discussed.[38]

---

[35] Hymer (1972) cited by Munro (1995) p.8.
[36] For an overview see Dunning (1993).
[37] See Williamson (2001).
[38] This is important for the empirical analysis on the macro-level which requires the inclusion of control variables for the empirical estimation of FDI flows. See Chapter 4.

2.2.2 Definition and Characteristics of FDI

Despite of the pressure of international organizations for uniformity there are still various definitions of FDI in the literature.[39] The USA provided a first definition in the year 1937 by defining inward FDI as "all foreign equity interests in those American corporations or enterprises which are controlled by a person or group of persons ... domiciled in a foreign country. Equity interest encompasses all holdings of common and preferred stock, advances, and inter-company accounts." Despite of its importance there is no precise definition of the term control. In the outward survey of 1950 the U.S. Depart-ment of Commerce gives a more precise definition of the characteristics of control. In this document direct investments are "United States equity in controlled foreign business enterprises... as statistically defined for the purpose of this survey". The definition includes four main categories:

1. Foreign corporations, the voting securities of which are owned to the extent of 25% by persons or groups, ordinarily resident in the United States
2. Foreign corporation, the voting stock of which was publicly held within the United States to an aggregate extent of 50 % but distributed among stockholders, so that no one investor or group owned as much of 25 %
3. Sole proprietorships, partnerships or real property held abroad by residents of the United States
4. Foreign branches of United States corporations

The definition of FDI endorsed by the OECD and the IMF avoids the idea of control. Instead, "Foreign direct investment reflects the objective of obtaining a lasting interest by a resident entity in one country (direct investor) in an entity resident in an economy other than that of the investor (direct investment enterprise)".[40] The term lasting interest refers to the existence of a long-term relationships between the direct investor and the enterprise and a significant degree of influence on the management of the enterprise. With this broad definition the OECD delivered a specification. A foreign direct investment enterprise is defined as an incorporated or unincorporated enterprise in which a foreign investor owns 10% or more of the ordinary shares or voting power of an incorporated enterprise or the equivalent of an unincorporated enterprise. Moreover, OECD points out that it does not require absolute control by the foreign investor. Instead, an effective voice, as evidenced by an ownership of at least 10%, implies that the investor is able to influence, or participate in the management of an enterprise.[41] FDI compromises not only the initial transaction but also all subsequent transactions between the investor and the direct investment enterprise. Therefore, also reinvested earnings are contained in FDI flows.[42]

This definition of OECD, that is also used by the IMF, is governing for all balance of payments compilations. The United Nations System of National Accounts however, provides a different definition of FDI which retains the idea of control. Subsidiaries that are to more than 50% owned by a foreign

---

[39] If not otherwise indicated the overview of FDI definitions is based on Lipsey (1999).
[40] OECD (1996b) p.7-8.
[41] See OECD (1996b) p.7-8.
[42] See UNCTAD (1999b) p.160 or Fischer (1999) p.22.

company are labeled with the term foreign-controlled resident corporations. If the share of foreign ownership is between 10 and 50%, the companies are classified as associates and may be excluded or included by individual countries according to their qualitative assessment of foreign control.[43] This definition refers more to the micro level focusing on the decisions of international investors and their impact on host country development. Unless stated otherwise data in this volume is based on the definition given by OECD and IMF. However, the discussion showed that the line between FDI and portfolio investment is not clear and that classifying real world investment flows is difficult. In spite of empirical problems of measurement the theoretical distinction helps to analyze the implications of different flow types for host economies.

A closer analysis of the characteristics of foreign investment flows suggest that the effects of FDI and portfolio investment on host countries are distinct. FDI differs from other investment flows in at least two main aspects. First, as the definition in the previous paragraph indicates FDI implies a lasting interest of the investing entity in the acquired object. Although the definition avoids the term of control, it means that the investing entity exerts a significant influence on the management of the company resident in another country.[44] Enterprises engaged in FDI usually have a motivation that exceeds the mere seeking of short-term profits. Instead, FDI implies the existence of a long term strategic interest of the investor in the acquisition. Second, rather than being just a capital flow, FDI involves the transfer of a package of assets or intermediate products which includes money capital, management expertise, technological know-how and human capital. FDI does not only complement local savings of the home country but in addition supplies more effective management and technology, in particular for developing countries.[45] Nevertheless, the impact of FDI on developing host countries is a topic that has been widely discussed for a long time.[46] Critics of FDI flows to developing countries state that in the case of imperfect markets with large barriers to entry MNEs can drive domestic producers out of the market and extract rents that eventually lower domestic savings and investment.[47] Even at present the theoretical literature on FDI does not offer a clear picture of the effects of FDI for recipient countries.[48] A positive impact on host countries depends on the market structure and the number of linkages of the investment project with the host economy. However, if enough forward and backward linkages exist and the investments induce technological spillovers, host countries will experience a growth stimulating effect. Various empirical studies indicate that FDI exerted a positive impact on

---

[43] See Lipsey (2001b) p.3
[44] For a discussion of the term "influence" see Dunning (1993) p.5.
[45] See Moran (1998) p.20, Lall (2002) and UNCTAD (1999b) p.195-228.
[46] The dependency theory, which predicts negative effects of FDI, was particularly influential in Latin America.
[47] See Moran (1998) p.20.
[48] The corresponding literature is far too large to cite here. A good overview of the existing contributions can be found in Munro (1995) p.33-62 and Lall (2002).

the welfare of host countries.[49] Although there is much empirical evidence that foreign investment "crowds in" domestic investment, the overall picture remains mixed.[50] Despite of the criticism concerning FDI flows, most developing countries are eagerly seeking to enhance incoming FDI. To ensure growth enhancing positive externalities the targeting of certain industries which are assumed to fulfill the exposed prerequisites has become an important topic.[51]

Besides its importance for the economic development of recipient countries the notion of lasting interest has yet another important implication. Since one characteristic of FDI is irreversibility, withdrawing quickly during a crisis becomes a less feasible option and investors stay in business. Several financial crises in the 90s showed that the volatility of financial flows is a potential threat for countries opening up for investment from abroad. Empirical studies show that FDI is indeed a less volatile source of capital than other investment flows.[52] Analyzing investment behavior in recent financial crises one observes that outflows of FDI are considerably lower than other outflows.[53] Therefore, FDI seems to be a more sustainable source of capital for host countries as the risk of a sudden reversal of flows is limited due to the long-term interest of investors. Despite of the criticism on FDI it remains an important potential stimulator of growth for recipient countries. This is in particular the case for developing nations, provided that the country's markets are competitive and the number of linkages with the host country economy are sufficient. If these requirements are met, FDI should theoretically have a welfare-increasing impact on host countries.

2.2.3 Theoretical Determinants of FDI
2.2.3.1 Overview
Rather than a single identifiable act the investment decision process is a complex succession of acts that involves many elements.[54] The theory of international investment has essentially been seeking to analyze two main aspects of this complex process. First, the factors that motivate firms to engage in international production and second, the factors that influence the choice of its location. These two basic questions have been studied by many scholars from various different perspectives. This paragraph briefly describes both theoretical approaches, the ones explaining the motivations of firms to engage in international investment and the theoretical contributions that seek to explain the choice of location for investment to developing countries.[55]

---

[49] See Moran (1998) p.24.
[50] See UNCTAD (1999b) p.171-173.
[51] See UNCTAD (1999b) p.183.
[52] See Lipsey (2001a).
[53] See Williamson (2001). During the Mexican financial crises in 1994 for example the outflow of FDI was limited. See Graham/Wada (2000).
[54] See Aharoni (1966).
[55] Empirical studies on the determinants of FDI location are reviewed in paragraph 2.2.4.2.

As most of the decisions to invest directly abroad are made by managers in multinational parent companies, the MNE is the dominant vehicle for FDI and the current theory explaining FDI is essentially a theory of MNEs.[56] A MNE can be defined as a parent company that engages in foreign production or other activities through its own affiliates, that exercises direct control over the policies of those affiliates, and that strives to design and implement business strategies and other functions that transcend national boundaries.[57] The first explanations for the behavior of MNEs were not completely embedded in a comprehensive theoretical framework. They are either descriptive or view international investment as a process that originates in the will of national companies to internationally diversify production. Following the latter approach the main determinant of international capital movements is the difference between the return on invested capital in different countries.[58] More recent theories to explain international firm activity may be divided into four main schools which are, together with important corresponding authors, depicted in table 2.1.

HYMER presented a criticism of the classical view that internationalization is just a means of portfolio diversification by pointing out that firms which want to operate successfully in foreign markets need to have a comparative advantage, if they want to be able to face their local competitors.[59] This competitive advantage is an important prerequisite for FDI given the fact that local producers possess better access to information about the local market than foreign companies giving them a considerable advantage vis-a-vis their international competitors. To make successful international investments possible the multinationals that engage in foreign markets need certain advantages in technology, marketing, management or organization processes that cannot easily be adapted by the local firms.[60]

KINDLEBERGER elaborates on the nature of the monopolistic advantages of MNEs and shows that they may arise in the goods market (e.g. marketing skills), the factors market (e.g. access to capital) or stem from the ability to achieve vertical or horizontal integration.[61] CAVES names the monopolistic advantage a "unique asset" and postulates that horizontally integrating firms acquire them via product differentiation. Moreover, he argues that vertically integrating firms do not rely on unique assets but are just interested in ensuring their long-time supply and pricing of input goods.[62]

---

[56] See Root (1994) p.583 and p.607-608. UNCTAD (1994) reports that in 1992 the 100 largest multinationals accounted for about one third of the combined outward stock of FDI of their countries of origin. See UNCTAD (1994) p.5 In a later report UNCTAD (2000) states that in 1997 the largest 50 multinationals accounted for over half of the outflows from their home countries. For some countries the share exceeded 90%. See UNCTAD (2000) p.71.

[57] See Root (1994) p.577.

[58] See Root (1994) p.608 or Dunning (1993) p.68.

[59] See Hymer (1990) and Hymer (1976).

[60] See Hymer (1990).

[61] See Kindleberger (1969).

[62] See Caves (1974).

Table 2.1: Theories to Explain International Investment

Theory	Authors	Main Arguments
1. Monopolistic Advantage Theory	Hymer (1990), Hymer (1976)	• Local firms have better information about the local market • MNEs that enter a domestic market must have a monopolistic advantage vis-a-vis their local competitors • Transactional market failure implies organization of production via hierarchies
	Kindleberger (1969)	• MNEs that enter a domestic market must have a monopolistic advantage vis-a-vis their local competitors • Source of monopolistic advantages can be the goods market, the factor market or the ability to engage in vertical or horizontal integration
	Vernon (1966b)	• FDI can be explained by changing monopolistic advantages of MNEs during the product cycle • Production is transferred abroad when a higher product maturity makes labor cost more important • Over time the location of production shifts from developed countries to developing countries
	Caves (1974)	• FDI may be classified in vertical, horizontal and conglomerate • The base for horizontal investments are unique assets of the firm • Vertical investment are made to secure availability and pricing of input
2. Oligopolistic Reaction Theory	Knickerbocker (1973)	• Risk avoiding members of an oligopolistic market will follow one another in any substantial foreign market • This parallel investment is most likely to occur in highly concentrated industries with heterogenous products • This investment behavior is also found in vertically integrated markets where firms check their competitors efforts to secure input supply
3. The Internalization Theory	Buckley/Casson (1976), Casson (1979), Rugman (1981), Buckley (1987)	• A firm will internalize the production of intermediate goods when markets fail • Firm will internalize markets as long as costs outweigh the benefits • Firm specific knowledge is an important reason for internalization
4. The Eclectic Paradigm	Dunning (1981), Dunning (1993)	• FDI takes place when three conditions are simultaneously fulfilled: a firm possesses ownership specific advantages, market failure implies internalization advantages and the host country offers location-specific advantages • location-specific advantages are not limited to natural resource endowments but also include the cultural, legal, political and institutional environment of host countries

Source: Own Table

VERNON relates the patterns of international trade and investment to the degree of maturity of the analyzed product.[63] He argues that FDI can be explained by the changing monopolistic advantages of firms during the product cycle. In the early stages of its development the product is still not standardized and because of the monopolistic situation the price elasticity of demand is comparatively low. Marketing of the product requires direct contact

---

[63] See Vernon (1966b).

to the customers and a high degree of flexibility. When international wage differentials outweigh the cost and uncertainty of producing in other countries production facilities are transferred abroad. Like this production facilities move to other developed countries and with further growing standardization to developing countries. With a highly standardized product at the end of the life cycle the innovator countries will import the products from abroad.

The oligopolistic reaction theory based on the work of KNICKERBOCKER postulates that international production occurs due to a strategic reaction of the firm to the behavior of its competitors. That is, firms in an oligopolistically structured market follow their competitors in any substantial foreign market. In doing so firms protect the exploitability of their firm specific assets and limit the scope for their competitors to strengthen their own firm specific advantages.[64]

Another group of theorists sought to provide an alternative and deeper micro-economic explanation for the existence of FDI. Starting from the theory of the MNE these authors are not only asking the question why firms engage in international transactions but also why firms choose foreign ownership instead of licensing. In this category of literature one can cite the internalization theory and the eclectic paradigm of international production. The internalization theory rises the question why international transactions are rather organized in hierarchies than in markets.[65] It tries to explain the fact that firms build production facilities in foreign countries instead of serving the market by exporting their products or by using the instrument of licensing. The core prediction of the approach is that with a given distribution of factor-endowments, the form of MNE activity is influenced by the cost of hierarchical organization relative to the cost of the market. The firms decide how to best serve the market by comparing the cost of using the market via exports with the cost of integrating production horizontally or vertically. The main explanation of FDI in this approach stems from market failures that render exporting or licensing (using the market) more costly than engaging in FDI (using hierarchies). Hence, the internationalization of firm activity is not entirely due to location specific variables but is explained by the benefits of internaliza-tion.[66]

The internalization approach is capable of explaining why firms choose FDI rather than serving foreign markets by licensing or exports. However, the empirical observation that some countries attract large inflows of FDI while others are largely ignored by MNEs suggests that also country specific characteristics are important for foreign investment decisions. When country specific factors play an important role in the decision process of MNEs, different country patterns have to be considered as a third dimension that in-fluences the firm's investment decision. In addition to monopolistic and inter-nationalization advantages the eclectic paradigm allows for the integration of

---

[64] See Knickerbocker (1973).
[65] For an overview see Dunning (1993) p.75-76 or Root (1994) p.618-620.
[66] See Buckley/Casson (1976), Casson (1979), Rugman (1981) and Buckley (1987).

country specific factors as determinants of FDI. In this paragraph no attempt will be made to provide for an exhaustive analysis of the literature on international location theory. Instead, the coverage of theories will be limited to those that offer an explanation for the location of FDI in developing countries. Table 2.2 provides an overview of important theoretical contributions to explain FDI in the developing world.

Table 2.2: Theories to Explain the Location of FDI Flows to Developing Countries

Theory	Authors	Main Arguments
1. The International Product Cycle Theory	Vernon (1966b)	• FDI can be explained by changing monopolistic advantages of firms during the product cycle • Production is transferred abroad when a higher product maturity makes labor cost more important • Over time the location of production shifts from developed countries to developing countries
2. The International Division of Labor	Fröbel/Heinrichs/Kreye (1981)	• Cheap labor and highly standardized production processes permit a transfer of production to developing countries • This transfer is not limited to labor intensive industries but also takes place in industries that rely heavily on energy or raw material as well as those that are the source of environmental pollution
3. Neoclassical Theory of Investment	Kojima (1973)	• FDI is determined by factor endowments of countries
4. The Eclectic Paradigm	Dunning (1981), Dunning (1993)	• FDI takes place when three conditions are simultaneously fulfilled: a firm possesses ownership specific advantages, market failure implies internalization advantages and the potential host country offers location-specific advantages • location-specific advantages are not limited to natural resource endowments but also include the cultural, legal, political and institutional environment of the host country

Source: Own table

VERNON'S approach has already been reviewed above. Another group of theorists state that factor costs play a decisive role in the process they call "the international division of labor". Stimulated by the availability of cheap labor in developing countries, lower transport costs and production processes that may be realized with minimum skills firms from developed countries are relocating their production into the developing world. Production takes place in those countries that provide for the most profitable factor combination.[67]

Focusing on a macro perspective one can ask why countries engage in FDI and what determines the attractiveness of countries for FDI in certain industries. KOJIMA extends the neo-classical theory of factor-endowments to international investment problems. He argues that outbound FDI is undertaken by firms that produce intermediate goods that require resources in which the home country has a comparative advantage, but that generate value added activities that require resources and capabilities in which that country is comparatively disadvantaged. To explain FDI between developed countries

---

[67] See Fröbel/Heinrichs/Kreye (1981).

Kojima distinguishes different underlying motives as trade barriers and transaction- as well as transportation costs.[68] Without neglecting the explanations of MNE activity the eclectic paradigm of DUNNING allows to integrate country specific factors as determinants of FDI. In recognizing the importance of firm specific, market specific as well as location specific factors the eclectic paradigm serves as a synthesis between these two approaches in the literature. Therefore, it may serve as an analytical framework for empirical research on FDI.

2.2.3.2 The Eclectic Paradigm as Analytical Framework

Although there are many potential motives for firms to engage in FDI that vary to a large extent with the industrial sector and the characteristics of the given firm, it is possible to provide a general overview of theoretical motives for FDI. DUNNING distinguishes four main reasons for a firm's decision to engage in international activity which are depicted in figure 2.17.[69]

Figure 2.17: Basic Motivations for FDI

Natural Resource Seeking	Market Seeking
Physical resources	Following suppliers or customers
Labor	Adaptation to local tastes
Technological or management capacity	Cost of production and transportation
	Presence on the market of competitors
Strategic Asset Seeking	**Efficiency Seeking**
Merging to face strong competitors	Exploit differences in factor endowments, cultures, market
Access to distribution channels	structures and institutional arrangements
	Exploit differences in consumer tastes and supply capabilities

Source: Own figure based on Dunning (1993).

The first possible motive is resource-seeking. Resource seeking enterprises invest abroad to acquire certain specific resources that cannot or only at higher cost be obtained in their country of origin. Those investments may be further distinguished by the type of resource which the firm desires to exploit. First, physical resources like minerals, raw materials, agricultural products etc. that are needed for the production process of international firms where investors are trying to acquire the necessary inputs at a low cost or to secure the sources of supply. Examples for these resources are oil, copper, tobacco, sugar, rubber etc. Second, the seeking of a supply of cheap labor. These engagements are undertaken largely by manufacturing firms that produce labor intensive products and are based in countries with high cost of labor. Examples for this kind of FDI are the labor intensive U.S. *maquiladora* production facilities in the north of Mexico or the production of textiles in low labor cost nations in the far east or Latin America. Third, firms may be interested in an acquisition of technological capacity or management

---

[68] See Kojima (1973) and (1977). For an overview see Dunning (1993) p.89-90.
[69] See Dunning (1993) p.56. In this chapter he presents 3 other reasons for FDI flows: escape investments, support investments and passive investments that have been left out by the author due to their lesser theoretical importance.

expertise. Examples for investments of this category are the alliances in R&D between MNEs from industrialized countries in the information technology sector.

Enterprises that invest abroad to supply the local market or the market of neighboring countries with their products are called "market seekers". First, market seeking may occur because the firm has to follow its main suppliers or customers to the foreign market. An example for this kind of investment is the increased number of cross border mergers and acquisition in the accounting, auditing and consultant sector with the objective of being able to offer a global service to multinational clients. Second, a motive for market oriented FDI is the fact that many products need to be adapted to local tastes and needs. This kind of presence on foreign markets is of particular importance for firms selling consumer goods like food, soft drinks or clothes where tastes vary considerably in different local markets. Third, a reason for the presence on local markets is the trade-off between economies of scale in production and transportation as well as transaction costs. If certain products, the transportation cost of which are high, can be produced efficiently in small scales, firms have higher incentives to be present in the destination market of these products. Eventually, "market seekers" may consider it as an important part of their international strategy to be present in important regional markets dominated by their competitors.

The motivation of efficiency seeking FDI flows is to rationalize the structure of established resource based or market seeking investment. There are two kinds of efficiency seeking investments. First, firms want to exploit different factor endowments. This implies that capital intensive products will be produced in developed and labor intensive products in developing countries. Second, the potential motive of the investment may be a reaction to different consumer tastes and supply capabilities of different markets and therefore not based on differences in traditional factor endowments. Such efficiency seeking usually becomes important, when a minimum level of market- and resource-seeking FDI has already been attained.

The final motive for FDI is the acquisition of strategic assets to promote the long-term competitiveness of international companies. The main motive of strategic investments is not to acquire precise advantages in production cost or marketing but to add assets to the firm portfolio that will strengthen their overall strategic position. It is for example imaginable that two companies merge to face the strong competition of a main competitor. Another realistic example might be the acquisition of a company to gain control of its distribution channels.

Summarizing, the expansion of a firm's activity to other countries can have various reasons. Therefore, it is difficult, if not impossible, to formulate an all-embracing theory capable of determining the driving forces of FDI activity. Although such a theory is desirable, it would always remain incomplete because it could not be applied to all kinds of FDI projects. As the determinants of FDI decisions vary considerably between industries and economic sectors a theoretical approach to explain FDI can only cautiously formulate a paradigm that is capable of providing a basic analytical framework for explaining FDI.

The eclectic paradigm seeks to offer a general framework for determining the extent and the pattern of foreign production by a country's own enterprises and the domestic production owned by foreign enterprises.[70] The paradigm is a positive approach that helps to explain the observable behavior of MNEs and accepts much of the results of neo-classical trade theory which explains the spatial structure of output by differences in factor endowments. Following this approach the international specialization of countries is a result of their relative factor endowments.[71] However, approaches built on the theory of competitive advantages cannot explain the ownership structure of international output since in traditional theory the different factor endowments would simply intensify international trade. The fact that foreign firms own domestic firms remains unexplained by this approach.

The eclectic paradigm starts from the existence of two kinds of market imperfections that allow for understanding why firms take part in international production. First, a structural market failure that discriminates between firms in their ability to gain and sustain control over property rights or to govern multiple and geographically dispersed value-added activities. Since firms are not, as neo-classical theory assumes, economic entities with identical production functions, in oligopolistic or monopolistic markets firms may possess advantages that competitors lack allowing them to face the competition of their local counterparts. In other words, to be successful firms investing abroad must possess some kind of innovatory, cost, financial or marketing advantages that are exclusive to the investing firm and that cannot easily be adapted by local firms. The market failure that allows the keeping of firm specific advantages over time is a prerequisite of FDI.[72] The second necessary market failure is transactional, that is, it is located on the markets for intermediate products and services. Firms choose the organizational structure of their engagement by weighting the cost of using the market or internal hierarchies for the trade of these intermediates. If the transaction costs of a market solution are too high firms are widening their degree of vertical or horizontal integration which can also imply the engagement in international production. This transactional market failure explains why firms choose FDI as

---

[70] The following paragraph is, if not cited otherwise, based on Dunning (1993) p.76-86.

[71] An explanation of the HOS-theorem can be found in every textbook of international economics. For the original papers see Heckscher (1950) and Ohlin (1933).

[72] This argument builds upon the work of Hymer (1990) and Hymer (1976) who argues that firms that engage in foreign countries need to possess some ownership-specific advantages to make up for the informational disadvantages vis-a-vis domestic firms.

a strategy of internationalization instead of serving foreign markets via exports or contractual arrangements.[73]

Starting from these basic convictions DUNNING identifies three conditions that have to be simultaneously fulfilled for a firm to engage in FDI. First, the possession of certain assets that are not or only at higher cost available to their domestic competitors. These assets, may they be tangible or intangible, are capable of generating a future income stream. Examples for tangible asset that offer this possibility are qualified labor, capital or natural endowments. Intangible assets can be access to technology or information as well as marketing or organizational skills. The assets that are specific to a firm are labeled ownership-specific assets or O-advantages. The possession of O-advantages is a necessary condition for a MNE to engage in FDI.

Nevertheless, it still has to be explored why firms, that own O-advantages do not serve foreign markets with exports. As well as there are certain assets that are specific to a firm there are assets that are specific to a particular location. These kinds of advantages will henceforth be referred to as L-advantages and MNEs that want to exploit these assets have to be present in host countries. L-advantages can take various forms, as for example natural factor endowments or cheap labor as well as a stable political environment for production or other favorable country characteristics.[74] Thus, the second requirement for FDI is the existence of a L-advantage in the potential host country.

However, the simultaneous existence of L- and O-advantages is not a sufficient condition for FDI because for exploring L-advantages it would be sufficient to integrate the company into international production via the market. Instead of taking the risk to make an investment abroad it could be advantageous to explore the L-advantages through buying cheaper inputs on foreign markets or letting foreigners produce via licensing. The third and last condition that has to be fulfilled before a company engages in FDI is the existence of transactional market failure. The main argument is drawn from internalization theory which has been reviewed above. For some reasons the use of the market as a coordination mechanism may be more expensive than the coordination by internal hierarchies. In this case it is the inability of the market to organize a satisfactory outcome for potential contractors and contractees of intermediate products that explains why firms choose the hierarchical route for exploring the differences in L-specific assets between countries. In other words, this kind of failure reflects the inability of the market to organize transactions in an optimal way. The reason for market failure may

---

[73] This argument has been pushed forward by authors that follow the internalization theory that was presented in paragraph 2.2.3.2. However, this argument is not specific for the decision to engage into international production as it goes back to the analysis of the firm by Coase who identified transaction cost as being responsible for the existence of firms in market economies. See Coase (1937).

[74] This volume is an analysis of the location specific assets of countries. Grosse (2003a) argues that the eclectic paradigm is a suitable theoretical framework for the analysis of FDI to Latin America.

be asymmetric information that eventually leads to problems of hold up, adverse selection or moral hazard as well as imperfections of the international capital market that makes vertical or horizontal integration more attractive. Whatever the nature of the market failure, firms choose integration to maximize the net benefits of lower production, transaction or governance cost or to reap the maximal rent from the O-advantages they possess. The advantages that a firm acquires by internationalization through hierarchies instead of the market are henceforth referred to as Internalization-advantages (I-advantages).

The implications of the eclectic paradigm are straightforward. At any moment in time the more one country's enterprises relative to those of other locations possess O-advantages, the more they have an incentive to internalize rather than using the market, and the more they are interested in exploiting the differences in location specific assets the more they are likely to engage in outward production. This means that enterprises only engage in FDI, if all three conditions that are summarized in figure 2.18 are simultaneously fulfilled.

Figure 2.18: Internationalization in the OLI-Paradigm

	TYPE OF ADVANTAGE		
FORM OF INTERNATIONALIZATION	O-Advantage	I-Advantage	L-Advantage
FDI	Yes	Yes	Yes
Exports	Yes	Yes	No
Contractual Arrangements	Yes	No	No

Source: Own figure following the classification of Dunning

To sum up, the combination of the aforementioned advantages in a given investment project determines the form of internationalization a firm eventually chooses. The analysis highlights that location specific assets of host countries play an important role for the investment decision of MNEs. When in turn, location specific assets are a decisive determinant for the decision of MNEs over their spatial distribution of production it follows that countries without L-specific advantages cannot attract FDI. The aggregate location specific advantage of a given country is influenced by various variables as for example the existence of resources, factor costs, and human capital formation. Besides these determinants the local investment climate, a proper protection of property rights, the absence of corruption as well as the existence of rule of law and political stability are variables that positively affect the investment decision of MNEs. High levels of political risks may outweigh other location specific advantages as the existence of natural resources, cheap labor, or low taxes. Summing up, the eclectic paradigm permits to theoretically derive potential location specific determinants of FDI which can be empirically tested with statistical models.

2.2.4 Empirical Studies of Aggregate FDI
2.2.4.1 Overview
The analysis of O-specific and I-specific advantages is an important topic for transaction cost economics and studies in industrial organization with a fruitful area for empirical research on the firm level. However, given the topic of this analysis and the focus on the macro-level, it is obvious to focus on the analysis of location specific advantages of developing countries to assess their attractiveness for FDI. Due to the importance of FDI flows for developing countries, it is important to analyze which location specific variables have an important impact on incoming FDI flows since studying the determinants of FDI decisions allows for conclusions about the design of economic policy.

Empirical economic research identifies many potentially influential determinants of aggregate FDI by analyzing investment flows to countries or country samples. Although the literature offers a great number of econometric studies about the determinants of FDI, their findings remain to a large extent ambiguous. Due to the wide range of perspectives, methods, samples and analytical tools there is no consensus about the relative importance and the direction of the potential location specific determinants of FDI. Moreover, econometric models often contain variables which lack a sufficient theoretical foundation but provide a good fit of the model for the analyzed sample. As the empirical literature on determinants of FDI is too large to be completely reviewed, only recent contributions are presented in this paragraph.[75]

The discussion of theoretical models explaining FDI concluded that there is no all embracing theory of FDI, from which potential determinants for empirical tests could be clearly derived. Furthermore the variety of motives for firms to take part in international production make econometric studies of aggregate FDI a difficult task, the results of which have to be interpreted with caution.[76] In addition location specific assets of countries differ widely making empirical tests with cross-country samples even more difficult. Nevertheless, theoretical plausibility and empirical evidence concerning the most influential potential determinants of FDI will be briefly discussed because despite of its drawbacks econometric analysis remains a powerful tool for the empirical analysis of FDI flows and alternative approaches are still missing.

2.2.4.2 Empirical Determinants of FDI
This paragraph reviews recent empirical evidence in the literature concerning the impact of potentially theoretical determinants of FDI. Table 2.3 summarizes these findings by depicting the impact of potentially influential location specific variables and the significance and sign of calculated coefficients. Moreover, the robustness of all potential determinants is assessed by reviewing the

---

[75] See the more complete overview of Chakrabarti (2001).

[76] Kwon (2002) argues that the ambiguous results of the empirical literature on FDI stem from the fact that many studies focused on aggregate FDI. For attaining better results he proposes to focus research on the project level.

impact and significance of the variables in different empirical investigations with different methodologies.[77]

Table 2.3: Empirical Evidence on Potential Determinants of FDI

ANALYZED VARIABLE	OBSERVED EFFECT ON FDI IN DIFFERENT STUDIES			ROBUST
	POSITIVE IMPACT	NEGATIVE IMPACT	INSIGNIFICANT	
Market Size measured by GDP	• Overview of older studies Chakrabarti (2001) • Kravis/Lipsey (1982) • Schneider/Frey (1985) • Culem (1988) • Wheeler/Mody (1992) • Sader (1993) • Tsai(1994) • Shamsuddin (1994) • Billington (1999)			Fully
Openness measured by Trade-GDP-Ratio or other variables	• Kravis/Lipsey (1982) • Culem (1988) • Edwards (1990)	• Wheeler/Mody (1992)*	• Wheeler/Mody (1992)*	Convincingly
Host Country Infrastructure (Various Indicators)	• Billet (1991) • Wheeler/Mody (1992) • Loree/Guisinger (1995) • Harms (2000) • Stein/Daude (2002)			Fully
Labor Cost measured by Host Country Wage Rate	• Swedenborg (1979) • Wheeler/Mody (1992)	• Schneider/Frey (1985) • Culem (1988) • Lucas (1993) • Shamsuddin(1994)	• Sader (1993) • Tsai (1994) • Loree/Guisinger (1995)	No
Human Capital of the National Workforce	• Frey (1984) • Schneider/Frey (1985) • Billet (1991)			Fully
Host Country Tax Rate	• Swenson (1994)	• Loree/Guisinger (1995) • Cassou (1997) • Kemsley (1998) • Billington (1999)	• Wheeler/Moody (1992) • Jackson/Markowsi (1995)	No
Host Country Barriers to Trade	• Lunn (1980) • Jun/Singh (1996) •	• Culem (1988)	• Blonigen/Feenstra (1997).	No
Host Country Exchange Rate	• Edwards (1990)	• Froot/Stein (1991) • Blonigen/Feenstra (1996)	• Sader (1993) • Tuman/Emmert (1999)	No
Host Country Growth Rate	• Lunn(1980) • Schneider/Frey (1985) • Culem (1988) • Billington (1999)		• Nigh (1988) • Tsai (1994)	Convincingly
Host Country Current Account Balance	• Schneider/Frey (1985) • Lucas (1993)	• Culem (1988) • Shamsuddin (1994) • Tsai (1994)		No

Source: Own Table, *The Wheeler/Mody Study is cited two times because they find different results for different sub-samples.

---

[77] Variables where the empirical evidence is clear are classified as fully robust while variables where the majority of studies find the same sign with a significant coefficient are considered as convincingly robust.

One of the most cited potential determinants of FDI is the market size of the host country. Recalling the market-seeking motive it seems plausible that the size of the destination market significantly influences the investment decision of MNEs. In addition efficiency seeking enterprises may find a better possibility to explore economies of scale in larger host markets.

Therefore, a proxy for market size can be found in nearly all empirical studies of FDI, the most popular ones being GDP or GDP per capita. The empirical evidence for a positive impact of market size, proxied by GDP, on FDI is overwhelming.[78] Thus, recent empirical evidence supports the theoretical assumption that incoming FDI is positively correlated with the size of the host country market. Moreover, market size turns out to be a robust determinant as the positive impact of this variable is confirmed by all reviewed empirical studies.

Likewise, there is good theoretical evidence concerning the influence of variables that measure the degree of openness of countries. Openness and investment flows should be positively correlated when FDI is concentrated in the tradable sector. Although the empirical evidence for the hypothesis is not clear cut, there are various empirical results that indicate a positive correlation of openness and FDI.[79] Therefore, openness is considered a convincingly robust determinant of FDI.

It is often argued in the literature that in developing countries the quality and the extent of the host country infrastructure are important determinants of incoming FDI flows. As the quality of the local infrastructure directly affects costs associated with the factors of production, the production process and the distribution of the products this argument is theoretically convincing. Empirical studies confirm the hypothesis that infrastructure development is an important criterion for FDI in developing countries indicating that infrastructure variables are robust determinants of FDI.[80]

Another theoretically important determinant of FDI is the cost of labor in the host country. As pointed out before a cheap labor supply or other low factor costs are potential determinants of FDI since resource seeking MNEs typically invest in developing countries with low wages or other factor costs to decrease production costs. In particular when products have already attained a significant level of maturity factor costs become important location specific determinants.[81] Even if theory predicts a negative correlation between variables measuring labor costs and FDI, empirical evidence remains mixed. Results range from a negative or insignificant impact to an even positive

---

[78] See the studies of Kravis/Lipsey (1982), Schneider/Frey (1985), Wheeler/Mody (1992), Sader (1993), Tsai (1994), Shamsuddin (1994) and Billington (1999). For the results of older studies see the overview of Chakrabarti (2001).

[79] See Kravis/Lipsey (1982), Culem (1988), Edwards (1990) who find a positive impact of openness. Wheeler/Mody (1992) find an insignificant impact of openness.

[80] See Billet (1991), Loree/Guisinger (1995), Harms (2000) and Stein/Daude (2002).

[81] See Vernon (1966b).

influence of labor costs on FDI.[82] Although host country labor costs are theoretically an important location specific determinant of FDI, the reviewed empirical studies do not confirm the theoretical prediction indicating that wages are no robust determinant of FDI.[83]

Immediately related to the influence of host country labor costs are the skills of the national workforce. When low levels of qualification and skills of the workforce imply low labor productivity, location specific advantages of low wage countries may be offset completely. Therefore, a measure of human capital should theoretically have a positive correlation with FDI. Several empirical studies confirm the hypothesis that the greater the availability of a skilled workforce the greater the flow of FDI.[84] Hence, the existing empirical evidence indicates that human capital of the national workforce is a robust determinant of FDI.

The literature also investigates if FDI flows are sensitive to a host country's tax rates. As low taxes are location specific advantages that efficiency seeking international enterprises can exploit, economic theory suggests a negative correlation between host country taxes and incoming FDI. Empirical evidence however, remains ambiguous. Although some empirical studies find the expected negative correlation, there is also a great number of studies that do not find a significant impact and reject the hypothesis.[85] To conclude, the ambiguous empirical evidence on the influence of taxation on FDI does not permit the classification of taxes as robust determinants of FDI.

The theoretical impact of variables measuring trade barriers of host countries on FDI is unclear. Following the tariff hopping argument a high degree of protection in the host country will imply an increase in FDI as foreign companies are trying to avoid high tariffs. In turn, an excessive protection of the host country market may deter FDI, when investors are export oriented or heavily rely on imports of intermediary goods. The review of empirical studies on the effects of trade barriers likewise is inconclusive. While some authors find empirical evidence for the "tariff hopping" argument, there are also studies that reject it.[86] Therefore, trade barriers cannot be classified as robust determinants of FDI.

---

[82] See Culem (1988), Sader (1993), Shamsuddin (1994) and Tsai (1994) who found a negative impact of wages on FDI. See the studies of Swedenborg (1979) and Wheeler/Mody (1992) that obtained a positive impact.

[83] Another important problem immanent to empirical studies of the impact of labor costs is the lack of sufficiently large comparable time series on labor costs in particular for developing countries, which suggests a sample selection bias of existing studies. Another problem of the empirical studies is that instead of unit labor costs national wage rates are used.

[84] See Frey (1984), Schneider/Frey (1985) and Billet (1991).

[85] See Billington (1999), Kemsley (1998), Cassou (1997) and Loree/Guisinger (1995) who find a significantly negative impact of a country's tax rate on FDI. Wheeler/Moody (1992) and Jackson/Markowski (1995) find an insignificant influence while Swenson (1994) even reported a positive correlation.

[86] See Lunn (1980) and Jun/Singh (1996) that accept the tariff hopping argument. For a rejection or an insignificant impact see Culem (1988) and Blonigen/Feenstra (1997).

Another potential determinant of incoming FDI is the evolution of the host country's exchange rate. Following the exchange rate-hypothesis countries with a weak or volatile exchange rate will receive less FDI because asset values and income streams from countries with a weak currency are subject to large devaluation risks. Therefore, income streams will be discounted at higher rates when they originate in countries with weak currencies. In turn, a weak host country currency may also attract FDI because acquisition prices for foreign investors are falling. As the empirical evidence remains mixed, it follows that the exchange rate cannot be classified as robust determinant of FDI flows.[87]

There is also mixed econometric evidence with respect to variables that measure the economic dynamics of host countries. Following the growth hypothesis rapidly growing economies provide better opportunities for making profits and attract more FDI. Although many econometric studies seem to confirm the hypothesis, the variable does not turn out to be robust in all settings.[88] Nevertheless, the review of recent empirical studies permits to classify the variable as being convincingly robust.

Another dynamic variable, the impact of which on FDI has been discussed in the literature, is the current account balance. Following the trade-surplus hypothesis a positive current account is a characteristic of a healthy and dynamic economy with export potential. Therefore, a trade surplus should exert a stimulating impact on FDI. However, empirical tests of this hypothesis are inconclusive. While several authors find the theoretically expected positive sign, some authors' results indicate the opposite.[89] In sum, the empirical evidence does not permit to classify the current account as a robust determinant of FDI.

In addition to these variables there is great number of other potential determinants that have not been explicitly reviewed here. Particularly relevant for the purpose of this study is the existing empirical evidence on the influence of indicators measuring political stability or political risk. All these empirical studies however, are reviewed separately in paragraph 2.2.5.4. To conclude, only a few variables that are supposed to be potential determinants of FDI turn out to be robust in a large number of empirical studies implying that the significance of many determinants depends to a large extent on the design of the econometric model and the selected sample. This empirical ambiguity implies that up to now the economic literature does not offer a widely accepted standard model for econometric research on FDI. Nevertheless, empirical

---

[87] See Blonigen,/Feenstra (1997), Froot/Stein (1991) that find a strong negative correlation of the exchange rate and FDI. Insignificant or positive effects were found by Edwards (1990), Sader (1993) and Tuman/Emmert (1999).

[88] See the studies Billington (1999), Culem (1988) and Schneider/Frey (1985) and Lunn(1980) for positive evidence. Tsai (1994) and Nigh (1988) find an insignificant impact of the growth rate.

[89] See Lucas (1993) and Schneider/Frey (1985) for results that accept the trade-surplus hypothesis. See Shamsuddin (1994), Tsai (1994) and Culem (1988) for a rejection.

evidence suggests that market size, openness, infrastructure, human capital of the workforce and host country growth rates are convincingly or fully robust determinants of FDI flows. In turn, other potentially influential variables being reviewed in this paragraph as host country wages, taxes, the exchange rate and tariffs are not robust to minor changes in the specification of empirical models.[90]

2.2.5 Political Risk and International Investment
2.2.5.1 Definition of Political Risk

Since the term "Political Risk" is used in various economic publications without precise definition, this paragraph provides a definition of political risk that is based on a review of the existing literature and will be used throughout the present analysis. It was already pointed out that neoclassical investment theory assumes that all actors are fully informed. Uncertainty, in turn, occurs in a world without full information and in reality, economic actors are daily confronted with various forms of uncertainty. Recalling the analysis in Chapter 2, introducing uncertainty did not necessarily imply a risk for the decision maker. Only if an actor has to make ex ante decisions which are not, or only at high cost, reversible a risk occurs because current decisions directly affect future earnings.[91] Therefore, risk can be broadly defined as uncertainty over future developments affecting future returns of economic actors.

In the economic literature the definitions of political risk vary largely with the underlying unit of analysis.[92] HOWELL/CHADDICK define political risk as the possibility that political decisions, events or conditions in a country will affect the business environment such that investors will lose money or have a reduced profit margin.[93] LESSARD defines political risk for foreign investors as the risk of political discontinuities resulting in losses through expropriation or major policy shifts.[94] Other definitions may be classified in two groups. The first group solely focuses on governmental action as a source of political risk. The second group of definitions also includes sources of risk which are outside the direct control of the host government.[95] For foreign investors political risk can be a combination of both, a government's inclination to opportunistically interfere in operations and the presence of societal factors as civil strife or ethnic tensions. Therefore, here political risk is defined in a broader sense which also includes risks that do not emanate directly from governmental action. Speaking of political risk in this volume refers to uncertainty about the future interference or non-interference of governments as well as abrupt changes or discontinuities in policy affecting the revenues from or the value of private assets. The notion of "non-interference of governments" covers all those risks that are caused by an insufficient action of public administrations or

---

[90] These findings have implications for the methodology of the empirical analysis in Chapter 4. See paragraph 4.2.1.
[91] See paragraph 2.1.3.2.
[92] Simon (1982) offers an overview of earlier definitions of political risk.
[93] See Howell/Chaddick (1994) p. 71.
[94] See Lessard (1993) p.452.
[95] See Howell (2001) p.1-5.

that do not originate in governmental action at all. Examples are lack of public order, riots, strikes or revolution which clearly affect returns on investment but do not originate directly in governmental action. In addition, all those political risk factors are covered which affect the return of investors due to international political tensions. Cross country warfare or terrorist attacks are examples for exogenous risks that are not caused by governmental behavior. In this sense political risk occurs, if the government is not able to fulfil the tasks of ensuring that firms can follow their normal economic activities.[96] Related to the term political risk is the term country risk. Since this term usually refers to the risk that an international loan defaults, it should not be confounded with political risk in general.[97] Consequently LESSARD defines general country risk as the risk of change in an asset's value due to sovereign policy that involve general or selective default on, confiscation of or taxation of claims in response to circumstances under which either or both the ability and willingness of the sovereign to meet all the claims placed on it is impaired.

It is important to stress that it is not only the existing set of regulations, restrictions and institutions that may reduce the attractiveness of countries for FDI. Governments can impose taxes on cross-border financial flows and payments, quantitative limitations or reserve requirements independently from the current status quo. Therefore, also the time dimension of the problem and the expectations of investors have to be considered. Independent from the existing political institutions the mere possibility of measures that reduce the investor's returns already implies a political risk.[98] Given the irreversibility that is inherent to the majority of investments, it seems evident that investors are rather concerned about the government's future policy than about the past.[99] It is straightforward to see that the aforementioned definition contains a large quantity of governmental action or non-action that may possibly affect the return on private assets. However, the term political risk is only applied to situations where the declining value of private assets is due to a change of the property rights structure. This excludes all political action which decreases the value of private assets indirectly and not specifically as for example the general design of fiscal or monetary policy.[100] Furthermore, this definition ignores all kinds of economic risks that may affect the returns of MNEs due to evolutions on international markets. Examples are changing terms of trade, variations in international interest rate, a global reduction in demand, and increases in oil prices and so on. It is important to stress that political risk may also arise although the existing *de jure* property rights structure of a society

---

[96] The author is well aware of the fact that there is no consensus about the tasks of the state in a market economy. Chapter 3 delivers a more detailed discussion of necessary governmental tasks.

[97] See Benmansur/Vadcar (1995) p.20-21.

[98] See Obstfeld (1995).

[99] See Harms (2000) p.72.

[100] This exclusion is only valid for a "normal course" of economic policy that does not lead to economic or financial crisis. Economic policies that lead to severe macroeconomic imbalances are a potential source of political risk. The weakness of this definition is to distinguish "normal" policy from a "false" policy leading to economic crisis.

remains unchanged. If for example the *de facto* structure of property rights is significantly changed by problems of contract enforcement, political risk emerges. Henceforth, aggregate political risk is defined as the sum of possible exogenous and endogenous risk factors where uncertainty about future governmental action or non-action as well as abrupt changes or discontinuities decrease the value of private assets due to an alteration of the property rights structure.

2.2.5.2 Categories of Political Risk and Anecdotal Evidence

The last decade saw an enormous increase of private capital flows to developing countries. This growing internationalization of capital markets and the experience of several emerging market crises during the 90s made the evaluation of country risk and political risk a leading issue in the world of international finance. However, already the expropriations of resource extracting foreign facilities in developing countries during the 30s, 60s and 70s made international investors aware of political risks as a relevant determinant of investment decisions. As a reaction to the suffered losses MNEs aimed at removing the contractual relationship with developing countries from the supremacy of local laws, by requiring that the contract be governed by general principles of international law recognized by civilized nations. However, various attempts to conclude multilateral conventions on the subject of foreign investment protection, such as most recently the Multilateral Agreement on Investment (MAI) were unsuccessful.[101]

Moreover, the high relevance of political risks as a problem of international finance is reflected by the specialization of several public organizations in risk bearing and forecasting on the national and multinational level as well as by the large sums covered by political risk insurers. By 1998 new coverage issued by members of the Berne Union for political risk insurance reached an amount of 42 billion US$.[102] When compared with the total volume of world wide FDI of 644 billion US$ for the same year, this figure underlines the importance of the political risk insurance sector. In addition to these public efforts the last years witnessed the emergence of a large private market for the insurance of political risks. In the last decade this market saw a fast growth of private insurance companies offering innovative solutions for private investors willing to invest in foreign markets that are perceived as risky.[103] Responding to the large demand private insurers considerably increased their confiscation, expropriation, nationalization insurance capacity (CEN) per project over the last years. The market leader Lloyd's of London for instance pushed its CEN to

---

[101] These contractual solutions began to flaw when developing countries proclaimed a „New International Economic Order" claiming the sovereignty of each state to regulate foreign investment and to nationalize foreign property. See Bernardini (2001) p.236-238.

[102] The Berne Union encompasses 24 national investment ensurers and Multilateral Investment Guarantee Agency (MIGA). See West/Martin (2001a) p.153.

[103] See Benmansour/Vadcar (1995) p. 149-170, West/Martin (2001a) and West/Martin (2001b). Most political risk insurance contracts focus on developing countries.

900 million US$ for the year 1999.[104] Besides their demand for political risk insurance recent research shows that most MNEs are simultaneously active in in-house political risk assessment.[105] The interest of private investors in organizations that bear parts of their foreign investment risks leads to the conclusion that political risk is a major impediment of international capital flows to developing countries. On the multilateral level organizations like the Multilateral Investment Guarantee Agency (MIGA) and the International Finance Corporation (IFC) are aware of this problem and offer solutions for investors willing to engage in developing countries or emerging markets with a high level of risk. While the previous chapter provided a theoretical definition of the term political risk, this paragraph is concerned with the different categories of political risks that may affect MNEs. Following SIMON political risk may be categorized by using three main characteristics. These criteria for classifying risks and real world examples for the resulting categories of risk are depicted in figure 2.19.

Figure 2.19: Typology of Political Risks

Macro Risks		Micro Risks	
Societal-related	**Governmental-related**	**Societal-related**	**Governmental-related**
Endogenous			
Revolution	Nationalization	Selective terrorism	Selective Expropriation
Wars	Expropriation	Actions against personnel	Changes in Regulation
Coups d'etats	Creeping expropriation	Selective strikes	Operational Restrictions
Violence	Repatriation restrictions	Selective protests	Discriminatory Taxation
Factional Conflict	Change of Public Priorities	National boycott of firm	Local content rules
Civil Unrest	Change of Party		Breach of Contract
Widespread riots	Change of Government		Loss of copyright protection
Nationwide Strikes	Change of Ministers		Price controls
Shifts in public opinion	Corruption		
Union activism	High inflation		
	Level of Public Spending		
	Exchange Controls		
	Labor Market Policy		
Exogenous			
Cross-National Guerilla	Warfare	International activists	Diplomatic stress between
International terrorism	Border conflicts	Selective international	host and home country
World public opinion	Alliance shifts	terrorism	Bilateral trade agreements
Disinvestment pressure	Embargoes	International boycott of firm	Multilateral trade
	International boycotts		agreements
	Protectionism		Selective Import/export
	Unsustainable external debt		restrictions
	International economic		Foreign government
	instability		interference

Source: Own figure based on Simon (1982) p.67.

---

[104] See the overview by West (2001) p.52-58, West/Martin (2001a) p.139-145 and West/Martin (2001b) p.207-230.

[105] In a survey of US multinationals Hashmi/Guvenli (1992) find that all respondents at least occasionally engage in political risk analysis. Over 50% of the multinationals have a regular (yearly or quarterly) political risk assessment pattern. In the words of a leading manager; " [Host country] governance is as important as value." Cited in Henisz/Zelner (2003a) p.2.

First, the source of political risks can be either exogenous or endogenous to the political process in a given host country. Cross national warfare, for example, is an exogenous risk factor while civil strife is an endogenous risk. Second, political risks can be related to governmental action like expropriations or rather to societal events like strikes or riots. Third, political risk may affect all firms in the host country (macro-risk) or just specific firms (micro-risks).[106] It follows that aggregate political risk is shaped by endogenous and exogenous risk factors which may differently affect firms present in the host country. Although figure 2.19 suggests that political risks can be precisely categorized, in reality all these different sources of political risk are interdependent.

Figure 2.20 shows the possible interactions of endogenous and exogenous political risk factors and gives real world examples for the interaction of these two risk types.

Figure 2.20: Dimensions of Aggregate Country Risk

| | NATURE OF ENDOGENOUS RISK FACTORS | | |
NATURE OF EXOGENOUS RISK FACTORS	Not significant	Sector-specific	General
Not significant	No Risk	Shift in regulation Targeted expropriation	Breakdown in Public Order General Expropriation
Sector-specific	Commercial Losses on firm-level	Creeping Expropriation through Windfall Taxes	More of the same
General	Economy-wide Commercial Losses	Commercial Losses	Economy wide Total Loss

Source: Lessard (1993) p.453

Both figures highlight that political risks are far from being homogenous. Instead, investors face such diverse forms of risks as wars, expropriations, strikes, shifts in regulation and so on. It follows that political risk is a complex multidimensional phenomenon implying that suitable political risk indicators have to contain several potential sources of risk. Furthermore, it is straightforward to see that even if an indicator pictures the main potential sources of risk in a given country, it can hardly be complete.

Another useful classification of political risk is provided by SCHIFFER/WEDER who distinguish between catastrophic and creeping political risk. The term catastrophic political risk refers to the classical risks that a host government expropriates the investor without offering compensation or that other catastrophic circumstances like wars, coups or civil unrest imply the total loss of private assets. This risk is usually closely related to significant changes in political power implying major policy changes. Creeping political risks or creeping expropriations in turn, contain all forms of unexpected changes in the

---

[106] See Simon (1982).

institutional framework that reduce the value of private assets without resulting in a total loss of the title on private property.[107] In other words, a creeping expropriation does not result in a formal dispossession of property by its owner. Instead, a creeping expropriation implies that governmental actions as for example regulatory policy reduce the profits of private assets by slowly diluting property rights. For a better understanding of the latter consider the example of an infrastructure investment which is subject to national regulation. By altering the conditions of regulation the government possesses a powerful tool to reduce the profits of private investors. As those investors cannot easily withdraw, the governments have a strong incentive to act opportunistically by ex-post changes of taxes or regulations.[108] This incentive to exploit the investor by altering the relevant framework, ex-ante becomes a disincentive for companies planning an investment. While from this point of view a long-term commitment of the regulating body is desirable, one has to be aware of the problem that the benefit of a short term commitment is the flexibility to rectify wrong decisions of previous administrations.[109] Faced with the large variety of political risks it is interesting to identify those political risk which are of particular importance for international investors. The easiest way to do so is to analyze for which kinds of political risks there is a demand or an offer of insurance contracts on the international political risk insurance market. For its guarantee and insurance business MIGA offers four big categories of political risks insurance contracts which are depicted in figure 2.21.

The risk of War and Civil Disturbance means that private assets are affected by a loss from, a damage to, or the destruction or disappearance of, tangible assets caused by politically-motivated acts of war or civil disturbance in the host country, including revolution, insurrection, coups d'état, sabotage, and terrorism. Protection against war and civil disturbance also extends to events that, for a certain period, result in an interruption of project operations essential to overall financial viability. This type of business interruption is effective when the investment is considered a total loss.[110] A good example for firms being affected by revolutionary disturbances are the U.S. firms based in Iran under the leadership of the U.S. friendly shah. Used to the former friendly policy

---

[107] See Schiffer/Weder (2000).

[108] As a leading manager put it: "... If there is regulated price, the price will be used for political purposes. If anyone assumes that there will be no changes it is naive. It is more than naive, it is stupid...." Cited in Henisz/Zelner (2003b). There are many contributions in the literature which analyze the "bargaining power" of multinational firms relative to host country governments. Already Vernon stressed that governments have an incentive to renege on initial contracts when multinationals capital is sunk and its technology has diffused locally. As Vernon puts it: " As long as a foreign-owned goose can still lay golden eggs, ... the policy of most developing countries has been to squeeze the goose, not to destroy it or to have it fly away. Accordingly, multinational enterprises that perform a unique function, such as providing access to some difficult technology or some otherwise inaccessible foreign market, have generally been less vulnerable to government pressures, while subsidiaries whose withdrawal is thought to entail very little national loss have been more vulnerable." Cited in Henisz/Zelner (2003b)

[109] See Laffont/Tirole (1994).

[110] See MIGA (2002).

towards foreign firms they were strongly affected by the riots and civil disturbances preceding the Iranian Revolution.[111] More recently one can cite the losses of U.S. firms in Haiti or in former Yugoslavia that were due to civil strife.[112]

Figure 2.21: Categories of Political Risk Insurance offered by MIGA

CATEGORY	DEFINITION
War and Civil Disturbance	Private assets are affected by a loss from, a damage to, or the destruction or disappearance of, tangible assets caused by politically-motivated acts of war or civil disturbance
Restricted Transfer of Profits	Loss of the investment as a result of acts by the host government that may reduce or eliminate ownership of, control over, or rights to the insured investment
Breach of Contract	Refers to losses arising from the host government's breach or repudiation of a contract with the investor
Expropriation	Transfer Restriction means losses arising from an investor's inability to convert local currency (capital, interest, principal, profits, royalties and other remittances) into foreign exchange for transfer outside the host country

Source: Own figure based on MIGA (2002).

With expropriation MIGA identifies the loss of the investment as a result of acts by the host government that may reduce or eliminate ownership of, control over, or rights to the insured investment. In addition to outright nationalization and confiscation, "creeping" expropriation, that is a series of acts that, over time, have an expropriatory effect, is also covered. MIGA insurance coverage is available on a limited basis for partial expropriation (e.g., confiscation of funds or tangible assets). Not covered are non-discriminatory measures by the host government in the exercise of legitimate regulatory authority.[113] There are many historical examples for expropriations of foreign investors. The nationalization of the oil industry, the banking sector and the sulphur industry in Mexico.[114] The nationalization of the International Petroleum Company and many other foreign firms between 1968 and 1975 by the Peruvian government or the wave of nationalizations under the presidency of Allende in Chile between 1970-1973. Another prominent example is the "Zairianization-Program" enacted by president Mobutu expropriating more than 1500 foreign-owned enterprises.[115] A more recent example is the expropriation of white farmers in Zimbabwe under Mugabe.

Breach of Contract refers to losses arising from the host government's breach or repudiation of a contract with the investor. In the event of an alleged breach or repudiation, the investor must be able to invoke a dispute resolution mechanism (e.g., an arbitration) in the underlying contract and obtain an award for damages. If, after a specified period of time, the investor has not received payment or if the dispute resolution mechanism fails to function

---

[111] See Kennedy (1991).
[112] See Howell/Chaddick (1994).
[113] See MIGA (2002).
[114] For a more detailed review of expropriations in Mexico see paragraph 5.1.2.2.
[115] See Kennedy (1991) and Markwick (2001) p.41.

because of actions taken by the host government, MIGA will pay compensation.[116] A historical example for a breach of contract is the case of Belco and Occidental, two oil corporations active in Peru. When Garcia was elected president in 1985 he forced the two companies to renegotiate their operating agreements on less favorable terms.[117]

The risk of transfer restrictions refers to potential losses arising from an investor's inability to convert local currency (capital, interest, principal, profits, royalties and other remittances) into foreign exchange for transfer outside the host country. The coverage of MIGA insures against excessive delays in acquiring foreign exchange caused by host government action or failure to act, by adverse changes in exchange control laws or regulations, and by deterioration in conditions governing the conversion and transfer of local currency. Losses that are caused by currency devaluation are not covered. There are many historical examples for the imposition of transfer restrictions. During the 60s South Africa reacted with capital controls to the massive flight of capital following riots in major cities. In the aftermath of the peso devaluation during the debt crisis Mexico imposed foreign exchange controls.[118] More recently China arbitrarily ended the allocation of foreign exchange to a Chinese-American joint venture for political reasons in 1989.[119]

Summing up, the aforementioned examples as well as the large private and public offer for the insurance of political risks highlight the importance of this topic for the structure of international capital flows. Furthermore this paragraph underlined the importance of political risk analysis in the investment decision process of MNEs. The next paragraph reviews existing economic models of political and country risk.

2.2.5.3 Modeling Political Risks for International Investors
2.2.5.3.1 Existing Models of Political Risks
The anecdotal evidence from the previous paragraph illustrated how political risk may adversely affect international investors and borrowers. The economic modeling of such risks was given a lot of attention in reaction to the debt crisis at the beginning of the 80s. However, being the most important form of inter-national capital flows at that time, most of the authors were concerned with debt flows. These models analyze problems that arise out of credit relations between developed and developing countries with a particular interest in the factors determining the default risk of countries. The main conclusion offered by these types of models is that the major problem of international lending is contract enforcement. As supranational institutions lack the power to ensure an efficient enforcement of international contracts, sanctions which are imposed on a country that defaults on its international debt are usually inefficient. To put it in other words, in international lending no mechanisms

---

[116] See MIGA (2002).
[117] See Kennedy (1991) p.44-61.
[118] See Simon (1982) p.67.
[119] See Howell/Chaddick (1994).

exist that would allow for a credible commitment to repayment as it is the case for national debt contracts.[120] Technically speaking host countries are confronted with a severe problem of time inconsistency, which means that the government has an incentive to ex post reverse its ex ante plans.

Compared to the abundance of literature on the impact of country risk or political risk on international lending there are fewer models that are concerned with the influence of political risk on international investment flows. Earlier models of political risk are mainly concerned with the question of how political risks emerge in host countries. and do not explain how political risks influence FDI flows.[121] Despite of the distinct characteristics of debt and investment, the problem of time inconsistency in the sovereign debt models can also be extended to investment problems being aware of one major difference. A debt contract usually contains a set of formal rules which are agreed on by the contracting parties implying that deviations from the agreements can easily be identified although contract enforcement remains difficult. In the case of FDI there is a great variety of possible host government interference with private assets which may not be explicitly covered in a contract. This fact makes the identification and sanctioning of deviations more difficult and renders the problem of time inconsistency more severe for FDI.[122] Despite of potential risks for foreign investors developing countries witnessed a growth of FDI inflows during the last decades. This, in turn, suggests that there must be at least indirect sanctioning mechanisms that prevent governments from the worst opportunistic behavior.

To explain this EATON/GERSOVITZ present a model assuming that expropriated investors will never invest again in the former host countries. As a reaction to opportunistic behavior of the host country government they consequently exclude it from foreign capital flows in the future implying that after an opportunistic deviation the host country exclusively relies on the domestic capital stock. One finds a similar line of argument in the more recent contribution of COLE/ENGLISH. Both models stress a "reputation effect" that reduces the incentive of governments to act opportunistically. Deciding over opportunistic behavior, governments have to consider the trade-off between the one time gain and the discounted future losses of their actions. So weighting the cost and benefits of an expropriation can prevent them from expropriating if the future losses are large enough.[123]

Inherent to the argumentation of these two models is the fact that greater independence from other countries increases a government's incentive to act opportunistically because the autarchy cost of being excluded in the future is lower. The implicit assumption is that the cost of opportunistic behavior is de-

---

[120] For a review of the older literature see Eaton/Gersovitz/Stiglitz (1986).
[121] See the overview in Oseghale (1993). This emergence of political risk is discussed in greater detail in paragraph 3.2.
[122] See Harms (2000).
[123] See Eaton/Gersovitz (1983) and Cole/English (1991).

creasing in the country's income and the size of the national capital stock. This, in turn, implies the awkward result that the risk of a country is growing in its level of development. Following this logic richer countries should turn out to be more riskier than poor countries which is clearly at odds with the existing empirical evidence that rather suggests the opposite. It follows that the cost of autarchy have to be influenced by more factors than just the national capital stock. Other sanctions that establish a positive correlation of income and cost of autarchy are reductions in the country's productivity, disruptions in its ability to trade or the seizure of assets or these assets' returns that a country holds abroad.[124]

KONRAD models the expropriation risk of foreign investors as the result of a competition between investors and several competing government groups which lack supreme power to fully reallocate property rights.[125] In a recent paper JANEBA uses a model in which investments can be made simultaneously in more than one country which do not only differ in terms of production cost but also in the degree of commitment power. In this framework MNEs face a trade-off between investing in a low-cost and low-credibility country on the one hand and a high-cost but high credibility country on the other hand. If the low credibility country cannot give a credible commitment to the existing tax rate the existence of a high credibility country allows the firm to produce in both countries or to hold excess capacity for strategic reasons. Doing so the firm can minimize the risk that the firm becomes a victim of opportunistic behavior in the low credibility country. Therefore, holding plants in politically stable countries reduces the firm's dependence on a single government. The power to shift production quickly reduces the influence of political risk on the amount that is invested. As expected lacking commitment of host governments leads to welfare-losses. Yet they are not due to mere under-investment but caused by the fact that the MNE produces and invest in the less cost efficient location.[126]

2.2.5.3.2 Implications of General Investment Models
The previous paragraph reviewed a set of models which focused on the special characteristics of FDI to explain the impact of political risks on the investment behavior of MNEs. The approach offered here focuses on the decision making process of the foreign investor. To do so the effects of uncertainty on investment decisions that were analyzed in paragraph 2.1.3 have to be recalled. The presented models permit to derive the result that uncertainty reduces investment spending, when investment projects are irreversible. Although decisions about FDI differ from decisions about domestic projects, the characteristics of the investment decision process are similar because rational economic actors only invest if a considered project is advantageous.

---

[124] See Harms (2000) p.95-100.
[125] See Konrad (2001).
[126] See Janeba (2001).

Hence, similar to the process of investing in their home countries foreign investors base their decisions on a calculus designed to assess the profitability of the project. Therefore, the results which have been derived for general investment problems are also valid for international investment decision. This, in turn, means that also foreign investors will react with a reduction of investment spending when uncertainty increases and investments are irreversible. Hence, it may be argued that a rise in host country uncertainty will affect FDI in the same way as it affects domestic investment decisions. In addition foreign investors face an informational disadvantage vis-a-vis their local competitors which means that the influence of rising uncertainty should have an even stronger influence on foreign investors than on their domestic counterparts. Accepting the fact that political uncertainties negatively affect local investors it is plausible to argue that their foreign counterparts are likewise or even more affected. Therefore, the policy implications derived from the DIXIT/PINDYCK model are essentially valid for international investment problems.

Assume that a firm is planning to invest in a foreign country and that during the decision process it analyzes the aggregate risk of the project. Assume that σ_A is the aggregate risk of the investment project which corresponds to the parameter that reflected uncertainty of expected payoffs in the DIXIT/PINDYCK model where higher uncertainty was characterized by a higher variance of future returns. Paragraph 2.2.5.1 defined political risk as uncertainty about the future interference or non-interference of governments as well as abrupt changes or discontinuities in policy affecting the revenues from or the value of private assets. To analyze how this type of risk influences the overall risk of the project I assume the possibility that every component of a project's aggregate risk can be separately identified. The historical examples in the preceding paragraph showed that political risks often severely influence the return of investment projects and in many cases even imply a total loss of the invested assets. Let σ_{PR} be the parameter measuring the influence of the level of political uncertainty in the host country on the planned project. Let the aggregate risk of a project σ_A be the sum of different independent partial risks σ_1 - σ_n and a product of this sum with general political risk affecting each independent risk of the project. The independent partial risks are determined by the characteristics of the project and the current situation on the world market. Hence, the sum of this independent partial risk reflects the inherent risk of the project without any intervention of the government or other non-economic events affecting its return. Political risk is an exogenous factor that may influence the profitability of the project independent from its inherent characteristics. The existence of political risk can imply that a project becomes disadvantageous that would be inherently profitable, if it was not affected by other exogenous risks. That is to say, if the project was realized in an environment that was perfectly stable its return would be positive. Exogenous political risk may arise in various forms. Expropriations, breach of contract, civil disturbances and other risk factors can imply a loss to the firm although the project in itself is profitable. For reasons of simplicity assume that σ_{PR} is the only source of political risk that has an influence on the independent inherent risks of the project. Hence, σ_A can be written as:

(2.26) $\sigma_A = (\sigma_1 + \sigma_2 + \ldots\ldots\ldots + \sigma_n)\sigma_{PR}$

or

(2.27) $\sigma_A = (\sum_{i=1}^{n} \sigma_i)\sigma_{PR}$

where σ_{PR} is a multiplier that can theoretically take every value between 0 and ∞ and captures the influence of aggregate political risk on the variance of a project's returns. It is straightforward to see from equation (2.27) that every change in the level of political risk immediately affects the aggregate risk of the project. If σ_{PR} exceeds unity aggregate political risk is increasing the variance of the project's returns which implies a higher level of aggregate project risk for the investor. A parameter value of unity in turn, would imply that the existing level of political risk is not significant for the return of the project and its risk is solely determined by its inherent characteristics. In this situation investors can focus on real commercial project risks rather than on policy risks created by potentially adverse government actions. A parameter value of $\sigma_{PR}<1$ is at first sight less intuitive because it means that aggregate risk of the project is decreased by the existing level of political risk. However, taking the example of a firm that is state-owned or at least backed by public guarantees and whose total debts in the case of default will be covered by the state it becomes imaginable that the individual risk is lowered by public intervention. In this case the institutional design of the host country reduces the de facto risk of the project.

Assuming that σ_{PR} enters as a multiplier as shown (2.26) and (2.27) is restrictive because it means that every partial risk of the project is affected by a change in the political environment. Although historical evidence shows that this assumption is realistic for many risks of a project, this is hardly valid for all. For example project risks due to technical characteristics or natural processes are not affected by a change in the overall political environment of the host country. If the independent partial risks that are influenced by political risk are denoted with σ_i and those that remain unaffected with σ_e, equation can be modified and becomes:

(2.28) $\sigma_A = \sum_{e=1}^{n} \sigma_e + (\sum_{i=1}^{n} \sigma_i)\sigma_{PR}$

It can easily be seen from (2.28) that the influence of a variation in σ_{PR} now has less impact on the aggregate risk σ_A. Although smaller, the impact of a variation in the level of political risk is, all other things equal, still evident.

The effect of political risk on investment decision is illustrated in figure 2.22 that is analogue to the graphical solution of the DIXIT/PINDYCK-Model from paragraph 2.1.3.4.

Figure 2.22: Effects of Political Risk in the DIXIT/PINDYCK-Model

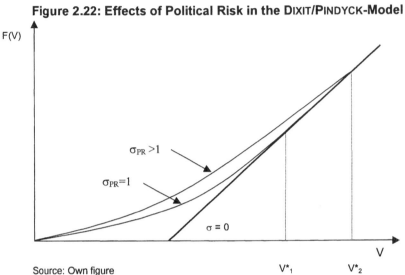

Source: Own figure

With σ_{PR} >1 the F(V) line shifts to the left implying that the value of the option to invest increases. Economically this means that higher variations of future earnings imply that for the firm the value of new information and thus the value of waiting increases. Being an opportunity cost of investing today the higher option value renders fewer projects advantageous because the critical value for the profitability of the project V* goes up. Hence, with a higher level of risk the tangency point between the F(V) line and the V-I line moves to the right. With V^*_2 as the new critical value including political risk, investments that would be favorable if just economic risks were considered generate losses to the firm. As a consequence firms reduce investment spending which implies that with a significant level of political risk, that is a value of σ_{PR} >1, all other things equal current FDI flows to host countries tend to decrease. It is obvious that the assumption that the aggregate risk of a given project can be precisely divided in sub-risks is not realistic. Nevertheless, this theoretical approach allows for a better understanding of how political risk affects profitability and private investment decisions.

2.2.5.4 Empirical Evidence
The previous paragraph presented a model studying the impact of political risk on the investment decision of MNEs. This paragraph reviews the existing empirical studies on the impact of political risk on FDI. There are various empirical methods that may be used to assess the importance of political risk in the investment decision process of MNEs. The most straightforward empirical approach is to ask decision makers in MNEs for their opinion about

the influence of political risk on their investment behavior. When surveyed about the importance of political risk managers usually rank moderate or low political risk among the most important criteria for an investment decision abroad.

Table 2.4 summarizes existing empirical studies using interviews or surveys to investigate the importance of political risk for investment decisions of MNEs. Already the pioneering studies of BASI, AHARONI, and ROOT indicate that political risk is a decisive variable for the decision of MNEs to start productive activities abroad.[127]

Table 2.4: Survey-Based Empirical Studies of Political Risk

Author	Method	Sample	Main Findings
Basi (1963)	Mail survey of international executives	International Companies	• A country's political risk and market potential are main determinants of FDI
Aharoni (1966)	In-depth interviews with company officials	38 U.S. corporations that were invested or planned to invest in Israel	• Political risk is a decisive variable for FDI decisions
Root (1968)	Mail-Survey of company officials	106 officials from UK, France, Mexico, Brazil and India.	• Political risk is an important determinant of FDI
Bass/McGregor/Waters (1977)	Survey asking executives to rate 44 variables concerning their relative importance for FDI decisions	175 firms contacted out of which 102 responded	• Host government policies and government instability are important determinants of FDI
Rolfe et al. (1993)	Survey of US companies asking for preferred investment incentives	103 US companies with operations abroad	• Officials ranked the absence of transfer restrictions and the existence of guarantees against expropriation as more important than tax incentives
OECD (1994)	Survey of company officials of investors and potential investors about motives of investment and faced barriers	291 company officials from an international pool of firms	• Bureaucratic, legislative issues and political volatility are mentioned as investment barriers
Tu/Schive (1995)	Mail survey of foreign companies in Taiwan asking for the relative importance of 18 factors for FDI decisions	1000 international companies contacted out of which 121 responded	• Political Stability, social order and governmental attitude towards FDI are important factors for FDI
Hatem (1997)	Combination of questionnaire and interviews	311 international firms (mostly US and European) answering the questionnaire and 100 firms giving direct interviews	• Political and social risk are important determinants of FDI
Hatem (1998)	Combination of questionnaire and interviews	311 international firms (US and European) answering the questionnaire and 100 firms giving direct interviews	• Political and social risk are important determinants of FDI
IADB (2001)	Survey asking for major obstacles to business	At least 100 companies in each of 73 countries	• Policy instability is a major obstacle to business operations

---

[127] See Basi (1963), Aharoni (1966) and Root (1968).

Table 2.4: Continued

Author	Method	Sample	Main Findings
MIGA (2002)	Global FDI-Survey	191 transnational corporations	• 64% of the surveyed companies see a stable political and social environment as a very influential determinant of FDI decisions, 36% see corruption and 33% crime and safety as very influential. • Between 40 and 60 % see war, security of staff, transfer restriction, breach of contract, ineffective enforcement of laws and expropriations as the greatest risks for FDI.
Ng/Tuan (2002)	Mail survey of foreign investors	124 foreign companies in China	• Stability and continuity of governmental policy are important for the investment environment • The absence of capital transfer restrictions is important for the investment environment
McKinsey&Company (2002)	Global Survey of Investor Opinion	Worldwide survey of 200 institutional investors	• 46% of investors think that effective enforcement of property rights is very important for investment decision • 32% think that efforts of the government to fight corruption are very important for investment decision

Source: Own table

Recent survey studies confirm these findings. ROLFE ET AL. asked U.S. companies for a ranking of their preferred investment incentives. Among twenty incentives the absence of transfer restrictions and the existence of guarantees against expropriation turned out to be more important than tax cuts.[128]

OECD asked 291 company officials of potential investors and investors in transition countries about motives for and barriers to investment decisions. The main obstacles that were mentioned by managers were bureaucratic and legislative issues as well as political volatility.[129] TU/SCHIVE surveyed the opinions of managers of foreign companies in Taiwan. Among 18 other potentially influential factors for FDI political stability and social order were consistently ranked at the top.[130] The international survey of over 300 questionnaires and 100 direct interviews with international companies by HATEM offers similar results. In particular, U.S. and Japanese companies ranked political and social risks as important determinants of their investment decision.[131] In a recent report the IADB published a survey asking 100

---

[128] See Rolfe et al. (1993).
[129] See OECD (1994).
[130] See Tu/Schive (1995).
[131] See Hatem (1997) and Hatem (1998).

companies in each of the analyzed 73 countries for major obstacles to doing business. Policy instability ranked on the third place after problems of financing and taxes. When analyzing the Latin American sample the result was even clearer as in Venezuela, Ecuador and Brazil around 70% of the surveyed business people think that policy instability is a major obstacle to business. For Colombia, Mexico and Peru around 50% hold the same view.[132]

Other empirical studies use historical data to explain the determinants of incoming FDI using econometric models. The empirical evidence of older econometric studies that vary largely in methodology, perspective and sample selection is mixed. Most of these econometric studies reject the hypothesis that political risk has a significant negative correlation with FDI.[133] More recent econometric studies are reviewed in table 2.5.[134]

SCHNEIDER/FREY use a variable that measures past and present policies (GNP) and the investors' perception of the future policy of the country. The latter is proxied by the Institutional Investor Country Credit Rating (IICCR) which is published by the Institutional Investor Magazine. Both variables' coefficients were significant at the 99% level. Moreover, the study shows a negative correlation between the number of political strikes and riots in the host country on FDI.[135]

In a panel-regression of manufacturing investment of U.S. firms WHEELER/MODY find that political risk had no significant impact on investment. The index Risk they added as a proxy for political risk is based on criteria like "terrorism risk", the "probability of opposition takeover", the "distribution of wealth" and the "attitude towards private enterprise". However, other crucial criteria like expropriation risk are missing.

HARMS argues that the insignificance of political risk maybe due to a sample selection bias as the sample consists of 22 high-income countries, 16 middle income countries and 4 low-income countries. This, in turn, implies that countries in which political risk is assumed to be of particular importance are clearly underrepresented.[136] Furthermore the study focuses on the electronics industry which may be considered as "footloose" implying low irreversibility. This, in turn, reduces the influence of political risk variables as the comparatively low levels of sunk costs enable a quick withdrawal if risks are increasing.

---

[132] See IADB (2001) p.27-33.
[133] For an overview of older studies see UN (1992) p.50-52 and Oseghale (1993).
[134] It has to be underlined that many of these studies do not explicitly focus on the analysis of political risk but just include risk indicators as control variables.
[135] See Schneider/Frey (1985).
[136] See Wheeler/Mody (1992) and the comment of Harms (2000) p.65.

Table 2.5: Econometric Empirical Studies of Political Risk

Author	Method	Sample	Main Findings
Green/Cunningham (1972)	Cross sectional analysis	25 countries	• Political Instability does not affect FDI
Schneider/Frey (1985)	Cross sectional analysis	54 developing countries	• Investors' perception of future policy of the country proxied by the Institutional Investor Country Credit Rating (IICCR) was significant at the 99% level. • Negative correlation between the number of political strikes and riots in the host country and FDI
Billet (1991)	Cross sectional analysis of various years for the period 1975-1986	108 developing countries	• Political Instability does affect incoming FDI • Political Repression does not have a positive impact on FDI
Wheeler/Mody (1992)	Panel Analysis	41 countries	• Political risk has little effect on FDI • Geopolitical risk is a significant determinant of FDI
Oseghale (1993)		Latin American countries	• adverse changes in host government policy have a significant negative correlation with FDI • political instability and conflicts with other states had significantly negative effects in many sub-samples but did not turn out to be robust in all tested model settings
Woodward/Rolfe (1993)	Panel Analysis	187 foreign investment projects in the Caribean	• An indicator of political stability was significant at the 10% level.
Jun/Singh (1996)	Panel Analysis	31 countries	• Both tested indices of political risk have a significant influence on FDI as a share of GDP • Average number of work days that are lost due to strikes or other events are significant for countries with low levels of incoming FDI
Harms (2000)		55 developing countries	• A significant effect of political risk on foreign investment • Splitting the sample into a low income and a high income group the coefficient is higher but less significant than in the middle-income sub sample
Drabek/Payne (2001)	Panel Analysis	52 countries	• Higher government transparency positively affects FDI flows
Hausmann/Arias (2001)	Panel Analysis	Latin American countries	• Country Risk has a strong and significant impact on incoming capital flows • Institutional quality has a strong positive and significant impact on FDI

Table 2.5: Continued

Author	Method	Sample	Main Findings
Harm/Ursprung (2002)	Panel Analysis	62 developing and emerging market countries	• High levels of individual freedom attract FDI. • Sum of three sub indices of the International Country Risk Guide measuring corruption in government, the quality of the bureaucracy and a country's law and order is a significant determinant of FDI
Sun/Tong/Yun (2002)	Panel Analysis	30 Chinese provinces	• The risk ranking of Political Risk Services Group used as a proxy for political risk is significant on the 1% level
Stein/Daude (2002)	Panel Analysis	63 countries	• Institutional quality of nations has a strong positive and significant impact on FDI • Lack of government commitment deters FDI
Jost/Nunnenkamp (2002)	Panel Analysis	Host countries for German FDI	• Country Risk has a significant impact on capital flows from Germany

Source: Own Table

OSEGHALE analyzes the influence of political risk on investment with time series examining U.S. FDI in Latin American Countries. A variable measuring adverse changes in host government policy has a significant negative correlation with FDI to host countries. Variables measuring political instability and conflicts with other states had significantly negative effects in many sub-samples but did not turn out to be robust in all tested model settings.[137] WOODWARD/ROLFE analyzed 187 foreign investment projects in the Caribbean Basin for the period from 1984-1987. They find an indicator of political stability to be significant at the 10% level.[138] JUN/SINGH test potential determinants of FDI divided by GDP using a panel of 31 countries for the period from 1970 to 1993. As a proxy for political risk they include the Political Risk Index (PRI) and the Operation Risk Index (ORI) of Business Environment Risk Intelligence (BERI). The PRI-index assesses the likelihood of political instability whereas the ORI-Index measures the general business environment. A panel of 105 experts evaluate a wide range of factors as the "enforceability of contracts", "nationalization" and the "attitude towards foreign investors and profits". JUN/SINGH find that both indexes have a significant influence. Furthermore, they find that the average number of work days that are lost due to strikes or other events are significant for FDI to countries with low levels of incoming FDI.[139]

BISWAS uses sub-indices published in the International Country Risk Guide of the Political Risk Services Group (PRS Group). The indices reflect the risk of

---

[137] See Oseghale (1993).
[138] See Woodward/Rolfe (1993).
[139] See Jun/Singh (1996).

contract repudiation by host country governments, the risk of expropriation, the quality of the bureaucracy, the degree of corruption and the rule of law. The study uses a panel of 44 countries for the period from 1983 to 1990 and finds a significant influence of the risk indices on U.S. FDI divided by GNP.[140] In a recent econometric study on FDI to China SUN/TONG/YU find strong evidence that political risk is a significant determinant of investment. Using a panel of 30 Chinese provinces for the period 1986-1998 and introducing the risk ranking of PRS Group as a proxy for political risk they find the coefficient to be significant on the 1% level. This result turns out to be robust for several model settings and sub-periods.[141]

HARMS uses a panel of 55 developing countries for the period from 1987 to 1995 to test for the influence of political risk on foreign investment measured as the sum of FDI and portfolio equity investment in per capita terms. Controlling for the quality of infrastructure, macroeconomic distortions, openness and the evolution of international interest rates he finds a significant effect of political risk on investment. Splitting the sample into a low income and a high income group he finds that the coefficient is higher but less significant in the middle-income sub-sample.[142] In a later paper HARMS/URSPRUNG tested the hypothesis that international investment is attracted by political regimes that deny their citizens political rights making it easier to suppress wages. In a panel analysis of 62 developing and emerging market countries for the period from 1989 to 1997 they find the opposite. Proxying citizens'political rights with the Freedom House Index of Political Rights and Civil Liberties they find that a high level of individual freedom attracts FDI. In the same analysis they also included a variable that is the sum of three subindices of the International Country Risk Guide (ICRG) measuring corruption in government, the quality of the bureaucracy and a country's law and order tradition which turned out to be significant determinants of FDI.[143]

This review of existing empirical studies shows that there is strong evidence for a decisive influence of political risk examining manager surveys while the results of econometric studies are less striking. These divergent empirical results indicate that the failure of many econometric studies to show a significant impact of political risk on FDI rather stem from methodological deficiencies than from the absence of a significant correlation between the two variables. There are many theoretical and methodological objections to existing econometric studies.[144] One important theoretical objection is the choice of the variables that proxy political risks. Although the reviewed studies vary considerably in their choice of dependent variables, most of them identify

---

[140] Harms (2000) delivers an overview of the study.
[141] See Sun/Tong/Yu (2002).
[142] See Harms (2000).
[143] See Harms/Ursprung (2002). Billet (1991) offers a discussion about the the influence of civil rights repression on FDI flows. In an empirical analysis he finds that in relatively richer developing countries like Latin American countries political repression does not create a better business climate. See Billet (1991) p.29-53.
[144] See Oseghale (1993).

political risk with some measure of political stability and social turmoil while other important components of political risk as for example the risk of expropriation are systematically not considered. Another theoretical drawback of these indicators of political risk is their exclusively backward-looking nature based on the implicit assumption that risk evaluations are mainly influenced by past policy events. However, if investors are rational, they should rather be concerned about the probability that policies may change unfavorable in the future. As a result most of these indicators should be weak predictors of the future investment climate.[145] Another reason for the deficiencies of existing econometric studies is the influence of other variables and a low quality of data.

Moreover, even if a significant influence of aggregate political risk indicators is detected, the sources of risk are not transparent and not further explored. Given these unsatisfying results, it is impossible to derive policy implications for developing countries seeking to attract more FDI. Applying different methodologies of political risk analysis simultaneously permits a better understanding of the sources of political risks and allows to formulate strategies for the mitigation of risk. Therefore, the author considers it useful to combine econometric analysis with an in depth analysis of a country case study.[146] Furthermore, the econometric methodology is modified to better suit the characteristics of empirical FDI models which permits to obtain more conclusive results on the impact of political risks on FDI.

2.3 Concluding Remarks
This paragraph postulates some primary hypotheses that may be drawn from Chapter 2 that are to be examined in greater detail in the following chapters. Investment models under uncertainty permit the theoretical conclusion that uncertainty reduces investment spending when investment projects are irreversible. Furthermore theoretical analysis and the review of the existing empirical evidence suggest that political risk is an influential variable for the investment decision process of MNEs. Given the fierce competition for FDI among developing nations, high national levels of political risk become a major obstacle for incoming FDI. Developing countries often lack an institutional structure that permits the creation of a stable and reliable business environment. Expropriation risks, corruption, populist policies, regulatory and judicial inefficiency as well as social unrest are all examples for factors causing investor uncertainty turning into obstacles for FDI.

Together these results indicate that shifting the focus of investment promotion policy of developing countries could imply welfare gains because investment incentives may be the wrong policy to attract FDI, as the sources of risks are not removed. Rather than granting special conditions and thus stimulating profits for investors a credible and transparent economic policy seems to be

---

[145] See Harms (1999) p.64. and Henisz/Zelner (1999). For a detailed discussion of political risk indicators see paragraph 3.3.
[146] See the empirical research in Chapter 4 and 5.

more efficient to enhance FDI. A policy reducing investor uncertainty may help to attract investment more efficiently and less costly than tax exceptions or other incentives. This is in particular the case for high risk countries with low levels of political credibility that do not receive FDI due to high investor uncertainty. For these countries attracting FDI is costly as investors will not invest unless they are adequately compensated for the high risk. Even if developing countries continue granting incentives, lower levels of political risk would require lower payments for risk compensation resulting in lower "cost of capital" of external financing. Additionally, a national risk reduction strategy would imply a "double dividend" as domestic investment is likewise positively influenced by risk mitigating reforms.

In turn, policies increasing investor uncertainty should always be avoided, given their depressing impact on FDI. This becomes of particular importance when FDI flows show signs of hysteresis meaning that even if risks are objectively absent, past policies still influence the present investment behavior and path dependency implies that errors of the past still have an influence in the future. The additional fact that reputation plays an important role for the attraction of international investment makes hostile policies towards FDI an even more severe problem. Hence, reducing perceived investor uncertainty is a key element of an efficient investment promotion policy. To reduce uncertainty economic policy must be transparent and predictable which means that policy makers have to avoid policy surprises which undermine their credibility and imply future investor uncertainty. Instead, in order to implement a long term strategy for the promotion of foreign investment credible commitments not to opportunistically interfere in private property rights have to be made.

The theoretical investment models captured uncertainty with an exogenous parameter σ the determinants of which were not further analyzed. As the preceding paragraphs indicate political risk may have diverse reasons. Warfare or expropriations could imply a complete loss of assets while other risk factors only slowly dilute property rights. The diversity of political risk factors requires a more detailed analysis of the origins of political risk that isolates the characteristics of a host country which lead to the emergence of political risk. Furthermore, it has to be investigated how these risks can be adequately measured and which societal institutions are important for the mitigation of risks. Therefore, Chapter 3 provides a detailed analysis of the determinants of political risk and their measurement.

It has already been pointed out that there are various sources of political risk that may affect foreign investors. Besides incentives, there is a great variety of measures which may be used for the mitigation of political risks which means reducing the probability of "bad surprises" for investors. To do so governments have to give credible commitment not to interfere in the activities of private investors. Even if the current institutional environment of the host country does not favor investment, it does not per se imply a risk. Surprises only occur, if the existing institutional structure of the economy changes without any possibility for the investor to anticipate these changes. Hence, it is not only the current institutional structure which causes a risks for the investor but also the feasibility of drastic policy swings in the future. It is straightforward to see that constantly changing policy restricts the capability of economic actors to plan future investments in a reasonable way. Consequently, continuity of economic policy and transparent and foreseeable policy instruments should be the guidelines of a risk-mitigating economic policy. Also tying the hands of the government by strict rules that limit the possibilities of intervention may be a good method to reduce uncertainty for investors. Essentially, there are two ways to approach this problem. First, one may establish measures which try to reduce the perceived degree of risk through domestic reforms. One measure may be to establish more veto rights in the political process resulting in a decline of discretionary freedom for politicians.[147] Thus, tying the hands of policy makers by binding them either by precise written laws or controlling institutions results in a higher degree of certainty for economic agents. However, changing the institutional setting of an economy is a lengthy, costly and difficult process. Furthermore, the introduction of vetoes in the political process on the one hand results in higher stability and investor credibility but on the other hand produces possible delays in decision making. Second, to avoid these problems host countries may reduce political risk by external commitments like the signing of international agreements or the membership in international organizations. In doing so governments externally tie their hands with the aim to reduce risks for private investors. These different strategies of risk mitigation are further analyzed in Chapter 3.

2.4 Chapter Summary
Paragraph 2.1 started with a definition of investment and a description of the different categories of investment. Thereafter, it reviewed the basic logic of investment theory and the most common models used in the literature. It criticizes the orthodox models for neglecting waiting options and irreversible investments. Introducing these two features into investment models permits deriving the result that uncertainty has an depressing effect on investment spending when investment are irreversible. Higher uncertainty implies further falling investment spending. Furthermore, the depressing effect is growing in the degree of irreversibility. The DIXIT/PINDYCK model used the analogy to option pricing as a microeconomic explanation for the depressing effect of higher uncertainty.

Paragraph 2.2 provided a definition of FDI and a review of common theories to explain MNE activity. Furthermore, it offers an overview of the empirical literature studying the determinants of incoming FDI. It defines political risk and shows that it negatively affects the investment spending of international investors. Moreover, a review of the existing empirical evidence highlighted the importance of political risk for FDI.

---

[147] This approach will be further discussed in paragraph 3.1.2.5.

Paragraph 2.3 briefly summarized some possible policy implications of the theoretical models and the empirical evidence and offered some concluding remarks. Furthermore, it provides a short outline of the topics that will be analyzed in Chapter 3.

"Men are powerless to secure the future;
institutions alone fix the destinies of nations."
Napoleon I, Imperial séance (1815)

3. Political Risk and National Institutions
3.1 Political Institutions and Economic Performance
3.1.1 Overview

This chapter deals with explaining how political risks emerge and offers a theoretical foundation for the analysis of the impact of social and political variables on private investment decisions. This basic theoretical framework permits avoiding the ad hoc hypotheses about the economic impact of socio-economic variables that are a common deficiency of many empirical analyses. Moreover, it is discussed how political risk may be adequately quantified and measured. Eventually, the chapter analyzes how host countries may efficiently mitigate political risk by discussing potential remedies against political risk and their political feasibility of implementation.

3.1.2 The Analytical Framework
3.1.2.1 Theoretical Foundations

The conviction that government and politics influence the economic performance of national economies is not new. In medieval Europe the rise of successful independent cities or city states, in particular in the north of Italy, demonstrated the importance of good government for economic welfare and prosperity.[1] A pair of frescoes in the Italian city of Sienna painted around 1340 by Ambrogio Lorenzetti captures this knowledge in an impressive allegory of bad and good government where good government is illustrated by wisdom, peace, justice and prosperity while bad government is identified with cruelty, treason, war and poverty. In spite of this common knowledge orthodox economics for a long time ignored processes inherent to the political system of countries as determinants of economic outcomes. Instead, state and govern-ment were treated as monolithic entities that were assumed to be benevolent and seeking to enact policies maximizing the welfare of society.

Economists of the Public-Choice-School first gave up this assumptions and based their writings on the central hypothesis that self-interested governments are maximizing their own utility functions instead of social welfare.[2] While the Public-Choice school analyzes economic behavior within a given set of rules, New Institutional Economics (NIE) and Constitutional Economics go one step beyond by analyzing the optimality and choice of rules as well as their impact on economic behavior.[3] NIE stresses the important role of institutions for the process of economic development and growth. Empirical evidence indicating that institutions are an important determinant of economic development is by now abundant.[4] The crucial role played by sociopolitical factors in determining

---

[1] One example is the Republic of Venice that became an important center of commerce. See Tullock (2002a) p.252-253.
[2] Tullock (2002b) gives an overview of the Public Choice Theory.
[3] Erlei/Leschke/Sauerland (1999) or Richter/Furubotn (1999) provide an overview of NIE.
[4] See World Bank (1997). For an overview of the large empirical literature see Worldbank (1998), Worldbank (2003) or IADB (2000).

the costs of bargaining, contracting, monitoring and enforcing has by now achieved the status of conventional wisdom not only in economic history but also in development theory.

NORTH argues that understanding the long run potential of countries for economic development requires a precise analysis of their institutional setting. Institutions can be defined as humanly devised constraints that structure political, economic and social interactions. They may consist of both informal constraints (taboos, customs etc.) and formal rules (constitutions, laws etc.). Organizations, in turn, are collective actors, usually with their own institutions of governance, that make choices subject to these institutional constraints.[5] Analyzing the history of Europe NORTH/THOMAS show that institutions deeply influence the capacity of nations to generate economic growth and welfare. Economic history provides many examples of countries which were failing to produce adequate institutions that could ensure sustained economic growth and prosperity.[6]

Figure 3.1 classifies societal institutions concerning their feasibility of change and their degree of formality. In addition important societal organizations are identified whose interactions with formal and informal rules shape the institutional environment of countries.

Figure 3.1: Social Norms, Rules and Organizations Coordinating Human Behavior

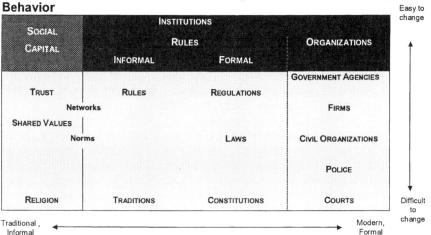

Source: World Bank (2003) p.38.

The political system of a country can be defined as a set of institutions that guides the government's current functioning and future evolution, and provides the society's governance structure. Therefore, the political system is the primary source of formal, legally sanctioned regulations and institutional

---

[5] See North (1990) and North (1991).
[6] See North/Thomas (1973).

change.[7] Considering the political system as an important part of the national institutional setting, it deeply influences the development perspectives of countries by defining the basic framework for the actions of private economic actors. As NORTH puts it

"...a theory of institutions also inevitably involves an analysis of the political structure of a society and the degree to which that political structure provides a framework of effective enforcement." [8]

COASE argues that all exchange implies transaction costs for the negotiation, control, and enforcement of contracts.[9] In developed market economies economic exchange usually takes place in an impersonal framework. Faced with high transaction costs individuals limit their exchange which, all other things equal, results in lower societal welfare. An important fraction of total transaction costs are the costs of contract enforcement. To enable wealth enhancing exchange, parties to an exchange must be able to enforce contracts at a cost that keeps the action worthwhile for them. While simple spot market transactions are usually self enforceable, complex contractual agreements require efficient third party enforcement. Third party enforcement involves a neutral party with the ability to measure the attributes of a contract and to enforce agreements such that the offending party has to compensate the injured party to a degree that makes it costly to violate the contract.[10] The risk of long term contracts for example where contractees may be confronted with opportunistic behavior of the other party may be efficiently mitigated if a neutral institution for dispute settlement exists.[11] Hence, institutions of enforcement evolve out of the necessity to reduce transactional cost of private economic activity. In spite of private contract enforcing institutions that developed historically, state-controlled bodies are usually the cornerstone of an enforcement system.[12] Effective public third party enforcement of private contracts considerably decreases transaction costs. The institutional environment of a country being the sum of the national humanly devised constraints essentially operates as a tool to facilitate trust and confidence so that high transaction costs may be overcome. National institutions become a major determinant of national economic activity because they shape the incentives of individuals and enable more complex contracting. NORTH draws the conclusion that

---

[7] See Haber et al. (1999).

[8] North (1986) p. 231.

[9] See Coase (1937).

[10] See North (1990) p.54-60.

[11] The idea that societies need an agent with coercive power to permit efficient societal outcomes goes back to the writings of Hobbes. See Hobbes (1966).

[12] An example for a private enforcement is the medieval institution of the "podesta". The podesta was an outside executive administrator with limited military command that was hired by communes and city-states in the 12th and 13th century to settle local disputes and to serve as an intermediary between communes and the emperor. See Nye (1997) p.130. Another example is the "lex mercatoria", a sophisticated privately enforced commercial code that was created in the early Middle Ages by European merchants and partly remains in effect. See World Bank (1997) p.45.

"the New Institutional Economics must not be only a theory of property rights and their evolution but a theory of the political process, a theory of the state, and of the way in which the institutional structure of the state and its individuals specify and enforce property rights." [13]

It follows that the political system is a decisive part of the institutional structure of a society or in other words, an important subset of the national institutional framework which has an important impact on its economic development prospects and the activities of private economic actors. [14] Political risks for investors arise when the institutional structure of the potential host country is inadequate since the institutional setting of a society with its formal and informal rules forms a framework for private investment decisions. Without well-developed contracts and no way of enforcing agreements between different societal groups, it is unlikely that specialization will emerge in forms that are conducive to production and economic development. Confronted with an inadequate institutional framework the incentives of private actors to invest are low and capital accumulation will be negatively affected. Investment in turn, is one of the key determinants of economic growth and welfare. If for example property rights are not properly assigned and protected, private investment incentives are lower which results, all other things equal, in lower growth. Therefore, political risks analysis essentially is an analysis of the institutional environment for private investment. In consequence a country's investment climate can be defined as the policy, institutional and behavioral environment, both present and expected, that affects the returns and risks associated with investment. [15]

The fundamental policy question is what forms of political and regulatory systems are required to ensure that a private market economy works efficiently and private investment is fostered. A normative approach to the analysis of the investment climate requires to determine the ideal institutional environment which maximizes private investment incentives. As this is hardly possible, only main prerequisites for high investment incentives and political actions which deter private investment may be identified in order to properly analyze political hazards for investors. This, in turn, requires a basic theoretical framework that helps understanding how institutions develop over time. It was argued before that the necessity of third party enforcement implies a central role for the state. This is of particular importance in two dimensions. First, as already pointed out, enforcing institutions have to provide a reliable framework for exchange between individuals reducing their transaction costs. National institutions here play the role of a catalyst for private economic activity stimulating national growth. The importance of the second dimension stems from the fact that the enforcing entity has a proper utility function. Put simply, if a state has coercive power, it may use it to serve his own interest at the expense of the rest of society. Therefore, it is necessary to establish an institutional setting which

---

[13] North (1986) p. 233.
[14] The constitutional economics literature is too large to cite here. Richter/Furubotn (1999) or Erlei/Leschke/Sauerland (1999) provide an overview.
[15] See Newfarmer (2002) p.258.

restricts the power of the enforcing institutions to limit the possibility of predatory activity. As MADISON put it:

"If men were angels, no government would be necessary. If angels were to govern men, neither external nor internal controls on government would be necessary. In framing a government which is to be administered by men over men, the great difficulty lies in this: you must first enable the government to control the governed; and in the next place oblige it to control itself."[16]

A state that opportunistically interferes in private economic activity eventually distorts individual incentives. Limiting possibilities for the abuse of state power is a challenge for every country since governments which are unrestricted and uncontrolled are likely to engage in predatory behavior. Economic history shows how limited power of sovereigns led to favorable economic outcomes compared to the distortionary effects of unlimited governmental discretion.[17] Figure 3.2 summarizes the aforementioned arguments and shows how national institutions influence the incentive structure for private investment and eventually economic outcomes.

Figure 3.2: Political System, Institutions and Incentives for Private Investment

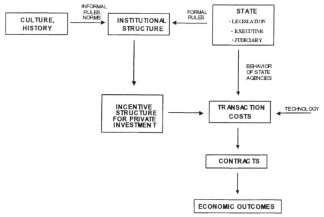

Source: Own figure based on World Bank (1997) p.30.

To explain how national institutions evolve over time one may use the theoretical approach of NORTH that explains the change of societal institutions with the interaction of institutions with national organizations. Its point of

---

[16] James Madison, Federalist No.51 (1788) cited in Henisz (2002a) p.17. Earlier claims for an effective control of government can be found in the work of Locke and Montesquieu. See Schmidt (2000) p.66-90.

[17] Levi (1988) argues that rulers maximize state revenue subject to the constraints of their bargaining power, their transaction costs, and their discount rates. She provides empirical evidence for this hypothesis in several case studies. Nye (1997) uses the term "parasitic rule" to name opportunistic governmental behavior. See Nye (1997) p.128-136. North/Thomas show how the parliament-controlled monarchy England economically outperformed other European countries with unlimited sovereigns. See North/Thomas (1973).

departure is the conviction that institutions and the standard constraints used in economic analysis determine opportunities in societies. Organizations are created to take advantage of these opportunities and alter institutions as they evolve. Institutional change is induced by changing perceptions of the members of these organizations realizing that they could do better by altering the existing institutional framework. If political markets were perfect, changes in the overall set of constraints, as for example changes in relative prices, should imply an alteration of the institutional environment to fit the new requirements.[18]

Real world institutional settings however, may remain inefficient for three reasons. First, informational constraints imply that actors may make suboptimal decisions that lead to the persistence of overcome structures. With regard to the complexity of reality mental models are necessarily reduced, have a limited processing capacity and only change slowly while ideologies may lead to a perpetuation of inefficient structures because they are perceived as being just or fair. Second, the symbiotic relationship between institutions and organizations implies that inefficient national institutions may persist because national organizations have an interest in keeping the status quo. If the institutional framework disfavors productive activity, it will in the long run strangle economic growth. Organizations that evolve in such a framework will become more efficient, but only in rendering the society even less conducive to productive activities. In the absence of functioning political markets such an unfavorable path of development may persist over time.[19] Third, since the creation of new institutions implies high fixed costs economies of scale favor established institutions. Moreover, individual behavior is adapted to the framework of established institutions which increases the pressure for the persistence of existing institutional arrangements. As institutions are only slowly changing over time the past of societies matters for the present. Therefore, the historical development of societies is path dependent which means that having chosen a particular path in the past influences development perspective in the future. Path dependency, in turn, entails the danger that societies can get locked into existing institutions which avoids the generation of new, more efficient national institutions.[20] The theory of institutional change highlights that the analysis of national institutions requires a dynamic perspective. Countries with unfavorable institutions for private investment can end up in a vicious circle of low investment and a further deteriorating institutional environment. On the other hand, countries can break out of this vicious circle by creating more favorable institutions that stimulate private investment incentives and over time permit a further amelioration of the institutional environment.

Based on this basic theoretical framework the next paragraphs further describe four important dimensions of societal institutional that are of particular

---

[18] This point is made by North/Thomas (1973).
[19] See North (1990).
[20] See North (1990).

importance for private investment decisions: First, the assignment and protection of individual property rights as a framework for individual interaction. Second, the establishment of a society where the rule of law prevails. Third, the capability of the sovereign institution to give a credible commitment to enable private exchange and to avoid opportunistic governmental behavior. Fourth, the capability of individuals in a society to facilitate exchange by trust or other forms of social capital that avoid conflict and diminish transaction cost.[21]

3.1.2.2 Property Rights

The previous paragraph describes how institutions form a general framework for all economic activity, how they evolve over time and what determines the process of change. It closes with the result that this framework forms the incentives for private actors in national economies and thus influences economic performance. It is evident that private ownership is one of the constitutive pillars of market economies. Private ownership however, may only be ensured if property rights are clearly assigned to the members of society and can be protected against arbitrary intervention of other individuals or the state. Property rights are a bundle of rights over the use and the income to be derived from property and the ability to alienate an asset or a resource.[22] Since well defined property rights entitle actors to use an economic good according to their interests and give the right to invest resources and to produce new products with physical and human capital, property rights are one decisive driver of investment and economic growth.

Without well defined property rights, individuals cannot fully reap the benefits from their investments. Poorly defined property rights or the risk of future dilutions imply poor incentives for engaging in private productive activity and thus eventually lead to lower investment rates. The greater the perceived risk of losing existing property rights, the less likely the holder of these rights will be to forego current consumption to accumulate property, thus slowing investment that contributes to growth.[23] As a consequence aggregate societal welfare is lower compared to a situation when property rights are well defined. The property rights structure of a society constitutes a basic set of economic

---

[21] It is important to note that a partial analysis of these different institutional subsets is necessary to reduce complexity. However, in reality these institutional subsets are interdependent which implies that ignoring these interdependencies means loosing explanatory power.

[22] As Alchian/Demsetz put it: "It is not the resource that is owned; it is a bundle, or a portion, of rights to use a resource that is owned." See Alchian/Demsetz (1973) p.17.

[23] See Weimer (1997) p.2-10. Already Adam Smith recognized the importance of property rights for economic efficiency. He writes: "...in all countries where there is tolerable security [of property], every man of common understanding will endeavor to employ whatever [capital] stock he can command. ... A man must be perfectly crazy who, where there is tolerable security [of property], does not employ all the [capital] stock which he commands. ...In those unfortunate countries... where men are continually afraid of the violence of their superiors, they frequently bury and conceal a great part of their [capital] stock ... in case of their being threatened with any of those disasters to which they consider themselves as at all times exposed." Smith (1976) p.301.

rules that shapes private incentives to invest and considerably influences the welfare of societies since it is a method of assigning to particular individuals the authority to select, for specific goods, any use from an unprohibited class of uses.[24] As an efficient assignment of property rights is a costly process, DEMSETZ argues that property rights only develop when gains from a better specification are larger than the costs. Therefore, individuals in society will promote a better specification of property rights up to the point where the marginal cost of the process equals its marginal benefits. That is, property rights emerge in a way that maximizes total surplus in society.[25]

However, an efficient assignment of property rights alone does not enable well functioning transactions between private actors. Property rights must also be enforceable to unfold their positive societal implications. To put it in other words, instead of being merely de-jure, there has to be a de-facto protection of private property rights. Societies have to establish a sanctioning mechanism that punishes the violation of private property rights by other members of the society, that is, it has to prevent individuals from interfering with the property of other individuals. At the same time the effective protection of property rights is of particular importance for the relationship of private actors with the enforcing institution. The fundamental task of property rights protection is not only to prevent property rights violations caused by other private individuals in society but also those that originate in public predatory activity. Summing up, not only the task of assigning property rights is central to economic development but also the enforcement of those rights.

3.1.2.3 The Concept of Credible Commitment

The term credible commitment is widely used in the economic literature.[26] A commitment can be defined as a promise, pledge, vow, convenant, guarantee, or bond to perform in a specified fashion. A commitment can be credible in either of two senses, the motivational and the imperative, respectively. A commitment is credible in the motivational sense if at the time of performance the committing party continues to want to honor that commitment. It is motivationally credible because it is incentive-compatible and hence self-enforcing. In turn, a commitment is credible in the imperative sense if the committing party is unable to act otherwise, whether the acting entity wants to act otherwise or not. In this sense the commitment is credible, not because it is compatible with contemporaneous preferences but rather because performance is coerced or discretion to do otherwise is disabled.[27]

Here credible commitment refers to the ability of governments to give a credible guarantee that private contracts are enforced and that opportunistic government interference in economic activities of individuals is avoided. First,

---

[24] See Eggertsson (1990) p.33.
[25] See Demsetz (1967) who shows with the example of North American fur hunters that better defined property rights evolved when the payoffs of a better specification were growing with a higher demand for furs.
[26] See North (1993), Olson(1993) and McGuire/Olson (1996).
[27] See Shepsle (1991).

a credible commitment of the state guarantees the existence of a credible and enforceable institutional framework that governs private economic interaction. NORTH stresses that credible commitment is a prerequisite for economic development because it allows for transacting in capital and other markets at low cost.[28] Political philosophers have long understood that external constraints on individual actions are credibility enhancing. HOBBES points out that man is the most savage of animals, and that a state of nature is a condition of a war of every man against every man. Therefore, in the absence of a state that establishes order the life of man becomes "solitary, poore, nasty, brutish and short."[29] Furthermore, HOBBES argues that private contracts can only be efficiently enforced by a third party holding coercive power.[30]

Assuming that self interested private actors will only engage in economic activity if they are sure that they will reap benefits from their engagement, it is necessary that agreements between individuals can be enforced. Since contracts between individuals are often incomplete and parties to the contract do not possess the power to enforce them, economic actors have to be protected against contractual hazards and opportunistic behavior of contracting counterparts by adequate institutional arrangements. National institutions have to provide for measures of settlement if conflicts arise which are not covered in the contract. Thus, an important part of the analysis of national institutions is the assessment of their ability to provide a credible framework for private economic activity.[31]

The second dimension of credible commitment stems from the fact that a government with coercive power to enforce an institutional framework for private economic transactions may itself expropriate rents from those transactions.[32] To put it in other words, creating an enforcing entity that provides credibility to private interaction poses the problem that it may misuse its power to serve its own interest. The danger of self interested governmental behavior may be well illustrated by citing MACHIAVELLI's advice to the ruler:

---

[28] See North (1990).

[29] See Hobbes (1966).

[30] Hobbes writes: "If a Covenant be made, wherein neither of the parties performe presently, but trust one another, in the condition of meer Nature, (which is a condition of Warre of every man against every man,) upon any reasonable suspicion it is Voyd: But if there be a common Power to set over them both, with right and force sufficient to compel performance; it is not Voyd. For he that performeth first has no assurance the other will performe after; because the bonds of words are too weak to bridle mens ambition avarice, anger and other Passions without the fear of some coercive Power; which in the condition of meer Nature where all men are equal, and judges of the justness of their own feats cannot possibly be supposed .... But in a civil estate where there is a Power set up to constrain those that would otherwise violate their faith, that feare is no more reasonable; and for that cause, he which by the Covenant is to perform first, is obliged to do so." Hobbes (1966) p.91

[31] Among the many examples for such a framework are a civil code, a commercial code, a banking regulation and an efficient judicial sector.

[32] Whiting argues that credible commitment can means trust of private investors that the government recognizes and upholds their claims to their assets. See Whiting (1998) p.168.

"A prudent ruler, therefore, cannot and should not, keep his word when keeping it is to his disadvantage and when the reasons that make him promise no longer exist." [33]

Applying MACHIAVELLI'S words to the analysis of investment incentives it becomes evident that governments that nationalize industries, tax income and affect private property rights in many other ways have a credibility problem concerning future investment. In the long run a government that expropriates private surplus or is not able to commit to not expropriating distorts the incentives of economic actors since individuals who cannot be sure of keeping the benefits of their invested capital will spend less money for productive activities. Actors will shift their focus from engaging in welfare-enhancing investment to securing the existing stock of capital they possess. Capital is then allocated to investment projects that offer lower but immediate returns because by doing so investors can reduce the risk of governmental expropriation. Additionally, capital may be shifted to the informal sector or abroad where it cannot unfold its positive impact on the development of the national economy. It is straightforward to see that in a situation without a limit on possible predatory behavior of the government allocative efficiency of the national economy is severely disturbed and future prospects for growth and welfare are reduced. In the long run a lack of governmental credibility can become a serious obstacle for economic development. Yet from an investor point of view credible commitment has another important dimension since it requires a basic continuity of policy. Governments do not only have to establish sound rules and enforce them but also to guarantee that those rules are not permanently changed. Frequent and unpredictable change of rules, the failure to implement announced changes, and the arbitrary enforcement of rules all produce uncertainties for investors that will end up depressing investment. To limit these uncertainties the process of rulemaking has to be predictable and transparent. [34]

It is argued here that property rights have to be protected against violations from other individuals or the state by a credible commitment of the government. The question however, of what determines the possibility of credible commitments in countries has not been answered. The following paragraphs analyze societal institutions that may ensure a credible framework for private contracting and avoid public abuses of power.

3.1.2.4 Rule of Law

The previous paragraphs stressed the importance of third party contract enforcement and credible commitments by governments to ensure an incentive structure that is favorable for stimulating investment and growth. It already identified the problem of creating an organization holding coercive power that is simultaneously capable of ensuring third party enforcement without abusing

---

[33] Machiavelli (1997) p.66.

[34] In a survey covering 69 countries and 3600 firms the entrepreneurs reported that they were seriously affected by policy surprises. In Latin America 60% of the interviewed voiced this complaint while in Southeast Asia only 30% of the respondents considered policy surprises a problem. See World Bank (1997) p.34-38.

its power. Therefore, the fundamental problem is to create a state with sufficient coercive power to lower the cost of private transactions which is at the same time bound not to opportunistically interfere in private economic transactions. This dilemma may be solved by a functioning and efficient legal system that provides a legitimate base for private and public behavior and establishes a state with prevailing rule of law. In this context the law defines the basic framework within which the pursuit of all other activities takes place.[35]

Essentially, rule of law refers to those established rules of a general and impersonal nature that order the relationship between state and society, between individuals in society, and within the state itself. Being more precise, rule of law means government by law and with adherence to a predictable and working legal order. Rule of law is in place when the government is constrained or bound by the law through effective limits or checks and balances on political power and public office. The institutional design of legal accountability may take the form of various arrangements of separation of powers usually prescribed in the constitution and control of public office holders through regular elections. In other words, rule of law characterizes those control mechanisms by which the government can be brought to account according to established normative criteria.[36] Rule of law requires that nobody is above the law and that public officials as well as private actors act *"secundum legem"*, that is in conformity with the existing legislation. When working properly, rule of law brings definition, specificity, clarity and predictability into human interactions. It establishes networks of responsibility and accountability entailing that all agents in society are subject to appropriate, legally established controls of the lawfulness of their acts.[37] For producing such results a necessary condition is that rules have certain characteristics: [38]

1. All laws should be prospective, open and clear
2. Laws should be relatively stable
3. The making of laws must be guided by open, stable, clear and general rules
4. Independence of the Judiciary must be guaranteed
5. The principles of natural justice must be observed (open and fair hearing; absence of bias)
6. Courts should have review powers to ensure conformity to the rule of law
7. Courts should be easily accessible
8. Discretion of crime-preventing agencies should not be allowed to pervert the law

The organization which underpins the establishment of rule of law and legal accountability to national legislation is the judiciary.[39] An independent and efficient judiciary is vital to ensure that legislative and executive authorities

---

[35] See Rawls (1971) p.236.

[36] See Domingo (1999).

[37] Acting within the law is not sufficient when basic rights are violated by the existing legislation. See O'Donnell (1998) p.13-16.

[38] The following listing is based on Raz (1977) p.198-201.

[39] See Domingo (1999). Prillaman writes: "...an independent judiciary serves as the ultimate guarantor of constitutionalism: sovereignty is derived from the people, but the courts ensure that no agency of government acting on behalf of the people violates the principles of the rule of law. See Prillaman (2000) p.1.

remain fully accountable under the law and to interpret and enforce the existing legislation. If a country is to enjoy the benefits of a rule of law, the mere passing of legislation has to be complemented by effective law enforcement because when private or public actors violate the law with impunity the rule of law becomes ineffective.[40] Thus, for the achievement of its functions a judiciary has to ensure enforcement while being independent and efficient.[41] One can speak of a properly functioning judiciary when it simultaneously demonstrates independence, efficiency and access.[42] Without an efficient legal system in turn, private property rights cannot be assigned properly, undesirable actions cannot be condemned and sanctions for the non fulfillment of societal norms cannot be established. An efficient system for the provision of these goods is the establishment of a "Rechtsstaat", a society where the principle of rule of law prevails.[43] A functioning "Rechtsstaat" is a bridge between limits on governmental power and limits on individual freedoms which legitimates the public use of coercion.[44] A "Rechtsstaat" ensures basic rights of the citizenry, provides for checks and balances through an effective division of powers in government and ensures legal certainty for citizens in their acts with public authorities or other citizens.[45] Although a society where the principle of rule of law is established has many virtues for its citizens, this analysis will be limited to its economic effects.[46]

Together with informal norms judicial institutions promote the economic development of societies by reducing uncertainty, diminishing transaction costs, facilitating the enforcement of contracts and protecting private property rights. In an environment of rule of law the government possesses sufficient power to implement its policy, to protect the rights of the citizens as well as to act with transparency and efficiency to create a climate of confidence and credibility. By creating an atmosphere of certainty, predictability, and credibility a functioning rule of law fosters the functioning of national markets.[47] A transparent and efficient legal system stimulates economic incentives for private investment by providing for an environment of certainty in which

---

[40] See O'Donnell (1998) p.15.

[41] See World Bank (1997) p.8 and p.99-100.

[42] See Prillaman (2000) p.15-29. Ungar characterizes a functioning judiciary that guarantees the rule of law with the attributes accountability, independence and universal access. See Ungar (2002) p.1-5.

[43] The concepts of rule of law, "Rechtsstaat" and "estado de derecho" are not synonymous. See O'Donnell (1998). There are slight differences between the british rule of law tradition and the continental European concept of a "Rechtsstaat". Theobald argues that the former is more oriented on the legitimacy of procedures in legislation and application of the law while the latter is largely focused on the establishment of precise individual rights that are codified in legislation. See Theobald (1999) p.63-69. Despite of these differences the terms will henceforth be considered as being synonyms. For an introduction to the German concept of a "Rechtsstaat" see Katz (1999) p.82-106.

[44] See López Portillo Vargas (2001).

[45] See Rubio et al. (1994).

[46] It is straightforward to see that a "Rechtsstaat" is also an important social and political achievement and thus per se desirable without analyzing its economic implications.

[47] See Ayala Espino (2002) p.121-143.

individuals can engage in economic activities without the fear of arbitrary intervention by other citizens or public authorities. The legal system is an important determinant of profitability for national firms as it directly affects the transaction costs on the micro-level.[48] Several empirical studies confirm the importance of an efficient legal system for economic growth and development.[49]

At this point it is important to stress that high levels of societal and political corruption may undermine the principle of rule of law. When legal norms and rules are not enforced due to the payment of bribes or the use of nepotism, the legal system is unable to unfold its positive impact on the development perspectives of societies. Although the current literature provides many definitions of corruption, the term may be broadly defined as the misuse of public power for private benefit.[50] For a long time it was argued among economists that corruption is a means of aiding the economy in the case of cumbersome regulation and excessive bureaucracy.[51] Meanwhile there is a large strand of literature that demonstrates the adverse effects of corruption on investment, economic growth and development.[52] Chapter 2 argues that higher uncertainty decreases investment spending if investment projects are irreversible. Besides increasing the direct costs of doing business, high levels of corruption in host countries increase uncertainty for a firm that operates in such an environment. In high corruption countries the return of a company depends to a large extent on the results of in-transparent transactions as for example bribery or nepotism. When the granting of certain licenses or permits or the winning of public contracts depends on corrupt behavior instead of on the efficiency of companies not only national welfare is diminished. Moreover, legal uncertainty will increase the variation of a company's future returns implying higher risks for companies when the decision making of the national bureaucracy is distorted by corruption.[53] As corruption is usually limited to a small circle of insiders, foreign investors may be more severely affected than their national counterparts as they lack the necessary connections to engage in bribery.

Furthermore, corruption affects the quality of the public administration. As it is put by PRS Group, corruption is "a threat to foreign investment by distorting the economic and financial environment, reducing the efficiency of government and business by enabling people to assume positions of power through patronage rather than ability, and introducing inherent instability into the

---

[48] See Rubio et al. (1994).

[49] See Dollar/Kraay (2001). Klapper/Love (2002) argue that the quality of the legal system and investor protection affects corporate capital costs. Firm level governance and performance is lower in countries with weak legal systems suggesting that improving the legal system should remain a priority for policy makers. Sherwood et al. (1994) estimate that growth losses due to inefficient legal systems amount up to 15%.

[50] See World Bank (1997) p.102. For an overview over different definitions and forms of corruption see Pritzl (1997) p.46-63.

[51] See Huntington (1989).

[52] For a recent overview of the literature see Lambsdorf (2001).

[53] See Lambsdorf (2001).

political process".[54] The literature offers extensive empirical evidence for the depressing impact of corruption on investment.[55] A recent study of the World Bank on several transformation countries highlights the important role of corruption as a determinant for investment behavior. On the macro level the study concludes that high corruption countries have lower levels of aggregate investment than medium corruption countries. Evidence on the micro-level suggests that firms operating in high corruption environments tend to have lower investment growth rates than firms operating in medium corruption environments.[56] Several earlier empirical studies confirm the result that high levels of corruption are an important impediment to investment.[57] In the medium or long run high levels of corruption further aggravate this problem by undermining the credibility of national institutions that are important determinants of long-run growth perspectives as for example the judicial system or the public administration.[58] Recent empirical work finds that political corruption also significantly reduces the volume of incoming foreign investment flows by acting like a tax on MNEs.[59]

To sum up, deficiencies in the rule of law are serious impediments for investment as private investors are affected in many ways by an inefficient legal system or high levels of corruption. Private contracts cannot be efficiently enforced and protection against opportunistic behavior of contractual partners or against possible predatory governmental behavior is low. Legal uncertainty is a particular serious disincentive for long term investments that require a foreseeable evolution of the national institutional environment. Therefore, an inefficient judiciary which is not able to create an environment where rule of law is established is an important impediment for potential investors. Another measure that is capable of determining the level of the government's ability to give a credible commitment to economic actors is its degree of discretionary freedom.

3.1.2.5 Discretionary Freedom of the Government
Above it was argued that ensuring private property rights and creating an appropriate incentive structure for economic actors requires limitation and control of governmental power. The ability to give a credible commitment not to seize private assets or to opportunistically interfere in private transactions has been identified as a central prerequisite for private investment incentives and successful economic development. A criterion that is capable of reflecting this ability is discretionary freedom of host country governments. The degree of governmental discretion measures to what extent the governing body is subject to external constraints that limit the scope of its decision making

---

[54] See PRS Group (2003).
[55] As an example see Word Bank (1997) p.102-109.
[56] See Worldbank (2000).
[57] See Mauro (1995) and Knack/Keefer (1995).
[58] See López Presa et al. (1998).
[59] See Wei (2000). He estimates that an increase in the corruption level from that of Singapore to that of Mexico would have the same restrictive impact like a 50 percentage point tax increase for multinationals.

process and policy implementation. In other words, governmental discretion measures to what degree a government is subject to checks and balances by other societal organizations.

For a better understanding assume for simplicity that government is a monolithic entity maximizing its own utility function. It is straightforward to see that the scope of government for future action depends on its level of independence. If the ruling body is not subject to any form of external control, the variety of possible future decisions is high because without any form of external auditing those policies will be implemented that best serve the interest of government. So without any form of checks and balances the ruler's decisions are solely based on his utility function.[60] Hence, the possible policy outcome may vary along the personal policy space that represents the preferences of the government. In such an institutional setting the risk that the ruler may interfere with the interest of other members of society is high.[61] The government however, may be limited in its choice by formal instruments of constraint. Important examples for restraining societal institutions are an efficient judicial system and horizontal or vertical separation of powers.[62]

Figure 3.3 illustrates possible variations of policy outcomes for the case of government with unlimited governmental discretion. If the government is not subject to control of other societal organizations with veto rights (Actor A, Actor B), it is free to implement any policy that is in line with its preferences that are represented by the arrow. Since other organizations in society do not enjoy a right to veto the decision of the government, private actors have to accept any possible policy outcome even if it is not in line with their own preferences. With a given initial distribution of preferences the ruling authority may choose every outcome between the dotted lines marking the upper and lower end of its preference-arrow. In this case the risk that the interests of private actors are violated by governmental action is high.

If, in turn, the government's decisions were subject to some form of external control, like a veto of a controlling organization, it would limit the scope of the ruler's decision. Introducing a veto for actors A and B should therefore limit the variation of future policy outcomes.

---

[60] If the governmental utility function is known to economic actors transparency and reliability are promoted.

[61] Shepsle writes "Discretion is the enemy of optimality, commitment its ally." See Shepsle (1991) p.246.

[62] See World Bank (1997) p.99-102.

Figure 3.3: Variation of Policy Outcomes with Unlimited Discretion

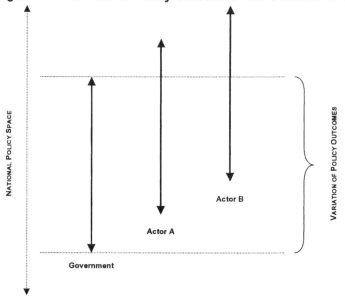

Source: Own Figure

Figure 3.4 illustrates the situation with the same preference structure when A and B have a right to veto the decision made by the government. Facing the veto power of A and B the ruling body can only implement a policy that can be agreed upon with both societal organizations. The need to reach a consensus with A and B limits the scope of governmental discretion and thus the possible variation of policy outcomes. Comparing the policy outcomes of figure 3.3 and 3.4 highlights that the introduction of constraints on government reduces the variation of future policy outcomes and reduces the risk that the interest of other societal actors is neglected.[63] The simple graphical example illustrates that the extent of governmental discretion is a determinant of future policy variations. The broader the separation of powers, the greater will be the number of veto points to be navigated to change any rule-based commitments. Separation of powers therefore increases confidence in the stability of societal rules.

The degree of governmental discretion also is a decisive variable for investors. If the level of governmental discretion is high, it means that their possibility to have an influence on future political decisions is low. This implies a higher risk of future changes that are not corresponding to their interest. Thus, unfavorable future changes from the current status quo become more likely when governments are comparably unconstrained. Therefore, unlimited govern-

---

[63] Already Montesqieu's work on the division of powers argues that supervising societal institutions limiting the discretionary freedom of governmental branches limit the abuse of public coercive power. See Montesqieu (1979).

mental discretion combined with an ineffective protection of basic individual rights is a source of political risk. States with too much flexibility and insufficient constraints will find that their actions are not viewed as credible, and investment will suffer.[64]

Figure 3.4: Variation of Policy Outcomes with Limited Discretion

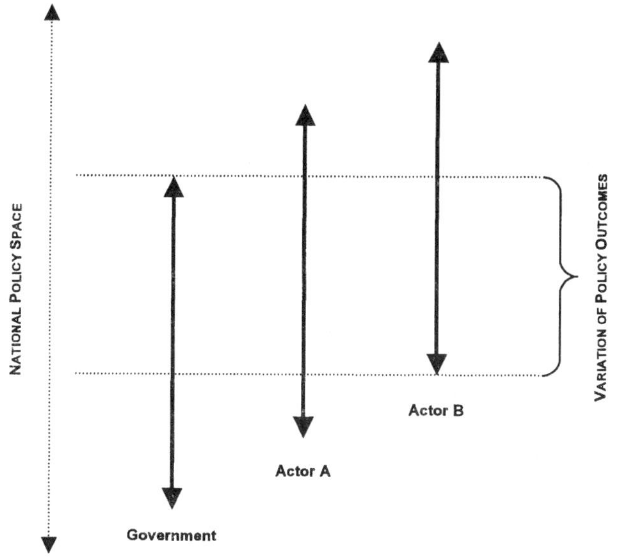

Source: Own Figure

However, excessive discretionary freedom of policy makers and public servants poses another important problem. If it depends entirely on the will of a public servant to grant a certain license or permit, his personal incentive to accept bribes or other personal favors as an exchange for his service is high. If, as often the case in developing countries, external monitoring is rare and public servants are poorly paid, this incentive is further intensified. In this case arbitrary public power is used to reap personal benefit rather than producing public goods.[65] Therefore, high levels of political discretion in government and administration create an environment that is highly susceptible for the development of institutionalized corruption.[66]

Discretion can be effectively limited if governing bodies and administrations are subject to the control of other institutions as the law or other societal veto players.[67] Veto players can be defined as those individual or collective actors

---

[64] See World Bank (1997) p.109.
[65] See World Bank (1997) p.25.
[66] See Jain (2001).
[67] See World Bank (1997) p.28.

whose consent is required to introduce a new policy.[68] There is a large variety of institutions and organizations that may act as veto players or legislative restraints in modern societies. First, a constitution which is binding for the executive and limits the discretionary freedom of policy makers and public servants by protecting basic individual rights and prescribing appropriate procedures for governance. Second, all political parties in parliament and in particular those of the opposition as well as independent courts. Although limiting governmental discretion is essential for a successful development of market economies, it is straightforward to see that this process may cause unwanted consequences if it is carried too far. Governments that are too limited by other veto organizations loose their power to implement programs that allow for the adaptation to changing circumstances. Excessive restraints may eventually lead to paralysis and as OLSON describes an interest group dominated society is economically less efficient.[69]

However, as important it may be, this argument does not affect the ex ante calculus of investors. When planning an engagement, the absence or low probability of political change due to high levels of constraints generates certainty for the investor because he can assume that societal variables will not change during his planning horizon. On the other hand, if constraints are low, the probability of political change is high which induces uncertainty because the investor knows that political change will probably affect the return of his project. It is straightforward to see that already a basic protection against public predatory behavior by vetoing institutions may be enough to protect investors and reduce uncertainty considerably.[70] A constitution that protects individual rights and an efficient judicial system that may enforce this constitutional protection are examples for limits on governmental discretion that do not lead to paralysis. However, if, like in many developing countries, judicial institutions are weak and the constitutional protection of property rights insufficient high governmental discretion should be resulting in higher levels of investor uncertainty.

3.1.2.6 The Concept of Social Capital
It was argued above that well functioning national institutions are important for the process of national development. However, it was already pointed out above that not only formal institutions may be influential for the process of national development but also informal institutions. Societal characteristics and norms and networks that govern the interaction of individuals may be seen as an influential part of the informal institutional framework co-determining national welfare. Recent literature in economics and other social sciences uses the term social capital in analogy to the notion of human capital to capture the economic effects of these variables. Although the term is widely used, there is no unique definition in the literature as available definitions range from focusing on microeconomic factors of societal relations to

---

[68] See Tsebelis (1995).
[69] See Olson (1982).
[70] It may be assumed that the marginal efficiency of additional veto points is falling over time.

macroeconomic factors or even political measures or psychological as well as sociological concepts.[71] Defining the term as norms and networks that facilitate collective actions the notion of social capital has some virtues which make it a valuable approach for studying problems in development economics.[72]

Lowering transaction costs of private actors has already been identified as an efficient mean to foster economic development. To understand the relevance of the concept of social capital for the following analysis it is helpful to briefly discuss an example concerning the impact of trust on transaction costs. If a society or a group in society is characterized by high levels of trust among its members economic transactions are facilitated because members of that group have no need to extensively refer to measures of precaution against opportunistic behavior of their contractual counterparts. Thus, functioning net-works of trust, as for example codices of business ethics among merchants, facilitate private economic transactions by lowering transaction cost.[73] Even if conflicts occur, functioning networks of trust enable a less costly process of conflict resolution by negotiation or by intervention of a third party. It is even imaginable that groups with high levels of internal trust may efficiently organize economic transactions without any form of third party enforcement. Therefore, it is to be expected that functioning networks of trust have all other things equal a positive impact on capital accumulation and growth.[74] If, in turn, a society or a group in society is characterized by low levels of trust, the opposite implications hold. Since contracting and conflict resolution are more costly in low trust environments, low levels of trust imply high levels of transaction cost which, all other things equal, decrease incentives to engage in welfare-enhancing private transactions.

Following the aforementioned definition societal levels of trust are a form of social capital that permits to lower transaction costs in society illustrating that low levels of social capital can become an obstacle to economic development.[75] This problem is even more severe when a lack of social capital coincides with weak institutions of third party enforcement. In such a situation transaction costs for private economic activity become prohibitively high creating an institutional framework which is detrimental to investment, economic growth and development. This unlucky combination however, is the reality for many developing countries implying a serious burden for private economic activity. The concept of social capital may also serve to describe those societal characteristics that cause high costs of transactions and may be defined as anti-social capital. This negative definition of the theoretical concept

---

[71] For a recent discussion of the varying definitions of the term social capital see Woolcock (2002) and Lin (2001).

[72] See Woolcock (2002).

[73] Putnam (1993) and Fukuyama (1995) have conceptualized trust as one component of social capital that can improve the efficiency of a society by facilitating coordinated action.

[74] Knack/Zak (2003) find that interpersonal trust has a positive growth effect and that trust can be stimulated by education, redistributive transfers and freedom.

[75] See Fukuyama (2001).

can be applied to capture the implications of societal characteristics with a supposed negative impact on transaction costs.

Possible sources of social capital are not limited to networks of trust or ethical communities. Instead, there are many potentially influential variables that determine the level of social capital. The absence of ethnic, cultural, linguistic or religious conflicts as well as severe distributive inequalities are all characteristics with a positive influence on societal levels of transaction costs. For the purpose of this analysis the concept becomes particularly valuable as it offers a simple analytical framework for studying the economic impact of societal characteristics. With this analytical tool socioeconomic variables that may have an influence on foreign investment decisions may be analyzed concerning their impact on the level of societal transaction costs. In other words, instead of ad-hoc postulating a causal relationship between societal variables and investment decisions, one may analyze the influence of a certain variable by judging its most likely impact on the level of societal transaction costs and eventually on incentives to invest. Consequently the concept of social capital offers a suitable theoretical framework for the analysis of the effects of societal variables on economic decision making that may be used for empirical research.[76]

> *"Who governs?" and "How well?" are the two*
> *most basic questions of political science.*
> *Robert Putnam (Making Democracy Work)* [77]

3.1.3 Political Regime Type and FDI
3.1.3.1 Systematic Order Of Political Regimes
Whether regime type has an impact on economic growth is a widely debated topic in the economic and political science literature.[78] Therefore, the impact of political regime type on private investment incentives is an important topic and political risk assessment inevitably requires an analysis of different real world political regimes.[79] I start with setting out a systematic order of political regimes that allows for a better theoretical analysis of their different characteristics. Although the author is aware of the fact that political systems in reality never own the properties of these ideal constructs, a theoretical distinction of different regime types is useful for further reflections on the impact of political systems on investment behavior.

The limited scope of this volume makes it impossible to give a complete over-view of the large literature on typologies of political systems. Instead, the

---

[76] See Chapter 4 and 5.

[77] Putnam (1993) p.63. cited by Nye (1997) p.121.

[78] An influential study is the work of Barro (1996). A review of the empirical literature is given by Kurzman/Werum/Burkhart (2002). For a complete literature overview see Przeworski/Limongi (1993) and Przeworski et al. (2000). Although it may be argued that unsatisfying empirical results stem from methodological deficiencies of existing studies, here there is no room for an extensive discussion of the impact of political regimes on economic growth. A critical evaluation is given by Durham (1999).

[79] Many political risk analysts consider regime type as an influential variable for the extent of political risk. See the discussion of political risk indices in paragraph 3.3.

concept of MERKEL permits the classification of political systems with regard to six criteria.[80] Using this approach nearly all existing political systems can be assigned to three basic categories: democracies, authoritarian systems and totalitarian systems. These ideal types of political systems and their corresponding characteristics are depicted in figure 3.5:

Figure 3.5: Typology of Political Systems

	DEMOCRACY	AUTHORITARIAN RULE	TOTALITARIAN RULE
LEGITIMACY OF RULE	Peoples Sovereignty	Mentalities (Nationalism, Patriotism etc.)	Ideology
ACCESSION TO RULE	Open, Universal Suffrage	Limited, Limited Suffrage	Closed, No Suffrage
MONOPOLY OF RULE	Democratically Legitimized Institutions	Leaders or Oligarchs, Ensured by Repression	Leaders, Ensured by Repression
STRUCTURE OF RULE	Pluralistic, Division of Powers	Semi-pluralistic, Limited Division of Powers	Monistic, No Division of Power
SCOPE OF RULE	Limited	Large	Unlimited
METHOD OF RULE	Rule of Law	Rule of Law or Repressive Rule	Repressive Rule

Source: Merkel (1999) p.28

Democracies are typically characterized by universal suffrage, a pluralistic structure of rule, a limited scope of rule and by the existence of rule of law. Government is based on the sovereignty of people and democratically legitimized institutions. Only political systems having these characteristics may be labeled as fully democratic. DAHL identifies six minimal requirements for a modern democratic system.[81]

1. Elected officials
2. Free, fair and frequent elections
3. Freedom of expression
4. Alternative sources of information
5. Associational autonomy
6. Inclusive citizenship

Democracy is a system of rule with open end, that is, outcomes of the political process are the result of a competition between different political forces.[82] The process of political competition takes place in a democratically legitimized framework of a priori fixed rules shaped by the constitution.[83] Democratic systems may be classified in ideal democracies, polyarchies, and defect

---

[80] See Merkel (1999) p.23-56.
[81] See Dahl (1998) p.85.
[82] Przeworski states that "democracy is a system in which parties lose elections." See Przeworski et al. (2000) p.16. The idea of democracy as a competition between different political groups in society for electoral support is based on the work of Schumpeter (1993) and Downs (1957).
[83] See Merkel (1999).

democracies. As ideal democracies largely remain a theoretical construct most of the existing democracies may be labeled polyarchic, that is, they differ to some extent from the theoretical construct but still possess most of the basic characteristic of democratic systems. In turn, defect democracies already show signs of authoritarian rule although they are still nearer to democratic systems than to authoritarian rule.[84]

In contrast, authoritarian rule may be defined as a system of government which is not democratic. Recalling the characteristics of authoritarian rule given in figure 3.5 shows that unlike in democracies legitimization of rule is not given by the population but instead by mentalities or beliefs and that the accession to rule is limited by religious, ethnic or other characteristics. Governance is not exercised by democratically legitimized institutions but by non-elected actors that often ensure their power by repression. The structure of rule is typically semi-pluralistic, that is, the division of powers is limited or non-existent while the scope of rule is large meaning that basic rights of the population may be easily violated. Although the degree to which rule of law is accepted may vary, arbitrary laws are a characteristic of authoritarian systems. Since political theory permits to classify various sub-categories of authoritarian rule, also real world authoritarian systems are far from being homogeneous. In fact the existing forms of undemocratic government are diverse.[85]

Distinguishing authoritarian rule from totalitarian rule is a difficult task because the essential characteristics of these two political system are similar. In addition to the criteria that have been depicted in figure 3.5 one may speak of totalitarian rule if the following criteria are fulfilled:

1. The existence of ideology
2. The existence of a single party
3. The existence of terror by party organizations or secret services
4. State monopoly in the media
5. State monopoly of force
6. Economic centralism

Using these ideal categories of political systems basically all historical political systems may be classified and allows for the construction of a continuum of political systems with the extreme regime types of perfect democracy and perfect totalitarian rule as polar cases.[86] Figure 3.6 depicts this systematic order of political systems giving historical examples of real world political systems.

---

[84] See Merkel (1999).
[85] See Tullock (2002a).
[86] It has to be stressed that even in western democracies citizen participation is far from being perfect. See OECD (2001).

Figure 3.6: Continuum of Political Systems

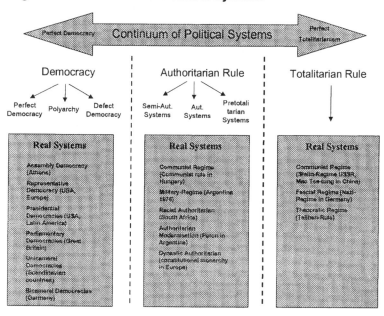

Source: Merkel (1999) p.55.

The systematic order of political systems which has been developed in this paragraph permits a closer economic analysis of political regimes.

3.1.3.2 Economic Analysis of Political Regimes

While the previous chapter distinguished different political regime types, this paragraph is dedicated to studying how these systems may influence private investment decisions. MCGUIRE/OLSON develop a three stage hierarchy of political regimes comparing anarchy, autocracy, and democracy. By providing public goods such as law and order and by limiting discretionary expropriation, an autocratic leader can obtain more resources for himself and at the same time leave his subjects better off than in the case of anarchy. This self-limitation of an autocratic ruler is due to his encompassing interest in the domain he controls meaning that he profits from every increase in production realized by his subjects as a consequence of his credible commitment.[87] MCGUIRE/OLSON speak of an "invisible hand", leading the rational bandit to settle down and replace anarchy with authoritarian government, which leads to an increase in output as citizens have more incentives to produce. Comparing the economic outcomes of such an authoritarian rule with the outcomes of democratic rule permits drawing conclusions about the influence of regime type on private investment incentives. MCGUIRE/OLSON show that a ruling majority in democratic systems will limit redistribution as a significant share of the market income of society is earned by the rulers themselves. As a

---

[87] See McGuire/Olson (1996).

consequence redistribution is comparably lower and private investment incentives should be higher.[88] WINTROBE'S review of common public choice models confirms the result that from a theoretical point of view redistribution in dictatorships tends to be higher than in democratic regimes. The same result holds for the extent of public corruption as there are fewer constraints on rent distribution.[89]

The McGuire/Olson model holds valuable insights into how the type of political regime influences economic performance by focusing on the problem of tax setting. However, their basic argument may be extended to all kinds of political actions which influence the national business climate as autocrats have an incentive to extract the maximum possible surplus from society because they can levy a monopoly charge on every economic activity. Historical evidence confirms that many autocratic leaders collected as much revenue as possible by pushing the tax rate to its maximum.[90] Moreover, McGuire/Olson argue that autocratic leaders only have an incentive to provide public order and basic protection of property rights when they are maximizing long run revenues. Although a long term thinking autocrat ensures that his subjects' profits are not wholly expropriated since he benefits from higher future output, this result is only valid if the autocrat's grip on power is secure. Assuming a short-time horizon of the autocrat or personal fear to be overthrown changes results significantly because it now becomes perfectly rational for the dictator to seize as many assets as he can while he is still in power. In this case, the leader has no reason to consider the future output of society and will abrogate contracts in order to maximize his short-run income.[91] Consequently the argument that autocratic leaders limit their theft does not hold for all imaginable situations, even more since an independent institutional structure which is capable of enforcing the leaders' promises does not exist.[92]

BARZEL argues that autocratic leaders have a vital interest in limiting the probability of a revolution against their rule. Therefore, a dictator limits societal welfare gains which could result in a demand for more civil rights and establishes a costly system of supervision and repression which suppresses possible revolutionary tendencies in society.[93] NYE shows that distorted out-comes and deadweight losses are inevitable by-products of strong rule with costly monitoring and uncertainties regarding current and future control of the

---

[88] See McGuire/Olson (1996). The existence of this "Olson-effect" is confirmed in the theoretical model of Lee (2003).

[89] See Wintrobe (1998). A simple argument for the tendency of higher redistribution is the mere fact that in authoritarian regimes the resistance of the taxed population is lower than in democracies. See Wintrobe (2001) p.43.

[90] See Olson (1993).

[91] See Clague et al. (1996). Abramovich (2001) argues that in general dictators and their loyal groups only have low incentives to implement sound economic policies and that therefore high growth dictatorships are rare phenomena. See Abramovich (2001).

[92] See Olson (1993).

[93] See Barzel (2000).

citizens.[94] To ensure a minimum degree of loyalty among followers and to avoid palace revolutions dictators have to redistribute rents to their followers which likewise has welfare-depressing effects. So ensuring power in an autocracy requires a policy-mix of repression and loyalty payments which can be used to characterize the nature of authoritarian governments.[95] Moreover, low levels of legitimacy may result in future civil strife as the discontent of citizens is growing over time.

There is abundant historical evidence for autocratic leaders having short–time horizons due to an insecure hold on power. Likewise there are many examples for costly systems of suppression (for example a secret police) which significantly reduced societal welfare. Furthermore, nearly all authoritarian governments had to redistribute rents to their followers to ensure loyalty to the regime.[96] The mere possibility that an autocrat has a short-time-horizon reduces confidence in government which all other things equal depresses investment because the promise of an autocratic leader not to seize private assets is never completely credible. Since authoritarian systems do not offer judicial protection of individual property rights, dictators who renege on given commitments cannot be sued implying that technically speaking dictators have a severe signaling problem.[97] From historical examples of dictatorships it is evident that succession crises further enhance uncertainty because economic actors cannot foresee the consequences of a leaders' death or removal from power.

All the aforementioned uncertainties should, all other things equal, decrease investment spending because private actors cannot be sure that they will fully reap the future benefits of their investment. If investment takes place anyway, it is likely that the structure of investment changes favoring projects that have short pay-off-periods even if potential returns are lower. In particular investments in developing countries need protection from violation of property rights by other individuals or from opportunistic government action. Since autocratic regimes have difficulties in giving credible commitments to private property rights, they fail to ensure right incentives for private investment decisions. A democratic system with constitutional protection of individual property rights seems more suitable to meet these expectations of private investors as the same institutions that ensure a proper functioning of democracy can also ensure the protection of property rights and the enforcement of civil and public

---

[94] See Nye (1997).

[95] Using these criteria Wintrobe defines four basic types of authoritarian government: tinpots (low repression, low loyalty), tyrants (high repression, low loyalty), totalitarian (high repression, high loyalty), and timocrats (low repression, high loyalty). See Wintrobe (2001) p.38-41. Abramovich (2001) argues that the dictator has an incentives to have a small group of loyal followers to facilitate supervision and to limit loyalty ensuring payments to a minimum. See Abramovich (2001) p.143-145.

[96] Several examples are given by Wintrobe (2001) p.39.

[97] See Wintrobe (1998).

contracts.[98] In addition to being prerequisites for democracies a constitution, an independent judiciary and rule of law provide investors with the required legal security for doing business because governments can more easily give a credible commitment to the protection of property rights when its hands are tied by independently controlling institutions that protect private property against private violations and governmental interference. Recalling the prerequisites for a favorable investment climate that have been derived in the preceding paragraphs, it follows that democracies should better allow for credible commitment, an effective assignment and protection of private property rights, as well as for the establishment of a political system with checks and balances based on the rule of law. Furthermore, societal participation in universal suffrage and legitimized rulers ensure lower levels of social tensions due to lacking social capital that could endanger private assets. Therefore, it is to be expected that investment incentives are more favorable in democracies.

Given these arguments the disappointing records of many democratic countries in the protection of investor rights are astonishing.[99] To understand this it has to be underlined that a *de jure* democratic system without the characteristics of a functioning democracy does not provide investors with credible commitments.[100] Hence, the pure labeling of a country as "democratic" is neither a necessary nor a sufficient condition for the ability to credibly commit and to protect investor rights. That is to say, if democratic institutions do not work properly, the investment enhancing effects of a reliable institutional framework will not materialize since an inefficient judiciary for example cannot effectively enforce legislation in commercial law suits. If existing laws cannot be enforced, legal certainty of investors is not increasing and if parliaments and the judiciary cannot effectively control the government the protection of individuals against public predatory activity is de-facto inexistent. Therefore, the empirical analysis of the institutional environment for investment cannot be limited to investigating if controlling institutions exist but simultaneously has to analyze if they work properly. The next paragraphs are dedicated to the analysis of models explaining the emergence of political risks.

---

[98] Empirical evidence by Claque et al. confirms that democracies in general provide greater security of property and contractual rights than autocracies. Moreover, they find that property rights in young democracies are weaker than in long lasting democracies. See Claque et al. (1996).

[99] In a recent study Kurzman/Werum/Burkhart (2002) only found a weak positive impact of democracy on investment. Tavares/Wacziarg (2001) in turn find a negative impact of democracy on physical capital accumulation.

[100] The fact that most public choice models do not distinguish between functioning and defect democracies is identified as a major problem by Wintrobe (1998). As examples for defect democracies he identifies among others the democracies of Latin America. See Wintrobe (1998) p.32.

3.2. Modeling the Emergence of Political Risks
3.2.1 Classical Political Risk Models

While the political risk models in Chapter 2 show how political risks influence private investment decisions, this paragraph analyzes how political risks emerge and what are its sources. I start with a review of influential classical models explaining the emergence of political risks in host countries. SMITH presents a model where political risk depends on the likelihood of civil strife in host countries.[101] He argues that civil strife emerges when the perceived relative deprivation of the population increases. With relative deprivation SMITH refers to the discrepancy between value expectations (living conditions that the citizens think they are entitled to have) and value capabilities (living conditions that the citizens think they will get and keep). If deprivation grows, that is, the discrepancy between expectations and capabilities becomes larger, citizens respond with discontent and anger leading to catastrophic events like riots, strikes or violent demonstrations. Other influential factors for the risk of civil strife are the coercive capacities of government, societal institutions, the historical tendency to civil strife and finally the legitimacy of the existing political regime. The model implies that high degrees of inequality in societies as well as weak and illegitimate governments and insufficient institutional structures are the most important sources of political risks. However, since the model defines political instability in the form of civil strife as the primary form of political risk, more subtle risks that originate in predatory governmental behavior are not covered. Therefore, the model is only suitable for the explanation of catastrophic political risks.[102]

The model of ROOT, in turn, identifies governmental action as the primary source of political risk since the government of a host country is constantly adjusting its policy to changes in the national economy and society.[103] Although the government itself also initiates political change, it is never wholly free in its process of decision making. Interest groups in society, their ideology and power as well as their relation to the government constitute a political process that shapes national policies towards foreign investors. To changes in this political game the government responds with an alteration of national policy towards MNEs. Therefore, the behavior of host governments towards MNEs is seen as a response to economic and social change mediated by their leadership, ideology, and capabilities. Changes in the political system or in society trigger governmental responses that determine type, nature and extent of political risk. Unlike SMITH, ROOT argues that political risks essentially emerge from actions of national governments implying that the model is not capable of explaining political risks that are not directly caused by governments but instead have their origin in catastrophic events like riots, strikes and violence. Nevertheless, the model is valuable because it indicates that political

---

[101] See Smith (1971) and the critical review in Oseghale (1993).

[102] Most of the older econometric studies of political risk are based on this restrictive definition of political risk in Simon's model. The inconclusive results of the studies may be due to this theoretical foundation. See Oseghale (1993) p.17.

[103] See Root (1973).

risks are influenced by the structure of the political system and societal characteristics.

SCHÖLLHAMMER provides a synthesis of the two previous models by assuming that political risks derive from governmental action that in turn is determined by changes in such factors as civil strife, economic conditions, institutionalization or the coercive potential of governments.[104] Extent and nature of political risks for MNEs are thus determined by the interplay of the societal situation and possible changes induced by the host country government. In sum, both, political instabilities and changes in host country policies are possible sources of political risk. SIMON argues that political risk may emerge from different sources, which have already been depicted in figure 2.19.[105] The individual risk factors may be classified in internal-societal factors, external-societal factors, internal-government-related factors and external-government related factors. Emanating from internal societal related reasons are risks of civil strife like revolution, civil war and strike which are often referred to as political instabilities in the literature. In turn, emanating from internal government-related sources are risks of host government policy alterations like expropria-tions or operational restrictions. Eventually, government or societal related external risks emanate from guerilla warfare, other armed conflicts or hostile diplomatic actions. For the MNE aggregate political risk is the sum of all this partial risks implying that its investment behavior is determined by its perception of the magnitude of political risk in these different environments. Having reviewed classical models of political risk the next paragraph presents a model which is capable of explaining in greater detail the risk of unforeseen host government policy changes.

3.2.2 The Political Constraints Model
Based on the concept of discretionary freedom HENISZ developed a theoretical framework for the analysis of political hazards for investors that focuses on the emergence of government related political risks. Studying market entry modes of foreign firms HENISZ derives a systematic order of potential hazards confronting the management of a company. First, if firms choose to enter a foreign market by engaging in a joint venture with a domestic company, they face the risk that partners act opportunistically which may be named inde-pendent contractual hazard. The second risk for MNEs stems from the fact that political actors may expropriate assets or profits and is labeled independent political hazard. Third, joint-venture partners may instigate political action that alters the investor's relationship with the local government to their favor resulting in a contractual hazard caused by the presence of political hazards.[106] The following analysis focuses on what determines the risk of independent political hazards for MNEs.

---

[104] See Schöllhammer (1978).
[105] See Simon (1982).
[106] See Henisz (2000a).

HENISZ presents a model that may be used for the analysis of political risk as a determinant of foreign investment decisions.[107] The analysis starts with the empirical observation that countries with comparable levels of infrastructure stocks and GDP per capita display vast differences in infrastructure investment. They argue that these major differences are caused by higher political risks which result from the failure of national governments to give credible commitments not to opportunistically interfere in private investment projects. Although a general prerequisite for investment, commitment is more essential for infrastructure projects, because opportunistic alteration of public policy has an tremendous impact on the expected profits of projects. As infrastructure projects usually imply a high share of sunk cost, politicians assume that investors will not divest when planned profits are not attained. In addition high economies of scale in infrastructure projects mean that markets are often served by a single producer who is subject to regulation. This, in turn, makes it easy for host governments to achieve popular reallocations of revenue streams by altering regulatory policies so that private investors are negatively affected.

Although more severe for infrastructure investments, all investors whose projects contain a considerable fraction of sunk cost essentially face the same problem.[108] HENISZ argues that a proper evaluation of the risk of an investment project in a foreign country requires more than a careful observation of the present situation or the past development. Instead, the ability to properly evaluate the risk of policy change in the future is more essential for private investors. Thus, the decisive variable for the MNEs' risk position is the government's ability to give credible commitments that future policy will not change the status quo in a way that private profits are affected. Therefore, HENISZ suggests that measuring the likelihood of future policy changes is a more appropriate form of measuring political risk than analyzing past oriented variables. Moreover, this approach forges an explicit link between the structure of the political system in host countries and likely policy outcomes by arguing that credibility and reliability of national policy determines investment spending.[109]

The proposed influence of institutional factors on investment decision passes via two channels. First, frequent arbitrary changes in taxation, regulation or other economic policy increase investor uncertainty. Chapter 2 showed that higher uncertainty results in higher real option values of investment opportunities as opportunity cost of investment. With private hurdle rates growing investment spending will decrease which eventually also affects national growth prospects. Second, an institutional environment with high discretion is more viable to political lobbying activities.[110] Foreign investors, who unlike their national competitors are not familiar with host country

---

[107] See Zelner/Henisz (1999).
[108] Chapter 2 showed that risks only occur if investments are irreversible.
[109] See Henisz (2000b).
[110] See Henisz (2000b).

characteristics, are potential losers in such a lobbying process. Accepting the argument that a higher probability of policy change leads, all other things equal, to lower investment rates the next step is analyzing the structural determinants of the feasibility of future policy change.

Recalling the argument from paragraph 3.1.2.5 that the variation of policy outcome is falling in the level of political constraints, the existence of an effective opposition to the host government is a decisive variable for the feasibility of policy change. Opposition increases when the number of national institutions that may veto decisions of government is growing. Veto players may be defined as those individual or collective actors whose consent is required to introduce a new policy.[111] A higher number of veto players like chambers of parliament, opposition parties or sub-national organizations make it harder for governments to implement policy changes. Therefore, additional societal veto players effectively reduce discretionary freedom of policy makers by setting up constraints for the implementation of new policies.

However, when aligned to the host government the effects of additional veto players are low since veto players with a similar preference structure are no effective constraint for the host government. Hence, the number of effective veto players does not only depend on the structure of political institutions but also on the preferences of actors and possible alignments between actors.[112] To adjust for alignments across the existing branches of government, the level of constraints has to be modified because when alignment increases, a higher feasibility of political change reduces the level of political constraints.[113] Figure 3.7 shows how these variables determine the existing level of political constraints, the discretionary freedom of governmental action and eventually the risk of policy change.

Instead of using private risk perceptions the political constraints model derives the risk of future policy changes from the structure of the national political system by determining the number of independent national vetoes constraining governmental discretion. In this model a detailed analysis of the structure of the national political system is crucial for the assessment of political risks.[114]

---

[111] See Tsebelis (1995).

[112] To illustrate this argument take the example of Mexico before the administration of president Zedillo. Although the Mexican political system had veto institutions as a judiciary, a parliament and federalism, de facto all veto players were aligned to or controlled by the executive branch. Therefore, de facto constraints of executive policy were nearly inexistent.

[113] In a different model by Zelner/Henisz (1999) also the intensity of interest group competition is seen as a decisive determinant of investment as it affects the likelihood that a firm's lobbying activities result in a favorable change of policy. In case of high interest group competition econometric evidence on electric utility investments shows that higher levels of political constraints (limited discretionary choice for policy makers) increases investment spending.

[114] An empirical measure that permits to measure the political constraints of the national government is presented in paragraph 3.3.5.

Figure 3.7: Determinants of Political Risk in the Political Constraints Model

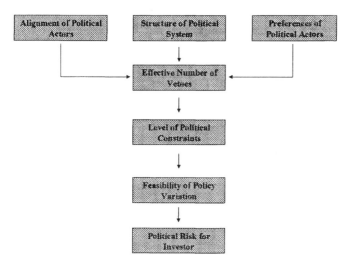

Source: Own figure.

The political constraint model uses no political science constructs such as autocracy or democracy, but reveals the ease with which a policy maker in a given country can change taxation, regulatory or other policies in a way that reduces the expected returns of MNEs. The interplay between political constraints and alignments between political actors is the decisive factor that influences investment spending.

3.2.3 The Effective Party Approach

DURHAM proposes a continuous measure founded on the concept of discretionary choice that permits to evaluate a government's ability to give credible commitments.[115] Similar to HENISZ, DURHAM argues that policy out-comes are determined by the degree of discretionary freedom of national governments. That is, regimes with constraints on governmental action can solve the aforementioned commitment problem by arranging political institutions in a way as to disable or render costly the exercise of discretionary authority of host governments. Based on this theoretical argument, DURHAM develops a measure capable of reflecting the discretionary freedom of politicians. He argues that the effective number of parties in government is a good proxy for the degree of discretionary freedom in a country because both internal party discipline and external competition between parties do limit the decisional freedom of politicians.

---

[115] See Durham (1999).

The effective number of parties N can be calculated by using the following simple formula:

(3.1)
$$N = \frac{1}{\sum_{l=1}^{n} Pl^2}$$

where N is the number of effective parties and Pl represents the share of the total number of parliamentary seats the l-th party holds. In the case that each party holds an equal share of parliamentary seats N equals the actual number of parties that do exist in government. In case of an authoritarian government N becomes unity as the ruling party possesses all seats in parliament. However, for many real world political regimes not only the number of effective parties in the legislation is decisive, but also the degree of discretion in the executive branch. Correcting the measure by including the executive branch of government one obtains:

(3.2)
$$N = \frac{\dfrac{1}{\sum_{l=1}^{n} Pl^2} + \dfrac{1}{\sum_{e=1}^{n} Pe^2}}{2}$$

where Pe is the number of effective parties in the executive branch. Like the model of HENISZ the effective party index has the great advantage to focus directly on the institutional characteristics of political systems, which are neglected by the traditional, outcome orientated, risk indices and to allow for distinguishing democratic countries according to their constitutional framework. A deficiency of this measure is that it is not possible to distinguish between benevolent dictators with the aim to foster economic development and malevolent dictators with the simple aim to maximize personal income. Comparing the growth rates of party-less dictatorships and single party regimes Durham finds that checks and balances limiting the degree of discretion are promoting economic growth. Furthermore, the econometric analysis shows that lower discretion in autocratic regimes increases invest-ment.[116]

3.2.4 Synthesis and Hypothesis
The previous discussion has shown that political risk is a complex multidimensional phenomenon. Since such diverse variables as a low protec-tion of property rights, lacking rule of law, corruption, unlimited governmental discretion, the risk of civil strife, and an inefficient judiciary are all potentially influential for the investment decision process of MNEs, it follows that political risk assessment necessarily needs a broad focus. Nevertheless, the reviewed models permit to derive more precise hypotheses which may be empirically tested. Given the diversity of possible political risk sources a grouping of different risk factors is useful to facilitate the empirical analysis. Throughout the literature it is generally agreed that aggregate country risk is the result of

---
[116] See Durham (1999).

political, social and economic risk factors.[117] Therefore, I formed three risk groups applying similar criteria. This clustering of risks indicators has the econometric advantage that degrees of freedom are preserved without loosing information about the sources of risk. However, it has to be underlined that these analytical categories of political risk are not intended to be mutually exclusive.

First, there are political risks which are a direct consequence of governmental action or deficiencies in public administration. Expropriations, lacking rule of law, governmental corruption or discriminatory taxation are illustrative examples for this group of risk. In the presence of high uncertainty due to institutional deficiencies investment suffers because investors are not willing to commit resources in highly uncertain and volatile environments. Unless firms are confident that policies will remain reasonably stable over time, they will fail to invest.[118] Unconstrained governments however, cannot guarantee a basic continuity of policy that would limit investor uncertainty.[119] That is, countries with governments that are not subject to any form of political control or checks and balances imply higher risks for international investors as the probability of adverse future policy changes is higher. The HENISZ model shows that the feasibility of policy change can be measured by the existing number of effective vetoes. Thus, theory suggests that lower constraints increase the risk of policy variation resulting in lower investment flows. The inspection of other sources of governmental related risks shows that a major part of aggregate political risk is inherent to the political structure of the host country. Rather than being accidental, corruption and legal uncertainty for instance may be rooted in the deficient institutional setting of the host country. For Latin American countries it is to be expected that governance related risks like a lacking rule of law, unconstrained governments and high levels of political corruption have an important influence on foreign investment decisions. Therefore, it is expected that a governance indicator pooling different governance ratings has a significant and positive impact on FDI.[120]

Second, there are political risks like civil strife resulting from societal events and characteristics which are not directly caused by governmental action. Potentially influential characteristics of a given society are high poverty rates, distributive inequalities or lacking political inclusiveness. Theoretically, social instabilities as riots, civil wars or other forms of social unrest are important

---

[117] See Oetzel/Bettis/Zenner (2001) p.129.

[118] See World Bank (1997) p.36-45.

[119] The World Bank writes: "... potentially the largest source of state-inflicted damage is uncertainty. If the state changes rules often, or does not clarify the rules by which the state itself will behave, business and individuals cannot be sure today what will be profitable tomorrow. They will then adopt costly strategies to insure against an uncertain future – by entering the informal economy, for example, or sending capital abroad- all of which impede development". World Bank (1997) p.32.

[120] To avoid confusion it has to be underlined that higher ratings of the governance indicator imply lower political risk. Therefore, higher governance ratings should have a positive impact on FDI. Unless explicitly mentioned the same logic applies to all other indicators that have been used.

potential sources of political risk as they lower social capital implying higher transactions cost or even cause a total loss of assets for investors. However, civil strife only becomes important for investors if assets or the production process are directly affected by societal tensions. If countries pass a critical threshold of political stability, as most emerging markets have, it is unlikely that societal tensions severely harm foreign investors. Therefore, it is to be expected that societal risk factors are of lesser importance for investors in Latin American countries. Despite of a high future potential for societal conflict caused by poverty and inequality, severe societal conflicts like civil wars, revolutions or riots that endanger foreign assets are not to be expected in the region.[121] Therefore, the importance of societal risk factors for aggregate political risk should be comparatively low. In consequence an indicator of societal risk is expected to have a weak or insignificant impact on FDI flows to Latin American countries.

Third, there are political risks emerging from factors that are studied by orthodox models of country risk focusing on hard macroeconomic data. High inflation, extensive national budget deficits, high volatility of the exchange rate or severe imbalances of the current account are good examples for influential variables in orthodox country risk analysis. Given the experience of foreign investors with a decade of severe macroeconomic imbalances following the debt crisis, it is to be expected that macroeconomic risk factors have an important influence on FDI flows to the region. Since sound macroeconomic policy, low inflation rates, moderate budget deficits and sound external debt contribute to lower political risks, an indicator of macroeconomic stability should be positively correlated with FDI flows to the region.

The formulation of these hypotheses highlights that the econometric analysis in Chapter 4 does not only focus on the impact of aggregate political risk on FDI flows to Latin America but instead also analyzes the influence of subgroups of aggregate political risk, namely the risk exposure of foreign investors due to governmental behavior, societal risk factors and the macroeconomic environment. The empirical investigations in Chapter 4 and Chapter 5 show which political risk factors are likely to have a major influence on the decisions of foreign investors in the Latin American region and Mexico respectively.

3.3 Empirical Measures of Political Risks
3.3.1 Overview
The large variety of political risk determinants entails the empirical difficulty of correct measurement since appropriate risk indicators have to contain those macroeconomic, political and social characteristics of a host country which are potential sources of corporate losses.[122] Although the political risk analysis and

---

[121] Of course there are exceptions from higher social stability in Latin America as for example Colombia with its massive presence of guerilla activity and the Chavez government in Venezuela that provokes massive resistance in the population.

[122] Since orthodox country or macroeconomic risk factors are economically intuitive the following paragraphs focus on governmental and societal related risk factors.

insurance market by now offers a large quantity of indicators which are widely used by both private companies and academic researchers, empirical evidence suggests that their forecasting performance is limited.[123] However, since alternate data sources are missing, political risk research, may it be for academic or for business purposes, requires the use of these indicators. Therefore, this paragraph discusses the efficiency of the most influential risk indicators which are used by managers and academics.[124] In general MNEs can choose between four different methodologies for the assessment of political risks in host countries which are depicted in figure 3.8.[125]

Figure 3.8: Methodologies in Political Risk Analysis

METHODOLOGY	CHARACTERISTICS	EVALUATION
"Old Hands"	Relying on opinions of professionals with a high level of experience in a particular region or country	High predictability, low comparability between countries
Delphi-Techniques	Builds on the Old-Hands method by polling various experts through a common format	Questionable operationalization of variables, low predictability due to the absence of an explicit model
Quantitative Measures	Employing macro-level statistics to generate models of political risk	Low predictability due to the absence of forecasts, not published often enough
Grand Tour	Investors visit the country to examine the micro-level variables with an impact their project	Cultural differences cloud perceptions, low comparability due to subjective methods

Source: Own figure

Given the better availability of data and the inter-country comparability, I use indicators based on Delphi-Techniques and quantitative measures for the empirical research in Chapter 4 and 5.[126] Most of these political risk indicators are component-indicators which aggregate various sub-indicators to an aggregate measure of political risk. The country evaluations are usually made by experts that subjectively assign scores to each sub-indicator. The aggregate risk of countries is then calculated by generating a weighted sum of the different sub-categories and is supposed to reflect the risk exposure for exporters or investors in a given country. Beside these perceptional measures a risk indicator, which is objectively derived from the political structure of the host country, is presented.

A country risk rating of the Economist which was first published in 1986 in the Economist Magazine received a lot of public attention.[127] Although a real theoretical underpinning was lacking, the chosen determinants of risk offered a

---

[123] See Howell/Chaddick (1994).
[124] Due to the large variety of political risk indicators this review necessarily cannot be complete. Therefore, only those risk indicators which are presented in the International Handbook of Country Risk Analysis will be reviewed. The indices that have not been used for the empirical research in Chapter 4 and 5 will only be briefly presented. Indices that exclusively focus on macro-economic data are not discussed.
[125] For a more detailed discussion of the methods see Molano (2001) p.20-27.
[126] The case study on Mexico in Chapter 5 also uses qualitative assessments.
[127] See the review of Howell/Chaddick (1994).

picture that is reflective of the prevalent thinking among international investors. The rating presents a list of factors that contain economic, political and social variables as well as a scheme for weighting them to assess the climate to invest in countries. The composite risk index has a maximum of 100 points where 33 are attributed to economic factors, 50 to politics, and 17 to society. High scores of the aggregate index indicate a high level of risk while low scores reflect a good institutional environment for investment. The four social and six political variables that were considered as important determinants of FDI are depicted in figure 3.9.

Figure 3.9: Social and Political Variables in the Economist-Index

COMPONENT	POINTS (MAX.)
Bad Neighbors	3
Authoritarianism	7
Staleness	5
Illegitimacy	9
Generals in Power	6
War/Armed Insurrection	20
Urbanization Pace	3
Islamic Fundamentalism	4
Corruption	6
Ethnic Tensions	4

Source: Howell/Chaddick (1994).

Staleness refers to the fact that after being in power for a certain period of time governments begin to get detached implying that the longer a government is in power the higher is the risk of complacency, delay and corruption so that a certain number of changes in government lowers political risk.[128] Illegitimacy measures the acceptance of the current regime by the population proposing that a high degree of acceptance reduces the risk of civil strife and upheavals. With illegitimate governments persisting in power for a long time the future risk of civil strife or violent resistance grows. Similarly military governments re-placing civilian governments reduce the probability of efficient governance. Apart from the physical destruction of the capital stock, war disrupts the economy in several other ways. Supplies of raw materials are delayed or allocated to war use, the principle of the rule of law is undermined, human capital is destroyed etc. Urbanization pace refers to the risks that accompany a rapid pace of urban centralization like for example an expansion of drug trade, crime and prostitution or extreme levels of urban poverty. Islamic fundamentalism is considered an important threat to foreign investors since host countries with a high fraction of Muslim radicals imply high risks for investors that are not Islamic. Corruption distorts economic incentives and poses a threat to foreign investors since high levels of corruption imply that investors have to use resources for political purposes that could otherwise have been used for value creating activities. Moreover, excessive levels of

---

[128] PRS Group explains high rates of governmental corruption in host countries with staleness.

corruption cause a low predictability of the future business environment. Ethnic Tensions imply risks for foreign investors because they may redirect government attention and lead to higher rates of crime and civil unrest.

The rating focuses on risks that have been classified as catastrophic and largely neglects relevant political risks of a more subtle nature. In particular the indicator does not include political risks resulting from creeping expropriations or a repudiation of contract which are of increasing importance in international finance.[129] HOWELL/CHADDICK tested the ability of the index to predict corporate losses for the period between 1987 and 1992. Examining the correlation of the risk index with a loss indicator constructed from US data provided by the Overseas Private Investment Corporation (OPIC) revealed that the ability of the Economist Rating to predict future corporate losses is low.[130] This permits the conclusion that the Economist Model is not particular useful for measuring political risks for MNEs.

Besides the risk rating published in the magazine the Economist Intelligence Unit offers a risk rating service for the private sector that is published periodically. The risk rating methodology of CRS examines risk from two distinct perspectives. First, aggregate risk is grouped in the analytical categories political risk, economic policy risk, economic structure risk and liquidity factors risk. Second, risk exposure associated with investing in particular types of assets, that is, specific investment risks, are distinguished. The published letter scores for risk range from A (lowest risk) to E (highest risk). The measure of political risk is divided into two subcategories: political stability and political effectiveness. While the former evaluates whether the political situation of a given country is free of external or internal threats to security the latter criterion focuses on issues of good governance. Each of the two categories consists of several subindicators which are depicted in figure 3.10.

Figure 3.10: Political Risk Variables in the CRS-Index

POLITICAL STABILITY	POLITICAL EFFECTIVENESS
War	Change in Government
Social Unrest	Institutional Effectiveness
Orderly political transfer	Bureaucracy
Politically motivated violence	Transparency, Fairness
International disputes	Corruption
	Crime

Source: Howell (1998).

With the additional variables that evaluate political effectiveness in host countries the CRS index avoids the drawbacks of the older index which largely focused on catastrophic political risks.

---

[129] Although it can be argued that the probability of opportunistic government behavior is implicitly represented by the regime type variable, the coverage remains inappropriate.
[130] See Howell/Chaddick (1994).

The Business Risk Service (BRS) which is published three times a year since 1978 by Business Environment Risk Intelligence (BERI) offers information on political risks in 50 countries of the world. BERI's comprehensive recommendation concerning the risk exposure of firms in given countries is an average of three separate ratings. The Political Risk Index (PRI) is composed of ratings for ten political and social variables. The other two, the Operations Index and the Repatriation-factor include weighted ratings on 15 economic, financial and structural variables as well as an assessment of the country's legal framework. While the former index reflects the operating conditions in host countries the latter pictures risks connected with the repatriation of profits and access to foreign exchange.

Like the Economist Index the BRS is based on scores assigned to different risk components by experts. For political risk variables experts can assign a maximum of 7 points to each of the ten subcomponents, with seven representing the lowest and 0 the highest of level risk. Therefore, an overall score of 70 corresponds to the lowest possible level of risk. The ten subvariables of the Political Risk Index are divided into three categories which are shown in figure 3.11:

Figure 3.11: Components of the BERI- Political Risk Index

CATEGORY OF RISK	COMPONENTS
Internal Causes of Political Risk	• Fractionalization of the Political Spectrum
	• Fractionalization by Language and Ethnic or Religious Groups
	• Restrictive measures to retain power
	• Mentality (xenophobia, nepotism, nationalism, corruption etc.)
	• Social conditions (wealth distribution, population density etc.)
	• Organization and strength of the radical left
External Causes of Political Risk	• Dependence on a Hostile Major Power
	• Negative Influences of Regional Political Forces
Symptoms of Political Risk	• Societal Conflict (demonstrations, strikes, violence etc.)
	• Instability

Source: Howell (1998).

The present evaluation of these risks is supplemented by an assessment of the most likely future situation in 1,5 and 10 years. A measure of aggregate political risk for investors is constructed by summing up the scores of each partial component weighted by their relative importance. Finally, 30 bonus points for particularly favorable business conditions may be added to the eight internal or external variables by the judging experts allowing for a maximum score of 100 points. The aggregation of the 10 subcomponents and the number of bonus points reflects aggregate political risk, with a score of 100 representing the lowest possible risk.

"Fractionalization of the political spectrum" represents the divisions among political perspectives in a society, with the number of perspectives seen as an indicator of low consistency and regularity in politics arguing that a high diversity of political or ideological thought results in an increased risk of political discontinuities.[131] "Fractionalization by language, ethnic or religious groups" parallels the ethnic tension variable in the Economist-Index where a high degree of fractionalization implies a higher risk of civil unrest or violence. "Restrictive measures to retain power" is similar to the criterion authoritarianism in the Economist rating.

The variable "mentality" includes such diverse dimensions as xenophobia, nationalism, corruption, nepotism and willingness to compromise making it a veritable "catch-all". Although each of the mentioned variables may intuitively be considered as a risk for MNEs, the aggregation of such diverse risk factors in one component makes an interpretation of the assigned score a difficult task and the rating somewhat arbitrary. The variable social conditions reflects the argument that high inequalities in society result in a higher probability of undesired societal developments as for example high crime rates, drug use and civil unrest.

The two external determinants for political risk are "dependence on a hostile major power" and "negative influences of regional political forces". The former criterion parallels the "bad neighbor" variable of the Economist-Index based on the idea that the influence of major powers increases political risk in host countries. The latter criterion reflects the negative influences of political forces in a certain region and parallels the "trouble spots" argument in the Economist rating. The two variables measuring societal risks are "societal conflict" and "instability" where the former pictures every relevant form of civil strife that may have deterrent effects on private investment as for example demonstrations, strikes, riots etc and the latter political instability in countries as perceived by the number of non-constitutional changes, assassinations, guerilla wars, ethnic tensions etc.

In addition to the quantification of each subindicator BERI provides score intervals as guidelines for the evaluation of political risks in host countries which are shown in figure 3.12. Like the Economist-Index the BERI-Index largely focuses on events that are society-related and of catastrophic nature implying that the index is subject to the same criticism than the Economist-Index. The capability of this index to correctly measure political risks however, is higher than that of the Economist index.

---

[131]This argument is at odds with the political constraints approach that has been reviewed in paragraph 3.2.2.

Figure 3.12: Guidelines of Political Risk According to BERI

BERI-INDEX-SCORE	LEVEL OF POLITICAL RISK
100-70	**Low Risk**
	Political changes will not lead to conditions seriously adverse to business. No major sociopolitical disturbances are expected.
69-55	**Moderate Risk**
	Political changes seriously adverse to business have occurred in the past, but governments in power during the forecast period have a low probability of introducing such changes. Some demonstrations and strikes have a high probability of occurring.
54-40	**High Risk**
	Political developments seriously adverse to business exist or could occur during the forecast period. Major sociopolitical disturbances, including sustained rioting, have a high probability of occurring periodically.
39-0	**Prohibitive Risk**
	Political conditions severely restrict business operations. Loss of assets from rioting and insurgencies is possible. Disturbances are part of daily life.

Source: Howell (1998).

HOWELL/BRADDICK empirically tested the predictive properties of the BERI index with the same loss indicator derived from OPIC-data. Although the BERI index performs considerably better than the Economist index in forecasting losses for private firms, its overall explanatory remains limited since it explains only 26% of the variance in the losses for the analyzed period from 1987-1992.[132]

3.3.2 The International Country Risk Guide (ICRG)

The International Country Risk Guide model for the forecasting of financial, economic and political risk was created in 1980.[133] Its rating comprises 22 variables in three sub categories of risk: political, financial and economic where the political risk category is given a 50% weight for the calculation of aggregate risk rating while the categories of financial and economic each have a weight of 25%. The political risk rating includes 12 weighted variables covering both political and social attributes where each component is assigned a maximum numerical value, with the highest number of points indicating lowest potential risk and vice versa. Political risk assessments are made on the basis of a subjective analysis of the available information by the PRS staff. Unlike other political risk indices the ICRG rating systematically considers the structure of the national political system as a determinant of political risk. Before evaluating political risks with a quantitative rating system analyzed countries are ordered by regime type. These classifications of political regimes are fundamental to the ICRG rating system as they reflect the basic premise that a growing degree of democracy in host countries reflects a higher

---

[132] See Howell/Chaddick (1994).
[133] If not cited otherwise the content of this paragraph is based on Howell (2001a).

accountability of national institutions which in turn implies a lower risk of political shocks.[134] The basic classifications of different regime types and their corresponding characteristics are shown in figure 3.13.

Figure 3.13: Political Systems in ICRG

TYPE OF POLITICAL SYSTEM	CHARACTERISTICS
Accountable Democracy	• Government or executive has not served more than two terms • Free and fair elections for the legislature and executives determined by constitution or statue • Active presence of more than one political party and a viable opposition • Evidence of checks and balances among the three elements of government: executive, legislative and judicial • Evidence of an independent judiciary • Evidence of the protection of personal liberties through constitutional or other legal guarantees
Dominated Democracy	• Government or executive has served more than two successive terms • Free and fair elections for the legislature and executives determined by constitution or statue • Active presence of more than one political party • Evidence of checks and balances between executive, legislative and judicial • Evidence of an independent judiciary • Evidence of the protection of personal liberties
De facto One-Party State	• Government or executive that has served more than two successive terms, or where the political or electoral system is designed or distorted to ensure the domination of governance by a particular government or executive • Holding of regular elections as determined by constitution or statue • Active presence of more than one political party • Evidence of restrictions on the activity of non-government political parties (such as disproportionate media access between the governing and the non-governing parties, harassment of the leaders and/or supporters of non-government political parties, the creation of impediments and obstacles affecting only the non-government political parties, electoral fraud, etc.)
De jure One-Party State	• A constitutional requirement that there be only one governing party • Lack of any legally recognized opposition
Autarchy	• Leadership of the state by a group or single person, without being subject to any franchise, either through military might or inherited right

Source: Howell (2001a).

---

[134] This premise is in line with the analysis of the influence of regime type in paragraph 3.1.3.

Having classified the country to a category of government type each of a fixed number of other indicators is evaluated with a scoring model. After a risk assessment has been awarded to each of the 22 risk indicators all subcomponents are aggregated in an aggregate risk rating for each of the three basic risk categories (Political Risk, Financial Risk, Economic Risk). The 12 components of the aggregate political risk rating and the maximum score which may be assigned to them are depicted in figure 3.14.

Figure 3.14: Components of the ICRG Political Risk Index

COMPONENT	POINTS (MAX.)
Government Stability	12
Socioeconomic Conditions	12
Investment Profile	12
Internal Conflict	12
External Conflict	12
Corruption	6
Military in Politics	6
Religious Tensions	6
Law and Order	6
Ethnic Tensions	6
Democratic Accountability	6
Bureaucracy Quality	4

Source: Howell (2001a).

Government stability with a possible maximum of 12 points is a measure that basically reflects two criteria. First, the government's ability to carry out its declared programs and second, its ability to stay in office. This will depend on the type of governance, the cohesion of the government and governing party or parties, the closeness of the next election, the government's command of the legislature and the popular approval of government policies. The component socioeconomic conditions in turn, refers to the general public satisfaction with governmental economic policy. The greater the popular dissatisfaction with the current government the greater are the chances that it will be forced to change policy or that the government falls. Socioeconomic factors cover a broad spectrum of factors ranging from infant mortality and medical provision to housing and interest rates. It is important to stress that within this range different indicators may have different weights from society to society.[135] Investment profile measures the government's attitude to inward investment and basically consists of an evaluation of expropriation risk, risk of contract repudiations, levels of taxation, restrictions on the repatriation of profits and labor costs. For the aggregate score expropriation and repudiation risks are weighted as most influential components of this subindicator.

---

[135] This implies that highly developed industrial countries may have a lower score than developing countries because a 2% rise in the unemployment rate is considered negligible in a society with unemployment rates around 30% but as politically influential in societies that are used to low unemployment rates.

Internal conflict is a measure that captures the degree of political violence and its influence on governance in host countries. The lowest ratings are usually given to countries with an ongoing civil war while the highest values are assigned to those where there is no armed opposition and the government does not indulge in arbitrary violence. Intermediate ratings are awarded on the basis of whether threats are posed to government and business or just to business, whether the violence has a political purpose (terrorism), whether violent groups are well-organized, whether the violence is sporadic or sustained and whether it is restricted to a certain area or region. External conflict in turn, is an assessment of risk to government or inward investment originating from actions outside the country. Possible sources are trade restrictions, embargoes, geopolitical disputes, armed threats, border incursions, foreign supported insurgency and warfare. External conflicts adversely affect investment in various ways ranging from restrictions on operations to violent changes in society.

The sub-index corruption is a measure of corruption within the political system of the host country. The most common forms of corruption met directly by business are demands for special payments and bribes connected with permits, licenses and tax assessments. Moreover, the measure takes into account corruption in form of excessive patronage, nepotism and secret party funding. According to PRS Group an additional risk for investors in such corruption is that at some time it becomes so overweening that a public scandal may provoke the fall or overthrow of the government, a major reorganizations of the country's political institutions or in the worst case a breakdown in law and order rendering the country ungovernable. The rating of the likelihood of corruption in the framework of the ICRG is subject to the assumption that the risk of corruption is correlated to the time the government is in power. The component military in politics assesses the involvement of the military in the political decision process. Besides a diminution of democratic accountability high military involvement poses the threat that elected govern-ments change their policy due to military pressure. The greatest risks are implied by the threat or the actual implementation of a military regime. Although a military regime may provide stability in the short run, the long run effect will be rather destabilizing as the system becomes corrupt or creates an armed opposition.

Religious tensions may stem from the domination of society or governance by a single religious group seeking to replace civil law by religious law in order to exclude other religious groups from the political process. Foreign investors may be affected by civil dissent or performance requirements due to religious reasons. The variable "law and order" describes the strength and impartiality of the legal system and the popular observance of law. The component "ethnic tensions" pictures the degree of tensions within a country attributable to racial, nationality or language divisions. "Democratic accountability" measures how responsive the government is to its people since durable low levels of responsiveness increase the probability that the government will fall. As democratically elected governments also implement policies that are not approved by the population it is important to note that democratic accountability is not guaranteed by fair elections. The quality of the bureaucracy tends to function as a shock absorber for the practical implementation of measures when government policy changes abruptly. Countries that have a strong bureaucracy receive higher ratings as the risk of drastic changes in policy is lower. On the contrary, countries with a weak bureaucracy intensify the risk of being subject to drastic policy swings.

HOWELL/CHADDICK evaluated the performance of the ICRG in predicting corporate losses for the period between 1987-1992 concluding that the ICRG performed better in forecasting losses than all other indicators that have been reviewed. Of particular influence were the sub-variables "exchange controls", "international liabilities" and "repatriation restrictions".[136] The ICRG has also been widely used as a proxy for political risk in empirical studies on the impact of national institutional quality on investment and growth. ERB ET AL. show that the ICRG performs satisfactorily in explaining expected fixed income returns.[137] Because of its good predictive performance, the good data availability and the coverage of the characteristics of the political system in the host country, the ICRG is a suitable measure for political risk caused by societal events or governmental action. The next paragraph presents a measure of political risk which is not based on the aggregation of subcomponents but instead directly derived from the structure of the political system in the host country.

3.3.3 The POLCON-Index

The POLCON-Index is based on the Political Constraints approach by HENISZ that has been presented in paragraph 3.2.2. It is based on the conviction that discretionary freedom of government increases the risk of future policy swings which negatively affects private investment. To test this hypothesis HENISZ created the political constraints index (POLCON) which may be used for empirical research. The index shows the extent to which the executive is constrained in its choice of future policies by other societal institutions. As argued earlier high constraints on host country governments imply that a future variation from the status quo policy becomes less likely. This in turn, reduces the risk that MNEs are affected by arbitrary policy changes of the current government, allowing for the conclusion that higher political constraints reduce the political risk of investing in a country and vice versa. As pointed out before governments are constrained most effectively by vetoes in the political system because effective veto players decrease governmental discretion resulting in a lower feasibility of abrupt policy changes.

The POLCON index takes values between 0 and unity. Values approaching unity represent high political constraints and low governmental discretion while values approaching zero reflect low levels of constraints and high

---

[136] See Howell/Chaddick (1994).
[137] See Erb et al. (1996).

governmental discretion. Because of homogenous preferences or possible alignments between actors, the number of *de-jure* veto players is not sufficient to picture the level of political constraints. If, for example, judges are appointed and controlled by the ruling party, a simple count of the number of vetoes would significantly over-evaluate the level of political constraints because the homogenous preferences of the two actors do not imply an effective constraint for the executive. It follows that veto players which have similar preferences or are aligned to other players only have limited constraining impact.

The POLCON index is constructed by using a spatial model of political choice based on data extracted from political science databases. For each nation it considers the number of independent branches of government with veto power over policy change (executive, lower and upper chambers, judiciary and sub-federal institutions). The preferences of these branches and the status quo-policy are assumed to be independently and identically drawn from a uniform, unidimensional policy space. Considering possible alignments between different veto players POLCON is modified using data on the party composition of executive and legislative branches. Denoting political actors with E for executive and L for legislative branch the preferences of each actor can be written as:[138]

3.3 $X_I, withI \in [E,L]$

Assume that the status quo policy X_0 and the preferences of all actors are independently and identically drawn from a uniformly distributed unidimensional policy space [0,1] and that every actor has a veto over the final policy decision. The utility of a political actor I with a policy outcome X is given by:

3.4 $U_I = -| X - X_I |$

where U_I ranges from a maximum of zero (when $X=X_I$) to a minimum of −1 (when $X=0$ and $X_I =1$ or vice versa. The variable of interest to investors is how much political actors are constrained in their choices of future policy, which may be calculated as (1-level of political discretion). Discretion is measured as the expected range of policy which all participating players can agree upon. Consider the case of a country where the executive is unchecked. Because the executive always attains the policy outcome X_E corresponding to its maximum of utility, discretion equals 1 and the level of political constraints becomes 1-1=0. With a growing number of independent veto players discretion decreases and political constraints grow. In a country with an executive that is controlled by an effective unicameral legislature L the executive has to win the support of the legislative chamber to implement policy change. Now to maximize utility the executive can only achieve the outcome

---

[138] The following is based on Henisz (2002a) and Henisz (2000b).

that is closest to X_E and in line with the preferences of L. Assuming that preferences are drawn independently and identically from a uniform distribution makes it possible to express the expected difference between two actors as

3.5 $1/(n+2)$

with n being the number of actors. Considering the two players E and L the initial draw yields an expected differential of preferences of ¼ (1/(2+2) resulting in six possible preference orderings in the policy space that are assumed to be of identical likelihood.[139] All possible preference orderings are depicted in figure 3.15 with the rows of E indicating the range of outcomes preferred by the executive to the status quo X_0 and the row of L standing for the outcomes preferred to the status quo by the legislative.[140] In the first and second ordering there is no other attainable policy outcome than the status quo because the preferences of the executive and the legislative do not over-lap. As both of them enjoy a definite veto power over final decisions the keeping of the status quo is the only attainable solution of the policy game and no change in policy is to be expected in this case. Therefore, discretion about policy change equals 0 which implies a value of political constraints of 1 (1-0=1).

In preference ordering 3 executive and legislative only agree upon a policy that is situated between ¼ and ¾ of the unidimensional policy space. Discretion of policy makers thus equals ½ implying a value of political constraints of ½. The same holds for the preference orderings 4-6 resulting in a political constraints score of ½ for each of these settings. When all six preference orderings have the same probability of occurrence the overall value of political constraints for the case of two veto players becomes (1+1+ ½ + ½ + ½ ½) / 6 = 2/3 compared to the score of 0 for an unchecked executive.

With growing numbers of veto players political constraints on the executive as measured by this index are increasing indicating that additional de-jure veto players reduce discretionary freedom of policy makers. However, it is important to stress that this value of constraints is solely based on the number of de jure veto points, that is, it neglects the de facto impact of the veto on the extent to which a policy maker is constrained in his choice. Therefore, POLCON has to be corrected by taking into account the preferences of the players and alignments between veto institutions.

---

[139] The Index measures the feasibility of policy change in a country. Therefore, the keeping of the status quo is considered as being a quasi player. Although the status quo is no veto-player, the POLCON Index considers it as being an alternative to change. Therefore, it has to be considered in the preference orderings of the game.

[140] Note that for reasons of expositional convenience the preference orderings are centered on the unit line. As long as the expected difference between any two preferred points remains one quarter, the quantitative results remain insensitive to the absolute location of these points.

Figure 3.15: Preference Orderings with Two Veto Players

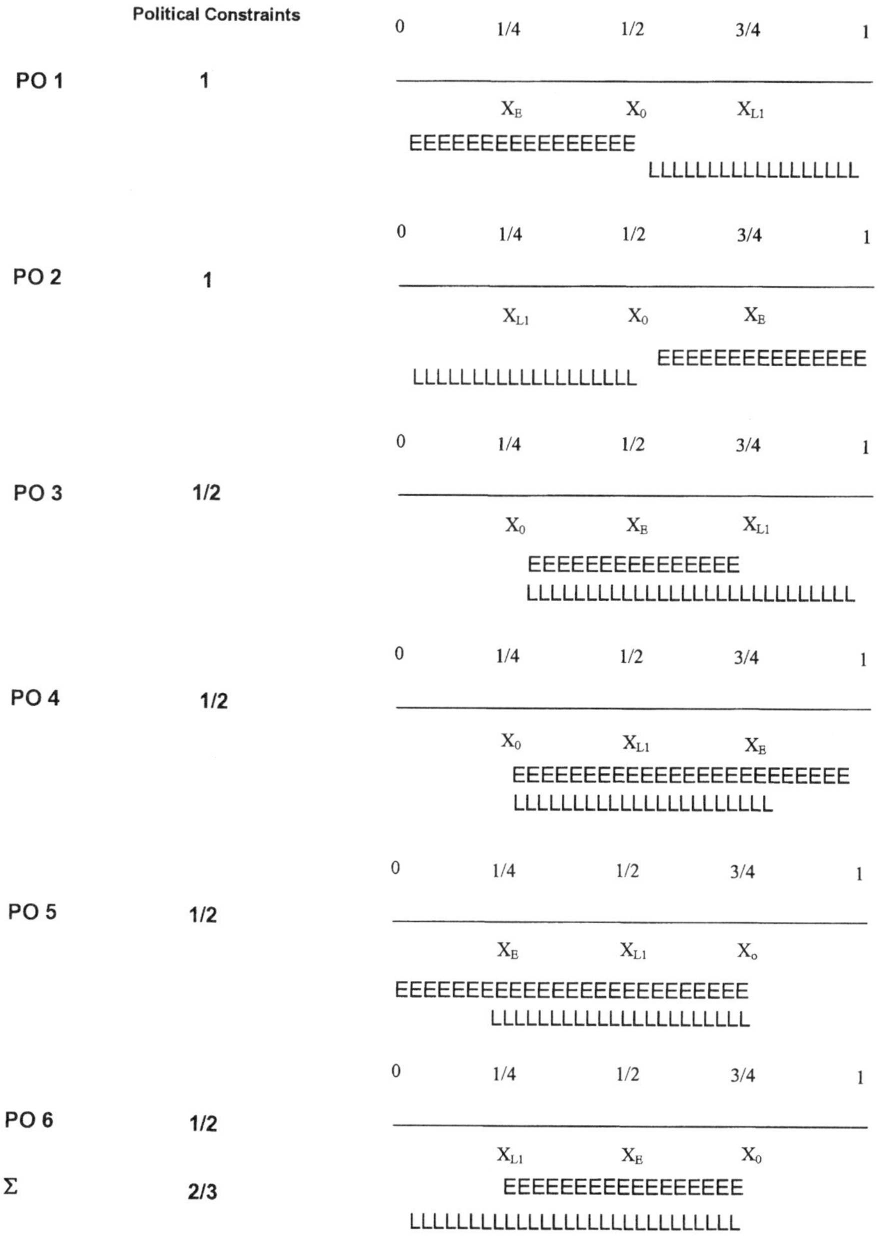

	Political Constraints	0	1/4	1/2	3/4	1
PO 1	1					

X_E X_0 X_{L1}

EEEEEEEEEEEEEEEEE

LLLLLLLLLLLLLLLLLL

		0	1/4	1/2	3/4	1
PO 2	1					

X_{L1} X_0 X_E

EEEEEEEEEEEEEEEE

LLLLLLLLLLLLLLLLLLL

		0	1/4	1/2	3/4	1
PO 3	1/2					

X_0 X_E X_{L1}

EEEEEEEEEEEEEEE

LLLLLLLLLLLLLLLLLLLLLLLLLLLLL

		0	1/4	1/2	3/4	1
PO 4	1/2					

X_0 X_{L1} X_E

EEEEEEEEEEEEEEEEEEEEEEEEEEE

LLLLLLLLLLLLLLLLLLLLLLL

		0	1/4	1/2	3/4	1
PO 5	1/2					

X_E X_{L1} X_o

EEEEEEEEEEEEEEEEEEEEEEEEEEE

LLLLLLLLLLLLLLLLLLLLLL

		0	1/4	1/2	3/4	1
PO 6	1/2					

X_{L1} X_E X_0

| Σ | 2/3 |

EEEEEEEEEEEEEEEEE

LLLLLLLLLLLLLLLLLLLLLLLLLLLLLLL

Source: Henisz (2002a) p.54

It is straightforward to see that for the previous example of two veto institutions an alignment between both players would significantly change the level of constraints. For the polar case that both actors are completely aligned the value for executive discretion would equal 1 resulting in a political constraints measure of 0 equal to the score of an unchecked executive and vice versa. Therefore, complete alignments may be analyzed without expanding the model.

Problems arise when political actors are neither completely aligned nor completely independent. To capture this effect the index has to be modified by incorporating the party composition in different branches of government. If the party controlling the executive also possesses a majority in the legislature, the level of political constraints is negatively correlated with the concentration of that majority because allied legislatures with great majorities are less costly to manage. If in contrast the legislature is dominated by a majority of the opposition party, higher fractionalization leads to a loss of opposition strength and diminishes political constraints. Hence, with higher fractionalization of an opposition which dominates the legislative branch political constraints are converging to the scores of a non-checked executive and vice versa. To cover these effects the de jure POLCON-Index is adjusted with a fractionalization index measuring the fractionalization of the legislature

3.6
$$FI = 1 - \sum_{i=1}^{n} \left[\frac{(n_i - 1)\frac{n_i}{N}}{N-1} \right]$$

where n is the number of parties, n_i the number of seats held by the nth party and N the total number of seats. Since this formula measures the probability that two random draws from the legislature are from different parties, a high value of equation 3.6 represents a highly fractionalized legislature and vice versa. The final score of the POLCON depends on the level of de jure veto rights and the extent to which political actors are aligned with each other. When the executive is aligned with the legislature the value of POLCON can be calculated by taking the sum of the political constraint value for full alignment and the product of the fractionalization index with the difference between the independent and the completely aligned values. Then POLCON becomes:

3.7 $POLCON = POLCON_A + FI * (POLCON_I - POLCON_A)$

Assume that the FI index is ¼, which means that congress is dominated by one party. With two national de-jure vetoes and the same party controlling executive and legislature a fractionalization index that equals ¼ implies that POLCON becomes:

3.8 $POLCON = 0 + 1/4 * (2/3 - 0) = 1/6$

The result 1/6 is intuitively correct because it reflects the higher discretion of the executive resulting from a less fractionalized legislature that is dominated by the same party. With falling levels of fractionalization the score of POLCON converges to the value for complete alignment. If in turn, the legislature is dominated by an opposition party, lower fractionalization has exactly the opposite effect because it strengthens opposition power and reduces governmental discretion. The formula for calculating POLCON changes to:

$$3.9 \qquad POLCON = POLCON_A + (1 - FI) * (POLCON_I - POLCON_A)$$

For our example of two veto players and a fractionalization index of 1/4 this implies the following value of POLCON:

$$3.10 \qquad POLCON = 0 + (1 - 1/4) * (2/3 - 0) = 1/2$$

For reasons of symmetry also this result is in line with expectations as a rather homogenous opposition in the legislature limits discretion of the executive resulting in high levels of political constraints. The next paragraph gives a critical evaluation of the risk indices that have been discussed before.

3.3.4 Critical Evaluations of Political Risk Indices
The preceding paragraphs discussed several political risk indicators and their ability to correctly predict future corporate losses for foreign investors. Table 3.1 summarizes the main focus, the weaknesses and strengths of these political risk indices. The indices that have been discussed in the previous paragraphs may be classified into two groups First, composite indicators consisting of several subvariables which have been assigned a score by country experts and second, continuous measures, namely POLCON, which may be objectively derived from the political system in the host country.

Although the predictive value of most composite indicators was found to be limited, they are widely used in international finance due to their intuitive logic and their comparably simple construction.[141] For many host countries and in particular for fairly developed emerging markets however, the large weight of catastrophic events compared to other risk factors is a drawback. Among the composite indicators that have been reviewed above the ICRG seems most appropriate for empirical purposes because it also recognizes more subtle

---

[141] Testing the ability to correctly predict major currency devaluation Oetzel/Bettis/Zenner (2001) found that most of the commonly used indicators had a weak predictive performance. In their analysis the ICRG performed best. However, as Drabek/Payne (2001) convincingly argue, even if risk indicators are weak predictors of company losses they still influence corporate investment decisions. That is, the considered indices are influential for investment decisions even if they rather mirror risk perceptions than real risk exposure.

political risks and its predictive capability was found to be comparatively high.[142]

Table 3.1: Main Characteristics of Political Risk Indicators

INDICATORS	INDICATOR TYPE	MAIN CHARACTERISTICS
Economist Index	Composite Indicator	• Focus on catastrophic events • Neglect of political structure in the home country (exception: authoritarian government and generals in power) • Expropriation risks and operational restriction risks are missing • Empirical analysis shows limited predictive capacity
Country Risk Services Index (CRS)	Composite Indicator	• Focus on catastrophic and structural risk factors • No empirical evidence on predictive capacity
BERI Index	Composite Indicator	• Focus on catastrophic and structural risk factors • Empirical evidence shows limited predictive capacity
ICRG	Composite Indicator	• Focus on catastrophic and structural risk factors • Convincing empirical evidence on predictive capacity
POLCON	Continuous Indicator	• Objectively derived from political system in the host country • Focuses on governmental-related political risk • Measures the feasibility of future policy changes • Neglects societal related sources of risk

Source: Own table

In addition to the criticism concerning each of the presented indicators, it is important to make a few general remarks about composite indicators. The Economist-Index, the CRS Index, the BERI-Index and the ICRG all share the common property of being the results of subjective perceptions about the current and future situation in host countries. Therefore, the quality of the risk assessment entirely depends on the qualification and the information processing capacity of the judging persons. Although the evaluation of risks is done by experts, it is important to stress that these country ratings are vulnerable for personal errors or manipulations.[143] Of particular relevance for foreign investors is the risk that the individual perceptions of experts are rather based on recent trends than guided by fundamental probabilities of political risk in the future. If investors invest in emerging markets with high growth rates leading to a reduction of risk perceptions for this country, it does not necessarily follow that the true risk exposure of these markets really declined. Instead, independent from past experiences the probability of opportunistic changes in governmental policy, which can imply hazards for foreign investors,

---

[142] Other risk measures have not been used for the empirical analysis either because it was cost prohibitive to purchase them, because country ratings were only available for short time periods or because the access was limited by the publisher.

[143] This argument is also made by Bubnova (2000) p.19-20.

remains unchanged.[144] Moreover, expert evaluations may be biased by hysteresis-effects meaning that past risks still have a considerable impact on present or future risk perceptions. In particular catastrophic political risks arising massive public attention are likely to influence long term political risk ratings even if the causes of risk are by now absent. The resulting path-dependency of risk ratings implies that current ratings may not picture the true risk exposure for MNEs and that investment decisions solely based on composite risk indicators may therefore result in missed business opportunities due to an unjustified over-evaluation of host country risk. Furthermore, perceptional indices have a tautological nature because it is hardly surprising that investors engage less in countries that are publicly perceived as risky. However, when experts err in predicting political risks in host countries perceptual measures of political risk only picture the expert's personal view of the country while hardly revealing anything about real sources of risk. If the predictions of the evaluating staff rely on models that lack the necessary sophistication composite risk indices may be totally misleading. All these drawbacks of composite political risk indices permit the conclusion that the predictive value of composite indices remains limited and that investment decisions should not be solely based on these measures.[145]

Another drawback of these measures becomes obvious when composite risk indicators are used for empirical research on FDI inflows because aggregation makes the derivation of policy implications more difficult. If aggregate index scores are found to be influential for FDI the results do not permit to precisely identify the underlying sources of risk since the mere result that political risk is influential for incoming FDI does not indicate which sub-risk are of particular importance and how those risks can be mitigated. In other words, finding a political risk index to be a significant obstacle to FDI does not reveal if the government has to improve the macroeconomic environment or to strengthen the enforcement of property rights to attract higher inflows of FDI. Therefore, empirical research on FDI should also determine the most influential risk factors in order to permit deriving strategies for the mitigation of political risks.[146]

Additional problems of many risk indicators stem from the fact that the characteristics of the political system in host countries and in particular regime type are largely ignored. Although economic theory argues that democracies should have higher investment rates than autocratic countries, the empirical evidence is often at odds with this conclusion.[147] While for example Russia receives significantly higher values for democracy than for example Taiwan or

---

[144] See Zelner/Henisz (1999).

[145] See Zelner/Henisz (1999).

[146] Therefore, the empirical part uses different categories of political risk that allow for the identification of the underlying risk sources.

[147] See the theoretical discussion about the influence of regime type in paragraph 3.1.3. that concludes that well functioning democracies in fact decrease risks for investors. However, these credibility enhancing effects only occur if democratic systems are well functioning, that is, if systems do not have to be considered as defect democracies.

Singapore the investment climate is obviously better in latter countries. Therefore, the pure classification of countries with political science constructs as democracy or authoritarian rule does not permit to evaluate a host country's investment climate. The POLCON Index avoids these problems because it is objectively derived from the structure of the political system in host countries. Therefore, it is not subject to the critique of being tautological or biased by the perceptions of experts. Instead of focusing on perceptions that may be influenced by past trends, it pictures the ability of governments to give a credible commitment to current policy. Since POLCON reflects the feasibility of arbitrary policy changes in host countries it should be capable of measuring the fraction of political risks that originates in governmental action, in particular risks of expropriation, creeping expropriation, repudiation of contracts, discriminatory taxation and so on. The forward looking nature of the index avoids the problems of backward oriented composite indicators. In turn, POLCON does not reflect risks that do not directly originate in governmental action. All risks with societal or external origins are ignored by POLCON which leads to a systematic underrating of risk when decisions are solely based on this indicator. As catastrophic risks can cause a total loss of assets the under-valuation of these risks is severe in politically unstable countries with a high probability of revolutions, armed conflicts, riots etc. Although many emerging markets currently have a low probability for catastrophic events, this argument clearly limits POLCON's suitability as risk indicator. Moreover, POLCON is not capable of picturing de facto political practices that deviate from the de jure rules of the constitution. Due to its technical derivation without a closer analysis of the political situation in host countries the index may over- or undervalue the level of political constraints.[148]

Therefore, a true political risk assignment necessarily has to consider both approaches, composite indicators and POLCON, as important determinants of risk for FDI projects. By applying a two-step-method which uses both indicators in the risk assessment process the danger of a misleading risk evaluation becomes lower. However, there is another important limit on the validity of all country risk indicators. As pointed out before determinants of FDI depend to a large extent on the individual characteristics of investment projects. In addition the theoretical analysis of investment decisions under un-certainty revealed that different degrees of reversibility imply different impacts of uncertainty on investment decisions. It is obvious that also the decisions of real world investors vary largely with the characteristics of the planned invest-ment project.[149] Investors with high shares of sunk cost for example should be

---

[148] The case study on Mexico in Chapter 5 shows that in the Mexican case POLCON systematically overvalues the level of political constraints because constitutional rules and de-facto politics differ considerably. See Chapter 5.

[149] See Howell (2001b) and Markwick (2001). The empirical research of Fatehi/Safizadeh (1994) reveals that sociopolitical instabilities had a different impact on FDI in manufacturing and extractive industries. The fact that the impact of political risk was higher in extractive industries indicates that higher irreversibility has an impact on the investment decision. Kwon (2002) argues that vertical and export oriented FDI are less sensitive to political risk than horizontal and market-oriented FDI because government

more sensitive to expropriation threats than investors in footloose industries. Therefore, an ideal political risk index should vary with the needs of the investor and the characteristics of the project. In other words, political risk indicators that perform well in the oil industry are not necessarily ideal for tele-communications investment and vice versa. Although highly relevant, this common problem can hardly be avoided in empirical investigations on the macro level. Nevertheless, an interpretation of empirical results has to consider this drawback of political risk indicators.

The discussion shows that political risk assessment is a complex process that should not be entirely led by standardized methods.[150] Although the econometric study of FDI in Chapter 4 requires standardization, the case study on Mexico in Chapter 5 permits to simultaneously use quantitative indicators and qualitative reasoning for the risk assessment. Summing up, despite of the indicated limitations of the reviewed risk indices they are the most powerful available tool for empirical research on the impact of political risks on FDI. Therefore, these variables are used in the panel analysis in Chapter 4 studying the impact of political risk variables on FDI inflows to Latin American countries as well as in the case study in Chapter 5 for the quantification of political risk exposure in Mexico. The next paragraph discusses risk mitigation strategies for countries with high levels of political risk.

3.4 Mitigating Political Risk
3.4.1 Overview
Having exposed the risks factors that are influential for the investment decisions of MNEs the following paragraphs analyze how political risk may be efficiently mitigated by host country governments. The emergence of risk mitigation and investment promotion efforts are a result of the fierce competition among host governments for the attraction of FDI. Although this competition is not an entirely new phenomenon, its aggressiveness and intensity is constantly increasing.[151] This development is of particular relevance to developing countries with a high demand for external finance because only those countries will attract considerable amounts of FDI that provide location specific assets as infrastructure, skills and an attractive institutional environment.[152] Consequently during the last years a process of policy adjustments and promotional campaigns initiated among potential host countries to attract foreign investors.[153] Even developing countries that traditionally did not have the necessity to compete for FDI due to the existence

---

incentives for expropriation are higher in the latter. His empirical findings however, only offer weak support for this theoretical hypothesis.

[150] As recognized in the Handbook of Country and Political Risk Analysis: "Political Risk analysis is an art, not a laboratory science which lends itself to precise predictions".... "Numerical ratings are of very little value unless they are backed by written, qualitative assessment, to explain how the analyst came to a conclusion." See Howell (1998) p.61.

[151] Wells et al. (2001) offer some reasons for the intensification of the competition for international investments. See Wells et al. (2001) p.1-7.

[152] See Lall (2002) p.331.

[153] See Wheeler/Mody (1992).

of vast natural resources or a large domestic market have begun initiatives to attract export-oriented FDI. This new competitive environment has prompted analogies between competition among governments for FDI and competition among companies for market shares. Given the similarities of the situations, countries may adopt marketing strategies that parallel those of private companies. In analogy to the variables product, price and promotion countries can essentially manipulate three variables to attract higher FDI flows:[154]

1. Intrinsic advantages or disadvantages of the investment site (Analogy to product characteristics)
2. The cost to investors of locating and operating within the investment site (Analogy to product price)
3. Activities that disseminate information about, or attempt to create a positive image of the investment site and provide investment services (Analogy to product promotion)

From these general investment promotion possibilities host countries choose the appropriate "marketing mix" which permits attracting the desired amount of FDI at the lowest possible cost. While industrial countries often initiate general campaigns to create a positive image of the national investment climate developing countries usually initiate promotion efforts which are more directly targeted at investors that are likely to be attracted.[155]

3.4.2 National Mitigation Strategies
3.4.2.1 Investment Incentives, Social Standards and Environmental Legislation

A widely discussed policy for the mitigation of political risks is decreasing location and operation cost of MNEs by granting investment incentives.[156] Investment incentives can be defined as a package of fiscal- and economic-related inducements that are offered by host governments with the goal of attracting higher FDI inflows.[157] The basic idea of this approach is straightforward. Instead of directly mitigating high levels of political risk by policy reforms international investors are compensated for their additional risk exposure by higher returns. Governmental incentives can take various forms as for example tax grants, lower prices for land, the provision of additional infrastructure etc.[158] Following a profit maximization view MNEs will invest more if they are confronted with relatively low taxes or other investment incentives as the net return on capital is increasing. According to this view economic and fiscal policies of host countries are a primary motivating factor for MNEs as these policies ameliorate or counter the risk and uncertainty found in developing countries. While in the first place the concept seems to be

---

[154] Therefore, Wells et al. speak of "marketing a country" when referring to investment promotion. See Wells et al. (2001).

[155] See Wells et al. (2001) p.42-47. The authors also argue that usually big countries need less marketing efforts as their large national market is sufficient to attract international investors. See Wells et al. (2001) p.178-180.

[156] Labelling investment incentives as national risk mitigation strategy is problematic because it is rather a means of curing symptoms than reasons. However, as it is a widely practised "national strategy" it is discussed under 3.4.2.

[157] See Billet (1991) p.64.

[158] See Guisinger (1986) p.82 –83 for an overview of possible investment incentives.

a suitable means of promoting FDI, a closer look identifies many drawbacks of such a strategy.[159]

First, whatever measure is taken to attract foreign companies incentives, imply a high cost to the host government.[160] Tax incentives for instance mean foregone future tax flows while other measures as the provision of additional infrastructure are a direct burden for public finances. Due to these fiscal losses the potential benefits of FDI on the host economy are reduced.[161] Moreover, incentive regimes usually impose high administrative costs which further reduce the net benefit of incoming FDI.[162] Thus, a rationally deciding government should carefully weight the potential benefits of the foreign productive engagement against the cost of incentive provision. Additionally, it may be argued that in some cases governments waste fiscal resources for the attraction of companies that would have invested anyway. Moreover, the offering of a generous investment incentive package may be even an adverse signal for MNEs deterring investment as international investors perceive the incentives as an effort to compensate for other major deficiencies of the investment climate.[163] Consequently, recent empirical evidence suggests that incentives only make a difference between competing countries when the basic, more important conditions are comparable. It follows that incentives will not make up for serious deficiencies in the investment environment which can often be found in developing countries.[164]

Second, as by definition incentives are limited to foreign investors their competitive advantage is fostered. In most developing countries local competitors already suffer from competitive disadvantages due to lacking financial resources and technology. If specific investment incentives are granted they are more severely affected by the lack of a level playing field. If, as a consequence, MNEs completely dominate the domestic market creating an un-competitive market structure the potential benefits of FDI are further reduced. While domestic reforms that ameliorate the investment climate in host countries offer a "double-dividend" investment incentives do not benefit

---

[159] The empirical evidence on the FDI enhancing impact of investment incentives is at best weak. See the overview in Moriset/Pirnia (2002). Although Guisinger (1986) and Loree/Guisinger (1995) find a significant positive impact of investment incentives, they argue that the incentives become inefficient when other countries also grant them.

[160] Oman (2001) reports that amounts spent on incentives rose considerably during the last years. While incentive payments ranged between 17000 to 51000 US$ per created job in the mid 80s during the 90s these payments ranged from 94000 to 420000 US$. It is estimated that Daimler-Chrysler received subsidies of 340000 US$ (largely in the form of tax holidays) per created job for an investment in the Brazilian state of Minas Gerais.

[161] Empirical research by Wells et al. shows that tax incentives are less cost efficient than other investment promotion techniques without transfers to MNEs. See Wells et al. (2001) p.121-129.

[162] See Moriset/Pirnia (2002) p.285.

[163] See Billet (1991) p.67 and Oman (2000) p.115. Investors with rational expectations would not invest in this case, because they anticipate to be affected by higher levels of political risk in the future.

[164] See Oman (2001) p.68 and Morisset/Pirnia (2002) p.277-288.

domestic investors which entails a skewed competition between MNEs and domestic producers. Moreover, these subsidies may act to reduce societal welfare.

Third, investment incentives do not eliminate domestic sources of political risk. Therefore, incentives are more a means of reducing symptoms than of curing the reasons for political risk. Even if the strategy of attracting FDI turns out to be successful, incentives are no sustainable solution for the problem of lacking investment due to high-risk environments.[165]

Considering these direct and indirect costs of an incentive-based strategy its overall long term efficiency seems at least questionable.[166] The ambiguous economic implications of an investment incentive strategy arises the question of why countries actually implement such a strategy. Policy reform often is a lengthy process that may produce results that are not as far reaching as initially intended. Furthermore, it is hard to demonstrate for a government that it is really intending to continue the reform path despite of popular pressure. Therefore, governments of high risk countries that are on the path of reform suffer from a serious credibility problem that may in the first place impede favorable reactions of international investors. To solve this problem, national governments may have to engage in granting incentives to compensate inter-national investors for their lack of credibility. Hence, incentives may indeed be efficient in the short run to compensate for the effects of lacking governmental credibility. Nevertheless, in the long run the strategy will rather produce undesirable results. Therefore, if they are granted at all, investment incentives should be timely limited to avoid these negative consequences.[167]

Theoretically, attracting investment to high risk environments by low social or environmental standards is similar to FDI promotion by incentives. Again the focus of governmental efforts is not to solve the problems that are entailing high risk levels but to compensate international investors by offering social or environmental legislation that is considerably weaker than in other countries.[168]

---

[165] Wells et al. (2001) argue that investment incentives are counterproductive because they tend to delay the implementation of reforms which are more likely to affect the investment decision. Oman (2001) argues that incentives may attract the wrong kinds of investors who do not stay beyond the duration of the subsidies limiting positive spillovers on the host country economy.

[166] This argument is used by the IFC. See CFI (1997). The empirical results concerning the effectiveness of investment incentives are ambiguous. See Billet (1991) p.61-80 and Moriset/Pirnia (2002). Blomström/Kokko (2003) state that investment incentives only have welfare enhancing effects for host countries when foreign direct investments generate positive externalities that outweigh the cost of granting incentives. They continue arguing that investment incentives which exclusively focus on foreign investors are not an efficient way to increase national welfare.

[167] Chapter 5 will analyze the importance of the investment incentive strategy for the case of Mexico.

[168] Oman argues that the effectiveness of low environmental and labor standards as tools to attract FDI are limited. In earlier work he does not find evidence for the hypothesis that

The cost difference that is generated by these lower standards is similar to granting incentives. It is straightforward to see that a national strategy based on lowering standards is not sustainable in the long run since environmental and social costs diminish societal welfare that is supposed to be created by the enhanced presence of foreign investors. Concerning the ongoing debate about social standards as measures of protection for industrial countries it is important to stress that it is unrealistic to demand similar environmental and social standards for industrialized and developing countries since lower standards in developing countries are not necessarily signs of social dumping or unfair competition but simply reflect different levels of economic and social development. Despite of this argument, the extensive use of social and environmental resources for the attraction of FDI does not seem to be an efficient strategy in the long run. Environmental damages have to, if it is possible at all, be costly repaired by using governmental resources. Low labor and social standards are not merely a moral problem but also have economic impacts by lowering the productivity of the labor force and by impeding human capital formation.

To conclude one may state that the strategies that have been outlined in this paragraph may only serve as aligning strategies that offer efficient results in the short run. As a long term strategy for the attraction of FDI low standards or investment incentives are not efficient.

3.4.2.2 Macroeconomic Stability

It is by now common knowledge that creating and ensuring macroeconomic stability is a prerequisite for successful economic development and that an un-stable macro-economic environment distorts private incentives to invest by producing uncertainty and insecurity. As pointed out in the analysis of the political risk literature the classical concept of country risk mainly focuses on macroeconomic indicators and their implications for international lenders or investors. Orthodox country risk analysis is thus basically an analysis of the current macroeconomic situation of a given country and as to which this situation implies risks for MNEs. Although the definition of political risk that has been presented above clearly extends this classical interpretation, it has to be underlined that macroeconomic indicators are still an important determinant of aggregate political risk. Therefore, the maintenance of a stable macroeconomic framework including sensible monetary and fiscal policy as well as a functioning exchange rate policy become an important part in a national risk mitigation strategy.

It is straightforward to see that macroeconomic problems as high levels of inflation or a highly volatile national currency are severe disincentives for inter-national investors. Although FDI usually reacts less volatile to macroeconomic indicators than portfolio investments, enduring instabilities may also induce lower levels of FDI. This is even more important considering possible

---

enhanced competition for FDI leads to a "race to the bottom", that is a severe lowering of social, environmental and labor standards. See Oman (2000) and Oman (2001).

hysteresis effects that may be caused by severe macroeconomic crises. That is, even if the most important sources of risk have been eliminated investors still perceive the country as being more risky than before. The Latin American debt crisis, for example, highlighted how severe macroeconomic imbalances reduce the attractiveness of countries for FDI. Therefore, since the outbreak of the debt crisis stabilization policies have been a main focus in the economic policy of many emerging market countries and an important tool for political risk mitigation. Moreover, sound macroeconomic policy does not only affect foreign investors but also their domestic counterparts which benefit to the same extent from low levels of inflation, sustainable fiscal deficits and external macroeconomic stability. Therefore, it can be concluded that the macroeconomic risk mitigation strategy is efficient and sustainable in the long run. The next paragraph discusses the efficiency of a risk mitigation strategy focusing on domestic institutional reforms.

3.4.2.3 Accountability, Transparency and Rules-Based Governance
The previous paragraphs focused on institutional prerequisites for the establishment of a favorable domestic investment climate and showed how risks for investors may arise if the institutional framework is not adequate. While many national risk mitigation strategies focus on the compensation of international investors for their higher risk exposure the strategy that is presented here is concerned with domestic institutional reform to directly tackle the problem of political risk.[169] As already pointed out in the previous paragraph one important part of this national beauty contest is the maintenance of macroeconomic stability. Nevertheless, domestic institutional reform goes far beyond this by aiming at the removal of institutional impediments to a favorable national investment climate. For developing countries possible goals of this policy are achieving a better assignment of property rights, promoting a better functioning of the legal system and enhancing individual constitutional guarantees. The more general objective of these reforms is the establishment of what the literature calls good governance. Here there is no room for a complete overview of the extensive literature on good governance.[170] Therefore, only those parts of the concept are mentioned here that are of particular importance for the incentive structure of private investors, namely accountability, transparency, predictability and the rule of law.[171] Important elements of good governance are a transparent and accountable government that on the one hand lowers transaction costs of private contracting and on the other hand is limited by a set of basic rules that protect individual rights against abuses of public organizations with coercive power. Since rule of law and predictability of governmental policy lower trans-action costs and reduce the probability of "policy surprises" for investors it is straightforward to see that the process of institutional reforms directly tackles

---

[169] In the literature this strategy of domestic policy reform to enhance the attractiveness for FDI has been referred to as national "beauty contest". This expression has been used by Eduardo Fernández-Arias in a comment on a paper by Oman (2001). See Fernández-Arias (2001).

[170] See World Bank (1994).

[171] See Isham et al. (1995) p.11.

the sources of low investor confidence.[172] Although theoretically the strategy of domestic policy reform is a means of reducing risks for investors, it poses several problems to host countries.

First, domestic institutional reform is a costly and lengthy process. As already pointed out adapting national institutions to the needs of national and international investors takes a long time and may face the severe resistance of societal forces as governmental organizations, parties, or other interest groups that may impede or at least slow down the reform process.[173] Reforming the national judiciary for example is a complex, costly and lengthy process that may mobilize the resistance of those powerful societal interest groups that do benefit from the existing inefficiencies of the current system.[174] Given these difficulties in the implementation of institutional reform it is necessary to think of an accompanying strategy that may reduce levels of political risk more quickly. Second, national actors and newly founded or reformed organizations may lack the necessary credibility to attract FDI since all contractual mitigation measures that rely directly on state investor relations do not resolve the credibility problem of developing countries. This implies that for countries with a negative track record of arbitrary governmental intervention and regulation of FDI the solution of domestic institutional reform is less feasible. In analogy to the literature on central bank credibility one may assume that newly created or reformed organizations that were associated with unstable policies in the past will not quickly gain the full confidence of international investors. Instead, building credibility is a lengthy process that needs accompanying measures if results of the reform policy are to be seen rapidly. Third, it is a major problem for national policy makers to lock-in reform programs. Politicians are usually under high public pressure and depend on the support of national interest groups. Unpopular reforms that imply losses for certain interest groups in society are therefore subject to high pressure of revision. Thus, for politicians a successful reform program is more likely to be implemented and maintained with accompanying measures that lock-in reforms, that is, make them unresponsive to populist pressure.

Summing up, the implementation of domestic institutional reforms and macro-economic stability are two main pillars of a successful national risk mitigation strategy. However, the implementation of institutional reforms is a lengthy and

---

[172] This strategy may also be directly focused on attracting foreign investors. In negotiations with multinationals the State could commit not to nationalize foreign assets or accept so-called stabilization clauses by which the state exempts foreign investors from changes it may introduce in its legislation or from administrative measures of general application whenever their effect would be to significantly reduce economic returns expected from the investment. Another possibility which less limits national sovereignty are the agreement to renegotiation clauses which permit to renegotiate the contractual terms and conditions in case of supervening circumstances as new legislative or regulatory measures. See Bernardini (2001) p.241

[173] North's theory of institutional change argues that institutional change is slow and that countries can get locked into inefficient institutional structures. See North (1990) and the brief summary in paragraph 3.1.2.1.

[174] See Ayala Espino (2002).

costly process so that results usually do not occur rapidly. Moreover, national institutions may lack credibility and politicians may face the problem to lock in institutional reforms against high populist pressure. Therefore, it may be efficient to accompany institutional reforms with other strategies to tackle these implementation problems.

3.4.3 International Strategies
3.4.3.1 Multilateral Agreements
International risk mitigation strategies focus on gaining credibility from signing international agreements or joining international organizations. The basic idea is that countries with weak institutions can restraint their government to precisely specified rules and lock it into international mechanisms that are costly to reverse. In addition to other goals international agreements are then used to successfully lock in institutional change.[175] Although sovereign countries still can reverse policies, international commitments force governments to not just calculate the costs and benefits of policy reversals, but also the broader cost of reneging on international treaties for which their partners will hold them accountable.[176] Apart from other consequences a membership of a country in an international organization implies that national political actors are no longer exclusively limited by national but also by international law. Multilateral agreements on trade, investment, environmental standards or any other topic submit national policy makers to the international law that has been agreed on and to the mechanisms of control and supervision of multilateral organizations. Thus, international commitment mechanisms can serve in enhancing credibility as a short-term substitute while national institutions are build up.[177] International agreements may therefore be valued for their "signaling" properties because member countries can demonstrate to potential investors that they are committed to play by the rules and that this commitment will not be easy to reverse.[178] Up to now however, various attempts to conclude multilateral conventions on the subject of FDI protection, such as, most recently the Multilateral Agreement on Investment (MAI) launched by OECD members, were unsuccessful.[179]

---

[175] See WTO (2003) p.50.

[176] See World Bank (1997) p.6 and p.101. The World Bank further argues that the mere integration of countries into the world economy helps sustaining macroeconomic stability as it becomes more costly to pursue inconsistent economic policies. See World Bank (1997) p.48.

[177] See World Bank (1997) p.109.

[178] See WTO (2003) p.50

[179] Exceptions are the multilateral investment protection agreements on the regional level such as ASEAN Agreement for the Promotion and Protection of Investment from 1987, the NAFTA investment chapter from 1992, and the agreement for the protection of investment under the MERCOSUR treaty from 1991. The only "true" multilateral conventions are the Convention on the Settlement of Investment Disputes between States and Nationals of other States (ICSID) and the Multilateral Investment Guarantee Agency (MIGA) convention insuring against political risks. See Bernardini (2001) p.236-238. For further details on the MAI see UNCTAD (1999a) and Robertson (2002).

While it may be argued that large and powerful countries or negotiating blocks may have the possibility to ignore international obligations it is less likely that developing countries or emerging markets can afford to neglect international obligations. Since multilateral agreements complement national legislation by defining binding international rules, efficient enforcement mechanisms of multilateral treaties imply constraints for national policy makers limiting their degree of political discretion. Therefore, multilateral agreements help mitigate political risks by providing higher legal certainty for investors through the establishment of transparent international rules that may be referred to when conflicts occur. Credible and efficient conflict resolution mechanisms imply a rise in investor confidence as they have the possibility to refer their claims and complaints to dispute settlement bodies of international organizations instead of just to the local judiciary. These legal guarantees on the international level are favorable for the investor even if local legislation for the protection of foreign assets already exists because in countries with low political stability risks for long term investments are not effectively diminished by domestic legislation that may easily undergo changes over time. The appointment of an international arbitrator reduces the risk that local courts deciding on investment disputes are influenced by political pressure of host governments.[180] However, multinational agreements are not only directly useful as a risk mitigation strategy. At the same time they can act as complements of a national institutional reform strategy since multilateral contracts facilitate the lock-in of domestic reform projects by tying the hands of national politicians through international law and making them immune against domestic populist pressure. Furthermore, the recognition of international agreements allows for a credibility gain of national institutions as they are subject to better international control and supervision. Therefore, the signing of international treaties additionally implies an "import" of credibility from the international organization. Moreover, if the international agreement that has been signed is a free trade agreement, the market that can be served by an investment in the region grows. Growing market size in turn, strengthens one of the key fundamentals to which investors attach great importance.[181]

Thus, the membership in international organizations may be an important means of accompanying domestic policy reforms by facilitating their local implementation. Gains in credibility, immunization against domestic populist pressure and higher legal certainty of economic actors are important measures that help ensuring the achievement of rapid and stable reform processes. Nevertheless, it is important to underline that in the long run a multilateral international risk mitigation strategy can only be successful if international obligations are honored and if the process of international integration is accompanied by successful domestic reforms. Violating or ignoring international obligations in turn, will result in undermining credibility and investor confidence.

---

[180] See Bernardini (2001) p.240-246.
[181] See Oman (2001).

3.4.3.2 Bilateral Agreements and Regional Integration

The functioning of bilateral agreements and regional integration blocks as a means of political risk mitigation is similar to that of multilateral integration strategies since national rules are complemented by international obligations and international mechanisms of control and supervision. Since national politicians are subject to higher controls, basic investor rights are guaranteed on the international level, and international obligations facilitate the domestic "lock-in" of reforms the mechanisms that cause the risk mitigation effect are similar. Faced with the failure to establish a multilateral agreement for the protection of investor rights many countries favored a policy of Bilateral Investment Treaties (BITs) for risk mitigation. Since the mid 90s the number of BITs increased enormously reaching a level of about 1500 agreements involving 180 states as contracting parties.[182] Rather than promoting a further liberalization of domestic FDI regulations most bilateral investment treaties are designed to protect basic rights of foreign investors as for example unrestricted monetary transfers or protection against expropriation.[183]

Despite of basic similarities, there is one difference between bilateral and multilateral treaties. Multilateral agreements are usually supported by a variety of international actors among them large industrialized countries. Therefore, international organizations and their mechanisms of enforcement and control in general enjoy a high degree of transparency and credibility which is not necessarily the case for bilateral treaties or other regional integration agreements. If integration agreements or bilateral treaties are signed by countries with high levels of risk and low credibility the process of risk mitigation by international integration may not turn out to be efficient. To put it in other words, international agreements between countries with a weak institutional framework will not necessarily result in the desired credibility enhancing effect of international integration, since it is unlikely that countries with low national credibility create international obligations that turn out to be reliable.[184] Even if such a treaty contains rules that are per se credible and honored in the long run it is unlikely that international financial actors do perceive it as a tool for fostering credibility and for locking in domestic reform efforts. This implies that the success of bilateral strategies for international risk mitigation or regional integration efforts largely depends upon the credibility of the signing parties. If all member states of the international agreement are characterized by weak domestic institutions and low credibility the potential for an import of international credibility remains limited. It is more probable that these effects occur if at least one of the signing member states possesses strong national institutions and enjoys international credibility. For developing countries this reasoning implies that joining forces with other developing

---

[182] See Bernardini (2001) p.238.

[183] See Sacerdoti (2000) and Bernardini (2001).

[184] This point is made by Grosse who comparing NAFTA and MERCOSUR argues: " Without a similar link to the US (like Mexico in NAFTA), Mercosur will never achieve a similar level of investor confidence, nor the integration of MNE activities that Mexico has experienced." Grosse (2003b) p.664.

nations will most likely not produce the credibility enhancing effect that may occur if international treaties are signed with developed countries.[185]

3.5 Conclusion

Chapter 3 gives a theoretical foundation for political risk analysis arguing that political risk analysis essentially consists of an analysis of the institutional environment in host countries and that the analysis of transaction costs for private economic activity permits to identify prerequisites and obstacles for a favorable investment climate. Based on these theoretical reflections several models explaining the emergence of political risk have been discussed. The synthesis of these models that classified political risk in three basic groups (societal risks, governmental risks and macroeconomic risks) aims at facilitating empirical tests of the main hypotheses in later chapters. Thereafter, the possibilities for empirical measurement of political risk have been discussed by identifying the strengths and weaknesses of existing political risk indices. Eventually, the chapter offered a brief discussion of potential risk mitigation strategies for high risk countries. It concluded that incentive based strategies have the drawback of being costly and inefficient in the long run while domestic risk mitigation strategies based on institutional reform were identified as efficient but lengthy and costly which means that their results take time to emerge. The chapter concluded by stating that international economic integration may help to quickly obtain positive results in risk mitigation. Complementing national efforts with "borrowing" credibility from multilateral organizations or industrial countries with high levels of national credibility is a way to more rapidly achieve positive results in terms of national credibility.

3.6 Chapter Summary

Chapter 3 of this volume focused on theoretical explanations for the emergence of political risk and analyzed the efficiency of potential empirical political risk measures. Paragraph 3.1 set the theoretical foundations for the analysis by showing that political risks emerge if the domestic institutional structure of a market economy is deficient and does not provide right incentives for private investment behavior. Based on NIE it developed a basic theoretical framework that permits to study the impact of political and socio-economic variables on investment behavior without having to refer to ad-hoc hypothesis. Additionally it discussed the influence of political regime type on investment incentives in host countries.

Paragraph 3.2 presents several theoretical models that explain the emergence of political risk in countries. Their strengths and weaknesses are discussed and the paragraph closes with a theoretical synthesis of the presented approaches that may be used as a base for the empirical investigations in Chapter 4 and 5 of this volume.

---

[185] Without entering into a detailed discussion about the potential benefits and problems of regional integration and bilateral treaties it has to be underlined that this result is limited to the credibility enhancing effects of international treaties.

Paragraph 3.3 is concerned with empirical measures in political risk analysis. It presents different commonly used measures of political risk and discusses their strengths, weaknesses and limitations. It closes with an assessment of indicator quality and argues which empirical indicators were chosen for the empirical analysis in Chapter 4 and 5 of this volume. The choice of the suitable indicators was governed by theoretical considerations and empirical concerns of data availability.

In paragraph 3.4 the chapter turns to the analysis of the efficiency of risk mitigation strategies for countries with high risk environments. It briefly discusses theoretical strengths and weaknesses of different risk mitigation measures and concludes that risk mitigation by granting investment incentives is a costly and unsustainable strategy that does not tackle the problems that are at the heart of high levels of political risk. Strategies that aim at promoting macroeconomic stability and the reform of national institutions have been identified as more suitable measures of national risk mitigation. I argue that the involvement in multilateral treaties or bilateral treaties where at least one signing member enjoys high international credibility theoretically are efficient strategies to attain higher levels of investor confidence and credibility.

Paragraph 3.5 holds a conclusion that summarizes the most important implications of this chapter for the following analysis.

4. Political Risk and FDI in Latin America
4.1 Stylized Facts on Foreign Investment in Latin America

Latin America has a long tradition as a destination of international capital flows. As a continent favorably endowed with natural resources, it inevitably arose the interest of foreigners since its discovery by the Spanish. The conquest and the colonial rule that followed were characterized by a focus of the European nations to exploit the rich national resources of the new world. Already before independence the American colonies of Portugal and Spain were heavily involved in international business in the form of exchange of raw materials as gold and silver for manufactured products from Europe. Spanish and Portuguese individuals and firms owned a variety of investments such as farms and raw material ventures in the colonies. This concentration of FDI in the primary sector, and in particular in extractive industries and large scale plantations also continued after independence. With the beginning of the industrial revolution FDI to the region accelerated with foreign participation in mining and infrastructure projects such as railways and telegraph systems. Nevertheless, most of the financial flows in the nineteenth century were related to bond issues by Latin American governments on European stock exchanges.[1]

In the twentieth century the production of natural resources such as oil, copper, bauxite and bananas attracted resource-seeking FDI to Latin America, in particular from the US, to build and operate large scale mines or plantations.[2] Until the past three decades market seeking FDI in the manufacturing sector, usually with low capital content, was largely attracted to the big three economies of the region: Argentina, Brazil, and Mexico. During the entire period up to the Second World War the United Kingdom and the United States were the sources of approximately two-thirds of long term capital flows to Latin America.[3] Inflows of FDI lost momentum when Latin American governments became more protective of their domestic natural resources during the 60s and 70s.[4] A dogmatic debate about the dependence of Latin American countries on MNEs based in industrial countries and the inward-looking industrialization of Latin America nations following the ECLAC model were responsible for a declining growth of international investment to Latin America. During the 70s many Latin American governments obliged foreign extractive and utility investors to sell ownership to nationals. Across a wide range of activities foreign firms were limited in their ownership and control of business in Latin America. These limits consisted of ownership restrictions,

---

[1] See Grosse (2001) and Grosse (1989) p.7-29.
[2] See Grosse (2003).
[3] See Grosse (1989) p.11-24.
[4] See Grosse (2001). The restrictions were accompanied by expropriations in many Latin American countries. Paragraph 5.2.2.2 reviews the changing political attitudes towards FDI for the Mexican case.

rules on profit remittances and royalty payments as well as of exchange controls, taxes and quantitative restrictions.[5]

In the following years FDI shifted from natural resources toward the manufacturing sector. During the lost decade of the 80s FDI to Latin America only grew slowly with investors still favoring manufacturing over other types of investment. The crisis of the Latin American development model after the debt crisis led to a new wave of economic opening and liberalization during the late 80s. In the 90s FDI was concentrated in services, partly induced by large scale privatization of former public service companies in telecommunication, financial services, electrical power generation etc.[6]

As figure 4.1 shows, Latin America and the Caribbean held the lion share of private resource flows to developing countries in the year 2001 indicating that the liberalization and opening strengthened the role of foreign investment in Latin American countries. The introduction already highlighted the stagnation of official net resource flows to developing countries compared to the dynamic evolution of private capital flows which peaked in the late 90s. Sustaining the level of external financing requires consistent national economic policies that do not decrease investor confidence about the stability and the economic prospects of the region.

Figure 4.1: Geographical Distribution of FDI To Developing Countries in 2001

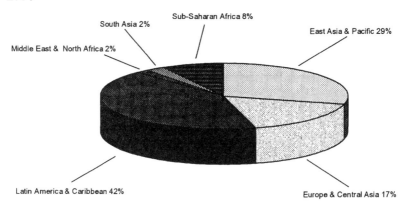

Source: Own figure using data of World Bank (2002): Global Development Finance

---

[5] See Grosse (2003b).

[6] Interestingly in these sectors foreign investors have a massive presence. In telecommunications Telefónica from Spain and US firms as GTE and Bell South are the dominant carriers. In electric power Endesa from Spain, Houston Energy, AES and Duke Power are leading distributors and generators of energy in the region. In banking Banco Santander_Central Hispano and Banco Bilbao Vizcayo from Spain along with Citybank and Hong Kong Bank have build regionwide networks of affiliates. See Grosse (2003b).

Therefore, similar to all other developing countries, Latin America's economic policy has to be designed in a way that permits attracting foreign investors. Given the importance of private external financing for the region and the volatility of international capital movements, inconsistent economic policies and public violations of basic investor rights imply enormous cost for the countries in the region in terms of foregone future investment flows. If FDI is deterred, a country also looses the benefits immanent to these long term investments as transfers of technology and management know how as well as growth and productivity enhancing linkages to the national market. As already argued in the introduction, high political risk in a given country is not only a major problem for MNEs eager to do business in the region but also for the countries themselves because it reduces their access to sources of external financing. The recent events in Argentina where the government abandoned the dollar parity and declared the inability to service its foreign debt impressively highlights the severe effects of inconsistent economic policy for countries of the region.

> *For every complex problem there is an easy answer, and it is wrong.*
> *H.L. Mencken*

4.2 Empirical Investigation of the Impact of Political Risk on FDI
4.2.1 Methodology

The following paragraphs present an empirical model which tests for the main hypotheses that have been derived in Chapter 2 and 3 of this volume by using the empirical measures of political risk that have been discussed in Chapter 3. For the empirical test I use a panel of all Latin American countries excluding the Caribbean covering the period from 1982 to 1997.[7] For isolating the impact of political risk indicators on FDI flows, variables are included in the model that control for other determinants of FDI. The discussion in paragraph 2.2.3.2 revealed that there is no theoretical consensus about the variables that determine FDI, since contemporary theory only offers a verbal eclectic paradigm for the explanation of FDI that is lacking an exact formalization and specification of influential parameters in the form of a mathematical model. Given this limitation empirical research on FDI has to follow what EDWARDS calls a pragmatic approach.[8]

This implies that empirical research has to focus on the use of proxy variables that control for the potential factors of influence that have been identified in theory. However, also the review of empirical studies leaves the reader with a rather ambiguous picture of the variables that explain FDI flows. This lack of consensus may be explained, to some extent, with the large variances in methodology, perspectives, sample selection and analytical tools that

---

[7] The choice of this period was determined by limited data availability and by the aim to gather a panel for a large number of Latin American countries. Belize that was originally placed in the sample has been removed as reliable political risk data was not available for the chosen period.

[8] See Edwards (1990).

researchers have been using. Moreover, the selection of independent variables often seems arbitrary and lacking sufficient theoretical foundation. As most authors only use a small subset of variables that are of particular interest to them, a wide selection of variables have been found to be correlated with FDI in different directions in different studies.[9] Therefore, the selection of appropriate control variables and the right specification of an econometric model for incoming FDI flows are difficult tasks.

In the presence of high uncertainty about the determinants of FDI inflows and with a sole interest in the influence of political risk variables on FDI flows to Latin America it is appropriate to use an econometric methodology that has been proposed by LEAMER.[10] Instead of choosing the classical econometric approach of specifying and respecifying empirical models according to the achieved results, he proposes to use a sensitivity analysis to test for the influence of a certain variable on an independent variable. LEAMER'S argument starts with the conviction that all empirical models are inevitably approximations of the real world and by any means incomplete. This implies that choosing one particular model and founding policy implications only on empirical testing of this particular model may be misleading, because the implications are just founded on one specification out of the thicket of possible specifications of the model. This implies that inferences derived from a given model about the impact of a variation in a particular explanatory variable on the dependent variable should be suspended if the explanatory variable does not turn out to be robust. An independent variable can be considered as robust, if it remains statistically significant with the same sign, when the conditioning information set is subjected to changes. To put it in other words, if the inferences drawn from the estimator of this variable are highly sensitive to small variations in the modeling framework, they are too fragile to serve as a basis for action. If the sign or the value of the estimator changes due to minor changes in the specification of the model, e.g. in the variables that are controlled for, the results of the estimation have to be interpreted carefully. An application of LEAMER'S approach is the so-called Extreme Bounds Analysis (EBA) which tests for the robustness of the influence of the variables of interest.[11] To do so I specify a simple empirical model including a "core model" with key determinants of FDI and the political risk variables of interest. In a second step it is tested, if the included political risk indicators stay robust when the specification of the empirical model changes slightly by including additional explanatory variables.

For the analysis potential determinants of FDI have to be classified in three groups of variables: X-variables, I-variables and Z-variables. X-variables are those variables that have been less controversial in the empirical literature and

---

[9] See Chakrabarti (2001).

[10] See Leamer (1983) and Leamer (1985).

[11] An example of an EBA for the explanation of FDI flows can be found in Chakrabarti (2001). Earlier applications of sensitivity analysis can be found in the literature on economic growth. See Levine/Renelt (1992).

can be referred to as robust determinants of FDI. The set of I-variables consists of variables that are of particular interest to the researcher. Z-variables in turn, are doubtful determinants that are chosen from a pool of variables that are claimed to be influential in the literature or the influence of which theoretically seems plausible. For the specification of the "core-model" I define X-variables as those variables that have come out with the same sign and significant coefficient estimates in various empirical studies. These so-called free variables are the "core" of the empirical model which is not adjusted during the process of testing. Examining the empirical literature on FDI the factors Market Size and Openness turn out to be the least controversial determinants influencing incoming FDI flows.[12] For developing countries also the quality of the local infrastructure has been identified as an important factor that influences the amount of incoming FDI to developing countries. Market size is usually proxied by the GDP of a given country while openness can be measured with the ratio of exports and imports to GDP. This openness measure also controls for the effect of opening and liberalizing the economy because higher trade flows are assumed to be correlated with more liberal legislation on FDI. However, including both measures into the right hand side of the equation causes a severe problem of multicollinearity which biases the regressions estimators and renders an usual interpretation of the coefficients impossible.[13] To solve this problem I divide the left hand side of the equation by GDP. So instead of considering market size as a determinant of total FDI flows, this equation estimates the determinants of the FDI/GDP ratio. This methodology controls for the large country bias without problems of multi-collinearity and with more degrees of freedom, since one explanatory variable is removed from the right hand side of the equation.[14] Furthermore it avoids a possible endogeneity problem as FDI may also be influenced by growth suggesting a symbiotic relationship between the two variable. The quality of the local infrastructure is proxied by the number of telephone lines per 1000 people as data on other variables like kilometers of paved roads is not available for all countries of the sample. Therefore, openness and the quality of infrastructure are the only X-variables of the empirical model.

I-variables are the variables of real interest in the sensitivity analysis. An initial set of I-variables is included into the equation and then a "base-regression" is run that contains only the X-variables and the I-variables of interest to the researcher. The resulting estimator is then tested for its robustness by varying the set of Z-variables that are included into the model and determining whether the considered coefficients stay significant and with the same sign. If this is the

---

[12] See the discussion of the empirical literature in paragraph 2.2.4.2.

[13] An observation of the correlation matrix confirms the presence of multicollinearity.

[14] Proceeding like this has the drawback that political risk may also affect the denominator of this ratio which potentially biases the regression results. An alternative for correcting for the large country bias is dividing by population size. However, as population size does not proxy in suitable way what theory identifies as market size regression results with the FDI/Population-Ratio did not offer convincing results. Therefore, the following analysis uses the FDI/GDP-Ratio.

case, the I-variable may be classified as robust. In cases where small variations in the model setting imply a change of sign or a loss of significance the variable has to be labeled as not robust. Besides determining the impact of different risk indicators on FDI I also study the impact of different sources of risk. Therefore, in addition to analyzing the impact of variables measuring aggregate political risk, in this study different subgroups of risk are analyzed to identify the sources of risk for international investors. The sub-variables of political risk that are introduced as I-variables to the model have already been described in Chapter 3 which identified potential political hazards to international investors and provided a theoretical analysis of different sources of political risk. To facilitate the empirical analysis of a complex multidimensional phenomenon as political risk I defined groups representing different sources of political risk. This procedure has the important econometric advantage that it preserves degrees of freedom without loosing information on the sources of risk. Thus, aggregate political risk has been subdivided in three groups according to the nature of underlying reasons. Despite of the fact that such a theoretical distinction is by definition incomplete and sometimes unclear it has been considered a useful simplification that facilitates the empirical analysis that follows. It is obvious however, that this classification cannot be rigid and has to be interpreted as one of multiple possible groupings for the analysis of political risks. Henceforth I distinguish between three main sources of political risk: macroeconomic risks, governmentally induced risks and socially induced risks.

The first category consists of classical variables of country risk that measure hazards resulting out of the macroeconomic environment in the host country. The risk factors are those that are generally used in orthodox country risk analysis as it is done by financial institutions. The index which is used here consists of "pure" economic variables that reflect the current macro-economic stability of the host country. It contains the rate of inflation, the national budget deficit as percentage of GDP, the reserves debt ratio, the interest rate spread over LIBOR, the fraction of short-term-debt in total debt and the current account balance. All these indicators proxy the risk exposure to macroeconomic imbalances which may have a detrimental impact on FDI. To better picture the influence of macroeconomic imbalances and to make the indicator comparable with the other score-model-based indicators that have been used in this study I transformed hard macroeconomic data into an indicator with a 0-10 rating for macroeconomic stability. This measure has been constructed by pooling information from different macroeconomic variables and using a methodology proposed by the World Economic Forum for the transformation of the hard data into numerical ratings. This transformation formulates a rating by comparing national indicator values to maximum and minimum benchmark values in the reference sample.[15] To ensure comparability between the indicators I chose the IRIS 3 sample based on PRS data, from which the other

---

[15] For the formula see Annex I.

political risk indicators have been taken, as reference sample for the transformation.

The second category of political risks contains all variables that reflect the part of aggregate political risk that directly originates in governmental action. The variables that are included in this section are the quality of the national bureaucracy, the level of governmental corruption, the risk of expropriation and the risk of repudiation of government contracts. These different indicators are pooled to obtain an aggregate governance indicator that permits to assess the influence of good governance on FDI flows. A second governance indicator additionally includes the level of political constraints which are imposed on the national executive.

The third category of risk consists of the variables that measure the part of aggregate political risk that has primarily societal origins. In this category I include variables that measure the part of risk that is not caused by direct governmental actions but that results out of the characteristics of the countries at study. It contains the variables rule of law tradition and the degree of ethnic tensions. Table A.1 in Annex I gives an overview of all variables that have been used for the analysis and their methodology of construction.

The last group of variables in the model is called Z-variables. Z-variables are variables that have been plausibly argued in the literature to be potential determinants of FDI. Empirical evidence on their influence however, remains mixed implying that they have to be considered as doubtful variables. These Z-variables are included in the model to test whether the I-variables remain robust, if the model setting is slightly changed. As potential determinants I only chose those variables that turned out to be significant in at least a few analyzed model settings.[16]

For the estimation of the panel I use a fixed effects model. There are two reasons for choosing this model instead of a so-called random effects model. The first reason is technical. The use of random effects model requires that the sample is selected randomly from an underlying population. If studies focus on large geographical regions, like in our case, the random sampling assumption is flawed implying that the estimation with the random effects model is not appropriate for this study. Second, the fixed effect approach has the advantage that the country specific constant term accounts for all those variables that affect FDI flows to a country that are not explicitly modeled and that do not change over time. In panel data analysis this constant term is called an unobserved effect. When different time periods for the same individual are studied this term captures exactly those features of the individual that do not vary over time. So when the particular interest of the researcher is only on time-varying explanatory variables, as it is the case in this empirical model, it is convenient not to have to model time-constant factors that are not

---

[16] Paragraph 4.2.3 holds a description of the included variables.

of direct interest.[17] Examples for time-invariant variables of different countries that may bias the results if they are not considered are the endowments of a country with natural resources, its climate or other geographical particularities. Including a fixed effect implies that the estimators in question are not biased by omitted variables of that type. However, when interpreting the results, one has to bear in mind that estimation with the fixed-effects model has the important drawback that only the within-country dimension of the panel is explored properly. If variables in question turn out to be insignificant, I estimate a model using a common intercept term to test, if the result is biased by this deficiency of the fixed effects model.[18]

Standard econometric tests are performed for each of the specified model settings to ensure that the coefficients may be interpreted as usual. In the presence of serial auto-correlation standard correction measures may be applied that allow for a correct interpretation of the estimated parameter coefficients. However, problems with auto-correlation have not been encountered indicating a satisfactory specification of the empirical model. Variance and standard errors of the estimators are also biased in the presence of heteroskedasticity which implies that standard t- and F-test are no longer valid. To avoid misleading inferences caused by this problem I use the matrix of heteroskedasticity-consistent standard errors based on the work of WHITE.[19]

Although not performed here some recent econometric articles propose the use of unit root and cointegration tests for panel data.[20] In time series analysis the testing for unit roots and cointergration have meanwhile become standard although even the standard tests which are usually applied only have limited explanatory power.[21] In panel data analysis however, this problem is aggravated as most of the currently proposed tests for panel data have the important drawback that they only test for the null hypothesis that all series have a unit root. Therefore, these tests are subject to the severe criticism that it is well possible that some individual series have a unit root while others are stationary. This possible heterogeneity of different time series in a panel has the convenient implication that problems caused by non-stationarity may be less severe. That is, even if the noise in some of the individual time series is strong, the fact that it is independent across individuals implies that by pooling the data the effect of the residuals can be reduced. Hence, the estimated coefficient is still a consistent estimate where the usual standard errors and t-ratios are valid and can be interpreted as usual. KAO shows that the LSDV estimator converges to its true value in the case of a spurious regression model.[22] Moreover, PHILIPS/MOON show that even in the presence of non-

---

[17] See Wooldridge (2002) p.247-298.
[18] It is important to stress that the estimation without country specific constants may bias the result due to a problem of omitted variables.
[19] See White (1980).
[20] For an overview see Baltagi (2002) p.233-256.
[21] See Pindyck/Rubinfeld (1991) p.440-471.
[22] See Kao (1999).

stationary panel data the pooled least squares estimator is consistent which also holds in the case of individual fixed effects.[23] It follows that the problem of spurious regression is of lesser importance if panel data is used.[24] Finally also the relatively small t-dimension of the data sample I use does not necessarily impose the use of stationarity and cointegration tests.[25]

4.2.2 Model Specification

Having presented the methodology of the study I now formally specify the empirical model that is used for the empirical test. The general structure of the model for an EBA analysis can be written in the following form:

4.1 $\qquad Y = \alpha_i + \beta X_{it} + \gamma I_{it} + \delta Z_{it} + \varepsilon$

where Y stands for the dependent variable, α_i is a constant that is specific for every country of the used panel, X is the set of free variables that have been classified as less controversial, I is the set of variables the influence of which is of particular interest, Z is the subset of variables that have been classified as potential determinants of FDI and ε is an error term. As the available data is a panel all used variables in the model vary in the cross sectional dimension and the time dimension which is indicated by the sub indices i and t. Using the variables that are defined in table A.1 the core equation of the fixed effects model becomes

4.2 $\qquad FDIS_{it} = \alpha_i + \beta_1 OPEN_{it} + \beta_2 TELE_{it} + \gamma POLITICALRISK_{it} + \delta Z_{it} + \varepsilon$

where OPEN and TELE are the only free variables and POLITICALRISK stands for a particular political risk variable or a combination of those variables the influence of which is to be tested. Each political risk variable or set of variables is then tested for its robustness by including all possible linear combinations of the identified z variables. If the coefficients of the variable at question are not changing sign and stay significant throughout all tested model settings, they are classified as robust. In the contrary case the I-variables are classified as not robust. If variables turn out to be not robust, in a second step a model with common intercept term is estimated to take into consideration a potential bias that may result from the neglect of the in-between dimension of the data that is immanent to the fixed effects model. The model with common intercept term may be written as

4.3 $\qquad FDIS_{it} = \alpha + \beta_1 OPEN_{it} + \beta_2 TELE + \beta_3 POLITICALRISK_{it} + \delta Z_{it} + \varepsilon$

where the only difference between 4.2 and 4.3 is the intercept term that is now a constant throughout the t and the i dimension. However, as the author

---

[23] See Phillips/Moon (1999) and Phillips/Moon (2000).

[24] Philips/Moon (1999).

[25] An F-type test based on Maddala/Wu (1999) to test for the stationarity of the panel could not be used because the number of observations was not sufficient.

considers the Fixed-Effects-Model as superior, results of the common intercept model are only reported if they indicate a bias caused by the drawbacks of the Fixed-Effects Model.

4.2.3 Data Issues

Although it would have been desirable to test for the impact of political risk on industrial sectors with different degrees of reversibility, this could not be realized due the lack of reliable disaggregated data for the countries of the sample.[26] To avoid problems resulting from unreliable local data sources, if possible, data from the World Bank and other multilateral institutions has been used. Table A.1 in Annex I gives a complete overview of the data sources that have been consulted, the definitions of the used variables and the sign that is to be expected theoretically. Note that also the variables that only have been used as subparts to form an indicator are listed. For the transfer of hard data to the 1-10 scale I used a method applied by the World Economic Forum for the calculation of the Macroeconomic stability subindex in the World Competitiveness Report 2001/2002.[27] However, to obtain reasonable results in some cases minor adjustments had to be made to account for extreme outliers in the data. For example countries with hyper-inflation or extremely high spreads over LIBOR due to financial crisis have been eliminated. Including these outliers would have implied a reduced explanatory value of the indicators as even moderate quality of the variable at question would have been rated with high scale values.[28]

Some potentially influential variables could not be taken into account because reliable data was either completely missing or limited so that sample size would have been decreased intolerably. In this case proxy variables with better data availability were introduced into the empirical model. One example is human capital formation in host countries where I use the illiteracy rate of the whole population to control for the skills of the national workforce. Another example is the quality of the national infrastructure that has been approximated by the number of telephone lines per 1000 people. A similar problem occurred, when the social political risk variable was constructed as reliable yearly data was not available for every influential factor. Concerning measures of poverty and income distribution I consulted information from the largest available data sets assembled by DEININGER/SQUIRE and the World Income Inequality Database (WIID).[29] Even in these most complete collections of data on income distribution and poverty, many observations are missing which complicates empirical work with the data. Thus, including the data,

---

[26] This test would also entail the difficulty to theoretically determine the reversibility of investments in different industries.

[27] See Annex I.

[28] If outliers had not been eliminated countries with three digit inflation rates would have received macroeconomic stability ratings better than unity. To preserve the explanatory value countries with hyperinflation were not considered in calculating the sample maximum.

[29] See Deininger/Squire (1996) and UNDP (2000).

although desirable, would have diminished sample size considerably. The same holds for data on national labor costs and tax rates. FREEMAN/OOSTENDORP compiled a large panel data set with comparable data on international wages.[30] Nevertheless, data for the Latin American sample was limited implying that there were not sufficient observations for the introduction of a variable controlling for labor cost. The same holds for data about national tax rates. The World Bank provides some time series that may theoretically serve as a proxy variable for the national tax burden as for example information on the share of income and corporate taxes of total governmental income. However, when included into the model, this proxy does not offer good results, because it obviously does not correctly proxy the tax burden of foreign enterprises. Anyhow the exclusion of these two variables is not an important shortcoming of the empirical model because in the recent literature the empirical evidence on the influence of labor cost and tax on FDI is not convincing.[31]

4.2.3 Results

The specification of the empirical model allows to test for the robustness of the different political risk indicators which are included as I-variables. Table 4.1 presents the results of a test for the influence of an aggregate political risk variable that has been constructed by using data from the International Country Risk Guide and the World Bank including macroeconomic risk factors, societal risk factors and governance-related risk factors. As Z-variables I chose the illiteracy rate to control for the quality of human capital, the GDP growth rate to control for the growth dynamic of the economy and the exchange rate to control for the influence of the weak currency hypothesis.

Table 4.1: Influence of Aggregate Political Risk on FDI

VARIABLE	(1)	(2)	(3)	(4)	(5)	(6)	(7)	(8)
	REGRESSION NUMBER							
OPEN	0.000917	0.000930	0.000898	0.000921	0.000908	0.000910	0.000929	0.000901
	(0.0155)	(0.0149)	(0.0166)	(0.0170)	(0.0176)	(0.0159)	(0.0164)	(0.0182)
TELE	0.000202	0.000231	0.000195	0.000206	0.000225	0.000227	0.000230	0.000199
	(0.0004)	(0.0001)	(0.0008)	(0.0003)	(0.0002)	(0.0001)	(0.0001)	(0.0008)
AGRISK	0.004889	0.006224**	0.004204	0.004849	0.005684*	0.005606*	0.006274**	0.004170
	(0.1271)	(0.0372)	(0.2090)	(0.1386)	(0.0798)	(0.0706)	(0.0461)	(0.2215)
ILLIT		0.001098			0.001270	0.001226	0.001124	0.000420
		(0.1103)			(0.0650)	(0.0806)	(0.0964)	(0.0544)
GROW			0.000422		0.000479	0.000476		
			(0.0537)		(0.0354)	(0.0381)		
EXCH				-1.02E-06	7.67E-07		4.64E-07	-9.27E-07
				(0.7359)	(0.7922)		(0.8738)	(0.7602)
R^2	0.55	0.55	0.55	0.55	0.56	0.56	0.55	0.55
OBS	288	288	288	288	288	288	288	288

Source: Own table, p-values corresponding to White-Heteroskedasticity-consistent standard errors are in parentheses, *estimator significant at the 10% level, **estimator significant at the 5% level, ***estimator significant at the 1% level, OBS are number of observations.

---

[30] See Freeman/Oostendorp (2000).
[31] See paragraph 2.2.4.2.

The same Z-variables will be used for every sensitivity analysis in this paragraph. Although the risk indicator turns out to be significant at the 5% level in two tested model settings, the risk variable looses significance when minor respecifications of the empirical model are made. Therefore, the empirical results indicate that AGRISK is not a robust determinant of FDI flows to Latin American countries. For a closer examination of the reasons for this insignificance I split the aggregate risk indicator into its sub-parts to analyze if particular sub-indicators of aggregate risk eventually turn out to be robust throughout minor respecifications of the empirical FDI model.

Table 4.2 depicts the results that the model yields, if political risk is specified as solely resulting from the quality of the macroeconomic environment, as traditional country risk evaluation methods would suggest. Recall that the indicator MACROI was calculated in transferring hard macroeconomic data to a 1-10 scale using a method proposed by the World Economic Forum.[32] It measures the risk that macroeconomic imbalances adversely affect the decisions of foreign investors to invest in a country of the region.

Table 4.2: Influence of Macroeconomic Risk Factors on FDI

VARIABLE	REGRESSION NUMBER							
	(1)	(2)	(3)	(4)	(5)	(6)	(7)	(8)
OPEN	0.000958	0.000962	0.000930	0.000959	0.000938	0.000938	0.000962	0.000931
	(0.0071)	(0.0101)	(0.0084)	(0.0084)	(0.0117)	(0.0107)	(0.0109)	(0.0099)
TELE	0.000260	0.000267	0.000244	0.000261	0.000261	0.000261	0.000267	0.000245
	(0.0003)	(0.0000)	(0.0009)	(0.0001)	(0.0000)	(0.0000)	(0.0000)	(0.0005)
MACROI	0.003102	0.003101	0.002541	0.003076	0.002503	0.002496	0.003088	0.002512
	(0.1367)	(0.1384)	(0.2316)	(0.1726)	(0.2790)	(0.2566)	(0.1632)	(0.2740)
ILLIT		0.000148			0.000390	0.000386	0.000142	
		(0.8620)			(0.6528)	(0.6702)	(0.8617)	
GROW			0.000473		0.000509	0.000509		0.000473
			(0.0233)		(0.0356)	(0.0367)		(0.0237)
EXCH				-3.30E-07	9.48E-08		-1.62E-07	-3.66E-07
				(0.9195)	(0.9734)		(0.9547)	(0.9115)
R^2	0.54	0.54	0.55	0.54	0.55	0.55	0.54	0.55
OBS	288	288	288	288	288	288	288	288

Source: Own table, p-values corresponding to White-Heteroskedasticity-consistent standard errors are in parentheses, *estimator significant at the 10% level, **estimator significant at the 5% level, ***estimator significant at the 1% level, OBS are number of observations.

Although the macroeconomic environment theoretically is an important risk factor for foreign investors, the results in table 4.2 do not confirm this hypothesis. The coefficient of the variable shows the right sign but is not significant on the 10% level in all tested model settings suggesting that the quality of the macroeconomic environment is not significant for the decisions of foreign investors interested in Latin American countries. To control if this result is caused by the drawback of the fixed effects model that only the within country dimension of the panel is explored properly, I performed the same regression using OLS with a common intercept term as given in equation 4.3

---

[32] See World Economic Forum (2002) p. 51. For the formula see Annex I.

which shows similar results. Obtaining similar findings BUBNOVA argues that risks caused by erratic or inconsistent economic policies can be more easily diversified than other risks implying that investors react less sensitive to macroeconomic imbalances.[33]

There are two other reasons for these counter intuitive results explaining the outcomes as a consequence of the characteristic situation of the Latin American countries in the analyzed time period. First, the macroeconomic environment only becomes an influential determinant of FDI in the presence of severe imbalances or instabilities. That is to say that, in the absence of crisis a poor quality of the macroeconomic environment may be overcompensated by the positive impact of other location specific variables. In other words, investors are willing to accept less stable macroeconomic situations, if other variables on which their decision is based are favorable and suggest an investment. Second, investors to the region might have been less sensitive to macroeconomic disturbances because basically all Latin American countries found themselves in the middle of stabilizing reforms after the experience of the severe crisis during the beginning of the 80s. As the most severe imbalances occurred in the aftermath of the debt crisis investors could have perceived in the following years that risks resulting from the macroeconomic environment already were in decline. Moreover, as the stabilization policies of the affected countries were subject to external control by international organizations their national economic policy gained credibility and investors did not expect a fallback into severe imbalances. Despite of these possible explanations the result is surprising.

As pointed out in the preceding paragraphs other potentially important sub-components of aggregate political risk are risks which are not directly caused by governmental behavior but instead result from societal characteristics of the host countries. Table 4.3 presents the results that were obtained when testing for the influence of societal characteristics on FDI flows to Latin American countries. The indicator of societal risk SOCII is composed by using a measure of ethnic tensions and a measure that evaluates the rule of law tradition in the country. This indicator of societal risks performed considerably better than its macroeconomic counterpart. While the indicator is significant at the 10% level in nearly all the performed regressions it is significant at the 5% level in four cases. Thus, societal risk factors seem to have a higher relevance for FDI to Latin American countries than macroeconomic risk factors but still the empirical evidence is not very convincing. There are many possible reasons for these results. To avoid bias caused by the use of the fixed effects model I reestimated the equation with a common intercept term to better explore the in-between dimension of the data. However, the results concerning the significance of the societal risk parameter did not change.

---

[33] See Bubnova (2000) p.20.

Table 4.3: Influence of Societal Risk Factors on FDI

VARIABLE	REGRESSION NUMBER							
	(1)	(2)	(3)	(4)	(5)	(6)	(7)	(8)
OPEN	0.000894	0.000907	0.000868	0.000899	0.000879	0.000879	0.000909	0.000872
	(0.0197)	(0.0191)	(0.0233)	(0.0205)	(0.0233)	(0.0222)	(0.0198)	(0.0242)
TELE	0.000240	0.000280	0.000221	0.000247	0.000268	0.000268	0.000282	0.000227
	(0.0001)	(0.0000)	(0.0005)	(0.0001)	(0.0000)	(0.0000)	(0.0000)	(0.0003)
SOCII	0.005094*	0.005971**	0.004773	0.005107*	0.005793**	0.005799**	0.005947**	0.004788
	(0.0809)	(0.0276)	(0.1037)	(0.0797)	(0.0351)	(0.0325)	(0.0306)	(0.1019)
ILLIT		0.001016			0.001249	0.001258	0.000982	
		(0.1759)			(0.1045)	(0.1006)	(0.1917)	
GROW			0.000482		0.000571	0.000572		0.000477
			(0.0115)		(0.0057)	(0.0055)		(0.0128)
EXCH				-1.85E-06	-1.81E-07		-7.49E-07	-1.63E-06
				(0.5172)	(0.9488)		(0.7887)	(0.5717)
R^2	0.55	0.55	0.55	0.55	0.56	0.56	0.55	0.55
OBS	288	288	288	288	288	288	288	288

Source: Own table, p-values corresponding to White-Heteroskedasticity-consistent standard errors are in parentheses, *estimator significant at the 10% level, **estimator significant at the 5% level, ***estimator significant at the 1% level, OBS are number of observations.

Therefore, the empirical analysis suggest that, like macroeconomic risk factors, societal risks are only of minor importance for FDI decisions in Latin America. These results are in line with the hypothesis of the author that societal risk variables should be of minor importance for the region as a minimum level of societal and political stability has already been attained in Latin America. The analysis indicates that the countries of the region already passed the critical threshold of political stability where catastrophic risks cease to be most relevant for MNEs. In fact during the analyzed time period most of the countries in the region did not experience severe societal instabilities that resulted in total asset losses of international investors. With the exception of Colombia where civil war constantly endangers public security, neither situations of severe civil strife occurred in the region. The absence of severe societal risk factors however, suggests that these risks should have a less important influence for the investment decisions of MNEs.

The last group of political risk indicators that has been derived are risks that are directly linked to the performance of the national governments. Table 4.4 presents the results of a test for the influence of governance related risk factors on FDI flows to Latin American countries. The indicator GOVII contains subvariables measuring the quality of the national bureaucracy, the level of governmental corruption, the risk of expropriation, the risk of repudiation of government contracts and POLCON as a measure for discretionary freedom of host governments. Unlike the risk factors that have been tested before the obtained coefficient for governance risk is significant at the 1% level in all performed regressions of the sensitivity analysis implying that the indicator is highly robust to respecifications of the empirical model. The results suggest that governance related risk is an important explanatory variable for FDI flows and a major source of risk for MNEs in Latin American countries.

Table 4.4: Influence of Governance-Related Risk Factors on FDI

VARIABLE	REGRESSION NUMBER							
	(1)	(2)	(3)	(4)	(5)	(6)	(7)	(8)
OPEN	0.000908	0.000931	0.000888	0.000913	0.000909	0.000908	0.000932	0.000894
	(0.0109)	(0.0098)	(0.0125)	(0.0112)	(0.0117)	(0.0112)	(0.0102)	(0.0129)
TELE	0.000144	0.000179	0.000138	0.000152	0.000175	0.000174	0.000181	0.000145
	(0.0182)	(0.0027)	(0.0265)	(0.0113)	(0.0041)	(0.0044)	(0.0025)	(0.0175)
GOVII	0.005054***	0.006890***	0.004678***	0.005115***	0.006559***	0.006565***	.0.006873***	0.004743***
	(0.0009)	(0.0000)	(0.0029)	(0.0007)	(0.0000)	(0.0000)	(0.0000)	(0.0024)
ILLIT		0.001802			0.001922	0.001938	0.001767	
		(0.0316)			(0.0206)	(0.0230)	(0.0303)	
GROW			0.000373		0.000457	0.000459		0.000363
			(0.0644)		(0.0312)	(0.0298)		(0.0736)
EXCH				-2.51E-06	-3.30E-07		-7.65E-07	-2.29E-06
				(0.3794)	(0.9011)		(0.7742)	(0.4234)
R^2	0.55	0.56	0.56	0.55	0.56	0.56	0.56	0.56
OBS	288	288	288	288	288	288	288	288

Source: Own table, p-values corresponding to White-Heteroskedasticity-consistent standard errors are in parentheses, *estimator significant at the 10% level, **estimator significant at the 5% level, ***estimator significant at the 1% level, OBS are number of observations.

Therefore, the quality of governance and the credibility of national governments are crucial elements of a policy designed for attracting international investors. Given the overall significance and robustness of governance related risk factors, it is interesting to test for the influence of sub-indicators of the governance indicators to assess which subvariables are of particular interest for international investors. An important subindicator of GOVII is POLCON measuring the discretionary freedom of host governments to adversely change national policy. To test if POLCON is a significant determinant of FDI flows the indicator is introduced as I-variable into the model. Table 4.5 shows the results which are obtained when POLCON is used as sole proxy for governance related political risks.

Table 4.5: Influence of Governmental Discretion on FDI

VARIABLE	REGRESSION NUMBER							
	(1)	(2)	(3)	(4)	(5)	(6)	(7)	(8)
OPEN	0.000994	0.001004	0.000966	0.00102	0.001002	0.000977	0.001029	0.000993
	(0.0219)	(0.0244)	(0.0252)	(0.0216)	(0.0261)	(0.0266)	(0.0239)	(0.0248)
TELE	0.000239	0.000267	0.000217	0.000282	0.000294	0.000255	0.000306	0.00026
	(0.0032)	(0.0007)	(0.008)	(0.0007)	(0.0012)	(0.0014)	(0.0006)	(0.0018)
POLCONIV	0.017566	0.018497	0.015503	0.015701	0.014738	0.016592	0.016565	0.013681
	(0.1224)	(0.1097)	(0.1839)	(0.1747)	(0.2142)	(0.1585)	(0.1558)	(0.2477)
ILLIT		0.000516			0.000696	0.000756	0.00046	
		(0.5891)			(0.4771)	(0.4458)	(0.6262)	
GROW			0.000489		0.000543	0.000554		0.000483
			(0.0852)		(0.0769)	(0.074)		(0.0868)
EXCH				-1.62E-05	-1.56E-05		-1.59E-05	-1.61E-05
				(0.0866)	(0.0976)		(0.0838)	(0.0969)
R^2	0.49	0.49	0.50	0.50	0.50	0.50	0.50	0.50
OBS	224	224	224	224	224	224	224	224

Source: Own table, p-values corresponding to White-Heteroskedasticity-consistent standard errors are in parentheses, OBS are number of observations.

As Chapter 3 suggested, theoretically the discretionary freedom of host governments measured by the existing veto points in the national political system is an important determinant of risk. The empirical results indicate a rejection of the initial hypothesis that governmental discretion is an influential variable for FDI flows to Latin American countries. The coefficient of POLCON has the expected positive sign but does not turn out to be significant at the 5% level in any of the specified model settings. Hence, the empirical evidence for the Latin American sample suggest that governmental discretion is of no major importance as a determinant of FDI flows to the region.

The insignificance of POLCON as determinant of incoming Latin American FDI flows indicates that the overall significance and robustness of GOVII stems from the other variables that have been used to build the indicator. All other subindicators of GOVII have been taken form the IRIS-3 database which in turn, is based on data provided by PRS Group. Therefore, I recalculated the governance indicator without including POLCON as a measure of governmental discretion. Table 4.6 shows the results, when the influence of the resulting new governance indicator GOVI on FDI is tested with the empirical model. The results seem to confirm that the country risk measures taken from the IRIS-3 data set are indeed responsible for the robust significance of the governance indicator GOVII.

Table 4.6: Influence of Governance-Related Risk Factors on FDI (excluding POLCON)

VARIABLE	REGRESSION NUMBER							
	(1)	(2)	(3)	(4)	(5)	(6)	(7)	(8)
OPEN	0.000904	0.000922	0.000882	0.000910	0.000896	0.000895	0.000924	0.000888
	(0.0127)	(0.0112)	(0.0149)	(0.0128)	(0.0136)	(0.0132)	0.0115	(0.0150)
TELE	0.000163	0.000198	0.000153	0.000171	0.000190	0.000189	0.000201	0.000161
	(0.0062)	(0.0008)	(0.0130)	(0.0038)	(0.0019)	(0.0020)	0.0007	(0.0086)
GOVI	0.004840***	0.007678***	0.004474***	0.004967***	0.007448***	0.007454***	0.007663***	0.004600***
	(0.0065)	(0.0000)	(0.0132)	(0.0048)	(0.0000)	(0.0000)	0.0000	(0.0100)
ILLIT		0.002252			0.002411	0.002440	0.002201	
		(0.0079)			(0.0043)	(0.0045)	0.0082	
GROW			0.000425		0.000530	0.000534		0.000412
			(0.0248)		(0.0076)	(0.0069)		(0.0303)
EXCH				-2.99E-06	-6.32E-07		-1.17E-06	-2.71E-06
				(0.2596)	(0.7986)		0.6367	(0.3103)
R^2	0.55	0.56	0.55	0.55	0.57	0.57	0.55	0.55
OBS	288	288	288	288	288	288	288	288

Source: Own table, p-values corresponding to White-Heteroskedasticity-consistent standard errors are in parentheses, *estimator significant at the 10% level, **estimator significant at the 5% level, ***estimator significant at the 1% level, OBS are number of observations.

GOV I is significant at the 1% level in all tested model settings and the R^2 of the model is similar to the values when GOVII was used as governance indicator. Hence, GOVI can be classified as being a robust determinant of incoming FDI flows to Latin American countries. These empirical findings indicate that subindicators of GOVI as the quality of the national bureaucracy and risks resulting from governmental corruption, expropriation and the repudiation of contracts are central determinants of political risk in Latin America.

Summarizing the results of the regressions performed above permits to derive some final implications about the sensitivity and robustness of the analyzed political risk indicators for the Latin American sample. For each tested political risk indicator table 4.7 depicts an interval in which the coefficient of the indicator varied to minor re-specifications of the tested model. A second interval is given that shows the variance of the p-value of the coefficient indicating the significance of the variable in different model settings. When indicators had the expected sign and were significant in some of the tested modeling frameworks, they have been classified as significant. Examining the interval of the p-value and verifying if the sign of the indicator changed permits to classify the different political risk indicators into robust and not robust indicators of political risk.

Table 4.7: Robustness of Political Risk Indicators

POLITICAL RISK VARIABLE	COEFFICIENT INTERVAL	CHANGING SIGN	P-VALUE INTERVAL	SIGNIFICANT	ROBUST
AGRISK	{0.004170; 0.006274}	No	{0.0372; 0.2215}	Yes	No
MACROI	{0.002505; 0.003102}	No	{0.1367; 0.2790}	No	No
SOCII	{0.004773; 0.005971}	No	{0.0276; 0.1037}	Yes	No
GOVI	{0.00474; 0.007678}	No	{0.00001; 0.0132}	Yes	Yes
GOVII	{0.004678; 0.006890}	No	{0.0000; 0.0024}	Yes	Yes
POLCONIV	{0.013681; 0.018497}	No	{0.1097; 0.2477}	No	No

Source: Own table

The table shows that only governance related political risk variables can be classified as robust determinants of FDI flows to Latin American countries. Splitting the aggregate governance indicator into its subparts reveals that POLCON is neither a significant nor robust determinant of FDI flows to Latin America. In turn, those subindicators which have been taken from the IRIS-3 data set turned out to be significant and robust determinants of FDI when pooled in the indicator GOVI. Macroeconomic risk factors as well as societal risk variables did not turn out to be robust determinants of FDI inflows to the region. The former result is surprising as the long periods of macroeconomic instabilities in Latin America would rather suggest an important influence of macroeconomic stability. However, this theoretical hypothesis could not be confirmed by the empirical results of this econometric study. In turn, the minor role of societal risk factors for inflows of foreign investment to Latin America is less surprising. During the 80s and in particular during the 90s Latin American countries made enormous progress in democratization and elimination of violent social conflicts. With the exception of Colombia the analyzed time period did not witness severe forms of civil unrest or strife. This explains the reduced importance of societal risk variables for that time period, as societal risk usually gain importance when a severe crisis or catastrophic events occur. In spite of these results, it is appropriate to underline the possibility that prevailing inequalities and high levels of poverty in the region may imply that these risk factors gain importance in the near future.[34] Moreover, the empirical evidence on the influence of societal risk factors on foreign investment decisions may be biased by a lack of reliable data on this matter.

4.3 Conclusion

The quantitative empirical investigations reveal that political risk has a high and significant influence on the FDI/GDP ratio in Latin American countries for the analyzed time period from 1982-1997. However, this result does not hold for all tested sub-parts of aggregate political risk which is in line with our criticism concerning earlier empirical studies. While those indicators that measure political risk resulting out of governance-related factors turned out to be of the expected (positive) sign and robust to small variations of the applied empirical model, measures accounting for societal and macroeconomic risk factors were not found to be robust in all tested model settings. These empirical results are in line with the hypothesis that governance related risk factors are nowadays gaining importance while the impact of societal political risk factors in Latin America seems to be in decline.[35] However, high societal inequalities, ethnic and religious conflicts and poverty may turn out to be important risks in the near future.[36]

The lacking robustness of the indicator measuring risks resulting from the existing macroeconomic environment is harder to explain.[37] It may be argued that progresses in stabilization policies during the 80s rendered macroeconomics a less influential risk factor for MNEs as the most severe problems that prevailed during the early 80s had already been tackled. That is, the macroeconomic environment only is an important factor in the calculus of MNEs when severe imbalances are to be expected. Once a certain level of stability has been attained, that is, severe imbalances as e.g. hyperinflation have been overcome, macroeconomic determinants loose importance for the direct investment decisions of international enterprises. Nevertheless, the present empirical results seem surprising and more empirical research is

---

[34] The empirical results suffer from the fact that reliable yearly data on income distribution or poverty levels was not available for all countries and time periods and therefore could not be considered.

[35] These empirical results are line with the findings of Bubnova (2000) who finds that the most relevant risk factors for investors were poor bureaucratic quality, corruption and the lack of institutional constraints on governmental action.

[36] Nevertheless the political risk analysis for Mexico confirms the result that societal risk factors are of lesser importance for foreign investors. See Chapter 5.

[37] Although counter intuitive also Bubnova (2000) finds that among different risk factors investors were least concerned about risks stemming from short-sighted economic policies.

needed to fully understand the declining role of the macroeconomic environment as political risk factor that is pictured in this analysis.

Without doubt the empirical findings permit the conclusion that the quality of governance is of particular importance for FDI flows to Latin America. The governance indicator that has been constructed for this analysis was found to be a highly significant determinant of the FDI/GDP ratio. It follows that an improvement in the governance index would lead to a significant positive change in the FDI/GDP ratio of Latin American countries. These inferences drawn from the analysis are most likely not biased by a misspecification of the empirical model, as the governance indicator stays robust at the 1% level, even if the model is altered marginally. Hence, the improvement of national governance seems to be the most powerful tool to foster inflows of FDI to the emerging economies in Latin America. This conclusion is of particular importance for host countries as the amelioration of domestic governance not only fosters FDI but simultaneously implies a "double-dividend" as also domestic investors do benefit from better governance. Therefore, the results of this analysis permit the careful conclusion that national policy should focus on the establishment of good-governance in Latin America.[38]

4.4 Chapter Summary

This chapter presented a simple econometric model to test for the influence of political risk variables on the inflows of FDI for a panel of Latin American countries in the period from 1982 to 1997. Data for the empirical analysis was largely collected from the publications of international organizations like the World Bank. The country risk measures I used were taken from the IRIS3 data set provided by PRS group and POLCON. A macroeconomic risk indicator was derived from disposable hard data that has been transferred to a 1-10 scale using a methodology developed by the World Economic Forum. This analysis distinguished risk originating in governmental behavior, societal characteristics and the macroeconomic environment. For the estimation a fixed effect model was used that incorporates time invariant coefficients of every analyzed country in a constant term. I find that measures of political risk that incorporate the quality of governance and administration are highly significant and robust determinants of incoming FDI flows. In contrast, political risks that originate in societal characteristics or the macro-economic environment were not robust in all tested models but usually showed the expected sign when estimators were significant. The surprising result that indicators measuring macro-economic risk exposure did not turn out to be robust may be explained considering that in the absence of severe imbalances macro-economic risk factors loose decisiveness. The analysis permits the conclusion that good governance is a decisive determinant of the quantity of FDI to Latin American countries. While societal risks can surely be influential in other countries this empirical analysis did not confirm that there is a systematic

---

[38] The case study on Mexico in Chapter 5 confirms the result that good governance is essential for the attraction of FDI flows.

statistical connection between societal determinants of political risk and FDI flows to Latin America for the analyzed time period.

5. Political Risk and FDI in Mexico
5.1 Politics in Mexico
5.1.1 Stylized Facts of Mexican Political History

After independence from Spain in 1821 Mexico experienced long periods of political instability, civil wars and quickly changing governments caused by the struggle for power that was unfolding between liberals and conservatives.[1] Moreover, Mexico experienced the invasion of the country by the United States followed by a loss of large territories as Texas, Alta California and New Mexico. Under the liberal rule of Benito Juárez from 1859 to 1872 that was based on the Constitution of 1857 important changes were implemented as for example the abolition of preferential treatments for members of the military and the church as well as the obligation of the church to sell its large possessions of land. As a reaction to this liberal policy Mexican conservatives eagerly tried to convince European powers of the necessity to provide aid for restoring their power. When Mexico asked for a two years moratorium on its external debt, the French government decided to invade Mexico in order to enforce its claims forcing Juárez to exile in the north of Mexico. After the successful invasion the French enthroned Maximilian of Habsburg who should later be executed by the eventually victorious liberals. This long period of political turmoil ended when Porfirio Díaz established his authoritarian government in 1877. Although de jure a democratic republic based on the constitution of 1857, the rule of Díaz was characterized by his personal dominance in all sectors of government. He used appointments to reward supporters and left a national administration with a high fraction of military officers and businessmen. This technique which was generously applied produced corruption in all levels of political life and enhanced the political culture that public office was rather a reward to be taken advantage of than a public responsibility. Díaz reversed the cautious process of decentralization that was begun under Juárez by concentrating power in the hands of the national government. To further strengthen the federal government Díaz engaged in largely expanding the national bureaucracy. The power of the judicial and the legislative branch were decreased making them subordinate to the presidency and public elections were merely held to anew the loyalty of the Mexican people to the regime of the dictator. Opposition was suppressed by imprisonment, threats and violence while the press was subject to censorship. Typically lower social groups, and in particular indians that were believed to be racially inferior and an obstacle to national development, were the victims of the most violent oppressions. As power was largely concentrated in the hands of Díaz, his successors inherited an institutionally weak political system that lacked legitimacy and an extremely large, corrupt state apparatus as well as a society with severe inequalities.[2] This inequality, the oppressive and racist nature of the regime that largely ignored the interests of workers and peasants as well as the favoritism towards foreigners and foreign corporations led to the outbreak of the Mexican revolution in 1910. The revolution of 1910-20 marks the beginning of modern Mexican political history with the revolutionary

---

[1] See Córdova Vianello (1994).
[2] See Camp (2003) p. 31-40.

constitution of 1917 still being in effect. Although the 1917 constitution draws very much on its predecessor from 1857, it additionally establishes revolutionary principles concerning the separation of church and state, labor regulation and rules that were aimed at reducing the foreign domination of the Mexican economy.[3]

The Mexican revolution again implied long years of political instability with quickly changing governments, large numbers of deaths in the population and a severe economic crisis. Although the military phase of the revolution ended around 1920, the time until 1940 was characterized by political instabilities and occasional violent societal conflicts. In an initiative of president Calles, who ruled from 1924-1928 but dominated political life during the so-called maximato for six more years the Partido Nacional Revolucionario (PNR) was founded in 1929. Calles designed a ruling party with corporatist structure which could channel the different ideological positions in the revolutionary movement to avoid the outbreak of further violence. This party that should later change its name to Partido de la Revolución Méxicana (PRM) in 1938 and then to Partido de la Revolución Institucional (PRI) in 1946 should remain in power until the year 2000 when Vincente Fox became the first Mexican president that was not a member of the former governmental party. The renaming of the party in 1938 by president Cárdenas was accompanied by an reorganization of the party in corporatist lines with separate sectors being created for labor, the peasantry, the military, and middle class groups.[4] If the initial goal of this reform was to provide a framework for the expression of popular demands, the system soon became an instrument of political control and electoral manipulation. In exchange for granting political and economic benefits to sector leaders the party could ensure its power. The change of the official party's name in PRI in 1946 signaled a turn away from the revolutionary upheavals of the Cárdenas years in favor of political stability and economic development.[5] Hence, the response of the Mexican leaders to the enduring political instabilities and the massive devastation of the revolution was as CHAND writes

"to create a highly centralized political system with an extremely powerful president and a dominant state-sponsored political party, whose function was to garner support for the revolutionary elite and ensure that social demands were channeled through the confines of the official party, where they were more easily controlled."[6]

Although the Mexican constitution proclaims the separation of powers and a system of checks and balances that allows for a control of the executive branch, the reality was characterized by a president ruling without any

---

[3] The constitutional rules are further explored in the paragraphs on the branches of government. Paragraph 5.2.2.1.1 discusses the economic implications of the 1917 constitution for FDI.
[4] See Whiting (1992) p. 37-45.
[5] See Chand (2001) p.13-25
[6] See Chand (2001) p.14.

effective control of the legislative branch or the judiciary.[7] This particular organization of the PRI implied that a clear distinction between the party and the state was no longer possible. The status as "official" party ensured the party's superiority vis-a-vis the opposition parties in terms of media presence, financial resources and government patronage. PRI candidates for public offices were not democratically elected but chosen by an intimate inner circle of the party usually led by the president. This political practice of handpicking candidates was also applied for presidential candidates. The so-called *dedazo* meant that the current president chooses the next PRI candidate to run for the presidency. Considering the dominant role of the PRI in Mexican politics picking the presidential candidate was equivalent to choosing the next president of Mexico.[8] If, despite of their superiority in every respect, PRI candidates failed at the polls, the regime took advantage of electoral fraud to ensure the victory of its candidate. Although violent repression has never been used systematically, the government occasionally recurred to coercive measures to suppress dissident movements.[9] During the 80s the PRI cautiously initiated reforms that should finally foster democracy and strengthen the opposition.[10] This process of democratization was in part initiated by the party itself but also a reaction to the popular demands for more democracy in Mexico. A starting point for massive public protests was the gubernatorial election in the state of Chihuahua in 1986 that was characterized by massive irregularities. This fraudulent election provoked a wave of protests among the Mexican population including many civil organizations and the catholic church that threatened to suspend service if the elections were not annulled. Protest continued after the fraudulent presidential election of 1988 where the popular PRI dissident Cuautémoc Cárdenas and the PAN candidate Manuel Clouthier challenged the PRI candidate Carlos Salinas de Gortari. Although there is some evidence that Cárdenas won the election, Salinas was announced winner and took the presidency.[11] Repeated experiences of electoral fraud and growing discontent with the regime finally obliged the PRI to enact electoral reforms that strengthened the role of the opposition and culminated in the election of the PAN candidate Fox in 2000.[12] The problem of electoral fraud

---

[7] See Penner (1999) p. 39-47. For a more detailed analysis of the president's, the legislatives' and the judiciary's role in Mexican politics see paragraph 5.1.2.2, 5.1.2.3 and paragraph 5.1.2.4 respectively. As Pritzl (1997) points out an inefficient separation of powers is a characteristic of many Latin American countries. See Pritzl (1997) p.64-80.

[8] The PRI stopped this practice in 1999 under the rule of president Zedillo when for the first time in the history of the PRI an open presidential primary was held that eventually chose Francisco Labatista as the PRI candidate for the presidential race in 2000. See Camp (2003). Despite of this move towards democratization it is argued that the primary was in fact a disguised "dedazo" because of the privileges Zedillo's candidate Labatista enjoyed. See Langston (2002) p.80.

[9] The most prominent example are the student massacre that took place in 1968 where hundreds of protesting students were shot on the Tlatelolco square in Mexico City and the violent repression of student protests in Corpus Christi in 1971. But there are several other examples for violent repression. See Philip (1992).

[10] Semo (1996) gives an overview over the initiating phase of the democratization process.

[11] See Chand (2001) p. 13-74.

[12] For a short overview of the electoral reforms see Swan/Martorelli/Molinar (1998).

was tackled by the creation of the Instituto Federal Electoral (IFE) to supervise the electoral process, the financing of parties and competitive access to the media.[13] The growing importance of opposition parties in congress and on the regional level slowly established a system of checks and balances that helped constrain the power of the federal government and to break the dominance of the PRI.[14] Consequently, from the late 80s onward Mexico changed from being an authoritarian one-party state to becoming a multiparty democracy with a competitive electoral process. Moreover, the extremely powerful position of the presidency was opposed by a stronger congress and a more independent judiciary which are now posing limits to the executive branch of the Mexican government.[15]

5.1.2 The Current Political System in Mexico
5.1.2.1 Overview
This paragraph describes the main characteristics and institutions of the current Mexican political system. Due to its high complexity the description will be limited to mechanisms that are important for the analysis of political risks emerging from its institutional characteristics.[16] Before the different branches of the system are reviewed in greater detail this paragraph offers a brief overview of important characteristics of Mexican politics. Mexico, the official name of which is the United Mexican States, is a federal republic of 31 states and one federal district with the states being divided into 2394 municipalities. The capital and seat of government is Mexico City which is also the cultural and economic center of the country. De jure Mexico is a presidential democracy with many similarities to that of the United States. It is based on a constitution that was passed during the Mexican revolution in 1917 which divides power between an executive branch, a legislative branch, the judiciary and the federal states. The executive branch of federal government is represented by the president of the republic who is publicly elected for a six year term and a cabinet of 19 agencies. The legislative branch consists of a bicameral congress that is divided into a 128-member Senate and a 500-member Chamber of Deputies. Senate elections are held every six years. Chamber of Deputies elections are held every three years. On the state level governors, town councils and mayors are directly elected by the population. The judiciary has local, state and national levels the last comprising a court of appeals and a supreme court that may overrule legislation that violates the constitution. The main parties of the political spectrum are the former state party PRI (Institutional Revolutionary Party), the conservative National Action Party (PAN) and the leftist Democratic Revolutionary Party (PRD) with 51 seats. Smaller fractions are the Labor Party (PT) and the Ecologist Green

---

[13] For a detailed description of the IFE and its role in ensuring fair elections see Prud'home (1998).
[14] For an overview of the growing influence of the Mexican opposition parties during the late 80s and 90s see Chand (2001) p.13-74 and Camp (2003) p.186-213.
[15] See Camp (2003) p.174-180.
[16] Camp (2003) and Castro Rea et al. (1999) offer an excellent initial overview over the Mexican political system.

Party of Mexico (PVEM). The seat distribution in the Senate is still characterized by a majority of the PRI with 60 seats followed by the PAN, PRD and PVEM with 46, 15 and 5 seats respectively. A general principle of the Mexican political system is the principle of no reelection to any political position in the Mexican government including all seats in the federal and state legislatures.[17] Although there was a lot of progress in this matter during the last years, the press and media remain partly controlled. For a long time the federal government retained direct control over the press through its monopoly of newsprint. In the second half of the 90s the ability to control government advertising remained. Too critical media or press coverage of political events may therefore be sanctioned with the withdrawal of government advertisement contracts.[18] Inherited from the interventionist past the federal government still operates public enterprises in economic sectors like petroleum, petrochemicals, electricity, communications, transportation, and agriculture.

> "La silla presidencial está embrujada: cualquier
> persona buena que se sienta en ella se convierte en mala"
> Emiliano Zapata

5.1.2.2 The Executive Branch of Government

One of the keys to understanding Mexican politics is the role of the national presidency because since independence all of Mexico's political systems have been based on presidentialism.[19] This means that the executive power lies in the hand of the president who is publicly elected for a six year term or *sexenio* without the possibility of being reelected.[20] Despite of similarities with the US system the powers of the Mexican president went far beyond those that are found in other presidential democracies.[21] In fact, the dominant role of the president is not a consequence of his constitutional powers but of a combination of de facto structures in Mexican politics. Many scholars refer to the presidency as an institution with "meta-constitutional" powers.[22] Therefore, the de facto rules of Mexican government differ to a large extent from the de jure rules of the Mexican constitution which establishes a strict division of power.[23] A close look on historical presidential governments reveals that since the official party PRI was founded in 1929 the Mexican president has been the dominant force in national politics. Before the reforms enacted by the administrations of Zedillo and Fox the position of the president in Mexico could

---

[17] This constitutional principle is a revolutionary heritage caused by the dictatorship of Porfirio Díaz who ruled the country from 1877 to 1911.

[18] See PRS Group (2003). The change of government in 2000 limited the possibility of the PRI to influence the press.

[19] For a history of Mexican presidentialism see Córdova Vianello (1994).

[20] The principle of no re-election has not been violated during the last years. See Philip (1992).

[21] See Sutherland (1999). The author does not enter here the controversial discussion of the political science literature if presidential governments are generally inferior to parliamentary democracies. For an overview of the discussion see Mainwaring/Shugart (1997). For a detailed criticism of presidential democracies see Linz/Valenzuela (1994).

[22] See Weldon (1997) for a detailed analysis of the factors that enable these meta-constitutional powers.

[23] See Penner (1999).

be compared to that of "an absolute monarch for six years".[24] Article 71 of the 1917 constitution enables the president to initiate legislation which comprises the right to initiate amendments of the constitution. Article 72 states that the president can veto legislation and only be overturned by a two-thirds vote of congress. In addition the president had the right to nominate ministers, the judiciary, high rank officials and important party leaders, to name the mayor of Mexico City and to remove state governors and congress members from office.[25] Between 1946 and 1996 presidents removed 67 governors and during the Salinas administration 17 publicly elected governors resigned "voluntarily" and were replaced by members of the presidents inner circle.[26] Thus, in spite of the federalist system established by the constitution Mexican politics are in fact highly centralized.[27] In addition to his legislative powers the Mexican president may issue regulations that serve as guidelines for the interpretation of existing legislation.[28] The president may nominate and remove all members of his cabinet, as well as name diplomatic officers, military officers of a certain rank and supreme court judges with the latter necessitating the approval of senate. Moreover, before Zedillo presidents made use of the so-called *dedazo* to name their successor. Although the constitution does not provide the president with extraordinary decree powers, he was granted the right to regulate domestic and foreign commerce including taxes, tariffs and subsidies on his own account as well as to intervene in monetary policy.[29]

However, more than the constitutional powers of the president, his partisan powers, that is, his ability to control congress and his own party, are responsible for the large extent of his power. It is highly probable that the powerful position of the head of state erodes when he faces a congress dominated by opposition parties.[30] In fact, an important reason for the strength of the presidency in Mexico was the fact that the disciplined PRI dominated congress and approved nearly all presidential bills without amendments.[31] In fact the PRI majority in congress made the legislation process in parliament a

---

[24] Daniel Cosío Villegas cited by Philip (1992) p.167.

[25] The mayor of Mexico City is now publicly elected.

[26] See Rodríguez (1999) and Weldon (1997).

[27] See Cornelius (1996) and Bolaños Guerra (1994).

[28] See Carbonell y Sánchez (1994).

[29] Currently, the Bank of Mexico is an independent organization. Since 1994 the NAFTA treaty also limits the presidential power in the design of economic policy. In the case of invasions and severe disturbances of internal peace the president gains extraordinary decree powers. The extraordinary powers of the presidency in economic policy relied on a constitutional amendment that has been passed under the rule of president Miguel Alemán. See Carbonell y Sánchez (1994).

[30] The experiences of president Fox who faces a congress that is dominated by opposition parties show that the power of the president is now effectively constrained by the legislative branch as several presidential bills have not been passed.

[31] See Weldon (1997). As Philip states:" The PRI was not designed to represent the views of an articulate membership, but to reward conformity and control elections; all efforts to reform the PRI by turning it into a members' party have been successfully resisted. Philip (1992) p.165. For a more detailed analysis of the role of congress see paragraph 5.1.2.3.

simple formality. To illustrate the latter point table 5.1 depicts the bill success rate of the Mexican president for two different legislative periods.

Table 5.1: Bill Success Rate of the Mexican Presidency

	1994-1997 LEGISLATURE	1997-2000 LEGISLATURE
Bills Presented	274	677
Executive Success Rate	99%	90%

Source: Camp (2003) p.173

The presidential control of congress and the minor role of opposition parties implied that the president was even able to change the constitution with high discretionary power. Since its establishment in 1917 the constitution has been changed more than 350 times according to the current political and societal necessities.[32] These constitutional amendments have been used to implement government policy or to further strengthen the power of the executive.[33] The presidential gain in power by the lacking control of congress over bills is enforced by the lacking control of the judiciary.[34] The weakness of the other branches of government implied that the Mexican president played the decisive role for all political decisions including economic policy. The joint responsibility of the presidential office for such diverse matters as fiscal policy, national health, ecological norms, national education, social policies and the national economic strategy made the president the veritable geometric center of the political system.[35]

Another important factor that influences Mexican presidential politics is the *camarilla*-system. A *camarilla* is a group of political actors who share political interests and rely on one another to improve their chances in political leadership. The Mexican political system is permeated by these clientelistic relationships that have been formed over long periods of time and are based on personal loyalty. A *camarilla* leader who ascends in an organization places the members of his group in other influential positions. As the Mexican political system does not permit a re-election of the president the supreme patron and his *camarilla* are removed every six years and replaced by the new presidents group.[36] One immediate consequence of this system of personal loyalties is that the responsiveness and accountability of officials is greatly diminished. Moreover, it is an important source of political discontinuity. A recent study reveals that 80 % of top office holders are replaced every 12 years and 90 % every 18 years. At the end of each administration nearly one third of top-level

---

[32] See Rubio et al. (1994) p.25. This extraordinary power was exercised until 1988 when the PRI lost the necessary two-thirds majority in congress. See Sutherland (1999).

[33] See Penner (1999).

[34] See paragraph 5.1.2.4.

[35] See Bolaños Guerra (1994).

[36] See Camp (2003) and Cornelius (1996).

players drop out of political life. So every six years 18000 publicly elected posts and 25000 designated posts are changed.[37]

The reforms of Zedillo and Fox as well as the loss of the PRI majority in congress marks the end of unchecked presidential rule. It remains to be seen how the role of the president will be changing subject to these alternate conditions. In any case the analysis of the president's position in Mexican politics shows that before the recent reforms the executive power was hardly limited or controlled by any other governmental branch.[38] This lack of checks and balances often led to arbitrary decisions of the president that highly affected the well-being of the Mexican people and implied a massive abuse of power for personal or political ends.[39] Therefore, the quality of Mexican policy depends to a large extent on the personal qualities of the currently ruling president.[40] According to the so-called pendulum theory the policy of Mexican presidents swings from left to right following the preferences of the president and his *camarilla*.[41] The most prominent example of an economic policy that has been essentially shaped by a president is the term of president López Portillo. One observer classified his economic policy as a presidential economy rather than a policy that was conducted following any specific economic doctrine. There is evidence that in the years preceding the debt crisis the president personally blocked necessary cuts in public spending that were proposed by his advisors.[42] However, the most prominent example for his arbitrary decisions is the nationalization of the Mexican banks in 1982 that was announced without warning. The president obviously decided on this matter without consulting sufficient advice and considering affected groups.[43] The nationalization of the banks and the exchange controls were imposed by an executive decree. Article 28 of the constitution that prohibits monopolies was amended with a new paragraph that allowed for the bank nationalization

---

[37] See Cornelius (1996) and Sutherland (1999).

[38] Rubio et al. state: ... nuestro sistema constitucional de frenos y contrapesos de hecho no funciona porque los distintos órganos de poder no tienen intereses contrapuestos ni capacidad institucional de defenderlos." Rubio et al. (1994) p.168.

[39] See Cornelius (1996). As one observer states: "No matter how irrational a project may be in the eyes of specialists, if the president approves it, it must be carried out". Cited by Morris (1991) p.37. The detailed analysis of four presidential terms by Philips (1992) confirms the result that presidents often carry out arbitrary acts that have an important impact on the economy.

[40] A British observer commented: "It seems to me that this system is workable only so long as the candidates successively selected by the retiring president are people of restraint and sound common sense. The opportunities for abuse of power and the apparent lack of any of the normal checks and balances usually associated with democratic regimes do not offer any guarantee of permanent political stability. Cited by Philip (1992) p.169. Philip (1992) argues that the presidential terms of Díaz Ordaz (1964-1970), Echeverría (1970-1976) and in particular López Portillo (1976-1982) were characterized by weak ruling performances.

[41] See Philip (1992) p.178-183. In contrast Whiting argues that despite of high presidential influence Mexican politics show a basic continuity. See Whiting (1992).

[42] See Philip (1992) p.115-132.

[43] See Camp (2003). For a detailed analysis of the bank nationalization see Elizondo (2001).

which was again suspended in 1990 when president Salinas initiated the reprivatization of the banks.[44] López Portillo announced his decision to the cabinet 12 hours before his address to the public and asked for resignation of everyone that objected.[45] The fact that a single political actor can make decisions that deeply influence the economy may serve to illustrate the inherent dangers of this massive concentration of political power.[46]

5.1.2.3 The Legislative Branch of Government

De jure the Mexican constitution provides the legislative body of the Mexican political system with great powers.[47] The chamber of deputies and the senate have the right to present fiscal initiatives, to control the annual budget and ministers as well as to participate in the designation of important officials in public administration. Considering these constitutional powers of the Mexican congress one is attempted to conclude that its power is similar to that of the US congress. However, as already pointed out, during the last 70 years the presidency exerted the central role in Mexican politics.[48] The reasons for this de facto weakness of the Mexican congress stem from the particularities of the Mexican political system. One important reason is the minor role of opposition parties. Between 1940 and 1961 the percentage of seats in the chamber of deputies attributed to the PRI attained 96%. Due to cautious political reforms that strengthened the role of opposition parties this percentage fell to 83% and 61% for the periods 1964-1976 and 1979-1994 respectively.[49] The distribution of seats in the senate during the last years followed similar patterns. Until 1988 the PRI controlled 100% of the seats in senate.[50] Opposition parties therefore had little influence on policy making.[51] However, it may be argued that the long time dominance of one party does not necessarily imply a weak position of the congress. What additionally reinforces the presidential power in the Mexican case is the principle of no reelection of legislators, the high internal discipline of the PRI and the fact that until 1994 the president was simultaneously head of the PRI.

To allow for a better understanding these particularities will be examined more closely. In the first place the constitutional principle of no reelection hinders the development of legislative knowledge by members of congress. The complete

---

[44] The nationalization of the banks is not the only example for arbitrary changes of the constitution according to political objectives. See Rubio et al. (1994).

[45] See Maxfield (1990).

[46] Elizondo (2001) argues that the expropriation of the banks was not an illegitimate violation of property rights since the Mexican constitution permits the discretional restriction of property rights by the president. Paragraph 5.3.3.4 gives a more detailed analysis of the risk of expropriation in Mexico.

[47] See Nacif (2003) p.2-4.

[48] In the 1960s Vernon commented the role of the Mexican legislature as following: "... in practice, the legislature is a passive creature which hardly ever fails to carry out the wishes of the president; independent action on its part is almost unknown." Vernon (1963) p.11.

[49] See Massicotte (1999) p.93-101.

[50] See Camp (2003) p.175.

[51] See Langston (2002) p.64-66.

change of congress members after every election avoids that legislators gain experience in the complex programs and procedures of government which impedes a continuity in legislative policy of congress. Moreover, this principle leads to strong incentives for legislators of the president's party to remain loyal as their political future entirely depends on the benevolence of the party leader to assign them to lucrative posts.[52] So every member of congress, independent of the party he belongs to, has an incentive to rather vote according to party discipline instead of representing the interests of his constituencies.[53]

Up to the times of Zedillo the president was simultaneously head of the PRI.[54] It may be argued that this fatal combination was the source of presidential dominance and the de facto irrelevance of the Mexican congress.[55] Consequently presidential bills to congress nearly always passed without substantial amendments of the legislative body. In fact there have been no serious conflicts neither between the two legislative bodies nor between the executive branch and congress in the past.[56] The bill success rates that were presented in table 5.1 are an important empirical evidence for the minor role of the Mexican congress in shaping governmental policy. Thus, the long year dominance of the PRI in congress, the president's role as head of the PRI and high internal discipline within the party combined with the principle of no reelection implied that the legislative's role to provide for checks and balances of the executive branch of government could not be properly executed.

The minor role of congress as an institution of democratic control of government is also reflected in the low esteem of Mexican citizens of congress that is illustrated in table 5.2. While 83% of US citizens expressed confidence in congress in 1990 the corresponding figures for Mexico are 16%, 28% and 21% for the years 1988, 1998 and 2000 respectively. Moreover, the confidence of Mexican citizens in national political parties is considerably lower than in the US although here the difference is less striking.

Despite of the negative view of citizens, the role of the Mexican congress is gradually strengthened by the growing importance of opposition parties. The first important step to a better control of executive power was the national election of 1988 where the PRI for the first time in history lost its two-thirds majority in congress that is crucial for constitutional amendments.

---

[52] See Massicotte (1999).

[53] See Nacif (2003) p.5-6.

[54] See Nacif (2003) p.6.

[55] See Weldon (1997) who analyses in greater detail the prerequisites for the meta-constitutional powers of the Mexican presidency.

[56] See Massicotte (1999). The exception in Mexican history is the time of the so-called "maximato" (1928-1935) when the former president and party leader Calles dominated congress and the direction of Mexican policy. See Weldon (1997). Morris states that "congress has historically served as a virtual rubber stamp to presidential desires". Morris (1991) p.27.

Table 5.2: Confidence of Mexicans and US Americans in Congress and Parties

	PERCENTAGE OF RESPONDENTS GIVING POSITIVE EVALUATION				
INSTITUTION	USA 1990	USA 2000	Mexico 1988	Mexico 1998	Mexico 2000
Congress	83	-	16	28	21
Political Parties	-	56	-	29	20

Source: Camp (2003) p.55.

In the midterm elections of 1997 the PRI even lost its majority to the opposition parties leaving president Zedillo faced with a majority of the opposition parties in congress. The experience of the first years with higher opposition control suggests that the role of congress in Mexican politics becomes more important.[57] The current president Fox essentially faces the same situation as congress is not controlled by a majority of the president's party PAN. Hence, the beginning democratic transformation of the Mexican political system implies that the traditional "presidencialismo" of former years is no longer existent. With this particularity of the semi-authoritarian past diminishing the importance of congress for the design of Mexican politics is expected to be growing in the future. This process implies that the Mexican legislative branch is changing from a de facto irrelevant institution to a legislative body that may be able to fulfill the tasks that it is contributed to in the constitution. That is to say, that for the years to come one may expect a more effective control of the national executive by the legislative branch of government that may better limit arbitrary executive actions.[58]

5.1.2.4 The National Judiciary

As already pointed out in paragraph 3.1.2.4 a functioning judiciary is essential for democratic countries with market based economic systems. Like in the US the Mexican judicial system has courts at the local, the state and the national level, the last comprising a court of appeals and a supreme court. At present the supreme court consists of 11 judges that may serve for up to 15 years and are appointed by the president with a two-thirds approval of the senate.[59] These current rules are the result of an ambitious judicial reform that has been enacted under the rule of president Zedillo to fight the inefficiency and the corruption that prevailed in the national judiciary. In part the reform is a reaction to the violation of the principle of the separation of powers which, although explicitly stated in the Mexican constitution, has never been achieved. As it was the case for the legislative branch of government, the role

---

[57] Lujambio (1998) reviews the effects of growing opposition party presence in congress since 1988.

[58] Nacif (2003) presents a formal model of the Mexican political system modeling an executive that is constrained by divided government. Despite of critics highlighting the danger of deadlock policy in this situation the model shows that efficient government is still possible through coalition building.

[59] See Camp (2003).

of the judiciary as an independent power in government has not been exerted in the Mexican political practice of the last years. In fact, also the judiciary has been largely dominated by the president as he played a decisive role in the process of the appointment of judges.[60]

At the governmental level a supreme court is influential for national decision-making when it is independent from other branches of government and when it can legislate through rulings. The German supreme court for example may declare that laws are violating the constitution which obligates the parliament to alter existing legislation. The Mexican constitution of 1917 establishes no legal base for annulling laws or decrees that violate the constitution. Thus, the power of the court to shape national policy and to control constitutionality by rulings was nearly inexistent or at best inefficiently exercised. The reforms of Zedillo strengthened the role of the judiciary by granting the supreme court the right to decide on the constitutionality of laws and regulations which implies that norms that violate the constitution may be suspended.[61] Individual constitutional guarantees however, only offer protection for the citizens if they can be effectively enforced.[62] In the past only few individuals could protect themselves against arbitrary governmental acts.[63] To foster independence of the court no politicians, government officials or congress members are allowed to be appointed. Additionally the power of the senate in the decision process on the appointment was enlarged to restrict presidential influence. The administration of Fox continued Zedillos policy of strengthening the supreme court which recently lead to some cases in which the judges qualified presidential initiatives as anti constitutional.[64] Thus, on the governmental level the reforms enabled the Mexican judiciary to better perform its constitutional role as a counterbalance to the executive power.

In spite of these reforms the lower levels of the judiciary are still taunted by severe problems of corruption, political manipulation and long duration of trials. The lack of transparency and consistency makes it nearly impossible for the average citizen to resort to the system to protect his or her individual rights.

---

[60] See Holland (1999). Rubio et al. (1994) state: "La división de poderes es una ficción, tanto en el   marco de las leyes como en la práctica política, sobre todo en lo que concieme al poder judicial." Rubio et al. (1994) p.34.

[61] What existed before was a limited form of judicial revision called *amparo* that was focused on the protection of individual rights. See Holland (1999). For a detailed analysis of judicial constitutional control see Castro (2000).

[62] As a Mexican jurist states: "La historia ha demostrado que un pretendido derecho sin el respaldo judicial no es más que una declaración en el papel. El problema central de la ley constitucional es encontrar un modo práctico de asegurar al individuo una protección plena y efectiva contra los excesos arbitrarios del poder. Esto sólo es posible mediante la intervención judicial." Tamayo y Salmorán (1989) p.248

[63] In 1992 only 11% of all amparo-lawsuits that claimed the inconstitutionality of laws or administrative acts were successful. 77% of the claims were revised because they lacked the necessary formal prerequisites of constitutional claims. In addition, the amparo could only protect individual rights but not declare the inconstitutionality of laws. See Rubio et al. (1994).

[64] See Camp (2003).

Criminal justice is still characterized by massive human rights violations up to the use of torture to obtain confessions. In particular citizens with low incomes or with indigenous origin are targets of human rights violations as they do not dispose of contacts or sufficient means to pay bribes.[65] A sufficiently large bribe in turn, may buy a verdict of innocence or the ignorance of law enforcing institutions towards crime. Additionally the judicial system is bureaucratic and slow which implies that bribes are not only paid for a favorable judgement but also for speeding up the decision. The fact that judges are badly paid further increases corruption and the payment of bribes to judges. The absence of transparency, reliability, integrity and consistency imply that the respect of the Mexican citizens for the law remains low.[66] Mexicans do not feel protected by the law since the impunity of criminals may be viewed daily. The same is true for the national police that is widely known for inefficiency and corruption. The low quality and efficiency of the system is confirmed by the low esteem that it enjoys in the Mexican public. Table 5.3 depicts the results of surveys in Mexico and the USA where people were asked if they had confidence in the judiciary and the police.

Table 5.3: Confidence of Mexicans and US Americans in the Judiciary

	PERCENTAGE OF RESPONDENTS GIVING POSITIVE EVALUATION				
INSTITUTION	USA 1990	USA 2000	Mexico 1988	Mexico 1998	Mexico 2000
Law/Courts	-	80	32	31	22
Police	88	87	12	33	22

Source: Camp (2003) p.55.

The results show that despite of the enacted reforms the trust of Mexicans in the judicial system has not grown significantly during the last years indicating that the efforts were not sufficient. As GONZÁLEZ GÓMEZ writes the unreliability and intransparency as well as the low levels of esteem for the law and the enforcing organizations creates a "culture of illegality" in Mexico.[67] Even the winning of the presidency by the PAN in 2000 did not result in higher levels of confidence for the national legal institutions. However, it is to be expected that growing pressure from interest groups inside and outside the country for a better functioning of the Mexican judiciary will improve the situation in the future.[68]

5.1.2.5 The Political Parties
Up to the year 1988 the analysis of Mexican political parties may be limited to an investigation of the PRI as the only party with a significant level of political influence in society. The official party held large majorities in both chambers of

---

[65] See Camp (2003) and Rubio et al (1994).
[66] See Holland (1999) and Castro (2000). A low respect for the judiciary is a common problem in nearly all Latin American countries. See Buscaglia/Dakolias/Ratliff (1995).
[67] See González Gómez (2001). For a closer analysis of rule of law in Mexico see paragraph 5.3.2.2.
[68] See Domingo (1999).

congress and dominated public administrations, the judiciary and other key governmental organizations. The long history of the PRI as the unique, corporatist party that had to integrate all parts of society implied that its influence spread to nearly every important interest group including unions and peasant organizations.[69] This dominant role led to a virtual fusion between the party and the state that resembled the former Soviet Union which is symbolically pictured by the fact that the PRI's emblem has the same colors as the Mexican flag (green, white and red) and that public social spending used to be accompanied by colorful propaganda evoking the party's emblem.[70]

The role of opposition parties was merely limited to enhance the legitimacy of the semi-authoritarian regime that was governing Mexico. Despite of their presence in congress their de-facto influence on the design of Mexican policy was severely limited either by repression of the regime or by their lack of unity.[71] The transformation of the Mexican society towards a true democracy during the 90s however, implied a steadily growing importance of opposition parties. The severe problems of inefficiency, corruption and the inability of the one-party regime to enhance public welfare initiated a process of democratization in Mexico that was partly rooted in the growing awareness of the Mexican population of the importance of democracy and partly due to cautious reforms inside the PRI. Faced by the devastating consequences of the Mexican economic crisis during the 80s the population offered massive resistance to the usual governmental practices of corruption, inefficiency and electoral fraud to ensure PRI dominance.[72] One important consequence of this democratic transformation was the enhanced role of the opposition parties in Mexican politics. The emergence of a multiparty system with higher electoral competition completely changed the characteristics of the Mexican political system as opposition parties for the first time faced a nearly level playing field to compete with the PRI. This democratic transformation reached a climax in the 2000 presidential election in which for a first time a non PRI member won the presidential race.

The current political system has five influential parties. The most important in terms of their current electoral support are the former governing party PRI, the conservative-center party PAN, and the left-center PRD that was founded by ex-PRI members. The other two with a lesser share in votes are the Mexican ecological or green party and the labor party.[73] The growing competitiveness and the erosion of the PRI's superior position imply that the role of the parties inside the political process grows. In the years of PRI dominance the role of

---

[69] For a detailed analysis of the structure and the functioning of the PRI see Rodríguez (1998b).

[70] See Otero (1996) p.11.

[71] See Gómez Tagle (1999).

[72] See Chand (2001) for an excellent analysis of the sources of the Mexican process of democratization.

[73] For an analysis of the party ideology and position in the political spectrum of PRI, PAN and PRD see Moreno (1998) and Rodríguez (1998a)

other parties was reduced to accept presidential bills in congress and to provide a stable basis for executive domination. This domination was further enhanced by the absence of democratic structures inside the PRI that would at least have ensured a competitive electoral process inside the party.[74] As the ancient regime's practices of executive dominance will no longer work in the current political environment the parties will inevitably become a more decisive force in the Mexican political system. The competitiveness of elections and the absence of fraud are most likely to produce governments that do not face majorities in congress which implies a need of cooperation between parties to enact legislation. Moreover, the former official party PRI will have to modify from being a corporatist party without real need of ensuring electoral success by good governance to an organization that is capable of competing in a multi-party framework. The former opposition parties in turn, have to show how they will perform in governing the country and to overcome the role of being just alternatives to the unique dominating party. Therefore, Mexican political parties will play a major role for the design of future Mexican politics.

5.1.2.6 The Federalist System

By the constitution of 1917 Mexico is a federalist republic where the states play an important role for the government of the country since articles 39 and 41 of the constitution divide power between federal government, state government and the municipalities. On the state level the governors, town councils and mayors are directly elected by the population and the constitution proclaims that local governments are sovereign and independent from the central government in its internal matters.[75] Despite of these constitutional guarantees during the years of PRI dominance, the autonomy of the states was subject to important limitations. To get nominated as candidate for a post as a local governor politicians usually had to show their loyalty to the federal government. Moreover, like on the federal level, local elections were influenced by fraud, manipulation and repression. In remote areas fraud was even more severe because due to lacking resources it was hard for opposition parties to guarantee free and fair elections.[76]

To avoid excessive autonomy of regional governors the president often made use of his right to remove state governors from office.[77] So in spite of the federalism prescribed in the constitution the Mexican political system is de facto highly centralized.[78] Despite of cautious decentralization efforts since the late 80s Mexico still remains a country where the local entities are in fact highly dependent of the federal government.[79] Another fact that underlines the reduced role of the states and municipalities is the distribution of fiscal

---

[74] See Gómez Tagle (1999).
[75] See Penner (1999).
[76] See Chand (2001). In some elections in remote rural areas the PRI obtained "soviet-style" results with nearly 100% of approval.
[77] See Rodríguez (1999) and Weldon (1997).
[78] See Bolaños Guerra (1994).
[79] See Penner (1999) and Cornelius (1996).

resources. In the past the federal government retained control of 85% of revenues that only under multiple control has been recently lowered by congress to 75%.[80] Like other characteristics of Mexican politics however, also Mexican federalism has been affected by the democratic transformation of the country. More and more local governments are now controlled by opposition parties which implies that the influence of the federal government on local affairs is slowly diminishing. In particular the economically important northern states are by now dominated by PAN governments.[81] In the year 2000 eleven states were controlled by the opposition parties PAN and PRD accounting for 33% of the population and 48% of national GDP.[82] Although the role of states and municipalities as a constraint for the central government is still limited, the ongoing process of decentralization and the establishment of opposition party rule in several states is likely to further strengthen the role of local entities.

5.1.2.7 Freedom of Speech, Press and Media

Freedom of speech as well as free press and media play a vital role in democracies in fulfilling the task of a proper information of the public and an external control of government and the public administration. It is obvious that these important task can only be properly fulfilled if the press and media are not subject to governmental controls or censorship and if individuals are free to express their point of view since only a free press and media may inform the citizens about corruption and other abuses of public office and evaluate properly governmental initiatives and programs. Hence, only a free press can exert external control over governmental action by mobilizing public opinion against violations of political principles or national law.

Freedom of press and media as well as the individual freedom of speech are guaranteed in article 60 and 70 of the Mexican constitution.[83] Nevertheless, in Mexico the freedom of media is a difficult topic. Although not directly controlled, politicians may exert considerable influence on the press by the placement and withdrawal of financially lucrative government advertising. Moreover, for a long time the national monopoly on newsprint ensured that delivery to unfriendly dailies could be suspended. Critical articles and commentaries could be answered by the canceling of government contracts that ensure the economic survival of the medium or by the suspension of newsprint supply. Besides, payments of bribes for political journalists and publishers were an institutionalized part of Mexican press and media. Therefore, much of the governmental control of the media relied on collusion instead of coercion.[84] A widespread practice in the Mexican printing press is the publishing of paid political announcements that are disguised as news

---

[80] See Camp (2003).
[81] See Chand (2001).
[82] See Camp (2003).
[83] See Carreño Carlón/Villanueva (1998).
[84] See Orme (1997). As Evelyn P. Stevens argues: "It would be an exceptionally courageous publisher, or a very foolish one, who would bite the hand which feeds him". Cited by Morris (1991) p.54.

stories, the so-called *gacetillas*. Although reliable data on the importance of *gacetillas* is not available, it is estimated that they are responsible for a large share of the newspaper's incomes and that the economic survivability of many papers would be endangered without these payments.[85] In addition pressure on critical journalists was also exercised by outright coercion as threatening, kidnapping, violence and even assassinations.[86] Although press freedom still remains limited, there has been great progress in this topic, in particular in the print media where many newspapers now show more independent reporting. Hence, the process of democratization was also influential for the media which implied that over time the coverage of governmental policy in the printing press became more critical. However, an important characteristic of Mexico is that the societal influence of the printing press remains limited as the number of sales of even the most renown national newspapers is comparably small.[87] Moreover, the high degree of government intervention discouraged the Mexican business community to invest in the press since a profitable press with independent reporting is too risky and a safe press without government criticism is hardly profitable.

Consequently television is the most important mean of information for Mexican citizens. Despite of growing independence in the printing press major television channels remained essentially pro-government.[88] In particular the dominating television broadcasting company TELEVISA had close ties to the PRI and for a long time favored the party in its media coverage of electoral campaigns.[89] There is also evidence that TELEVISA broadcasting of the Chiapas uprising was heavily pro-government biased.[90] During the years of PRI dominance the official party heavily relied on its priority access to the media to stabilize its influence in the Mexican society and to ensure a positive outcome of elections. Thus, more equal access to the media was one of the most important achievements that allowed for the success of Mexican opposition parties. Other reforms of the press were already enacted under the rule of Salinas when the government newsprint monopoly was ended, direct government payments to journalists were cut and privatizing a government

---

[85] See Keenan (1997).

[86] See Conger (1997), Moynihan (1997) and Solomon (1997). Assessing the number of attacked or murdered journalists is a difficult task. Some of the cited authors nevertheless compare the level of violence against journalist with Colombia. Though it cannot be guaranteed in all cases that violence is connected to the reporting of the journalist and enacted by the government investigation on the cases is nearly always unsuccessful or even intentionally delayed by officials which creates a situation of impunity for the masterminds of the attacks.

[87] See Riva Palacio (1997).

[88] See Sarmiento (1997) and Castañeda (1997).

[89] See Belejack (1997), Miller/Darling (1997) and Castañeda (1997). After the 1994 presidential election the PAN candidate Diego Fernández stated that the success was not the PRI's but a triumph of PRONASOL (a program for poverty alleviation), PROCAMPO (a program of rural subsidies) and TELEVISA. See Otero (1996) p.15.

[90] See López (1997).

television network created the first competitor for TELEVISA. The government of Zedillo cautiously followed the course of reform.[91]

Despite of these successes compared to other countries the freedom of press and media is still severely restricted in Mexico. The Freedom House press freedom indicator that is depicted in figure 5.1 confirms this statement suggesting that recent improvements and reforms were not sufficient. An index value of 100 represents a fully controlled press while 0 stands for a fully free press though the average index scores of western democracies usually vary around a value of 10. The inspection of the data for Mexico reveals that the enacted reforms of press and media only had a minor impact on the freedom of Mexican press and media.

Figure 5.1: Freedom House Press Freedom Indicator for Mexico (1994-2000)

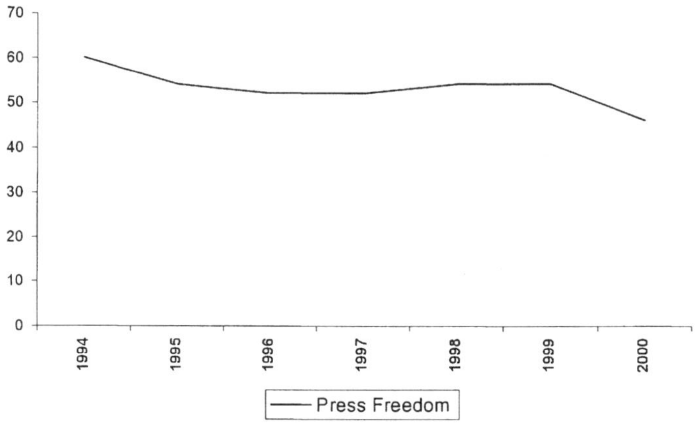

Source: Own figure using data of Freedom House (2003).

The comparison of Mexico with other Latin American countries in figure 5.2 reveals that its degree of press freedom is one of the worst in the region since only press freedom in the authoritarian Peru of Fujimori received a lower rating.

---

[91] See Orme (1997). It has to be stated that the number of violent aggressions against journalists increased heavily in the Salinas administration. See Conger (1997).

Figure 5.2 Freedom House Press Freedom Indicator for Major Latin American Countries (1994-2000)

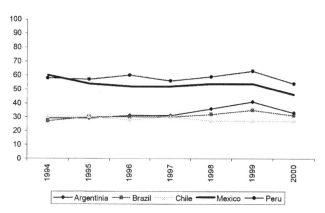

Source: Own figure using yearly data of Freedom House (2003).

With index values varying around 50, that are comparable to those of Pakistan, Nigeria or Tanzania, Mexico still has a long way to go to establish a free and reliable media sector comparable to Western democracies. In this context it is interesting that the NAFTA contract limits the foreign equity participation in Mexican television companies and newspapers to 49% with the exception of simply translated foreign-edited newspapers.[92] One may conclude that the important task that a free press plays in democracies can still not be properly executed by the Mexican press. Despite of the considerable progress during the last years information of the public and control of government by the Mexican press are still unsatisfactory.

5.2 Foreign Capital Flows to Mexico
5.2.1 Brief Economic History
5.2.1.1 Overview

The independence of Mexico in 1821 and the preceding wars marked the beginning of a weak nation state that still suffered from the long years of Spanish paternalism. The years following independence were characterized by durable political instability and economic stagnation. In the last quarter of the nineteenth century the authoritarian rule of Porfirio Díaz (1876-1911) restored political stability for the first time since independence. As a consequence Mexico experienced higher growth which was mainly stimulated by the dynamic export sector.[93] Although the dominating development strategy was characterized by a "desarollo hacia afuera", the 1890s mark the beginning of Mexican Industrialization in sectors as textiles, steel, cement glass etc. The

---

[92] See Orme (1997).

[93] The export sector grew at an annually average rate of 6,1% during the years of Diáz's rule. See Knight (2000). For a short analysis of the economic policy of Díaz see Haber/Razo/Maurer (1999).

socio-economic situation which was characterized by the authoritarian and racist political regime, an agricultural sector linked to peasant dispossession and labor coercion and the inequality in the distribution of benefits from the development process led to growing social unrest and finally to the outbreak of the Mexican revolution.[94] During the long period of armed conflict and social tensions the economic downturn reached its peak in 1917 with collapsing exports, high inflation and growing poverty. Short periods of recovery and decline followed until Mexico was hit by the consequences of the great depression. The fall in global demand harshly affected the export sector and between 1929 and 1932 Mexican exports fell by 64.9% leading to a general economic downturn.[95]

The presidency of Lázaro Cárdenas from 1934-1940 was marked by a complete restructuring of the state and its relation to the economy. The focus of the public sector shifted from the wealthy groups to peasants and workers leaving the private industrial sector largely untouched. An agrarian reform[96] that benefited a large part of the population shifted additional resources from commercial agriculture to industry which in turn fostered the process of industrialization. During the Second World War the increasingly centralized and authoritarian government focused on the expansion of public infrastructure and urbanization for the benefit of the industrial sector and commerce.[97] Mexico experienced high growth due to the increasing demand for Mexican commodities and natural resources during the war period.[98]

In 1948 the Mexican minister of economy obtained the right to change the list of goods under protection reinforcing the restrictive policy on imports. Throughout the 50s the protection scheme was gradually enlarged culminating in the practice that every industry which substituted imports automatically enjoyed full protection implying that the scope of protection changed from being a tool for the management of balance of payment-problems to a development strategy. By protecting domestic industries the government sought to foster the national process of industrialization and to reduce Mexican dependence on imported capital goods which in turn would diminish the vulnerability of the Mexican economy to external shocks.[99]

The decade of the fifties saw real aggregate investment growing with an average annual rate of 17% while GDP grew at a rate of 6.2%. Growth rates of

---

[94] See Knight (2000) p. 124-131. Many developments of Mexican politics in the 20th century can only be understood being aware of the revolutionary heritage of the Mexican society. The emergence of "Mexicanization" as a form of economic nationalism for example is based on revolutionary principles and has been very influential for the debate about foreign investment in Mexico. See paragraph 5.2.2.1.1 for an analysis of its influence on the national FDI legislation.

[95] See Cárdenas (2000a) p.197-201 and FitzGerald (2000).

[96] For a detailed analysis of the land reform of Cárdenas see Gordon (1975).

[97] See Cárdenas (2000b) p.182-185

[98] See OECD (1992) p.15.

[99] See Cárdenas (2000b) p.185-190.

real GDP continued to be high throughout the 60s stimulated by a dynamic industrial sector despite of declines in agriculture and the traditionally strong mining sector. At the same time inflation rates kept at a moderate level. The Mexican development model during this time (*desarollo estabilizador*) may be seen as a success.[100] However, already the late 60s mark a turning point for the economic development of Mexico by bringing to light the first signs of weaknesses of the chosen national development strategy. As a reaction to the considerable entries of foreign firms the Mexican business community was seeking further governmental protection. So, instead of protecting the domestic market the government now switched to a strategy of protecting domestic producers. Among other restrictive measures foreign control of shares in Mexican companies was limited to a maximum of 49%.[101]

Over time the extensive protection of domestic firms led to a steady decline in competitiveness of Mexican producers. Many businesses were inefficient operating with high profit rates and high cost to public finances due to subsidies at the expense of tax-payers. The "infant industry protection" of domestic sectors finally implied a total loss of international competitivity and a high inefficiency of Mexican firms. Nevertheless, the national government did not review its development policy by gradually liberalizing and opening up to foreign trade and investment. A result of maintaining this strategy was the growing dependence on external borrowing. The oil boom of the 70s and the excess of investment seeking liquidity from banks in industrial countries fostered a growing external debt throughout the seventies.[102] When economic growth was slowing in the 70s and political tensions mounted after the 1968 massacre of students, the governments of Luis Echeverria (1970-1976) and López Portillo (1976-1982) embarked on a populist strategy of heavy public spending and expansion of the public sector. This tendency was aggravated when large oil reserves were discovered in the wake of the first oil shock.[103] The important increase of international interest rates and the elevate level of external debt finally led to the outbreak of the great Latin American debt crisis causing severe economic problems not only in Mexico but throughout Latin America.[104]

Mexico declared a moratorium on external debt in 1982 which led to important disturbances of the international financial system as the credit exposure of many international banks was considerable. In a last desperate struggle to manage the crisis Mexico announced the complete nationalization of the banking system leading to an even bigger loss of investor confidence. As a consequence of the debt crisis Mexican growth rates fell sharply and remained low for the rest of the 80s. Inflation rates grew reaching three digit rates and

---

[100] See Ros (1993).
[101] See the review of the Mexican FDI legislation in paragraph 5.2.2.1.
[102] See Cárdenas (2000b) p.191-199.
[103] See OECD (1992) p.16.
[104] For a general review of the Latin American debt crisis see Ffrench-Davis (2000). For an overview of the events in Mexico see Krämer (1997) p.112-152.

real wages declined leaving the country in a deep economic crisis.[105] The outbreak of the debt crisis ended the strategy of import substitution and initiated a period of profound economic reforms that deeply influenced the economic performance of the years to come. Hence, the great debt crisis of the 80s marks a watershed in the economic history of Mexico because the following liberal reforms were to endure until the beginning of the new millenium.

5.2.1.2 The Reform Period 1982-today

The policy responses to the 80s debt crisis involved drastic exchange rate and fiscal adjustments as well as a complete change of the national development strategy. The government of de la Madrid initiated an austerity program to overcome the crisis and liberal reforms were implemented to bring the Mexican economy back to economic stability and growth. In 1982 three devaluations took place that were designed to cut the unsustainable balance of payments deficit. Fiscal adjustments relied on a decrease in public investment, real salary reductions for government employees, and increases in indirect taxes and public prices. Long negotiations with the IMF and the consortia of lenders followed to achieve a rescheduling of Mexican external debt.[106] Figure 5.3 shows that the aftermath of the debt crisis was characterized by a severe fall of per capita growth rates which only showed signs of recovery during the late 80s.

Figure 5.3: GDP per Capita Growth between 1980-1990

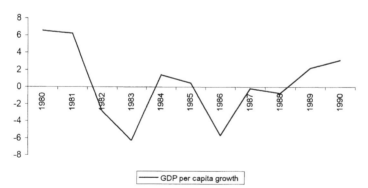

Source: Own figure using data from World Bank Development Indicators 2002

Although by the end of the 80s the Mexican government succeeded in assuring macroeconomic stability, the adjustment policy implied high costs to the population since in particular already deprived members of the Mexican society had to shoulder the heavy burden of the national stabilization policy. Low growth severely affected poverty levels in the country. As public spending

---

[105] See Krämer (1997) p.112-121.
[106] For an overview of the management of the debt crisis in Mexico see OECD (1992) and Krämer (1997) p.121-144.

was cut people depending on public transfers were heavily affected by the adjustment process. Throughout the 80s real incomes were on average 30% lower than in the years preceding the crisis.[107] As an reaction to the surge in poverty and the resulting potential for social unrest the Salinas administration initiated the PRONASOL program with the objective of alleviating poverty and strengthening the legitimacy of the PRI government.[108]

Following the short term management of the debt crisis the Mexican government started important economic reforms aiming at liberalizing and opening the economy to foreign trade and investment. Under the de la Madrid administration import liberalization measures were initiated that culminated in Mexico's signing of GATT in 1986. Besides to fighting inflation, the Economic Solidarity Pact of 1987 led to a further reduction of tariffs and import licensing requirements.[109] As a consequence of these liberalization measures Mexican non-oil exports rose from 5.5 billion US$ in 1981 to over 16 billion in 1990 with the automobile and maquiladora sector being the most important drivers of growth.[110] Moreover, large privatization programs reduced the enormous number of public enterprises in Mexico. Between 1983 and 1988 the government sold 122 state-owned enterprises. In this period the Mexican government was involved in only 13 of the 28 productive sectors in which it was active in 1982.[111]

During the sextenio of de la Madrids successor Salinas de Gortari the process of opening and liberalizing the economy accelerated and efforts were concentrated on promoting macroeconomic stability and a continuing opening of the economy to the world market. Tariffs were reduced and the restrictive FDI legislation was reviewed.[112] The output coverage of import licenses was reduced from 92% in 1985 to 20% in 1990. Average tariffs fell from 24% to 13% over the same period. An additional focus of Mexican efforts was to promote the export sector. The production coverage of export restrictions fell from 25% in 1987 to below 18% in 1990.[113] For the period between 1988 and 2000 Mexican exports grew at a yearly average of 15,1%. Public sector-specific industrial policy was reduced to allow for a better functioning of market processes.[114] From 1989 on the Mexican government continued the process of privatization by starting the sale of large public enterprises, some of them monopolies. Among the privatized enterprises were the telephone company TELMEX, the airlines MEXICANA and Aéro Mexcio, the copper mining

---

[107] See Krämer (1995a).
[108] For an overview of the PRONASOL program see Krämer (1995b). Otero (1996) states that PRONASOL was rather a political tool for avoiding electoral success of the opposition. He shows that PRONASOL tended to spend more where electoral competition from the PRD was more intense. See Otero (1996) p.15.
[109] See OECD (1992) p.30-36 and Lustig/Ros (1999) p.19-27.
[110] See Ros (1993) and Peters (2001).
[111] See Sánchez et al. (1993) and Krämer (1997) p.147-150.
[112] See paragraph 5.2.2.1.1.
[113] See OECD (1992) p.137-141.
[114] See Peters (2001) p.224-227 and Lustig/Ros (1999) p. 30-32.

company CANANEA, the insurer ASEMEX, several steel companies and 18 commercial banks.[115] The absolute number of public enterprise fell from 1155 in 1982 to 223 in 1992.[116]

By 1990 Mexico succeeded in bringing inflation down to rates around 20%. Low international interest rates as well as growing investor confidence in the Mexican reform process stimulated massive inflows of portfolio investment to Mexico leading to a real appreciation of the Peso. The current account deficit rose quickly and capital inflows led to a domestic credit boom in the absence of prudential supervisions in the financial sector. The enhanced international credibility Mexico gained through the signing of the NAFTA treaty was reflected in an enormous increase of FDI and other capital flows. The armed uprising in Chiapas and the assassination of the PRI presidential candidate Colosio in 1994 provoked the first foreign capital withdrawals finally leading to the substantial depreciation of the Peso. The dollar parity went from 4 pesos in December 1994 to 7.55 pesos in March 1995 when finally stopped by an emergency economic program involving the US government, the IMF and the Bank of International Settlements.[117] The so-called "Tequila-Crisis" was followed by a sharp recession of the Mexican economy. GDP dropped by 6.6% ,capital formation even by 30% and open unemployment nearly doubled in 1995. The Mexican crisis had a negative impact on Latin America as a whole.[118] However, recovery from the crisis was quick with growth rates of 5.1% in 1996 and 6.8% in 1997 due to growing export revenues and high fixed investment growth.[119]

Despite of the problems caused by the Tequila-Crisis for Mexico the decade of the 90s is characterized by a further integration of the country into the world economy and a continued liberalization of the foreign investment regime.[120] In the 90s Mexico negotiated the NAFTA and pursued various other bilateral free trade agreements with a variety of countries or regions. Mexico now participates in 13 free trade agreements (FTA's) and is currently engaged in negotiation with other partners.[121]

Figure 5.4 gives an overview over the multilateral and bilateral treaties Mexico signed recently. The large amount of bilateral agreements reflect the efforts of the Mexican administration to reduce the dependency of the national economy from the evolution of the US markets. Nevertheless NAFTA and the treaty with the EU are of particular importance to the Mexican economy given the large potential for further trade with and investment from these regions.

---

[115] See Sánchez et al (1993) p.102-104 and Lustig/Ros (1999).
[116] See OECD (1992) p.88-93.
[117] See OECD (1996a) p.20-25, Lustig/Ros (1999) p.34-39 and Ffrench-Davis (2000) p.195-205.
[118] See Ffrench-Davis (2000) p.195-205.
[119] See Lederman et al. (2001).
[120] For an overview of the Mexican trade liberalization see OECD (1996a).
[121] See WTO (2003) p.63.

Figure 5.4: Mexican Bilateral and Multilateral Free Trade Agreements

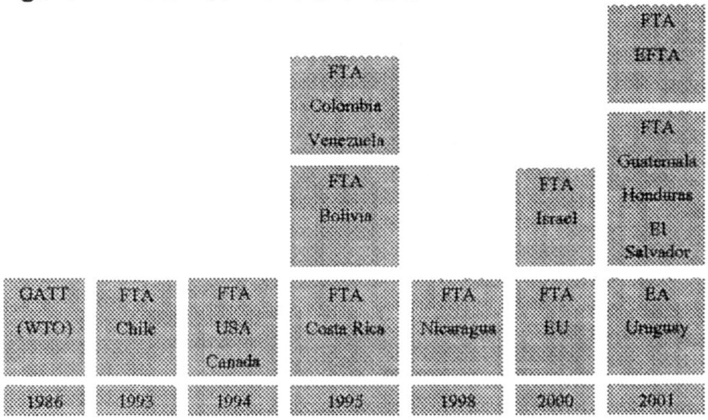

GATT (WTO)	FTA Chile	FTA USA Canada	FTA Colombia Venezuela / FTA Bolivia / FTA Costa Rica	FTA Nicaragua	FTA Israel / FTA EU	FTA EFTA / FTA Guatemala Honduras El Salvador / EA Uruguay
1986	1993	1994	1995	1998	2000	2001

Source: Consulado General de México, Hamburg, FTA stands for Free Trade Agreement while EA refers to Economic Agreements

Although Mexico up to now showed an impressive success in the implementation of economic reforms during the 90s, there still remains an important agenda of reforms. Modernizing the education sector, reducing the reliance on oil-revenues, enhancing the efficiency of public spending and fighting poverty are just a few examples that may be given here.[122] After having drawn a broad picture of the evolution of the Mexican economy during the last years the next paragraph is dedicated to the analysis of incoming FDI flows to Mexico and to the attitude towards foreign investors, as well as to developments in the national FDI legislation.

5.2.2 The Evolution of Foreign Investment to Mexico
5.2.2.1 The Mexican Foreign Investment Legislation
5.2.2.1.1 The Evolution of the National FDI Legislation
The policy of regulating FDI flows to Mexico can be traced back to the passing of the Mexican constitution in 1917 which already established restrictions and conditions on foreign acquisitions of land and concessions. Article 73 empowers congress to encourage the promotion of Mexican investment and regulation of foreign investment. However, the legal foundation for most regulation of foreign investment activity were the articles 27 and 28 of the constitution. Article 27 has three important provisions that have impacted the regulation of foreign investment. First, it grants sovereignty over national resources which in fact abolishes foreign private property rights for all subsurface mineral and petrol deposits. Second, it implements the so-called Calvo clause to which foreigners wishing to own property or to engage in business in the country had to agree. With this agreement the investor limits his rights with respect to a contract or his property and the means available to him of enforcing those rights to the same as are accorded by Mexican law to its own citizens. All other means like the right to seek diplomatic intervention or

---

[122] See OECD (2000).

the help of an international claims tribunal are waived. The breaking of this agreement implied the expropriation of the investor's assets or the ending of the contract or license.[123] Third, article 27 defined the so-called restricted zone that forbid foreign ownership within a zone of 100 km along the borders and 50 km along the shores. Article 28 identified strategic sectors of the economy that were reserved for the Mexican government and was the legal basis of many expropriations during the 20s and 30s with the most prominent example being the oil sector in 1938.[124]

The articles of the 1917 constitution reflect the revolutionary principle of "Mexicanization" and explain the tendency of Mexican politics to restrict the influence of foreigners on the economy. This fear of exploitation in turn, is a national heritage that resulted from the excessive dominance of foreign investors during the time of the Porfiriato. These constitutional rules based on revolutionary principles supported a restrictive Mexican policy towards FDI that predominated until the middle of the 80s when the aftermath of the debt crisis marked the beginning of a liberalization of the FDI regime in Mexico.[125]

In addition to these constitutional norms explicit legislation on FDI did not exist until the year 1944. Based on an executive decree from this year foreign investors had to obtain a permit issued by the Mexican Foreign Ministry for the acquisition of Mexican firms or other property.[126] In 1945 the Ministry issued an interim list of industries where a majority of Mexican capital would be required. Sectors mentioned on this list were transportation, radio broadcasting, motion pictures, publishing, advertising, fishing, and beverages.[127] In 1947 a commission composed of several Mexican ministries formulated general norms for the application of the 1944 decree. The aim of the commission was to "maintain the right equilibrium between national and foreign capital in investments that are made in Mexico". Eventually, the commission decided that Mexican capital should participate with at least 51% of total capital in any foreign investment although the application of this rule was subject to

---

[123] See Sandrino (1994), Wright (1971) and Vázquez Tercero (1971) p.111. The Calvo clause gained importance on the international stage when in 1974 the United Nations passed several resolutions for the establishment of a new economic order. A key component was the Charter of Economic Rights and Duties of States intended to strengthen the independence of developing nations. One main principle of the charter was that every state has the right to regulate foreign investment including the activities of multinational corporations and the right to expropriate alien property upon the payment of adequate compensation. Currently there is a consensus that an expropriation is a legitimate act of national autonomy provided that public welfare is fostered and that a fair compensation is granted. See Gudofsky (2000).

[124] The nationalisation in particular hit British and US investors. See Sandrino (1994) and Wright (1971) p.61-70. For a detailed analysis of the expropriation during the 20s and 30s see Gordon (1975).

[125] See Sandrino (1994).

[126] See Sandrino (1994).

[127] See Whiting (1992) p.71.

enormous discretion, that is, the Mexican government often granted exceptions.[128]

The strategy of import substitution led to an even more restrictive policy towards FDI during the 70s. FDI was limited in many important industries as steel, cement, glass, aluminium paper and fertilizers.[129] To facilitate the transfer of know-how and technology the government passed several laws that regulated the purchase of technology and licenses by Mexican and foreign firms. The law on inventions and trademarks that was passed in 1976 included restrictions on the use of international trademarks in Mexico.[130] The "Law to Promote Mexican Investment and Regulate Foreign Investment" passed in 1973 reflects this general tendency. The law restricted FDI in product groups that were reserved for public Mexican investment which included petroleum and other hydrocarbons, basic petroleum products, radioactive and strategic materials, nuclear energy, electricity, railroads, telegraphic and radio communications as well as banking. Moreover, FDI was restricted in product groups reserved exclusively for Mexican public or private investment. Among these sectors were radio, television, agricultural activities, road, air and maritime transportation as well as forestry, gas distribution and financial intermediation. In addition the law defined product groups in which FDI was only allowed up to a specific share of the firm's capital. For instance in mining FDI was limited to a 49% share of the firm's total capital. For secondary petrochemicals and the fabrication of automobile components the maximum share was at a level of 40%.

Although in absence of a specific regulation foreign equity participation should not exceed 49% of total capital, the law contained a grandfather clause according to which foreign holdings that already existed prior to the effective date of the new law were allowed to continue to exist as long as the proportion of local and foreign capital remained unchanged.[131] Table 5.4 gives an overview of the restrictions of the 1973 FDI law.[132]

Moreover, the law created two organizations to supervise and regulate FDI. The Comision Nacional de Inversiones Extranjeras (CNIE) was in charge of determining and regulating potential investment projects according to the national development strategy while the Registro Nacional de Inversiones Extranjeras was designed to provide statistical data about the operations of

---

[128] See Sanchez-Gamper (1989) and Pescador-Castañeda (1971).

[129] See Secretaría del trabajo y previsión social (1994) p.14.

[130] The most controversial part of the new law was an obligation to use international trademarks jointly with a trademark originally registered in Mexico. General Electric for example had to link its trademark with the partner of a Mexican joint venture: General Electric/Esamex. See Whiting (1992) p.108-136. Most of the laws that targeted technology transfer were revised when the Salinas administration prepared the joining of NAFTA and passed the Law for the Promotion and Protection of Industrial Property in 1991.

[131] See Whiting (1992) p.99.

[132] See paragraph 5.2.2.2 for an analysis of the law's effects on FDI flows to Mexico.

foreign companies in Mexico. Moreover, the CNIE had the power to pass regulation as to clarify the application of the law.[133]

Table 5.4: Restrictions of the 1973 FDI Law

Restriction	Sector
Foreign equity participation must not exceed 49% of total capital	All sectors (if no other regulation has been established)
Economic activity is reserved for the state	Petroleum and other hydrocarbons
	Basic petroleum products
	Radioactive and strategic materials
	Nuclear energy
	Electricity
	Railroads
	Telegraphic and radio communications
	Banking
Economic activity is reserved for Mexican citizens or the state	Radio
	Television
	Agricultural activities
	Road transport
	Air transport
	Maritime transport
	Forestry
	Gas distribution
	Financial intermediation

Source: Own Figure

Following the debt crisis Mexico embarked on a strategy of economic reform aiming at macroeconomic stability, privatization and liberalization. Part of the liberal reform program was opening the economy to foreign trade and investment. Nevertheless, the de la Madrid administration maintained the 1973 law on FDI and only changed the approach as to how the law was to be interpreted and applied. In 1984 the CNIE issued new guidelines for FDI with the objective to encourage investment in high priority areas as heavy machinery, electronic equipment, high technology products and tourism.[134] The guidelines were complemented by a list of activities in which foreign participation could foster national development and the CNIE signaled that it would even allow a foreign equity share of more than 50%.[135] These new guidelines mark a watershed for the evolution of Mexican foreign investment legislation. Following Mexico's *apertura* in 1985 the government further liberalized FDI by eliminating restrictions for petro-chemical investment and by engaging in a debt-equity swap program.[136]

---

[133] See Secretaría del trabajo y previsión social (1994) p.15.

[134] See UNCTC (1992) p.13-15.

[135] See Peres-Nuñes (1990a) p.41-46. One of the first multinational that took advantage of the liberalization was IBM that build a 100% owned production plant in Guadalajara in 1986. However, the negotiations with the Mexican government to obtain the permission for the majority ownership took nearly two years. See Whiting (1992) p.194-210.

[136] See Munro (1995) and Peres-Nuñes (1990a).

Efforts to open Mexico to foreign trade and investment continued under the succeeding administration. The National Development Plan of Salinas de Gortari assigned a key role to foreign capital since FDI was expected to create new employment, to provide the country with financial resources, to provide modern technology and to advance the country's efforts to increase manufactured exports.[137] Consequently the Mexican government further liberalized the investment law of 1973. The most important changes to the 1973 law were made in 1989 (Law for the Promotion of Foreign Direct Investment), 1993 (Law for Foreign Direct Investment),1996 (Reform of the Law for Foreign Direct Investment) and 1998 (Amendment to the Law for Foreign Direct Investment).[138] However, up to 1993 FDI was liberalized without changing the restrictive law of 1973 but by imposing liberal regulations for its application.[139] The new investment law issued in 1993 already anticipated Mexico's joining of NAFTA in 1994 and consequently continued to promote a further opening of the Mexican economy.[140] It was designed to "permit the opening of industries where foreign capital is desirable" and "to remove discretional administrative practices that led to uncertainties for investors".[141] Although the NAFTA investment chapter defined many restrictions on FDI to Mexico, most of them were determined to be phased out in the future.[142]

The basic framework of the current investment legislation in Mexico is still the Law for Foreign Investment of 1993. With the new law coming into effect the old law of 1973 and the decree of 1944 requiring the necessity for foreigners to obtain a permit by the government to acquire assets are repealed. Furthermore, Article 27 of the Constitution that established the Calvo clause and restricted private ownership of national resources was changed.[143] Although as a principle access to the Mexican market is free, the current legislation defines various exceptions from this general rule. The oil industry as well as the market for petrochemicals and electricity are still reserved for the state and not open to FDI. For several other sectors like for example television and radio broadcasting as well as development banks the law only permits investment from Mexican citizens or corporations. Furthermore, the Mexican investment law defines sectors with specific regulations where investments up to a certain threshold of 10%, 25% or 49% of total capital are allowed.[144] For certain sectors like for example the construction and operation of airports the CNIE is in charge of controlling investment from abroad. Moreover, the commission establishes policy guidelines regarding foreign investment,

---

[137] See UNCTC (1992) p.7.

[138] See UNCTC (1992) and Peters (2000) for an overview over the legislative changes.

[139] See Secretaría del trabajo y previsión social (1994) p.17-20. Munro (1995) states that regulating but not repealing the law was a strategy of Salinas de Gortari to avoid a battle in congress over liberalization.

[140] See Alexander (1995) for an overview of the 1993 Foreign Investment Act.

[141] See Secretaría del trabajo y previsión social (1994) p.21-22.

[142] See Rugman/Gestrin (1994). For a closer examination of the NAFTA Investment Chapter see paragraph 5.2.2.1.2.

[143] See Alexander (1995) p.77-79

[144] See Peters (2000).

determines its terms and conditions and establishes criteria for the application of the legal and regulatory provisions of the investment law. The CNIE is comprised of several ministers of government and a commitee of representatives that carry out daily functions.[145] Table 5.5 provides an overview of the current foreign investment legislation in Mexico.

Table 5.5: FDI Legislation in Mexico

FOREIGN INVESTMENT LAW (1993)

1) Foreign investment may participate in ANY proportion in the social capital of Mexican societies (Article 4) excepting:

I. Activities reserved for the State (Article 5)

II. Activities reserved for Mexicans (Article 6)

III. Activities that have a special regulation where specific percentages are determined (Article 7)

IV. Activities that need a favorable resolution from the Commission to participate in a percentage higher than 49% (Article 8)

2) Any acquisition of an interest in a Mexican corporation exceeding 49% of its capital stock requires a permission of the Commission, but only if the total value of the assets of such corporation is higher than an amount that is fixed annually by the Commission (Article 9)

3) Neutral Investment (Article 18):

Is a specially regulated investment, where foreign flows are not taken into account to determine the percentage of a foreign investment to a Mexican company. In the case of Fiduciary Institutions, it may be done through investment instruments which allow a monetary return for investors, but a limited right to vote in assemblies of the institutions. In other societies, neutral investment may be accounted for actions without the right to vote.

REFORM OF THE FOREIGN INVESTMENT LAW (1996)

1) Reforms to the specially regulated sectors are introduced:

Article 7, III includes a complemented list of activities that may participate up to a percentage of 49% in Mexican companies, which replaces the one existing in 1993.

In Article 8, the sectors which need a special permission from the commission in order to receive more than 49% FDI changes.

2) Regulation of acquisition of real property and trust is extended

3) The foreign individuals and entities intending to acquire real estate outside of the restricted zone or to obtain concessions for the exploration and development of mines and waters anywhere within Mexico, shall previously submit before the Ministry of Foreign Affairs and obtain the corresponding permit from that Ministry.

REGULATIONS TO THE FOREIGN INVESTMENT LAW (1998)

In this regulation procedures for applying the Foreign Investment Law are stated:

1) procedures needed to constitute societies, acquire permissions of neutral investment, register foreign investment and generally register as a society

2) In the list of reserved activities, some exceptions are determined.

3) Acquisition of real estate, exploitation of mines and national territorial waters, and trusts are further regulated

Source: Own figure

Investors who are willing to hold more than 49% of total shares of Mexican companies in these industrial sectors require a permission of this commission. As a general rule the law states that acquiring a majority stake (>49% of total capital) in a Mexican company requires a permission of the CNIE if the total

---

[145] See Alexander (1995) p.72-73 for an overview of the CNIE.

value of such a company exceeds an amount which the commission itself determines on an annual basis.[146]

Table 5.6: Restrictions on FDI to Mexico

Restriction	Sector
Economic activity is reserved for the state	Petroleum and other hydrocarbons
	Basic petro-chemical products
	Electricity
	Radioactive and strategic materials
	Nuclear energy
	Emission of money
	Telegraphic and radio communications
	Control and supervision of airports
Economic activity is reserved for Mexican citizens	National road transport
	Commerce of gasoline and petrol
	Radio and television broadcasting
	Credit unions
	Development banks
Sector specific regulations	International road transport (maximal foreign share of 49% of total capital)
	Cooperatives of production (10%)
	Satellite communication (49%)
	Automobile parts (49%)
	Construction (49%)
	Fishing (49%)
	Local and long distance telecom services (49%)
	Pension funds (49%)
	Water transport (49%)
	Production and distribution of explosives and arms (49%)
Investment of more than 49% of total capital requires an authorization of the NCFI	Exploration of minerals
	Shipping companies
	Construction of pipelines for the transport of petrol Oil-or gas-seeking
	Services related to railways and ports operation
	Administration, construction and operation of airports
	Private educational services
	Legal services

Source: Own Figure based on Peters (2000).

Currently there are no limitations for the repatriation of profits to home countries or other restrictions on balance of payment operations for foreign companies. Table 5.6 gives a short overview of the current sectoral restrictions for FDI in Mexico.[147]

---

[146] See Alexander (1995) p.69. In 1999 this asset value was 394 million peso, at that time about 40 million US$. See PRS Group (2000) p.23.

[147] A comprehensive overview of the current sector restrictions is given in table A.3 in Annex II.

Despite of liberalization and a further opening of the country, current legislation still leaves considerable power to the government for the control of FDI inflows. In particular the required permission of the CNIE for the acquisition of majority stakes leaves room for an influence of the government on foreign investment policy. In modifying the critical asset value which requires a permission of the CNIE the government possesses a powerful tool to influence amounts and structure of foreign investments to the country. To put it in other words, the government did not fully commit to a liberalization of FDI because it reserved considerable discretionary freedom to decide on a case to case basis. Although FDI to Mexico is highly welcome at the moment, the current legislation may also be applied in a more restrictive way if this general attitude changes in the future. This may be the case if the government is subject to high societal pressure as it was the case in 2003 when peasant organizations demanded a re-negotiation of the NAFTA regulations concerning agrarian products.[148] National FDI legislation however, is currently complemented by international law that will be reviewed in the next paragraph.

5.2.2.1.2 Investment Legislation of NAFTA and other Bilateral Agreements

In addition to national investment laws Mexico signed various multilateral and bilateral agreements which contain regulations on investment matters.[149] Among them the most prominent are NAFTA and the free trade agreement with the EU. Therefore, the content of the investment chapters of these two treaties will be briefly reviewed here. The signing of NAFTA not only confirmed the further integration of Mexico into the system of international trade but also marked the beginning of a new approach towards foreign investors. Beside the liberalization of trade the signing parties agreed to significant disciplines of how nationals of other parties are to be treated on another party's territory. Enhanced legal certainty and better protection of foreign property are essential elements of this convention. In Mexican law international treaties may be signed by the president and have to be ratified by the senate of the republic. Once ratified and being consistent with the national constitution international treaties become a full part of the national legislation and are comparable to constitutional norms.[150] As a consequence the provisions of NAFTA may be seen as a measure that enhances credibility of the Mexican government because they tie its hands on the international level. Opportunistic government behavior which has a long tradition in Mexican policy towards foreign investors

---

[148] Rubio et al. (1994) highlight that articles 25 and 28 of the Mexican constitution still permit the regulation of every field of economic activity including the nationalization of so-called strategic industries implying that Mexican constitution would allow for a step backward in economic liberalization. This is of particular importance in Mexico as demanding restrictions on FDI is still a viable tool for gaining populist votes. In 1996 for example members of the left wing opposition party PRD and even conservatives demanded new legislative limits on FDI. In addition, all efforts to permit foreign investment in petrochemicals and petroleum have been denied by the government. See PRS Group (1999) p.A10.

[149] For an overview see Siqueiros (2001).

[150] See Castro (2000) and Carbonell y Sánchez (1994).

thus becomes less likely. If arbitrary government intervention occurs, investors have the possibility to put forward a claim to an international dispute settlement tribunal.[151] Therefore, NAFTA ensures an enhanced protection of foreign property rights and fosters legal certainty of foreign investors by creating an organization with decisional power in international investment disputes.[152]

Chapter 11, the NAFTA Investment Chapter, extends significant protection to Mexican, US and Canadian investors who own or control investments in the territory of another party. The NAFTA Investment Chapter covers a NAFTA party or state as well as all business entities which are constituted or organized under the laws of a NAFTA Party. Moreover, the provisions of the NAFTA Investment Chapter are not only valid for investors from NAFTA parties but also for those having substantial business activities in NAFTA states. This implies that for example European enterprises with considerable activities in the U.S. also enjoy enhanced legal protection. Furthermore, the treaty covers past, present and future investors extending the protection of NAFTA also to those investors that have already been present in a member country before the agreement was signed and to those that are in the process of making an investment.[153]

Since chapter 11 includes 39 articles and 4 annexes, table 5.7 provides only an overview of the most important regulations of the NAFTA investment chapter. As a general rule signing parties are obliged by Article 1102 to treat NAFTA investors and their investments no less favorably than domestic investors. Article 1103 extends this general rule by stating that the signing parties have to treat investors from NAFTA states at least as favorable as other investments from third parties which is known as the most favored nation principle. Additionally NAFTA assures in Article 1105 that investors have to be treated "in accordance with international law including fair and equitable treatment and full protection and security."[154]

The imposition of performance requirements like domestic content, sourcing or trade balancing rules or technology transfer regulations is limited in Article 1106. Moreover, all monetary transfers of investors to their home countries related to investments are guaranteed in article 1109 of the treaty. Article 1110 of the Investment Chapter provides for the protection of foreign investment against nationalization, expropriation and other measures that lead to a

---

[151] For an overview of the NAFTA dispute settlement process in investment matters see Siqueiros (2001).

[152] For an overview over the policy towards foreign investors see paragraph 5.2.2.2. The NAFTA Investment Chapter represents a major change of policy towards international investors because adherence to the Calvo clause is given up and Mexico accepts general principles of international law concerning the protection of foreign property. Moreover, Mexico may be hold accountable for its conduct through a binding dispute settlement mechanism that is described in greater detail in this paragraph.

[153] See McIlroy (2002).

[154] This article reflects giving up adherence to the Calvo-clause.

"creeping expropriation" of investors. Confronted with the legacy of many expropriations of foreign property by Mexican administrations in the past this contractual safeguard is of particular importance for investors.[155] According to general international law, a state is free to adopt measures of expropriation given the existence of a public interest, a due process and the payment of a fair compensation.[156]

Table 5.7: Overview of the NAFTA Investment Chapter

Article	Content
Article 1102	NAFTA investors have to be treated like domestic investors
Article 1103	Most-Favored-Nation Principle
Article 1105	Investors have to be treated in accordance with international law
Article 1106	The imposition of performance requirements is limited
Article 1109	Guarantees all financial transfers that are related to an investment
Article 1110	Protection against expropriation, nationalization and creeping expropriation

Source: Own table

Adhering to these general principles article 1110 states that investments of NAFTA members may not be expropriated except for a public purpose, in accordance with due process of law and upon the payment of a fair compensation. Although the precise definition of creeping expropriation remains unclear, the article extents the protection beyond the coverage of direct expropriations implying a total loss of assets. The difference between a direct expropriation and a creeping expropriation is, that, unlike in the case of the former, the latter does not result in a property owner relinquishing title to his property, that is, a creeping expropriation does not result in a formal dispossession of property by its owner. Instead, a creeping expropriation

---

[155] For a short overview over the expropriations in Mexico see paragraph 5.2.2.2.

[156] Also de-facto expropriations are covered by international law. An OECD draft for the protection of private property states: "...applied in such a way as to deprive ultimately the alien of the enjoyment or value of his property, without any specific act being identifiable as outright deprivation. As instances, may be quoted excessive or arbitrary taxation; prohibition of dividend distribution coupled with compulsory loans; impositions of administrators; prohibition of dismissal of staff; refusal of access to raw materials or of essential export or import licenses." Cited by Sacerdoti (2000) p.120. A general problem of identifying creeping expropriation is drawing the line between general and discriminatory regulation. Likewise the determination of a legitimate public interest is problematic. Due compensation should correspond to the value of the property taken, be paid speedily and in a currency which the owner can transfer from the expropriating state. Under general international law States do not have to compensate for losses suffered in case of war or civil disturbances. See Sacerdoti (2000) p.121-125

implies that governmental action reduces the benefits which an investor may receive from his property by diluting his property rights.[157] This, in turn, is of particular importance as in the past the actions of the Mexican government to harm foreign investors have been far more subtle than outright expropriations.[158] For the settlement of investment disputes the NAFTA treaty provides a system of international arbitration. Investors who are convinced that a member government has broken the commitments of NAFTA can put forward a claim to an international dispute settlement institution that will decide on the matter. Furthermore, the treaty, as most of the other agreements as well, includes a section devoted to the resolution of private commercial disputes among parties in the free trade zone.[159]

The negotiation of a Free Trade Agreement with the EU extends the level of NAFTA investor protection to European MNEs implying that European firms now face a level playing field for investments in Mexico. Besides the progressive and reciprocal liberalization of trade in goods, in conformity the agreement also sets up a consultation mechanism with respect to intellectual property matters. Like the NAFTA treaty, it further provides for a liberalization of investment and related payments and establishes a dispute settlement mechanism for the case of conflicts.[160]

Investment chapters of bilateral agreements are important instruments to enforce legal certainty and property rights of foreign investors. The massive increase of FDI flows to Mexico following the passing of the NAFTA investment chapter shows that foreign investors took advantage of the

---

[157] For a detailed description of the legal situation see Gudofsky (2000) p.257-286.

[158] See paragraph 5.2.2.2 for a few examples. A wide spread practice was for example to restrict the import of necessary inputs for foreign firms to force them out of business. In their final statement on the arbitration case Metalclad vs. Mexico where the US firm claimed a violation of the NAFTA treaty before the investment dispute settlement tribunal the judges argued: "Thus, expropriation under the NAFTA includes not only open, deliberate, and acknowledged takings of property, such as outright seizure and/or formal or obligatory transfer of the title in favor of the host state, but also covert or incidental interference with the use of property which has the effect of depriving the owner, in whole or in significant part, of the use or reasonably-to-be effected economic benefit of property even if not necessarily to the obvious benefit of the host State". Cited by Weiler (2001) p.694.

[159] See Sandrino (1994), Rugman/Gestrin (1994) and Siqueiros (2001). For legal details of the investment settlement procedure see Gudofsky (2000). For an overview of the Mexican experiences with the arbitration mechanism see González de Cossio (2002). The up to now most prominent case of the investment dispute settlement process has been the case of the US waste disposal firm Metalclad. After acquiring a local waste disposal firm Metalclad was denied necessary permits for the operation of the facility. Later Metalclad was de-facto expropriated when the local governor declared the region of the facility an ecological reserve. The dispute settlement tribunal saw a violation of the NAFTA treaty and awarded 16.685 million dollars of indemnization to Metalclad. Mexico then initiated a suit before the revision court and part of the award was set aside. See Weiler (2001) and González de Cossio (2002) who argues that challenging the award Mexico send a negative message to the international investment community.

[160] See Consulado General de México (2001).

enhanced security of their investment projects. It further shows that the intensification of legal protection and the reduction of hazards for investors has proven an efficient strategy for Mexico to make it a more attractive destination for direct investment. In this respect the international agreements for the enforcement of investor rights have been an important step towards a better institutional framework for FDI in Mexico.[161]

> *"En vista de la experiencia de México en materia de inversiones extranjeras en la época de Porfirio Díaz, cuando México fue llamado madre de los extranjeros y madrastra de los Méxicanos, dados los sucesos dramáticos relativos al caso de la experiencia petrolera, y el fondo económico colonial de México, sería en verdad sorprendente que la masa de la población mexicana no viera al capital extranjero con suspicacia y hostilidad"* [162]

5.2.2.2 Mexican Foreign Investment Policy and Inflows of FDI to Mexico

Basically all Latin American countries have a long tradition of skepticism towards the presence of foreign companies which has affected local foreign investment policies in many ways.[163] As the citation above demonstrates, also for the Mexican population foreign investors have long been a symbol for the economic exploitation of the country from abroad. Hence, past and present Mexican foreign investment policy can only be fully understood being aware of the historical development of foreign business in the country.[164] Therefore, this paragraph briefly sketches the historical evolution of FDI flows to the country within the broader context of changing attitudes towards foreign investors in Mexico.

Since the aftermath of Mexican independence was marked by a massive loss of foreign capital due to political instability, politicians of both of the two prevailing streams of political thought at that time, liberalism and conservatism, were convinced of the necessity to implement policies that would attract FDI to make up for the massive flight of capital during the post-independence years.[165] In reaction to this policy France and Britain were the origins of the first modest FDI flows to Mexico which were mainly destinated to mining and

---

[161] The bilateral investment agreements are part of an international strategy of risk mitigation. See paragraph 5.4.2.

[162] Mosk (1951) cited by Pescador-Castañeda (1971) p.99.

[163] An early explanation of this scepticism is given by Wionczek (1966).

[164] See Vernon (1966a) who describes the Mexican dilemma with the following lines: "Confronted with a great flow of industrial investment coming principally from the United States, the reaction of a succession of Mexican administrations has been understandingly ambivalent. On the one hand, no president of Mexico could afford to embrace the presence of the foreign investor; on the other hand, this particular breed of investor was obviously being helpful to the Mexican economy in a number of different ways: in helping to tide over the short-term pressures on the Mexican balance of payments; in helping to meet the challenges of the import replacement program which Mexico so badly wished to achieve; and in bringing technology of an advanced kind into the Mexican economy." Vernon (1966a) p.112. In this context Root speaks of the necessity for host governments to balance economic benefits and political cost of FDI. See Root (1994) p.640-644. Fayerweather (1973) discusses how host country nationalism affects MNEs.

[165] See Camp (2003) p.33.

retail trade.[166] Despite of earlier efforts to promote FDI Mexico experienced the first wave of FDI flows under the government of Porfirio Díaz (1876-1911) which for the first time ended the political instability of the post-independence years. Díaz and his economic advisors (científicos) were convinced of the need to achieve higher economic growth through enhanced FDI from Europe and the United States.[167] Restored political stability and the liberal economic policy of the Díaz administration that largely neglected the interest of workers and farmers led to large inflows of foreign capital from those regions, in particular for infrastructure projects as railways and other transports or electricity. FDI however, was not limited to infrastructure projects but also went to mining, the construction of farms and to the oil sector. Although the available data is not fully reliable, it is estimated that in 1910 FDI represented a share of approximately 70% of total investment in Mexico.[168] Despite of the presence of European companies in Mexico the inflow of US capital dominated during the Porfiriato.[169] Much of the US capital went to the north of the country for example to the mines of Sonora and Chihuahua or the smelting industry dominated by Guggenheim interests as well as to the construction of railways.[170] In 1911 total foreign investment amounted to 1.7 billion US$ of which 650 million was from the US, 500 million from Britain and 450 million from France. The liberal policy during the Porfiriato eventually led to a massive concentration of national wealth in the hand of foreigners. It is estimated that by the end of the Díaz era foreign capital dominated every area of productive enterprise except for agriculture and the handicraft industries.[171] It is estimated that the participation of foreign capital in mining was 97.7%, in petroleum 100%, in electricity 87.2%, in railroads 61.8%, in banking 76.7%, and in industry 85%.[172] Moreover, the agricultural policy of the government implied that substantial amounts of Mexican territory fell into foreign hands which should later turn out to be an important reason for upcoming antiforeignism during the revolution.[173] Even before the end of the Díaz rule there was evidence of a growing discontent both within and outside government with this foreign domination that culminated in expropriations in the railway sector and an attempt to limit foreign ownership in mining and the extraction of petrol.[174] Growing domination of foreign investors and a strict laissez-faire liberalism of the government finally provoked the outbreak of social unrest among the

---

[166] See Pescador-Castañeda (1971) p.69-73. The author neglects that in fact the Spanish conquest of the Aztec empire already marked the beginning of an integration into the international economy and flows of foreign investment.

[167] For an overview of the FDI policy of the Díaz administration see Wright (1971), Gordon (1975) or Pescador-Castañeda (1971).

[168] See Peters (2000) p.10.

[169] Among the European companies was Siemens that produced Electricity in the Valley of Mexico. British investment was concentrated in mining with many Mexican mine shares being listed on the London Stock Exchange. See Pescador-Castañeda (1971).

[170] See Pescador-Castañeda (1971) and Knight (2000) p.128.

[171] See Wright (1971) p.53-57.

[172] See Whiting (1992) p.60.

[173] See Wright (1971) p.53-57. It is estimated that in 1910 foreigners owned roughly one seventh of the land surface of Mexico. See Vernon (1963) p.50.

[174] See Wright (1971) p.60 and Vernon (1963) p.40.

Mexican citizens initiating the Mexican Revolution. It is argued that to a certain extent the revolution was a reaction to excessive foreign presence with MNEs being accused of "exploiting" the country and transferring excessive monopoly profits abroad.[175]

The revolution marked the end of the period of liberal policies towards foreign investors since the revolutionaries eagerly sought to enforce national sovereignty and to reduce foreign dependence of Mexico. The new Mexican constitution of 1917 embodied the main principles of this revolutionary movement and was the beginning of a period of more than 60 years of extensive foreign investment regulation by Mexican governments.[176] Following the military phase of the revolution foreign investors were hesitant to risk much new capital in the country. The oil industry was the only sector where the value of foreign investment exceeded pre-revolution figures. The decline in FDI continued with the onset of the great depression. Besides the depressing impact of the world wide economic crisis a main reason for declining investment flows was the presidency of Cárdenas who proclaimed a "Mexicanization" of the economy as policy goal. In reaction to the enormous influence that MNEs exerted in Mexico, in particular in the oil sector, the Cárdenas administration was characterized by outright hostility towards foreign capital flows. This hostility culminated in the nationalizations of the late 30s which included major redistributions of private owned land, the railroad system and the oil industry leading to a further decrease in investor confidence.[177] Between 1926 and 1940 most of the large multinational investments in agriculture were expropriated.[178] In contrast to the preponderant rule of foreign investment under Díaz, during the Cárdenas administration the share of foreign capital fell to approximately 15% of total investment. In 1940 total foreign investment reached an amount of under 500 million being only slightly more than one quarter of the level in 1920.[179] Despite of the decline in total numbers FDI increased in the manufacturing sector with firms like Ford and General Motors establishing plants in Mexico during the 20s and 30s.[180]

Cárdenas' successors Camacho and Aleman tried to improve the climate for foreign investment by settling the obligations, as for example the

---

[175] See Munro (1995) p. 121. Vernon argues that the economic policy of the Díaz rule deeply influenced later Mexican policy: "The stamp of Porfirian policy was so deep on Mexico's economy that the traces can still be glimpsed in the 1960s. The Porfirian policy regarding foreign capital, for instance, still provides part of the emotional backdrop against which foreign investors are judged today in Mexico's economy." Vernon (1963) p.39.

[176] See Sandrino (1994).

[177] See Pescador-Castañeda (1971) p.88-94. For a detailed analysis of the expropriation of the oil industry see Knight (1988). Vernon (1966a) argues that the nationalizations of the 1930s reflect the public opinion of the time. Indeed Diego Rivera's mural in the presidential palace of Mexico City where greedy and debauched Wall Street millionaires are depicted confirms this argument.

[178] See Munro (1995) p.130.

[179] See Wright (1971) p.61-70.

[180] See Cárdenas (2000b) p.181-182.

compensation of American Oil Companies, inherited from the previous government. During the war years FDI increased slowly with total foreign investment rising from 450 million US$ in 1940 to 575 million US$ in 1946.[181] In particular Alemán tried to attract foreign capital that was needed to promote economic development by convincing foreign investors, in particular from the US, that their capital was safe in Mexico.[182] In spite of the urgent need for investment in the electricity industry the government did not succeed in attracting investment of foreigners because they saw their assets endangered due to the in the long run unstable political environment in Mexico.[183] Nevertheless, during the rule of Alemán FDI accelerated again reaching an amount of nearly 730 million US$ by 1952. Growing FDI inflows went hand in hand with a drastic change in the preferred target sectors of foreign investors whose main focus shifted from primary materials to manufacturing to take advantage of the growing domestic market. Whereas in 1940 the share of the traditional sectors like mining, public utilities and transportation accounted for 90% of total FDI this value fell to only 41% in 1956. For the same time FDI in manufacturing rose from a share of below 1% in 1940 to a share of 46% in 1956.[184] The enormous increase in manufacturing FDI reflected the beginning protection of the domestic market initiating the strategy of import substitution. Faced with rising tariffs, MNEs that used to export to Mexico, established plants in the country to take advantage of the dynamic and protected Mexican market.[185]

Figure 5.5 depicts the evolution of FDI flows to the Mexican economy from 1940 to 1970 clearly indicating the dynamic development of FDI during the late 60s.[186] However already the upward swings of FDI during the 40 and 50s led to demands of Mexican industrialists represented by the industrial chambers Canacintra and Concamin for limiting FDI and fostered "mexicanization".[187] The skeptical attitude towards FDI gained momentum during the sextenio of López Mateos who limited foreign participation in certain industries and promoted the nationalization of the electric power industry by means of discriminatory regulation policy although the government was careful to avoid the public offending of foreign investors by offering a compensation.[188]

---

[181] See Wright (1971) p.71-76.

[182] See Sanchez-Gamper (1989).

[183] See See Pescador-Castañeda (1971) p.97. Vernon argues that since the late 1930s new foreign investment in electricity was low due to continuous expropriation threats by the Mexican government. As a consequence dim-outs and failures grew common in Mexico. See Vernon (1966a) p.105-109.

[184] See Wright (1971) p.71-76 and Sanchez-Gamper (1989). For a detailed analysis of the structure of Mexican FDI see paragraph 5.1.2.3.

[185] See Cárdenas (2000b) p.187-188.

[186] It has to be noted that the reliability of the older data on FDI to Mexico is questionable. Therefore, it has to interpreted carefully. However, the data set that has been used here was published by the Mexican central bank and is therefore the best available data set as most of the other consulted publications also rely on it.

[187] See Cárdenas (2000b) p.192-193.

[188] See Whiting (1992) p.75. The nationalization was celebrated by the Mexican public with posters reading: Land-1917, Oil-1938, Electricity-1960".

Figure 5.5: FDI inflows to Mexico 1940-1970 (in Million US$)

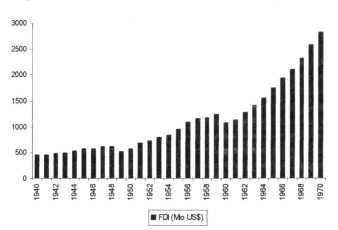

Source: Own figure using data from Sépulveda/Chumacero (1973).

In 1961 the government continued its efforts to "mexicanize" by forbidding new mining concessions and limiting the duration of existing concessions of foreign investors. The policy to displace foreign investors also continued in other sectors of the economy.[189] Also foreign ownership of forestry and real estate was further restricted under the López Mateos rule.[190] Despite the absence of legal restrictions on FDI the Mexican administration found other ways to limit foreign participation for example by withholding tax concessions or necessary import licenses. As a consequence of this policy and an general economic downturn foreign investment at the beginning of the 60s fell to levels below amounts in 1956. The decline of FDI flows provoked various governmental efforts to regain investor confidence and in the second half of the López Mateos rule FDI flows rose again.[191] Despite of these efforts, the share of FDI in total capital accumulation fell to 5% during the 60s.[192]

The new government of Díaz Ordaz proclaimed that FDI was welcome but that it should be preferably associated in a minority position. His term initiated with the lifting of restriction on incoming FDI flows in sectors as fertilizers, insecticides, basic chemicals and food products.[193] Due to this declarations and promising outlooks for the Mexican economy FDI flows accelerated during the second half of the 60s. Nevertheless, the Mexican government continuously promoted its goal of further "mexicanizing" the economy with the biggest example being the nationalization of the sulphur industry. Although the transaction consisted in a public bid for 66% of total capital of foreign enterprises, there is evidence that the Mexican government exerted pressure

---

[189] See Wright (1971) p.80-86.
[190] See Whiting (1992) p.75.
[191] See Wright (1971) p.80-86.
[192] See Cárdenas (2000b) p.192-193.
[193] See Whiting (1992) p.76.

to achieve the nationalization of the US company. Moreover, the government limited the acquisition of Mexican firms and forbid foreign participation in Mexican financial institutions. The sulphur case and the other restrictions on FDI contributed to cooling investor enthusiasm of the previous years.[194] In 1965 a series of decrees forbid any foreign participation in the capital of Mexican banks, insurance companies, bonding companies and investment companies.[195]

During the 70s skeptical attitudes towards foreign investors grew which was reflected in the passing of a new investment law in 1973 that restricted foreign participation to 49% of total capital.[196] This law was a reaction to the rapid growth of FDI in Mexico, a large part of which were acquisitions of Mexican firms by foreign companies.[197] Nevertheless capital inflows to Mexico did not totally loose momentum. Instead, the years preceding the debt crisis were marked by a massive upswing in FDI flows spurred by the pre-crisis boom of the Mexican economy. High domestic growth rates and the oil boom attracted foreign investors and by 1981 FDI reached a peak.

Figure 5.6 and figure 5.7 depict the evolution of FDI flows to Mexico since 1970 as yearly flows in constant US$ and as percentage of GDP.

Figure 5.6: FDI Inflows to Mexico 1970-2000 (in Million US$ of 1995)

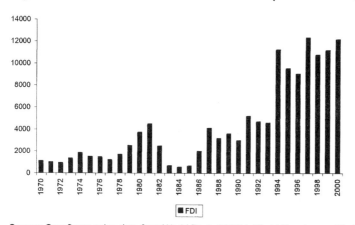

Source: Own figure using data from World Bank (2002b), World Development Indicators.

Despite of the restrictive policy on FDI that culminated in the 1973 law, FDI experienced no important declines and showed an upward dynamic that, with a minor decline between 1976 and 1978, continued during the early 80s. The

---

[194] See Wright (1971) p.86-94 and Whiting (1992) p.77-79.

[195] See Whiting (1992) p.77.

[196] For an overview of the legislation of 1973 see paragraph 5.2.2.1.1.

[197] Whiting describes in greater detail the positions of different Mexican interest groups towards a new legislation on FDI. See Whiting (1992) p.80-107.

decline during the 1976-78 period may not be solely attributed to the 1973 law since FDI also has been influenced by the global recession following the 1973-74 oil crisis. Between 1978 and 1981 excellent growth prospects of the Mexican Economy that were bolstered by the discovery of large oil reserves implied an enormous stimulation of FDI flows and average flows doubled compared to the 1974-1977 period.[198]

Figure 5.7: FDI Inflows to Mexico as a percentage of GDP 1970-2000

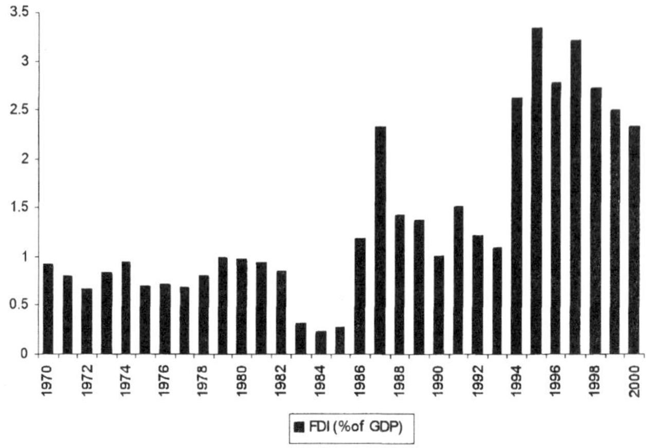

Source: Own figure using data from World Bank (2002b), World Development Indicators.

As the analysis of Mexican FDI data does not reflect a negative impact of the restrictive legislation of 1973 it is interesting to see if Mexico lost FDI relative to other host countries. Mexico's share in worldwide FDI is depicted in figure 5.8. Though it must be stressed that there is no way of knowing for sure what the level of FDI would have been without the passing of the legislation the analysis of Mexico's share in worldwide FDI does not confirm the hypothesis that Mexico lost FDI in relation to other countries. Instead, it may be argued that, since Mexico already passed restrictions on FDI in the years preceding the new law, the 1973 law was more a codification of yet existing rules than complete new legislation.[199] In contrast figure 5.8 clearly mirrors the increase of FDI preceding the debt crisis.

---

[198] See Peres-Nuñez (1990a).
[199] See Whiting (1992) p.90.

Figure 5.8: Mexico's Share in Worldwide FDI 1970-2000

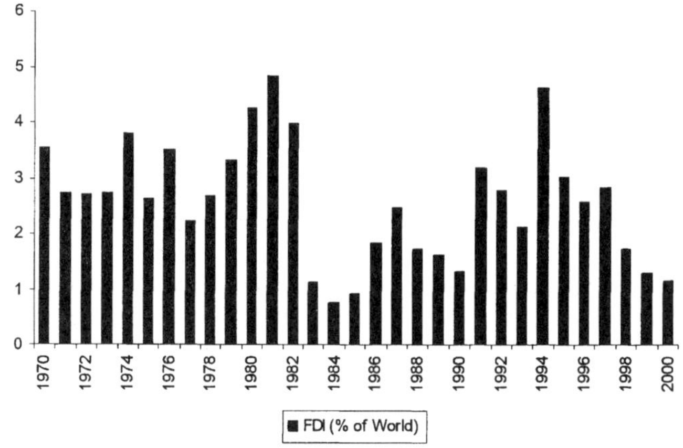

Source: Own Figure with data from World Bank (2002b), World Development Indicators.

Therefore, the new legislation only formalized more drastic actions by the Mexican government that had already been taken earlier when foreign equity participation was limited in many industries and foreign copper mining firms were nationalized during the late 60s and early 70s.[200] This governmental policy and the hostile rhetoric of president Echeverría against foreign corporations, that according to his view created "chains of dependency", already increased concerns of international investors before.[201] Falling FDI flows in the period from 1969 to 1972 are a support for the hypothesis that the actions that preceded the passing of the law were more influential than the law itself.[202]

The massive decline of FDI in the first half of the 80s is due to the outbreak of the Latin American debt crisis that began with Mexico's moratorium on international debt in 1982. Nevertheless, it also reflects the perception of industrialized countries that legal protection of FDI in developing countries in a time of such political and economic uncertainty was insufficient.[203] The value of FDI flowing to Mexico dropped from an annual average of 2.5 billion US$ in 1980-1981 to 0.4 billion US$ in 1983-1985.[204] The liberal reforms of the post-crisis years were accompanied by a consecutive opening of the economy to FDI leading to growing inflows from the mid 80s on. However, it must be stressed that the extremely high inflows of FDI in 1986 and 1987 are biased by the introduction of a debt-equity swap program that permitted the swap of public debt against shares in public or private enterprises. Consequently, flows

---

[200] See Munro (1995).
[201] See Philip (1992) p.81.
[202] See Munro (1995).
[203] See Sandrino (1994).
[204] See OECD (1992).

in 1988 decreased heavily when the program was suspended in 1987.[205] The implementation of the Brady plan to tackle the Latin American debt problem and a further liberalization of the investment law in 1989 accelerated FDI.

During the 90s growing inflows continued as a consequence of growing stability, further liberalization of the investment regime but also due to the growing worldwide investment flows to developing countries. While worldwide FDI flows between 1985 and 1990 averaged 142 billion US$ annually the annual average for the years 1990 to 1998 was 336 billion.[206] Mexico participated successfully in this upswing of FDI to developing countries. The joining of NAFTA in 1994 led to a further increase in FDI, reflecting higher investor certainty due to the protection of the NAFTA Investment Chapter and the access for investors to the US market. However, already the negotiations of NAFTA that were begun in 1991 and the new investment law of 1993 stimulated FDI in Mexico as is depicted in figures 5.6 and 5.7.[207] With the starting of NAFTA in 1994 FDI inflows to Mexico attained levels of around 3% of GDP, a level that with exception of 1987, a year that is biased by debt-equity-swaps programs, has never been attained before. Mexico's stock of FDI rose from 37.1 billion US$ in 1990 to 81.5 billion US$ at the end of 1998 and average flows represented more than 15% of the country's gross fixed capital formation.[208] In 1999 Mexico was the third important recipient of FDI in Latin America and the Caribbean.[209] FDI inflows maintained a high level with a short decline in investment in 1995 and 1996, which may be attributed to the recession following the Tequila crisis. However already in 1997 FDI flows were superior to 1994 when the effect of the Asian crisis implied lower inflows in 1998 until flows consolidated again in 1999 and 2000. For the next years the projections for FDI flows to Mexico seem positive. The further liberalization in the framework of NAFTA and the continuing efforts to enhance investor confidence point to a further growth of FDI in the future.

To sum up, Mexico's policy towards foreign investment has undergone drastic changes during the last century. The liberal economic policy of the Porfiriato was followed by a occasionally aggressive nationalistic policy that limited and restricted FDI in Mexico. This nationalistic development policy has been pursued for many decades until the outbreak of the debt crisis highlighted the economic inefficiencies of this model. Despite the initial success, economic reforms and liberalization of FDI are relatively new phenomena in Mexican economic policy implying that societal resistance against this policy is still high. Growing electoral support for the left-wing PRD in the midterm election 2003

---

[205] See Peres-Nuñez (1990a). Schinke estimates that from 1985 to 1989 on average 43% of FDI and Portfolio Investment in Argentina, Brazil, Chile and Mexico were financed by debt equity swaps. See Schinke (1993) p.97.

[206] See Ramirez (2002).

[207] The Bank of Mexico writes: "Direct investment into Mexico has increased substantially, owing to improved confidence, structural change, and the prospect of a North American Free Trade Agreement with the United States and Canada." Banco de México (1993) p.8.

[208] See Ramirez (2002).

[209] See UNCTAD (2000).

and the resistance of "conservative" politicians inside the PRI, which promote a halt of liberal reforms may serve as a hint to demonstrate the existence of these societal forces. In presence of this revisionist forces in the Mexican society international lock-in mechanisms like NAFTA gain fundamental importance for the country.[210]

5.2.2.3 The Structure and Geographical Origins of FDI to Mexico

Traditionally FDI flows to Mexico have been largely concentrated in the primary sector and in particular extractive industries since for the Spanish the extraction of precious metals from the colonies of the New World was the main focus. This traditional pattern changed slightly when the government of Porfirio Díaz promoted the development of the national infrastructure and in particular the construction of railroads. Apart from railways FDI was largely concentrated in mining, the oil industry and other agricultural products whereas manufacturing and commerce only received a minor share.Figure 5.9 depicts the structure of FDI to Mexico in 1911, the last year of the Díaz rule.[211]

Figure 5.10 depicts the geographical origins of FDI flows to Mexico for the same year. Due to the geographic proximity and the great economic an political influence the United States were the most important source of FDI being responsible for more than 40% of total FDI. The second rank was taken by British investors with a share of slightly more than 30% whose investments were largely concentrated in mining and the oil industry. French investors followed on the third place holding a share of 20%.

Figure 5.9: Structure of Mexican FDI in 1911

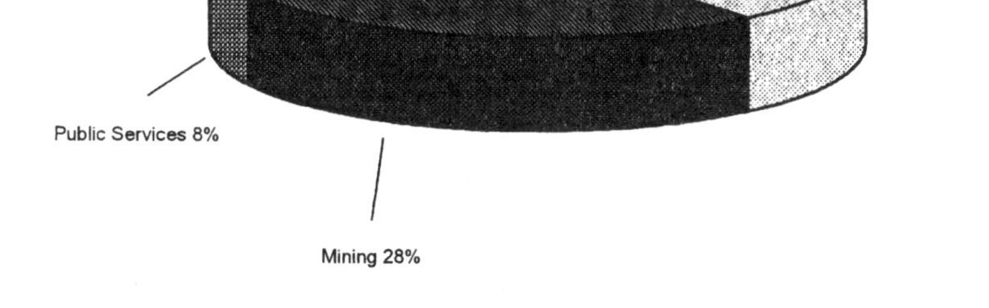

Source: Own figure based on data of Wright (1971) p.54.

---

[210] See paragraph 5.4.2 for an analysis of the effects of Mexico's internationalization strategy.
[211] It has to be noted that the reliability of the older data on FDI to Mexico is questionable. Therefore, it has to interpreted carefully.

While the geographical origin of foreign investment did not alter considerably and the dominant position of US FDI should prevail in the future, the sectoral distribution of FDI flows to Mexico experienced a considerable change.

Figure 5.10: Geographical Origins of Mexican FDI in 1911

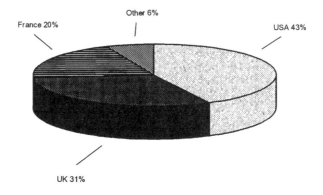

Source: Own figure based on data of Wright (1971) p.54.

More and more foreign investors began to invest in the manufacturing sector while traditional strong sectors as for example mining experienced a sharp decline. There are many reasons for this continuous upgrading of the sectoral FDI distribution. First, since the railway sector and the petroleum industry were nationalized in the 1930s Mexican governments made enormous efforts to mexicanize "strategic" industries of the primary sector. Although already the constitution of 1917 stated that all subsoil wealth belonged to the Mexican people, it took several years before these sectors were totally in the hands of Mexicans.

In the mining sector for example, laws that limited foreign ownership were not passed before the 1960s although over time the government ensured Mexican ownership in the primary sector and in other industries which were considered as strategic. Second, the growing domestic market protection induced tariff hopping FDI in the manufacturing sector since foreign firms that used to export manufacturing products to Mexico now transferred their production across the border to avoid tariffs and to benefit from the protected and fast growing domestic market.

Figure 5.11 depicts the structure of cumulated incoming FDI to Mexico between 1940 and 1950. Compared to 1911 FDI in the industrial sector rose significantly to a share of 19%, which was nearly equivalent to FDI in the mining sector. At the same time the share of FDI in commerce experienced a fast growth.

Figure 5.11: Structure of Mexican FDI in 1940-1950 (cumulated flows)

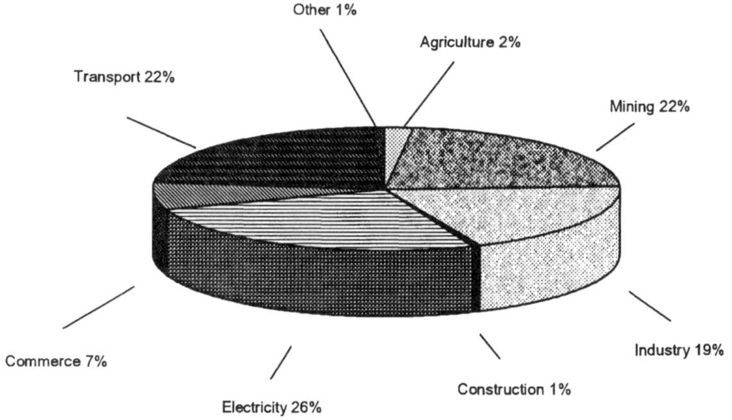

Other 1%

Agriculture 2%

Transport 22%

Mining 22%

Commerce 7%

Industry 19%

Electricity 26%

Construction 1%

Source: Own figure based on data by Sépulveda/Chumacero (1973).

These structural changes of FDI to Mexico endured during the 60s and 70s. As figure 5.12 shows for the period from 1960-1970, FDI in the industrial sector passed to an impressive share of 69% while FDI in commerce rose to levels of 17% of total incoming flows. On the other hand, mining that still made up for 22% between 1940 and 1950 passed to a share of 8% of total flows from 1960-1970. FDI in transport and communication passed from a level of 22% to a share of below 1% of cumulated inflows.

Figure 5.12: Structure of Mexican FDI in 1960-1970 (cumulated flows)

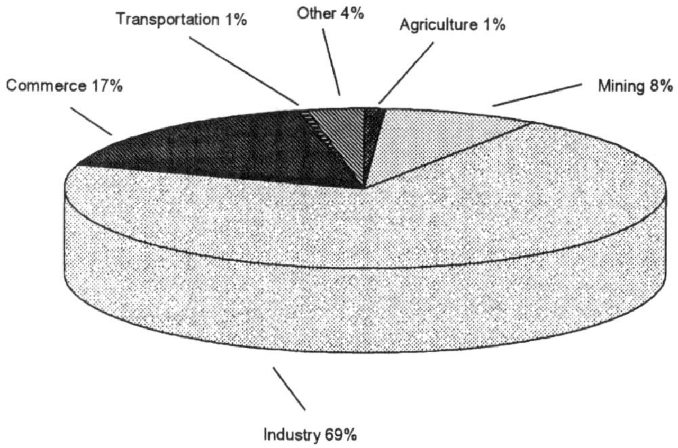

Transportation 1%   Other 4%   Agriculture 1%

Commerce 17%

Mining 8%

Industry 69%

Source: Own figure based on data by Sépulveda/Chumacero (1973).

The nationalization of the electricity sector implied a decline of FDI from a share of 26% for 1940-1950 to levels of below 1%. The share of FDI to construction remained constant at a low level. Therefore, between 1940 and 1970 the fastest growing recipient sectors were commerce and the industrial sector while traditional sectors as mining, transport or communication were in constant decline. Although already low in 1950, the share of agricultural FDI further fell to levels of around 1%.

During the 70s and 80s this general trend continued since the manufacturing sector continued to receive the lion share of incoming FDI. From the mid 70s to the end of the 80s the share of the industrial sector in total FDI reached 75%. For the same period the share of the mining sector constantly declined from 6.3% in 1975 to 1.5% in 1989. Likewise the share of commerce declined from 11.4% in 1975 to 7.1% in 1989. The share of FDI in agriculture constantly kept at a low level of under 1%. The fastest growing sector for this period has been the service sector rising from a share of 7.0% in 1975 to 24.7% in 1989.[212] Figure 5.13 showing the sectoral distribution of cumulated FDI for the time period 1994-1998 highlights that during the 90s the role of the manufacturing sector remained strong since its share of FDI was 62% with 28% of it flowing to the maquila sector.

Figure 5.13: Structure of Mexican FDI from 1994 - 1998 (cumulated flows)

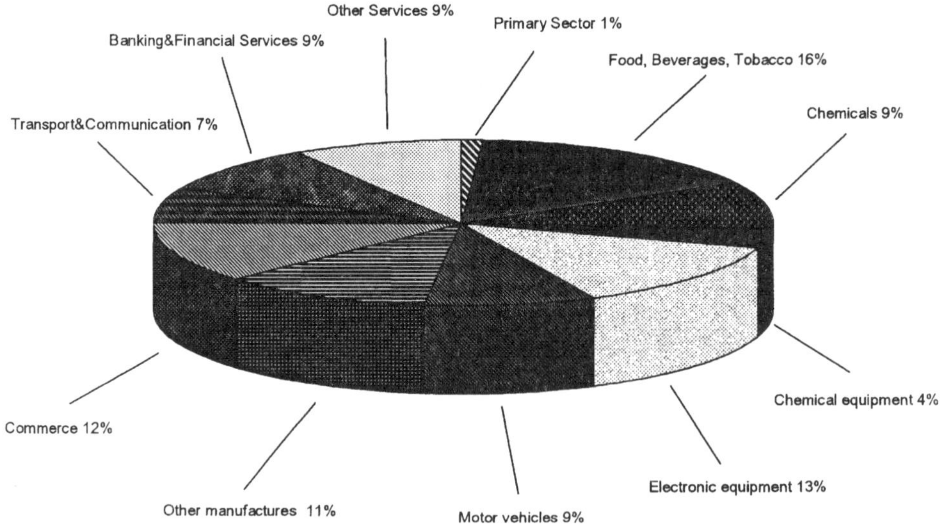

Source: CEPAL (2000) p. 102.

---

[212] See Ortiz (1994) p.168-171.

During the 90s the structure of FDI flows to Mexico has been affected by the continuing liberalization of the national FDI legislation. In particular the service sector in Mexico experienced a fast growth of incoming FDI flows. For the period 1994-1998 37% of total FDI went to the service sector with commerce, telecommunication and the financial sector being the most important recipient sectors. A great fraction of these FDI flows to the service sector consisted of international M&A transactions as many foreign investors entered the Mexican market by purchasing blocks of shares in financial institutions or local retail chains.[213]

Figure 5.14 illustrates the geographical origins of FDI flows to Mexico from 1994-2002. Despite of considerable changes in the sectoral structure of FDI geographical origins of FDI only changed slowly as the lion share of FDI flows to Mexico still comes from the US making up for 63% of total FDI. Among European nations the share of British FDI declined considerably over time with the Netherlands and Spain now holding higher shares of FDI to Mexico.

Figure 5.14: Geographical Origins of Mexican FDI 1994-2002 (cumulated flows)

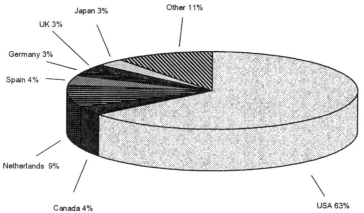

Source: Own figure based on data from Dirección General de Inversión Extranjera

Analyzing the local distribution of FDI flows inside Mexico reveals that not all regions of the country equally profited from the dynamic evolution of FDI flows to Mexico. Table 5.8 indicates that the Federal District (Mexico City) received the lion share of incoming FDI with 60.8% of incoming flows for the period from 1999 to 2002. If the State of Mexico is added, the share of the Federal District increases to 65.3% of total incoming FDI. Moreover, the nearby Puebla which is an important center of automobile production receives 2% of incoming FDI. For the rest of the country the structure of incoming FDI clearly mirrors the north-south divide of economic development in Mexico. While the northern

---

[213] See CEPAL (2000) p.101-105.

states Nuevo León, Baja California, Chihuahua, Tamaulipas and Sonora received shares of 9.2%, 5.7%, 4.4%, 2.5% and 1.4% respectively, southern states like Chiapas, Oaxaca, Michoacán or Campeche received 0.1 or less of total FDI.

Table 5.8: Regional Distribution of FDI in Mexico (in thousands of US$)

States	1999	2000	2001	2002	Accumulated 1999-2002	Share %
FDI Total	12,856,062.6	15,484,403.8	25,334,517.0	9,696,385.2	63,371,368.6	100.0
Aguascalientes	68,152.4	59,991.7	86,268.8	8,032.0	222,444.9	0.4
Baja California	1,133,124.8	952,735.8	775,594.9	772,580.4	3,634,036.0	5.7
Baja California Sur	87,340.3	54,609.8	64,928.6	97,033.4	303,912.1	0.5
Campeche	3,035.7	11,353.2	-21,414.4	17,981.1	10,955.6	0.0
Coahuila	166,699.1	201,426.2	128,130.7	109,071.2	605,327.2	1.0
Colima	4,203.3	7,045.0	1,382.0	4,153.2	16,783.6	0.0
Chiapas	3,326.8	2,209.5	-902.8	978.4	5,612.0	0.0
Chihuahua	583,975.3	940,386.8	693,771.0	585,155.0	2,803,288.1	4.4
Distrito Federal	5,915,599.1	7,582,778.4	19,478,996.7	5,525,381.3	38,502,755.5	60.8
Durango	7,113.6	5,255.4	4,214.6	80,571.7	97,155.2	0.2
Guanajuato	135,909.0	71,123.7	206,300.6	123,146.6	536,479.9	0.8
Guerrero	34,228.7	10,203.0	11,039.7	6,552.9	62,024.2	0.1
Hidalgo	747.8	4,731.8	8,705.3	966.8	15,151.7	0.0
Jalisco	526,638.0	1,028,372.1	257,996.4	129,916.4	1,942,922.9	3.1
Estado de México	1,369,628.2	426,952.9	687,617.1	368,669.1	2,852,867.4	4.5
Michoacán	5,236.9	28,062.7	3,066.1	3,651.5	40,017.2	0.1
Morelos	145,997.2	44,922.5	3,114.1	123.5	194,157.3	0.3
Nayarit	14,287.5	37,539.7	32,130.6	12,714.2	96,672.0	0.2
Nuevo León	1,317,145.7	2,017,144.6	1,562,063.6	918,416.7	5,814,770.6	9.2
Oaxaca	691.3	-1,739.9	-1,855.3	1,559.2	-1,344.8	0.0
Puebla	132,021.3	546,510.5	206,825.2	395,844.6	1,281,201.5	2.0
Querétaro	135,337.1	156,910.3	140,622.8	44,721.1	477,591.3	0.8
Quintana Roo	91,641.1	22,305.9	45,482.3	3,063.1	162,492.5	0.3
San Luis Potosi	209,754.8	276,449.8	166,776.8	3,119.8	656,101.2	1.0
Sinaloa	40,819.4	12,182.5	36,695.9	-1,127.1	88,570.7	0.1
Sonora	186,974.3	385,122.7	161,836.3	146,585.6	880,518.9	1.4
Tabasco	52,734.8	38,413.4	4,088.3	827.5	96,064.0	0.2
Tamaulipas	460,701.2	475,857.2	329,359.2	321,752.7	1,587,670.3	2.5
Tlaxcala	43,859.4	4,421.5	12,701.6	127.8	61,110.3	0.1
Veracruz	-73,266.0	21,767.8	117,192.6	2,561.1	68,255.6	0.1
Yucatán	41,303.8	47,205.9	126,272.3	6,962.2	221,744.2	0.3
Zacatecas	11,100.6	12,151.6	5,515.4	5,292.0	34,059.6	0.1

Source: Dirección General de Inversión Extranjera (2003).

The only southern state with a considerable share of FDI is Jalisco with a share of 3.1%, most probably related to the presence of the state oil company PEMEX in this federal state. These regional pattern of FDI implies that the capital and the 5 northern states account for 90.5 percent of total incoming FDI flows to Mexico.

It has been shown that Mexico has been constantly upgrading its locational specific advantages, inducing changes in the structure and motives for FDI although the debt crisis in 1982 and the financial turmoil in late 1994 implied a short break in this general transition of the FDI structure towards manufacturing and services.[214] While in the beginning of the century FDI was largely natural-resource-seeking investment, the import substitution period was characterized by a dominant position of market seeking foreign investors avoiding high national tariffs and profiting from the protected domestic market. Access to the local market still seems to be the dominant motivation for FDI in financial services, telecommunication, retail trade and some industrial sectors as food, beverages and tobacco. Despite of these market-seeking investments, the more Mexico became integrated to the North-American market through the signing of NAFTA the more FDI changed to being led by efficiency seeking motives. In sectors as automotive, computer, electronics and the clothing industry the need to cut costs and potential opportunities for exports to the NAFTA market stimulated the location of productive investments in Mexico.[215] Fostered by the continuous opening of the economy to foreign trade Mexico more and more became an export-platform for MNEs profiting of the cheap but comparably skilled labor in the country. For MNEs located outside the US in turn, NAFTA was an important motive for productive engagements in Mexico as it implied access to the large and dynamic US market.

In general the empirical literature indicates positive implications of increasing FDI flows for the Mexican economy. Empirical work of RAMIREZ confirms the hypothesis that Mexico attracted FDI in sectors where international trade links are strong and potential positive spill-over effects associated with the transfer of technology and learning-by-doing are high. Consequently, he shows that FDI has a positive impact on labor productivity.[216] Other empirical investigations likewise suggest that the presence of technological spillovers of FDI enhance economic efficiency in Mexico.[217] To sum up, the changing structure of FDI in Mexico towards manufacturing and services suggests that Mexico profits from transfers of technology and managerial know how. As recent empirical research indicates the overall impact of FDI on Mexican economic performance seems to be positive. Problematic is the regional concentration of FDI around the capital and in the northern states which further increases the regional divide of economic development in Mexico.

---

[214] See Calderón/Mortimore/Peres (1995).
[215] See CEPAL (2000) p.101-105.
[216] See Ramirez (2000) and (2001).
[217] See Blomström/Persson (1983), Blomström/Wolff (1994) and Burger (1998).

5.3 Political Risk in Mexico
5.3.1 Overview
The following paragraphs evaluate political risks for foreign investors in Mexico between the years 1984-2003 using the available risk data and analyzing the relevant literature. Although it would have been interesting to analyze the impact of political risk in different industrial sectors with different degrees of reversibility, these tests could not be performed due to the lack of reliable disaggregated data.[1] Due to the small size of the political risk data set methods of advanced time series analysis have not been considered a viable methodology for this empirical analysis. Instead, to show initial evidence for the influence of political risk indicators on FDI simple statistical correlations are reported in scatter plots. All numerical statistical results are depicted in table A.2 in Annex II. It is obvious that due to the lack of a reasonably sized data set and the resulting methodological deficiencies results have to be interpreted with caution.[2] To facilitate the empirical analysis I use the three groups of political risk that have already been used for the empirical analysis in Chapter 4. Paragraph 5.3.2 analyzes the evolution of macroeconomic risk factors in a similar fashion as orthodox country risk analysis would propose. Paragraph 5.3.3 in turn, is dedicated to the analysis of risks that result from governmental behavior or the structure of national institutions. Eventually, paragraph 5.3.4 is dedicated to the analysis of politic risk that originate in societal characteristics of the host country. The last paragraph offers a general evaluation of the institutional environment for FDI in Mexico and an analysis of Mexico's risk mitigation strategy since the outbreak of the debt crisis.

5.3.2 The Macroeconomic Environment
It has been argued that the establishment and maintenance of a stable macroeconomic environment is one of the basic economic tasks of a national government and an important prerequisite for national economic development.[3] However, macroeconomic stability has been a problem in Mexico since the beginning of the time period that is analyzed here. In 1982 Mexico's moratorium on its international debt initiated the outbreak of the Latin American debt crisis and left the country with nearly unacceptable business conditions for foreign investors.[4] In the following years a central focus of national economic policy was to overcome the effects of the severe crisis that had affected the country. Nevertheless, it took the Mexican government nearly 10 years to overcome the effects of the economic crisis that hit the country during the early 80s. Following the stabilization policy that was implemented in the aftermath of the crisis the country entered into a severe recession and living standards fell drastically. During the early 90s Mexico successfully continued the economic reform process and macroeconomic stabilization,

---

[1] Furthermore, this test entails the difficulty to theoretically determine the degree of reversibility of investment projects in different industrial sectors.

[2] Excluding 2003 the number of available observations is 19.

[3] See World Bank (1997) p.26-27.

[4] In 1986 BERI rated Mexico as a country with "unacceptable business conditions" for foreign-owned businesses. In this year Mexico's index scores were similar to those of Egypt, India, Iraq and Kenya. See Howell/Chaddick (1994) p.80-81.

economic liberalization and debt rescheduling over time restored investor confidence.

The most suitable indicator for measuring the evolution of macroeconomic country risk is the interest spread that is charged on a country's sovereign debt since spreads measure the difference between interests charged for sovereign debt of highly credible international debtors and emerging market countries. For taking the higher risk of default inherent to investments in government bonds of emerging markets investors are compensated by this risk premium.

Figure 5.15: Mexican Interest Spreads on Sovereign Debt 1993-2000 (in %)

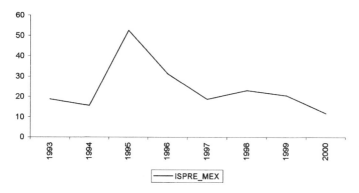

Own Figure using data of the World Bank (2002b).

When investing in riskier assets, investors demand higher spreads in order to cover expected losses from default. Therefore, interest rate spreads are good indicators of country risk as they picture the expectations of international financial markets about the default risk of country bonds and other obligations of emerging market countries. Figure 5.15 shows the evolution of Mexican interest spreads over LIBOR during the 90s and highlights the near tripling of Mexican spreads during the financial crisis that hit the country in late 1994. Following the Tequila-Crisis however, Mexican spreads have been constantly declining. In 2000 and 2001 the three major rating agencies Moodys, Standard and Poors, and Fitch assigned Mexico an investment-grade rating on its long-term foreign currency debt. Now being an attractive investment destination for a broader range of investors interest rates on public debt fell and country risk further decreased. Between September 1998 and March 2003 Mexico's score in the institutional investor country risk index rose from 45.4 points to 58.5 points indicating a marked improvement in the country's fundamentals.[5] In may 2003 Mexican interest spreads reached the all time low of 233 basis points.[6]

---

[5] See Blázquez/Santiso (2003).
[6] See BBVA (2003).

Figure 5.16 illustrates the evolution of Mexican interest rate spreads over US treasury bonds from 1997 to 2003 indicating the important decline in spreads between 1999 and 2001.

Figure 5.16: Mexican Interest Rate Spreads over US-treasury bonds (in basis points)

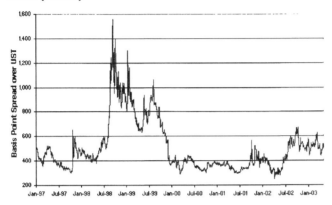

Source: BBVA (2003), Latinfocus.

Besides the inspection of hard data one may use pooled information about the macroeconomic situation given by political risk indicators that focus on macroeconomic risk. An indicator that pools the information of several sub-indicators to a single measure of macroeconomic risk is the Economic Risk Rating developed by PRS Group. This measure is " a means of assessing a country's current economic strengths and weaknesses. In general, where strengths outweigh weaknesses, a country will show low risk and where weaknesses outweigh strengths, the economic risk will be high. To ensure comparability between countries, risk components are based on accepted ratios between the measured data within the national economic/financial structure, and then the ratios are compared, not the data. Risk points are assessed for each of the component factors of GDP per head of population, real annual GDP growth, annual inflation rate, budget balance as a percentage of GDP, and current account balance as a percentage of GDP. Risk ratings range from a high of 50 (least risk) to a low of 0 (highest risk), though lowest de facto ratings are generally near 15".[7]

Figure 5.17 depicts the evolution of this risk indicator for the period from 1984 to 2003. An inspection of the data indicates that the economic risk indicator shows an upward trend since the beginning of the economic reforms in the mid 80s that is interrupted twice. The first time due to the recessive effects of the financial crisis in late 1994 and the second time in 1999. With exception of these two periods the economic risk rating mirrors the efforts of the national government to maintain macroeconomic stability. Despite of its obvious

---

[7] See PRS Group (2003).

success it took the national government a long time to see the results of its stabilization policies as Mexico needed 19 years for an increase of 10 index points.

Figure 5.17: Economic Risk in Mexico 1984-2003

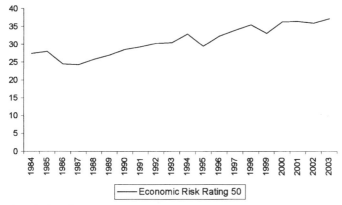

Source: Own figure and calculations using yearly averages of monthly data by PRS Group (2003). Index values for 2003 are calculated using data for January and February.

To assess the impact of the economic risk rating on the inflow of FDI the two scatter-plots in figure 5.18 depict the correlation between the economic risk indicator and FDI flows on the left as well as between the indicator and the FDI/GDP ratio on the right. The statistical correlation suggests a positive impact of lower economic risk on FDI flows as well as on the FDI/GDP ratio.

Figure 5.18: Correlation between Economic Risk and FDI

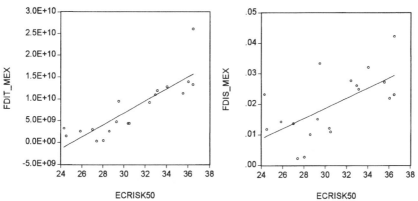

Source: Own figure using yearly averages of monthly data by PRS Group (2003) and yearly data of the World Bank (2002b).

Although lower risks pictured by the index coincide with higher FDI flows to Mexico, it has to be underlined that the correlation has to be interpreted with caution due to the limited data sample. Since the economic risk indicator has not been available for all Latin American countries included in the panel analysis in Chapter 4 there is no additional empirical evidence about the influence of this indicator on FDI. Nevertheless these results give an indication that economic risk exerts an important influence on FDI which seems to confirm the relationship between the two variables that has been postulated theoretically.

Another approach to assess macroeconomic risk is to measure a country's ability and willingness to fulfil its financial obligations. Again one could examine several macroeconomic indicators to analyze the current situation or pool relevant data in one single measure of financial risk. The Financial Risk Indicator of PRS Group is a "means of assessing a country's ability to pay its way by financing its official, commercial and trade debt obligations. To ensure comparability between countries, risk components are based on accepted ratios between the measured data within the national economic/financial structure, and then the ratios are compared, not the data. Risk points are assessed for each of the component factors of foreign debt as a percentage of GDP, foreign debt service as a percentage of exports of goods and services, current account as a percentage of exports of goods and services, net liquidity as months of import cover, and exchange rate stability. Risk ratings range from a high of 50 (least risk) to a low of 0 (highest risk), though lowest de facto ratings are generally near 20".[8]

Figure 5.19: Financial Risk in Mexico 1984-2003

Source: Own figure and calculations using yearly averages of monthly data by PRS Group (2003). Index values for 2003 are calculated using data for January and February.

Due to the country's severe problems with external debt, in particular during the 80s, it seems highly probable that financial risk in Mexico influenced the

---

[8] See PRS Group (2003). Due to the sub-components of the indicator it is comparable to the macroeconomic risk indicator that has been used in Chapter 4.

decisions of foreign investors. The evolution of the financial risk indicator between 1984 and 2003 that is depicted in figure 5.19 shows that following the debt crisis Mexico's financial risk rating reached highest possible de facto levels indicating that the country's moratorium on external debt and difficult negotiations about debt rescheduling obviously rendered financial risk of the country prohibitively high.

However, after the process of debt rescheduling had been agreed on and efforts of stabilization showed first success Mexican financial risk experienced a steady upward movement reaching its summit in the mid 90s which reflects the successful implementation of macroeconomic stabilization policy by the Mexican government. The unstable development since the mid 90s however, illustrates the volatility of financial risk on the Mexican market. Although the financial crisis in 1994 and its aftermath affected the financial risk rating since the late 90s, financial risk has been maintained on a stable level. To analyze the impact of financial risk on FDI to Mexico the correlation of the index with FDI is reported in figure 5.20. The two scatter-plots illustrate the correlation between financial risk and FDI flows and the FDI/GDP ratio respectively. Both graphs indicate a positive relationship which implies that Mexican data confirms the hypothesis of a positive correlation that has been postulated before.

Figure 5.20: Correlation between Financial Risk and FDI

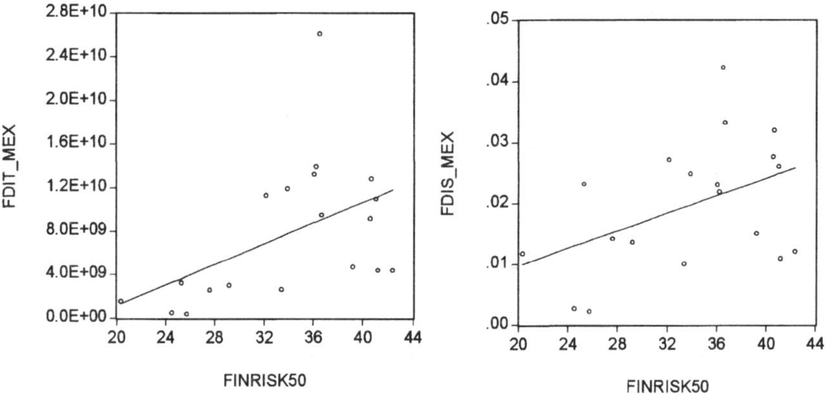

Source: Own figure using yearly averages of monthly data by PRS Group (2003) and yearly data of the World Bank (2002b).

Again it has to be underlined that the small data set limits the viability of these findings. However, as additional empirical evidence from the panel analysis on the impact of the indicator is not available it may be cautiously concluded that financial risk has an impact on the decisions of foreign investors in Mexico. Since the same result holds for the economic risk rating the analysis of Mexican data leads to different results than the panel analysis in Chapter 4. While the results of the panel analysis did not permit to label macroeconomic risk factors as robust determinants of FDI, the empirical analysis of the

Mexican data suggests an influence of macroeconomic risk variables on FDI. These deviating results for the Mexican case may be due to the preponderant role of macroeconomic risk factors in Mexico during the 80s. That is to say, the severe imbalances that Mexico experienced during the "lost decade" may have been a major impediment to incoming investment flows. However, despite of severe macroeconomic problems in Mexico during the debt crisis also other Latin American countries suffered from macroeconomic distortions. Therefore, explaining the diverging results with characteristics of Mexico is not very convincing. Another possible explanation for the diverging results is the different indicators that were used. Although the construction of the indices and the sub-indicators are similar, it is possible that the two indicators differ. Whatever the reason for this results the analysis of this paragraph permits the conclusion that macroeconomic risk factors have been an influential determinant of FDI flows to Mexico.

5.3.3 Mexican Institutions and Risk
5.3.3.1 Government Stability, Political Constraints and Regime Type
The analysis of the Mexican political system showed that for a long time power was largely concentrated in the hands of the executive branch of government. Although formally a democracy, the "meta-constitutional powers" of the president dominated every aspect of Mexican politics including economic policy. In turn, congress and the judiciary were found to be weak institutions without sufficient power to efficiently control the executive branch. In sum, the PRI dominance of Mexican politics reduced the checks and balances that are established in the constitution to not more than a mere theory.[9] Although universal suffrage existed, elections were often fraudulent to ensure the victory of the PRI. Nevertheless, the assessment of regime type in Mexico is a difficult task because the political system is as MORRIS states "neither fully democratic nor blatantly authoritarian; public policies are neither wholly capitalistic nor decidedly socialistic; interest groups both mobilize and demobilize; and elections are neither honest nor completely fraudulent".[10] Although the institutional design laid down in the Mexican constitution is undoubtedly democratic, de-facto policy was characterized by dominant authoritarian-corporatist patterns.[11] Using the criteria that have been presented in paragraph 3.1.3.1 for characterizing democratic systems Mexico before the presidency of Zedillo can hardly be labeled as democratic. The division of power was at best incomplete, press and media partly controlled and elections fraudulent.

---

[9] See Penner (1999). Moreno Ocampo (1993) argues that this is a common Latin American problem: "El obstáculo fundamental es nuestra pesada tradición de poder hegemónico, que no desapareció junto con los gobiernos autoritarios. Los nuevos gobernantes ya no llegan al poder por golpes militares sino por el voto, pese a que luego pretenden ejercer el poder del modo irrestricto y discrecional con que actúa un gobierno de facto." Moreno Ocampo (1993) p.38

[10] Morris (1991) p.21.

[11] See Morris (1991) p.25. Elizondo writes: "Formalmente México es una democracia: tiene elecciones periódicas, un sistema de partidos y un presidente y un congreso electos; sin embargo, aunque existe un pluralismo limitado, la sociedad estuvo administrada hasta hace muy poco de manera autoritario por el gobierno y por el presidente, quien dirige el gobierno." Elizondo (2001) p.73.

Although violent repression has not been systematically used and freedom of speech and political participation were not severely restricted, Mexico did not have the characteristics of a democratic political system.[12] Consequently in an investigation on democracy in Latin America MAINWARING classifies Mexico as authoritarian from 1821 to 1988 and as semi-democratic from 1988 onwards.[13] This classification is confirmed by ratings of Freedom House. Since 1972, Freedom House has published an annual assessment of freedom by assigning each country and territory the status of "Free," "Partly Free," or "Not Free" as an average of political rights and civil liberty ratings. Those whose ratings average 1-2.5 are generally considered as "Free," those with ratings between 3-5.5 as "Partly Free," and those with scores between 5.5-7 as "Not Free." For all periods between 1972 and 2000 Mexico has been rated as partly free which confirms the picture of an intermediate status that has been drawn above.[14] Using the terminology of WINTROBE before the reforms enacted by Zedillo Mexico was a "timocracy" with comparatively low levels of repression but high loyalty due to the distribution of rents by the corporatist party system. However, with the strengthening of the opposition parties and electoral reforms in the second half of the 90s the country made a transition towards a true democratic system with fair elections as well as checks and balances for the executive branch. Although since the electoral victory of Fox in 2000 Mexico's Freedom House-rating has been upgraded to the status "free", the credibility enhancing effects of a functioning democracy which have been exposed in paragraph 3.1.3.2 are largely absent for the analyzed time period.[15] In other words, the institutional environment for investors has not been characterized by a proper protection of basic constitutional rights and effective checks on the actions of the national executive that should be given by a functioning democratic system.

A careful examination of the political system of Mexico has many implications for the analysis of political risks for MNEs. Following PRITZL one may distinguish three levels of institutional instability in a political system: regime instability, policy instability and arbitrary actions of government officials.[16] The first object of study for political risk analysis is therefore the stability of the political system. It is straightforward to see that an unstable government may

---

[12] Guillermo O'Donnel called Mexico a "dictablanda" (soft dictatorship). Cited in Peeler (1998) p.119. Przeworski et al. argue that Mexico was not democratic because the opposition had no realistic chance to come to power. See Przeworski et al (2000) p.17.

[13] See Mainwaring (1999) p.7. In the same paper he argues that many democracies in Latin America are defect in the sense that minorities like indigenous or the rural population have formal citizenship rights but are frequently marginalized. Furthermore, countries in the region face the problem of weak democratic institutions and a limited rule of law.

[14] See Freedom House (2003). Mainwaring (1999) offers a critical discussion of the Freedom House Index.

[15] Mainwaring finds that for the Latin American countries democracy measured by the Freedom House Index weakly positively correlates with the level of per-capita income which is an initial indication for the potential wealth enhancing effects of democratic governance in the region. Interestingly this correlation is lower than in other regions of the world. See Mainwaring (1999) .

[16] See Pritzl (1997) p.72-76.

imply risks to investors. Governments that only have a weak hold to power or that may be easily removed by other societal forces are a possible source of instability that may affect the economy as well as the returns of private investment projects. In the worst case political stability is undermined by revolutions, violent protests or upheavals. In less severe cases rapidly changing governments cannot guarantee a basic continuity of policy that produces a reliable framework for private economic activity. Radical policy swings induced by quickly changing governments produce a climate of discontinuity and instability that depresses private investment because governing institutions cannot give a credible commitment to protect private assets.[17]

Unlike in many other Latin American countries in Mexico stability of government has not been a problem.[18] Since the political instabilities of the revolutionary period had been overcome the establishment of the one party government produced a stable political climate.[19] The corporatist one party state which effectively channeled societal conflict by occasional repression and distribution of rents to system loyalists produced a political system that did not suffer severe problems of instability.[20] Since the presidential term of Cardenas (1934-1940) the political system of Mexico has not undergone periods where the volatility of governments was high.[21] Unlike other Latin American countries Mexico neither experienced revolutions, coup d'etats or military governments. Even during the years of severe economic crisis the grip of the PRI to power has not been seriously menaced.[22]

Although it is obvious that the empirical measurement of government stability is not straightforward, I use an indicator that has been constructed by PRS Group. The index is a measure of the government's ability to stay in office and carry out its declared programs, depending upon such factors as type of governance, cohesion of government and governing parties, approach of an election, and command of the legislature. Figure 5.21 depicts the evolution of

---

[17] Empirical research has confirmed the link between political instability and expropriation. Between 1960 and 1979 40% of all expropriations followed revolutionary transformations of socioeconomic and political systems. See Kennedy (1991) p.21.

[18] Rodríguez (2000) argues that political instability was an important impediment for growth in Latin America.

[19] See Philip (1992) p.1-17 and Semo (1996) p.107-109.

[20] See Peeler (1998) p.113-124. Whiting argues that Mexico's political system has a high degree of resilience which permitted the survival of the system despite of major changes in its environment and the society. See Whiting (1992) p.43-45. Langston (2002) argues that four central factors ensured regime stability in Mexico. The president's control of the succession process, the successive passing of the generation of revolutionary leaders, the combination of growth and a strong state and the restrictive electoral rules. See Langston (2002) p.72-74.

[21] Langston (2002) argues that the sharpest threats to the stability of the system came from internal splits inside the PRI. Hence, the ruptures of 1940, 1952 and 1988 when party dissidents challenged the official PRI candidate were the greatest threat to political stability in Mexico. See Langston (2002).

[22] The only exception were the events of 1988 when PRI candidate Salinas de Gortari was challenged by the PRI dissident Cuauhtémoc Cárdenas.

government stability from 1984 to 2003. Despite of its comparative stability the inspection of the empirical data for Mexico suggests that there have been variations of government stability in the analyzed time period.

Figure 5.21: Government Stability in Mexico 1984-2003

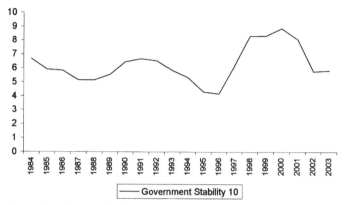

Source: Own figure and calculations using yearly averages of monthly data by PRS Group (2003) normalized to a 1-10 scale. Index values for 2003 are calculated using data for January and February.

However, when the consequences of the debt crisis reduced government stability during the second half of the 80s recovery to old levels of stability was rapid. In the early 90s however, in particular following the dramatic political events of 1994, government stability dropped to all time lows. After the effects of the political and economic crisis had been overcome stability ratings accelerated again reaching a peak in the year 2000, which is unusual for election years. The change of presidency in 2000 and the difficult situation in congress afterwards reduced index values again to levels of the early 90s.

To determine if government stability has an impact on FDI flows to Mexico I examine the correlation of the index and yearly FDI flows and FDI/GDP ratio respectively. The two scatter-plots in figure 5.22 depict the relationship between the government stability index and Mexican FDI data. The data does not permit a decisive conclusion about the impact of government stability on FDI although the statistical correlation between the two variables indicates a weak positive correlation. However, it has to be underlined that this result may be due to the lack of econometric sophistication that has been caused by the small sample of available data.

Figure 5.22: Correlation between Government Stability and FDI

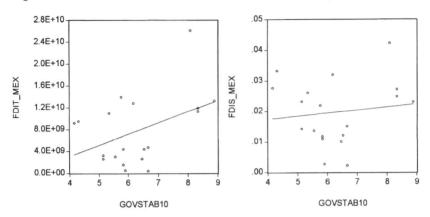

Source: Own figure using yearly averages of monthly data by PRS Group (2003) and yearly data of the World Bank (2002b).

Besides regime instability, other important sources for institutional instabilities are lacking policy stability and arbitrary actions of government officials. BILLET argues that a high degree of government intervention in the host country economy increases risks for MNEs as governments most likely want to regulate key corporate decisions once the investment is made.[23] The theoretical analysis in Chapter 3 identified political discretion and the absence of checks and balances as an important source of risk for current and potential investors since arbitrary changes of the status quo are more likely if constraining societal institutions are lacking.[24] Thus, investors face a higher risk of opportunistic policy changes when governments are not subject to an efficient control of other societal institutions. In other words, unlimited governments do not succeed in giving credible commitments not to interfere in the investor's property rights. A detailed analysis of presidential politics in Mexico during the last years indeed reveals an abundance of anecdotal evidence that arbitrary presidential decisions repeatedly affected the Mexican economy.[25]

Although the exact quantification of governmental constraints remains a difficult problem, I use POLCON to proxy checks and balances in national politics.[26] Chapter 4 already offered econometric evidence on the effects of political constraints on FDI concluding that political constraints were no robust determinant of FDI for a sample of Latin American countries, although it turned

---

[23] See Billet (1991) p.37. In fact a survey of private sector senior managers shows that in Latin America more than 38% of the respondents spent more than 15% of their working time with negotiations with government officials compared to 10% in OECD countries. See World Bank (1997) p.43.

[24] See Pritzl (1997) p.73.

[25] See Philip (1992).

[26] See paragraph 3.3.5.

out to be robust as part of a governance indicator.[27] Despite of these findings analyzing the influence of governmental discretion on FDI to Mexico is interesting. As already pointed out POLCON measures veto points in the political system corrected by current partisan powers in the legislative chambers. The indicator is normalized to a value between 0 and 1 where a level of 0 represents the theoretical case of an absolute absence of checks and balances while a value of 1 represents the theoretical case of a fully constrained executive. Although it has to be noted that the upper extreme value is not often observed, authoritarian regimes approach values around zero which indicates a massive concentration of power in the hand of the executive.[28] Figure 5.23 depicts the evolution of this indicator for the period between 1960 and 2001:

Figure 5.23: Political Constraints in Mexico 1960-2001

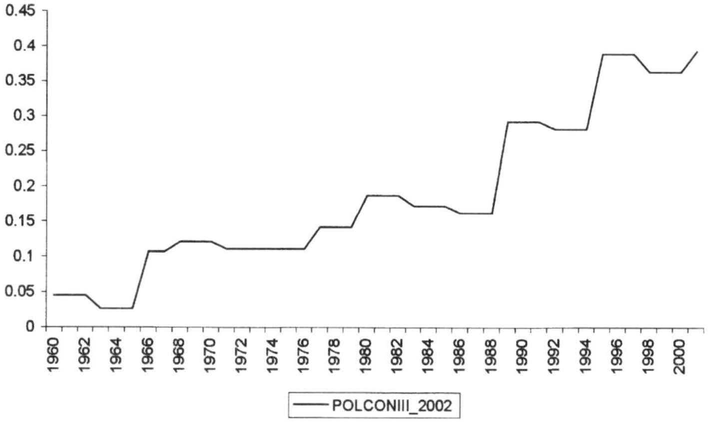

Source: Own figure using yearly data from POLCON.

The Mexican data shows that initially the level of checks and balances in the political system was extremely low which implies that the Mexican government ruled nearly unchecked by other societal institutions. For the early 60s the indicator attains levels that are only slightly higher than zero representing an absolutely unchecked government which is usually characteristic for personal dictatorships. In fact the level of political constraints in Mexico for that time is similar to that during the authoritarian rule of Díaz. Insofar the indicator is in line with the previous analysis of the political system that highlighted the meta-constitutional powers of the Mexican president and the irrelevance of other governmental branches. Despite of cautious political reforms constraint levels remained low throughout the 70s and 80s implying that the executive branch could still implement policies without any effective control of other political branches. With the PRI loosing its grip on power, the level of constraints for

---

[27] See paragraph 4.2.4.

[28] For Castro's Cuba, Mexico under Porfirio Díaz, Spain under Franco and Chile under Pinochet index values score 0.

the federal government was growing constantly. The first important upward move of the indicator occurred in 1988 when the PRI lost its constitutional majority.[29] With higher presence in congress and a growing importance in the political process opposition parties successfully limited the discretionary freedom of the Mexican government. In other words, growing political constraints were caused by political reforms in Mexico. The process of democratization during the 90s resulted in a more limited government that faced higher levels of checks and balances and was more effectively constrained in its implementation of policy. The similar higher rankings of the PRS Group's democratic accountability ranking which is depicted in figure 5.24 demonstrate that higher levels of democracy coincided with higher constraints for the executive. Currently the levels of political constraints in Mexico already roughly resemble average values of the USA.

Figure 5.24: Democratic Accountability in Mexico 1984-2001

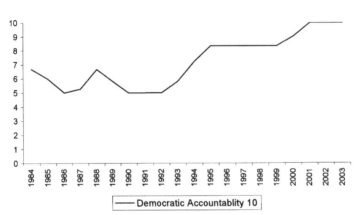

Source: Own figure and calculations using yearly averages of monthly data by PRS Group (2003) normalized to a 1-10 scale. Index values for 2003 are calculated using data for January and February.

Having in mind the theoretical implication of strengthening political constraints this analysis indicates lower risks for MNEs of becoming victims of opportunistic government action since additional mechanisms of control make radical policy swings less likely. Nevertheless, there are two important additional arguments. First, it has to be stated that the POLCON indicator for Mexico is systematically upward-biased as the objectively derived indicator is not able to picture the characteristics of the Mexican political system. Since compared to the US system all governmental branches except for the executive are still weak, the objective derivation of the indicator does not properly picture the characteristic role of the Mexican presidency. The high bill success rates of president Zedillo who already faced an opposition majority in congress may serve to illustrate this point. In addition, the inability of the judiciary to act as a contra-weight to executive dominance shows that the level of checks and balances in Mexico is still considerably lower than in the US.

---

[29] For an overview of the political events see Nacif (2003) p.8.

The other important objection to the use of the indicator is the integration of Mexico into the world economy by signing free trade agreements and other multilateral treaties. Since these agreements imply obligations that limit governmental discretion by international law the sole focus on national institutions neglects checks and balances by international law which produces a systematic downward-bias of the indicator.

Figure 5.25: Correlation between Political Constraints and FDI

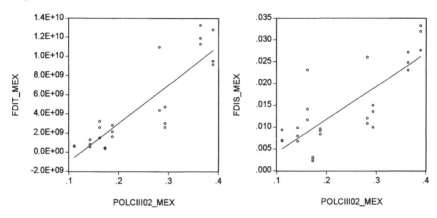

Source: Own figure using yearly data of POLCON 2002 and the World Bank (2002b).

Despite these limitations POLCON permits to calculate the statistical correlation between political constraints and FDI flows to Mexico. Although sophisticated econometric evidence is missing, the correlation in figure 5.25 suggests a positive influence of political constraints on FDI to Mexico as higher level of constraints appear to coincide with higher inflows of FDI or higher FDI/GDP ratios.

Given the positive correlation between growing constraints and higher values of democracy it will be analyzed if this results also holds for the index of democratic accountability. Figure 5.26 depicts the correlation between the values of democratic accountability and FDI to Mexico. The inspection of the two scatter-plots also suggest a positive correlation between democratic accountability and FDI flows and the FDI/GDP ratio respectively. Despite of the already mentioned difficulties in interpreting these results one may come to the conclusion that higher democratic accountability and political constraints go hand in hand with higher FDI flows and FDI/GDP ratios. Therefore, the correlation may be seen as a weak empirical indication for an impact of democratic accountability and political constraints on FDI flows to Mexico.

Figure 5.26: Correlation between Democratic Accountability and FDI

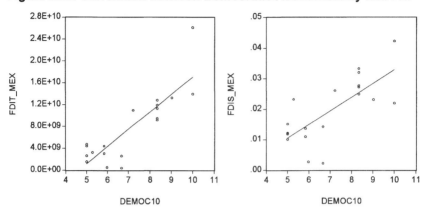

Source: Own figure using yearly averages of monthly data by PRS Group 2003 and yearly data of the World Bank (2002b).

Another risk factor that traditionally has been influential in Latin American countries is the involvement of the military in political decisions. Military governments or military controlled governments can become a threat for investors because democratic reliability is severely diminished, basic citizen rights may be suspended and property be expropriated if an individual's political ideology does not coincide with the beliefs of the military government. Moreover, military governments can initiate politics that rather aim at ensuring power and redistribute wealth to members of the junta instead of promoting general societal welfare.[30] To quantify the military's involvement in politics I use an indicator that has been provided by PRS group that measures the risk for foreign investors that their businesses will sooner or later be affected by military rule.[31] In Mexico military involvement in politics has traditionally been more scarce than in other countries of the region. Moreover, unlike other countries in Latin America, since the end of the unstable revolutionary period Mexico has neither experienced a military coup or a military government.[32] Nevertheless, it is interesting to analyze the potential impact of political

---

[30] Wintrobe (1998) writes "... the military regimes in Latin America in the 1970s and elsewhere, whose most concrete and lasting achievement has been to increase military salaries and the military budget." Wintrobe (1998) p.26.

[31] PRS Group writes: "Since the military is not elected, involvement, even at a peripheral level, diminishes democratic accountability. Military involvement might stem from an external or internal threat, be symptomatic of underlying difficulties, or be a full-scale military takeover. Over the long term, a system of military government will almost certainly diminish effective governmental functioning, become corrupt, and create an uneasy environment for foreign businesses." See PRS Group (2003).

[32] Langston (2002) argues that president Alemán (1946-52) made an important step to ensure civil primacy over the military by breaking with the habit to recruit politicians with revolutionary background from the military. Instead, he started to recruit university trained bureaucrats that were usually trained at the Universidad Nacional Autónoma (UNAM). See Langston (2002) p.

involvement of the military on FDI and figure 5.27 depicts the evolution of this indicator for Mexico between 1984 and 2003.

Figure 5.27: Military in Politics in Mexico 1984-2001

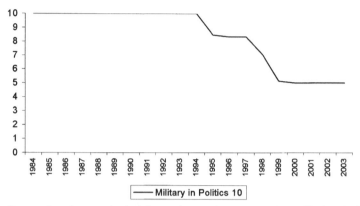

Source: Own figure and calculations using yearly averages of monthly data by PRS Group (2003) normalized to a 1-10 scale. Index values for 2003 are calculated using data for January and February.

The inspection of the data suggest that indeed the degree of military involvement in Mexico has traditionally been low as ratings picture the lowest level of risk until 1994. After 1994 however, the risk of military involvement in political decision making has been considerably growing implying that in only nine years Mexico's rankings in military involvement dropped by 50%. Since in the late 90s and the first years of the new millenium military involvement in Mexican politics has been constantly growing, the rating may reflect the tendency of the Zedillo administration to assign many additional task to the military that have formerly been the responsibility of civilian institutions.[33] There are many reasons for this development. First, the violent uprising in Chiapas entailed a more important role for military decision makers in politics. Second, the rising problems with drug trafficking in Mexico has been answered by higher military presence and involvement of the armed forces.[34] In addition, Zedillo also assigned military leaders to lead the demoralized and corrupt national police force.[35] Third, migration problems at the northern and southern border imply a massive presence of the military in border regions. Therefore, the role of the military in Mexican political life seems to be growing unless these problems have been tackled. In spite of the growing influence of the military during the last years the army fulfilled its role without seeking to increase its political power as an institution. This implies that the Mexican tradition of civilian dominance over the military seems to be secure.[36]

---

[33] See PRS Group (2000) p.41-42.
[34] See Covarrubias Velasco (2000) and Alvarado/Davis (2001).
[35] Since then reports of human rights abuses have multiplied. See PRS Group (2000) p.41.
[36] See Whiting (1992) p.48. and PRS Group (2000) p.41-42.

Figure 5.28: Correlation between Military Involvement in Politics and FDI

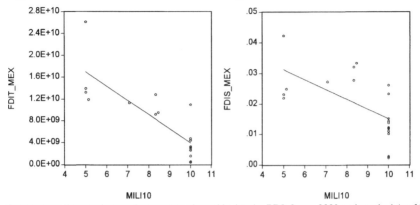

Source: Own figure using yearly averages of monthly data by PRS Group 2003 and yearly data of the World Bank (2002b).

To analyze the potential impact of higher military involvement in Mexico on FDI figure 5.28 reports the correlation between military-in-politics and FDI as well as the FDI/GDP ratio. The Mexican data indicates an inverse relationship between the two variables suggesting that higher levels of military presence coincide with higher levels of FDI. If this counter-intuitive evidence is a product of the bias that arises due to the lack of reliable data or due to growing levels of public insecurity which cause a positive effect of higher military presence on investor security, is unclear.

Summing up, I find weak empirical evidence for the hypothesis that the degree of government stability has a positive impact on FDI. At the same time the hypothesis that higher military involvement depresses FDI is rejected by the analysis of Mexican data. On the other hand this paragraph offers empirical evidence for a positive impact of democratic reliability and political constraints on FDI flows to Mexico. This is of particular interest, as not only the direct implications of unconstrained government and lacking democratic reliability for incoming FDI are important. Instead, lacking constraints and low levels of democratic accountability might as well have an impact on other institutional variables. For example, unlimited governmental discretion may be detrimental for a functioning rule of law since high levels of discretion and lack of control by other societal institutions make it unlikely that the government restricts itself by obeying to existing legislation. Moreover, as has been argued in the literature high levels of corruption are fostered by a political system that lacks functioning mechanism of control since lacking checks and balances facilitate the establishment of a system of institutionalized corruption that is harmful for foreign investors.[37]

---

[37] See Morris (1991).

"La movida para mis amigos, y la ley para mis enemigos." [38]

5.3.3.2 The Rule Of Law

As argued before lacking rule of law may not only be caused by domestic legislation but also by inefficient institutions of law enforcement. The short analysis in paragraph 5.1.2.4 already highlighted that the judiciary and other institutions of law enforcement are not efficiently working in Mexico. Like in other Latin American countries this lacking rule-of-law-tradition is partially a heritage from Spanish colonialism. As laws and regulations were passed in Spain but had to be applied by local administrations in the New World legal norms were usually interpreted with high levels of discretion. This situation over time led to a lack of respect for the law which may be illustrated by the common Latin American sayings "obedezco, pero no cumplo" and "la ley se acata, pero no se cumple".[39] In Mexico the divergences between de-jure and de-facto rules including constitutional norms imply that many national laws loose relevance because they are not properly enforced. Despite of judicial reform Mexico today is still characterized by an enormous discrepancy between de-jure norms and legal reality.[40] Non enforcement of the law however, fosters a societal culture where the respect of citizens for the law is constantly decreasing. That is, if the benefits of breaking the law are higher than the cost of doing so, individuals have a constant incentive for violations of the law.[41] Furthermore, Mexican laws are inconsistent and sometimes even contradictory. The excessive legislation is often unclear and applied with high levels of discretionary freedom by the authorities. Access to the law is not equal in the sense that poor people often do not have the possibility to successfully enforce legal claims undermining the legal principle of equality before the law.[42]

In criminal justice enforcement problems imply that criminals are seldom convicted which leads to a situation of continuous impunity. Furthermore, like in many other Latin American countries the national police, which is essential for the enforcement of the law, is perceived as inefficient, underpaid, poorly qualified, corrupt and not being respectful of basic citizen rights and liberties.[43]

---

[38] Latin American saying cited in Buscaglia/Dakolias/Ratliff (1995).

[39] See Pritzl (1997) p.64-80 and Peeler (1998) p.25-42. A Mexican observer writes: "It would be naive to think that the ghost of the old Spanish colonial state – with its enduring paternalism, corruption, bureaucracy, and extreme centralization – can be exorcised completely ... The best effort would be a new legal system modeled frankly and unashamedly on the Anglo-Saxon pattern." Cited in Buscaglia/Dakolias/Ratliff (1995) p.2.

[40] See Rubio et al. (1994).

[41] See Ayala Espino (2002) p.137.

[42] The hourly salary of a qualified lawyer in Mexico equals the value of 21 to 42 daily minimum salaries. The services of public lawyers are of low quality and in general do not permit successful access to the law. Other cost that potential claimants have to bear are bribes, administrative fees and bails. See Rubio et al. (1994). This situation may be illustrated with the Mexican saying: "El código civil se aplica a los ricos, y el codigo penal a los pobres." Cited in Rubio et al. (1994) p.18. This characteristic of many Latin American countries leads to a situation that Mario Vargas Llosa once called legal apartheid. Cited in Pritzl (1997) p.141.

[43] See Frühling Ehrlich (2001) and Sarre (2001).

In 1990 91.4% of the crimes that have been committed in the federal district remained unresolved.[44] Informal vendors are active throughout the capital selling smuggled goods, pirated products or other contraband without being harmed by local administrations.[45] Moreover, the police often applies torture to coerce confessions and prisoners are detained without conviction in precarious social conditions due to an overcrowding of state prisons.[46]

In Mexico the second half of the 90s is characterized by a steady increase of crimes with a particular growth of robbery and theft. The growing crime rate went hand in hand with a growing number of complaints of Mexican citizens before the National Human Rights commission about lacking efficiency and human rights violations of the national police force.[47] Increased public insecurity and high levels of crime that go hand in hand with an inefficient national police force affect any type of commercial activity by simply increasing costs of doing business.[48] In a survey conducted in 1999 in Mexico City 47% of the interviewed people stated that crime and public insecurity were the most important problems, well ahead of economic problems with a percentage of 22% on the second rank.[49] A fact that indicates growing public insecurity is the large number of private security firms that operate in Mexico to protect private

---

[44] See Rubio et al. (1994) p.94.

[45] See Gilespie/McBride (1996) p.46-48.

[46] In 1992 49% of Mexican prisoners were yet unsentenced and thus in preventive detention. In 1993 Mexican prisons were at 126% of capacity, in 2001 at 136 %. See Bekker/Patrick (1998) p.1-3 and INEGI (2003). Police violence and abuses of power are widespread in Latin America. See Bekker/Patrick (1998) p.5-9.

[47] Denounced crimes per day in Mexico City increased by 57% from 445 daily cases in 1994 to 700 daily cases in 1997. Moreover, it has to be underlined that these figures are downward-biased because not all committed crimes are reported by the victims. Complaints about the police increased by 45 % from 1812 in 1995 to 2623 in 1997. See Alvarado/Davis (2001). According to a recent survey reported by PRS Group 90% of the crimes are not reported because citizens think they will receive no help or will even be harmed by a police force that protects criminals. See PRS Group (1999) p.D3. In 1983 a group of police was discovered operating a large ring of auto-theft and bank-robbery, in 1989 the Mexico City office of the Federal Intelligence Directorate (ID) was accused of kidnapping, extortion, robbery, torture and homicide. During the 80s reports of police and military involvement in criminal activities grew common. The severe involvement of Mexican police and military in crime led one observer to the conclusion that "society has come to fear the police more than it fears the criminals". See Morris (1991) p. xvi. When the opposition party PRD took control of Mexico City's government, they discovered a pyramidal structure of institutionalized corruption in the Mexico City police department where lower levels were coerced to make payments to their superiors and promotion to midlevel positions required the payment of bribes. Therefore, members of the police force had to engage in various forms of illegal activities. See Garibaldi (2001) p.12-14.

[48] In a large scale firm survey conducted by Brunetti/Kisunko/Weder nearly 90% of the respondents from Latin America stated that crime and theft substantially increase their costs of doing business. Nearly 80% of all surveyed persons from Latin America did not feel confident that state authorities would protect their person and their property from criminal actions. According to the same survey businesspeople from Latin America ranked crime and theft as the third most important obstacle to business after corruption and an inadequate infrastructure supply. See Brunetti/Kisunko/Weder (1997) p.17-18 and 25.

[49] See López Portillo Vargas (2001).

property and businesses as banks, malls or restaurants.[50] With around 2000 kidnappings every year Mexico has the second highest kidnapping rate in Latin America after Colombia. Although kidnappers generally target wealthy Mexicans, executives of MNEs are also at risk.[51] Only these few facts impressively highlight the problem of public security in particular in major Mexican cities, remote rural areas and border regions. Currently Mexico encounters a situation where high levels of crime, violence, low protection of individuals against arbitrary government actions and an unpredictable judiciary severely endanger the rule of law and the governability of the country.[52]

However, these inefficiencies of the legal system have more far reaching consequences for the Mexican economy than just augmenting the direct cost of private security and doing business.[53] In private law the outright consequences of an inefficient judiciary are severe distortions for private business activities. The theoretical analysis of prerequisites for credible commitment revealed the crucial role of third party enforcement for complex economic transactions. Assuming that self interested private actors will only enter in welfare-enhancing economic activity if they are sure that they will reap the benefits from their engagement it was pointed out that it is necessary that agreements between individuals are enforceable. In other words, incomplete contracts, contractual hazards and potential opportunistic behavior of contracting counterparts require an efficient institution for conflict resolution. To lower the cost of wealth enhancing private transactions national institutions have to assure by coercive power that contracts between individuals are honored. Thus, economic theory suggests that the judiciary plays an important part in providing a suitable framework for private economic activity.

Therefore, the poor performance of the Mexican judiciary severely limits the possibilities of economic actors to engage in welfare-enhancing transactions.[54] As the enforcement of private contracts cannot be ensured by national institutions Mexican firms often limit their business activities to those contract partners that are well known as family and friends because if contracts with unknown partners were negotiated, the need to investigate the commercial reputation of the contractual partner would imply a considerable increase of transaction costs. Hence, the inefficiency of the legal sector implies an inefficiency of markets because potentially wealth-enhancing transactions are

---

[50] See Alvarado/Davis (2001).

[51] See PRS Group (2000) p.20.

[52] The World Bank refers to the combination of these factors as "lawlessness syndrome". See World Bank (1997) p.41.

[53] In a survey conducted by Brunetti/Kisunko/Weder over 70% of the surveyed firms from Latin American countries state that an unpredictable judiciary is a major problem for their business operations. See Brunetti/Kisunko/Weder (1997) p.19.

[54] Poor law enforcement is a common Latin American problem. In a regionwide survey of business court users 55% responded that they prefer to negotiate a partial settlement rather than adjudicate in the formal court system. See Buscaglia/Dakolias/Ratliff (1995) p.6.

not performed due to high levels of transactions costs.[55] In Mexico the resolution of private law conflicts is the task of the local and federal judiciary. However, the quality of the first local instances is that low that in a great number of cases the decisions of the local courts are overruled by federal tribunals.[56] Further empirical evidence highlighting the inefficiency of Mexican jurisprudence is that US companies doing business with Mexican firms usually negotiate the responsibility of the US judiciary in the case of contractual conflicts.[57] Although there recently has been progress in tackling the problem of severe judicial corruption, enormous trial lengths imply that private parties to a conflict try to negotiate private agreements to avoid lengthy court decisions.[58] This incapacity of the Mexican judiciary to provide for credible enforcement of private contracts limits national commercial activities. At the same time it becomes an important obstacle for foreign investors since it is obvious that the situation of foreign firms that are doing business in Mexico does not differ from the one their national competitors face. One may even argue that foreign firm activity is more severely affected by the prevailing legal insecurity as foreign managers lack the necessary local information or personal ties to promote a quick resolution of legal conflicts between contracting parties. Impediments to foreign firms however, are not limited to private contracting as Mexican law neither offers effective protection against

---

[55] Thus, in the absence of an efficient third party enforcement individuals rely on social contract enforcement which is based on long-term personal relationships. See World Bank (1997) p.45. There are many examples for market inefficiencies in Mexico resulting from high transaction costs. The excessive legal protection of individuals renting apartments in Mexico City implies that landlords are extremely cautious to rent to strangers and most of the time do not rent at all explaining the insufficient offer on the market. The inefficient enforcement of the commercial code implies that legal suits against debtors take a long time and imply legal insecurity as well as high costs. This situation leads to many "private" solutions that avoid courts and at the same time limits the offer for credit contracts. See Rubio et al. (1994).

[56] In 1994 over 35% of local courts decisions have been revised by federal judges. Local judges are often not very well qualified, poorly paid and often subject to pressure from the local political elite. Nevertheless they are the first instances in commercial matters. Therefore, for improving the Mexican judiciary it is crucial augmenting the quality of the local courts. See Rubio et al. (1994).

[57] See Holland (1999).

[58] In a survey about judicial corruption where a score of 10 represents a completely honest and a score of 0 a completely corrupt judiciary Mexico received a rating of 3.18. Canada in turn received 8.87, Chile 7.94, the US 7.79 and Colombia 3.44. See Buscaglia/Dakolias/Ratliff (1995) p.40. It usually takes up to 304 days to settle a simple commercial matter before Mexican tribunals. If the contractual partner disposes of "competent lawyers", commercial law suits may take up to 5 years. Additionally the low transparency of the system makes it hard to ex ante anticipate the legal outcome. In the case of financial contracts the fact that the opportunity costs of the trial length which the creditor has to bear are not adequately covered aggravates this problem. In most legal suits against the public administration there are no indemnifications for commercial losses that occurred due to administrative actions. This fact further increases the vulnerability of private citizens for illegal and arbitrary interventions by the government and contractual violations by business partners. See Rubio et al (1994). The Mexican saying "Un mal areglo es mejor que un buen pleito" impressively highlights the effects of lacking legal certainty.

predatory governmental actions. Therefore, the negative impact of the inefficient judiciary extends to the relation between government and private investors. To put it in other words, if the judiciary is not able to protect property rights of private investors against arbitrary predatory interference by governmental authorities, potential risks for foreign investors are further growing.[59] Summarizing it may be concluded that the high cost of contract enforcement as well as the low degree of legal security for investors are a potentially important disincentive for incoming FDI.

It is straightforward to see that the exact quantification of political risk that is caused by lacking rule of law is hardly possible. Nevertheless, data provided by the PRS Group gives an impression of how rule of law in the Mexican society developed over time. The rule of law measure of PRS measures two characteristics of the rule of law where each of the sub-components has a weight of 50%. The "law" sub-component assesses the strength and impartiality of the legal system whereas the "order" sub-component assesses the popular observance of the law.

Figure 5.29 depicts the evolution of the rule of law rating from 1984 to 2003. Analyzing the PRS rating the judicial reforms enacted by the Zedillo were not particularly successful in providing higher rule of law in Mexico.

Figure 5.29: Rule of Law Rating in Mexico 1984-2003

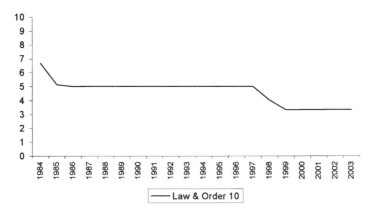

Source: Own figure and calculations using yearly averages of monthly data by PRS Group (2003) normalized to a 1-10 scale. Index values for 2003 are calculated using data for January and February.

Likewise the reforms of the Fox administration do not seem to have produced measurable progress in rule of law in Mexico. It has been shown in the literature that usually the powerful interest groups in societies with lacking rule-of-law show resistance to reforms as they are the ones that most profit from

---

[59] See paragraph 5.3.3.4 for the evaluation of property rights protection in Mexico.

legal uncertainty and impunity.[60] In addition, reforming the judiciary is a lengthy and costly process that is difficult to implement.[61] Therefore, possible reasons for the lack of positive results is the resistance of mighty interest groups in the Mexican society that benefit from the existing status quo as well as the limited availability of financial resources for judicial reforms.

To assess the influence of the rule of law indicator for FDI flows to Mexico figure 5.30 depicts the correlation of FDI and the PRS rule of law indicator. In contrast to the expected sign the correlation between the indicator and yearly FDI flows as well as the FDI/GDP ratio indicates a negative relationship between the two variables.

Figure 5.30: Correlation between Rule of Law and FDI

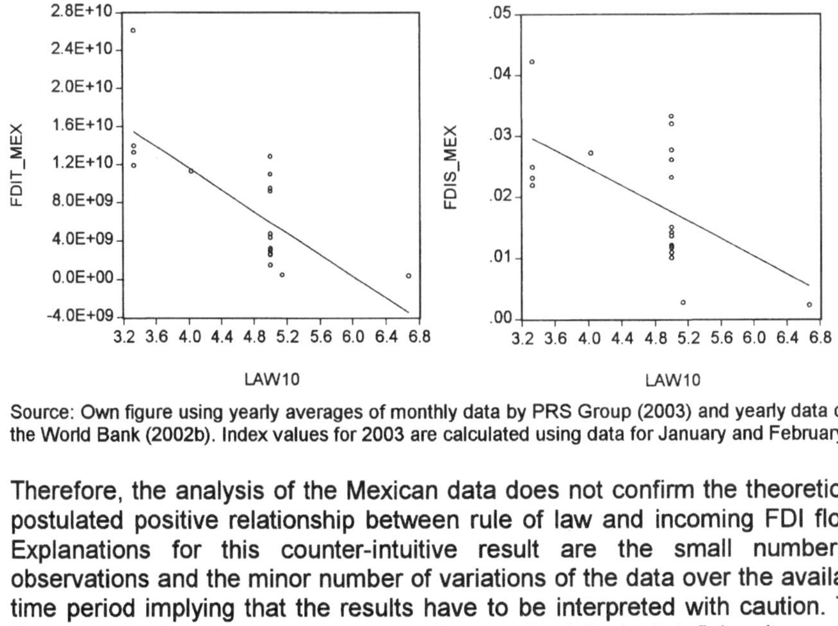

Source: Own figure using yearly averages of monthly data by PRS Group (2003) and yearly data of the World Bank (2002b). Index values for 2003 are calculated using data for January and February

Therefore, the analysis of the Mexican data does not confirm the theoretically postulated positive relationship between rule of law and incoming FDI flows. Explanations for this counter-intuitive result are the small number of observations and the minor number of variations of the data over the available time period implying that the results have to be interpreted with caution. The interpretation that these results stem from methodological deficiencies seams reasonable since the empirical evidence drawn from the panel analysis in Chapter 4 indicates a significant influence of rule of law on FDI flows to Latin America.

An important variable that is related to rule of law is the quality of the national bureaucracy since a reliable and competent public administration offers a favorable framework for private economic activity and fosters legal security and continuity in state business relations. Institutional strength and quality of the bureaucracy therefore are a shock absorber that tends to minimize revisions of policy when governments change. Typically, in low-risk countries,

---

[60] See Pritzl (1996) and Buscaglia/Dakolias/Ratliff (1995).
[61] See Ayala Espino (2002) p.135.

the bureaucracy is somewhat autonomous from political pressure. In turn, low quality public administrations produce legal uncertainty and are an obstacle to forming a reliable framework for private economic activity.

Figure 5.31: Bureaucratic Quality in Mexico 1984-2003

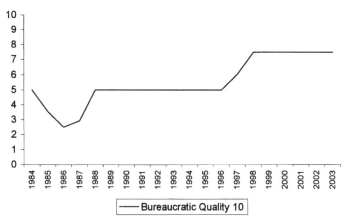

Source: Own figure and calculations using yearly averages of monthly data by PRS Group (2003) normalized to a 1-10 scale. Index values for 2003 are calculated using data for January and February.

Foreign investors in Mexico are often daunted by bureaucratic impediments as well as by a lack of clear regulations.[62] Figure 5.31 depicts the indicator values of bureaucratic quality for the time period 1984-2003. While deteriorating temporarily during the mid 80s bureaucratic quality experienced a considerable upward swing during the mid 90, most likely as a result of the reforms enacted by the Zedillo administration. The change of government in 2000 however, up to now did not result in a better rating for the public administration compared to the ratings of the mid 90s.

Concerning the impact of bureaucratic quality on incoming FDI flows the scatter-plots in figure 5.32 show the correlation between the index values and total FDI flows as well as the FDI/GDP ratio. The inspection of the graphs suggests a positive impact of bureaucratic quality on FDI flows to Mexico with a more convincing evidence for the correlation between the index value and total incoming flows as depicted in the left graph of figure 5.32. Again it has to be stated that these results have to interpreted carefully as evidence from sophisticated econometric analysis is missing due to the lack of data.

---

[62] See PRS Group (2000) p.23.

Figure 5.32: Correlation between Bureaucratic Quality and FDI

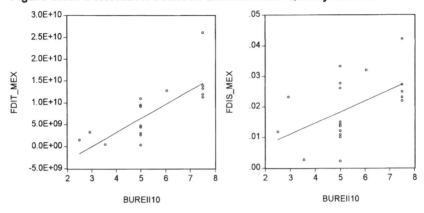

Source: Own figure using yearly averages of monthly data by PRS Group (2003) and yearly data of the World Bank (2002b).

However, as the results of the panel data analysis in Chapter 4 provides additional empirical evidence it is most likely that the depicted correlation for Mexican data is not spurious. Therefore, it may be plausibly argued that the quality of public administration is an influential factor for FDI flows to Mexico.

Con dinero baila el perro...
Sin dinero uno baila como perro.[63]

5.3.2.3 Corruption

An analysis of Mexico's history shows that political and administrative corruption have a long tradition in the country.[64] Although several times leading intellectuals of the country publicly denounced the excessive corrupt practices of governments and public administrations, corruption is still an ubiquitous phenomenon in the modern Mexican society that may be found on

---

[63] Mexican saying cited by Morris (1991) p.1.
[64] For an overview of the older literature see López Presa et al. (1998). For more historical details on corruption in Mexico see the contributions in Lomnitz (2000). For Vernon corruption in Mexico is a heritage of colonial rule: "As long as the [colonial] law was so pervasive in its scope and so particularistic in its application, it was inevitable that corruption would exist. First of all, the pervasiveness of regulation meant that any operating business was at the mercy of the law. There was always some provision or other that constituted a threat, actual or potential, to the continued existence of a going business; so any business that hoped to stay afloat had to find some way of securing immunity from a hostile application of the regulations. ... So bribery in one form or another was an unavoidable part of the system; ..." Vernon (1963) p.30. For Daniel Cosío Villegas corruption originates in revolutionary times: "La deshonestidad administrativa de México tiene sus causas (....) ellas no quitan adarme a su monstuosidad social, ni mucho menos reducen en nada los funestos efectos políticos que ha tenido, pues (....) ha sido la deshonestidad de los gobernantes revolucionarios, más que ninguna otra cosa, la que ha rajado el tronco mismo de la Revolución Mexicana."

all levels of societal activity.[65] On low administrative levels the famous *mordida* (literally: bite) is paid to low rank officials (as policemen) to avoid the payment of fines as for example for the violation of traffic rules, to buy impunity in criminal justice, or to receive favorable treatment in public administration. However, corruption in Mexico is not restricted to lower societal levels but also widespread among high rank government officials including the president. Incentives for the corrupt misuse of public power are particularly high in Mexico as the principle of no re-election dilutes the responsibility of politicians. Office holders that are not restricted by the need to get re-elected and only have a limited time for the misuse of public power have a higher incentive to engage in corrupt transaction to ensure their personal benefits.[66] Indeed there is evidence that corruption levels augment in the final year of a *sexenio* which is publicly referred to as the "Year of Hidalgo" while the influence of anti corruption campaigns is decreasing with the approaching end of the term.[67] During the last years there have been several serious accusation of governmental corruption or personal enrichment of presidents and other high ranked government officials.[68] Likewise other governmental organizations, the judiciary and the police force are accused of corrupt practices in office.[69] In particular the public administration is characterized by severe problems of corruption.[70]

The long history of corruption in Mexico suggests that the public abuse of power in this country is no sporadic phenomenon that can be described by the existence of a few "bad apples". Instead, the long years of PRI dominance, the lack of controlling institutions like opposition parties or a free press and the importance of public posts as the most important way to make a career shaped a system where corruption was widespread.[71] It was argued above that whenever public officials have wide discretion and little accountability incentives for corrupt behavior arise. In Mexico high discretionary freedom of politicians and public servants and lacking controls combined with a high level of governmental intervention in the economy produced a climate that was

---

[65]The literature denouncing political corruption in Mexico is too large to cite it completely. Representative works are Elizondo (1987) and Moheno (1979).

[66] See Pritzl (1997) p.147.

[67] See Morris (1991). A popular Mexican saying is: este es el año de Hidalgo, chin-chin el que deje algo" ("this is the year of Hidalgo, he is a fool who leaves something"). Cited by Morris (1991) p.85.

[68] There have been several serious accusation of presidential corruption with the most prominent case being the rule of president Salinas whose private wealth is estimated around 400 Mio. US$. The private wealth of Mexico's ex-president López Portillo (1976-1982) is estimated to amount between 1 to 3 billion US$. It is estimated that president de la Madrid transferred between 10 and 20 million US$ outside the country in the last year of his sexenio. See Morris (1991).

[69] See Morris (1991) and Garibaldi (2001) p.12-14.

[70] See the examples in López Presa et al. (1998).

[71] In 1977 a major Mexican newspaper commented the strengthening of opposition parties by López Portillo with the words: "the political monopoly of the PRI has been a determining factor in corruption". Cited by Morris (1991) p.94.

conducive for extensive corruption.[72] Rather than being a rare societal event corruption in Mexico showed patterns which allow for the conclusion that corruption is instead deeply rooted and institutionalized.[73] The high involvement of the state in the economy, excessive regulation and the inefficiencies in the public administration further stimulate levels of corruption.[74] Indeed an empirical investigation of the patterns of corruption in Mexico concludes that 59.5% of discovered corruption cases involved extortion or fraud of government officials.[75] The inefficiencies of the national judiciary that have been exposed in the previous paragraph imply that corrupt practices are often not properly sanctioned which further increases private incentives for the misuse of public power.[76] In addition the partly controlled press could not efficiently fulfill its role of discovering and publicly denouncing corrupt practices and misuse of power by government officials.[77]

In the Mexican literature on the matter it is often argued that high levels of corruption resulted from the need to stabilize the corporatist political system that has been exposed in paragraph 5.1. This system that organized loyalty to government with stick and carrot experienced a crisis when the economic downturn during the 80s rendered the financing of corrupt practices more difficult.[78] Moreover, high levels of political corruption slowly eroded the credibility and the legitimacy of Mexican political institutions.[79] Eventually the process of liberalization and democratization in Mexico reduced the potential for this kind of institutionalized corruption. The fight against high level political corruption has been initiated by the establishment of controlling organizations like the Federal Electoral Institute (IFE) and the strengthening of the national congress. Another important factor that helped limit excessive corporatist corruption is the growing independence of the electorate, the emergence of civil organizations, effective opposition parties and the growing role of public opinion that permit a better societal control of corrupt practices.[80] To combat corruption in public administration several reforms were initiated to allow for a better persecution of corrupt government officials. Usually every incoming

---

[72] See Jain (2001) and World Bank (1997) p.102-109 who argue that high levels of discretionary authority lead to high levels of corruption.

[73] See Morris (1991). Pritzl claims that in many Latin American countries corruption has an institutionalized structure. See Pritzl (1996).

[74] See Rubio et al. (1994) p.31-34.

[75] See Morris (1991) p.56-64.

[76] In a recent study the World Bank finds a negative correlation between an index of corruption and an index measuring the predictability of the national judiciary. See World Bank (1997) p.104.

[77] The World Bank argues that exposure of corruption in the media is a viable tool for checking abuses of power. See World Bank (1997) p.108.

[78] See the overview in López Presa et al. (1998).

[79] See Morris (1991) p.16-20.

[80] See López Presa et al. (1998) and Morris (1991) p.115-137. As Morris states: "In sum, the Mexican state embarked on a series of reforms that envisage greater limitations on the power of the state, a greater reliance on the private sector, and greater political openness. Forces in society, in the meantime, pushed their own autonomy and demands with greater vigor than ever before. As an integral part of the political system, corruption is clearly affected by both the economic and political changes of the decade". Morris (1991) p.130.

administration promises to fight the high levels of political and administrative corruption and initiates anti corruption campaigns.[81] However, measures to combat the sources of corruption in a preventive manner were scarce.[82] In the past the results of the anti-corruption campaigns have been at best limited and high levels of corruption persisted despite of the reforms that have been initiated.[83] As MORRIS argues over time the composition of corruption changed from extortion and fraud to bribery of government officials and a growing importance of drug-trade related corruption which more severely endangers political stability.[84]

The best method to assess national levels of corruption is the use of population surveys. When in 1986 Mexicans were asked how often it is necessary to pay a bribe when dealing with the government, 40.4% said always and another 38.3% indicated that it was required much of the time.[85] More recent quantitative empirical evidence on corruption is offered by the "Encuesta Nacional de Corrupción y Buen Gobierno" (ENCBG), a recent national survey on corruption realized by Transparency International. The survey registered 214 million acts of corruption in the use of public services during the year of the investigation. The average cost of a "mordida" for a Mexican household was 109.50 Mexican pesos (ca.10 US$) which implies a sum of 23.4 billions of pesos (2.34 billion US$) annually paid to the public sector in the form of bribes. This sum is equivalent to 0.4% of Mexican GDP and it is estimated that the total societal cost of corruption amounts to 15% of total annual tax income or 30 billion US$. The survey also reveals that the average Mexican household uses 6.9% of its personal income for the payment of bribes to the public sector for obtaining services. For poor households living on minimum salary this percentage goes up to 13.9% of total income. The survey found that on average, Mexicans pay bribes for 10.6 percent of the public services they receive. The services for which bribes are most frequently paid are related to cars: retrieving an impounded car required a bribe 57.2 percent of the time; avoiding traffic tickets, 56 percent; and avoiding other traffic offenses, 54.5 percent. In the Federal District 80% of the surveyed people confessed having paid bribes to the local police for avoiding fines for traffic offenses.[86] However, corruption also affects other levels of social and

---

[81] For an overview of anti-corruption campaigns see Morris (1991) p.83-101.

[82] In 1983, as a part of his moral renovation campaign, the Penal Code has been reformed by the de la Madrid administration to allow for a more efficient persecution of corruption in the public administration. In the following years several controlling organizations, like in 1994 the Secretary for Control and Administrative Development (SECODAM) and in 1995 an auditing commission for fiscal matters, were created to ameliorate the supervision of the public administration. In 1995 a program for the modernization of the public administration was launched to ameliorate the efficiency and reduce corrupt practices. See López Presa et al. (1998). However, de la Madrid refused to arrest high PRI officials on charges of corruption including ex-president López Portillo who was likewise not put to trail. See Philip (1992) p.136-137.

[83] See Morris (1991) p.83-101.

[84] See Morris (2000).

[85] See Morris (1991) p.71

[86] See Transparency International (2001).

political life in Mexico. National programs to fight corruption in the Federal District discovered extensive corrupt practices in the granting of licenses, the supervision of businesses, the public control of environmental pollution, the issuing of driving licenses, the operation of the Mexico City Airport, the police force and the distribution of fuel by the state-controlled oil company PEMEX.[87] According to a recent report by the national radio network, Radio Red, some Mexico City high school students even purchase their grades from teachers with the current rate for an A being 10 US$. Empirical evidence on regional differences in corruption levels indicate that the Federal District and the State of Mexico show the highest levels of corruption. For the rest of the country the survey suggest a slight north-south bias with the northern states like Chihuahua, Sonora and Baja California showing lower levels of corrupt acts than their southern counterparts.[88]

To quantify the extent of corrupt practices in Mexico over time figure 5.33 shows the evolution of the Corruption Perception Index (CPI) that has been developed by Transparency International.[89]

Figure 5.33: Corruption in Mexico 1980-2003 measured by the CPI

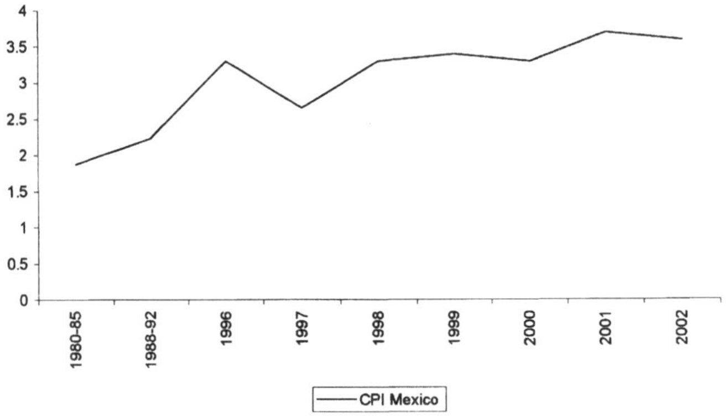

Source: Own figure using data by Transparency International (2003).

The CPI ranks countries concerning the degree to which corruption is perceived to exist among public officials and politicians. Index values vary between 0 (high corruption) and 10 (low corruption). In the 2002 rating Mexico ranked on the 57th place with a score of 3.6 among 102 ranked countries. As a benchmark Finland on the first place has been rated with a score of 9.7 for the same year. An inspection of the Mexican data reveals a continuous downward trend in the levels of perceived corruption since the middle of the 80s that has only been interrupted by a short decline of index values during the year 1997.

---

[87] See López Presa et al. (1998).
[88] See Transparency International (2001).
[89] For details of the methodology of the index see Lambsdorf (2002).

Since compared to the situation in the 80s perceived levels of political corruption are considerably lower in the 90s the CPI-Index suggests a success of the anti-corruption campaigns that have been initiated by the federal government. Among other OECD member countries however, Mexico still holds the penultimate position in the ranking only being surpassed by Turkey which indicates that the level of corruption in Mexico still by far surpasses average corruption ratings of industrialized countries.

Another index to quantify the evolution of corruption in Mexico during the last years is the index of governmental corruption that has been constructed by PRS group. The difference between the latter indicator and the CPI is that it does not determine a country's level of corruption but the political risk involved in corruption, two factors that may differ considerably. Figure 5.34 depicts the evolution of the PRS index for the period from 1984 to 2003. Indeed the inspection of the data paints a completely different picture of corruption in Mexico. Since from 1984 to the mid 90s index values remain unchanged the data suggests a total failure of public anti corruption campaigns initiated during this period indicating that despite of reforms political risk due to corruption has not significantly diminished. The last years even show rising levels of political risk from corruption although the Fox government made the fight against corruption one of the most important points on its political agenda.[90] The distinct empirical evidence about the extent of corruption offered by the PRS indicator and the CPI-index highlights the severe problems that are related to the empirical measurement of national corruption levels.

Figure 5.34: The PRS Corruption Index in Mexico 1984-2003

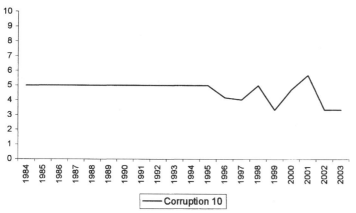

Source: Own figure and calculations using yearly averages of monthly data by PRS Group (2003) normalized to a 1-10 scale. Index values for 2003 are calculated using data for January and February.

---

[90] This empirical finding is in line with the hypothesis that societal levels of corruption are not necessarily influenced by regime type. Nevertheless it has to be underlined that a better functioning democracy may limit corrupt practices by establishing better mechanisms of control. See López Presa et al. (1998). Morris (2000) argues that corruption has changed from misuse of public power to drug related corruption.

To analyze the impact of political corruption on FDI I use the governmental corruption index that has been constructed by PRS Group which has been normalized to values between 1-10 where higher values represent less corruption.[91] The scatter-plots in Figure 5.35 depicts the relationship between the corruption index and FDI flows to Mexico.

Figure 5.35: Correlation between Corruption and FDI

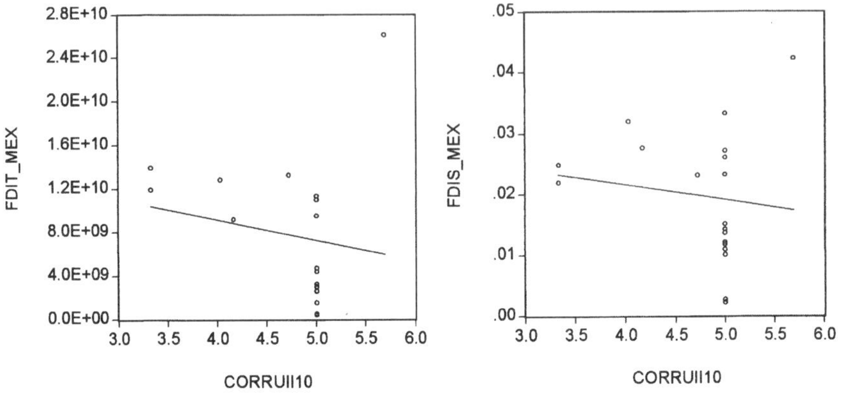

Source: Own figure using yearly averages of monthly data by PRS Group (2003) and yearly data of the World Bank (2002b).

Mexican data does not confirm the theoretical hypothesis of a negative correlation between corruption and FDI. Instead, the scatter-plots as well as the numerical statistical correlation indicate a counter-intuitive positive correlation implying that higher levels of corruption would attract higher FDI flows. These result are clearly at odds with empirical evidence of the panel analysis in Chapter 4 and other empirical research on this matter.[92] Therefore, it is most likely that the counter-intuitive results for the Mexican case are due to the lack of econometric sophistication of the analysis or the small data sample. Given other empirical results and the qualitative empirical evidence on corruption in Mexico it is in turn most likely that foreign investors are, like their national counterparts, affected by corruption. Nevertheless, this analysis does not provide empirical evidence for the theoretical hypothesis postulating a negative correlation between corruption and FDI.

5.3.2.4 Protection of Property Rights
Economic theory argues that property rights protection is a necessary prerequisite for a functioning market economy since weak protection of

---

[91] The CPI index is not used here because the number of available data is considerably smaller.

[92] See Wei (2000) who uses corruption indices provided by the Economist Intelligence Unit, ICRG, and Transparency International. His results indicate an important influence of corruption on FDI flows. As Wei also used data from PRS Group his findings also indicate that the counter-intuitive results for Mexican data are not biased by the use of the PRS corruption indicator.

property rights distorts incentives for private investment. Therefore, well defined and enforceable property rights are an important prerequisite for a favorable national investment climate. As the historical review of Mexican policy towards MNEs demonstrated, the protection of property rights in the country has long been feeble.[93] ELIZONDO argues that in contrast to the United States the constitutional protection of property rights in Mexico is weak since national interests (represented by the state) are valued higher than private interests, namely private property rights.[94] In particular article 27 of the constitution may serve as a legal basis for dilutions of property rights as it permits expropriations for reasons of public utility and through indemnification.[95] Although article 27 guarantees indemnification, in the past the inefficient judiciary only offered weak protection of individual constitutional rights.

Furthermore, in line with these constitutional principles the expropriation law from 1936 gives the president the right to expropriate private property to achieve a more equitable income distribution. In addition a law from 1950 permits an extensive regulation of prices by the executive branch. Based on these legal norms it takes nothing more than a simple signature of the president to expropriate private property.[96] Since in the past the Mexican government extensively used this capacity to expropriate foreign property MNEs are aware of potential problems caused by predatory intervention of the state.

Although the risk of expropriation is hard to quantify, I use an indicator that has been constructed by PRS Group. Figure 5.36 depicts the evolution of this indicator that is available for the period 1982-1997. After the large scale nationalization of Mexican banks in 1982 expropriation risk showed a decline during the mid 80s until a liberal policy initiated a steady process of diminishing expropriation risks. Expropriation risk further declined with the initiation of the NAFTA negotiation process due to the fact that the treaty contained explicit regulation forbidding expropriations without due reasons or proper indemnification of affected parties which helped strengthen legal security for foreign investors in Mexico by recognizing common principles of international law.

---

[93] Elizondo (1999) argues that high degree of liquidity on Mexican financial markets and the preference for US dollars are signs of weak property rights and fears of inflation or devaluation.

[94] See Elizondo (2001).

[95] Article 27 states: "The nation shall have at all times the right to impose on private property such modalities as the public interest dictates, and the right to regulate the use and exploitation of all natural resources susceptible to appropriation, in order to preserve and to effect an equitable distribution of the public wealth." English translation cited by Whiting (1992) p.243-244. Conflicts with Mexico over the implications of Article 27 for US investors led the US government to refusing the recognition of the Mexican government until 1923. See Whiting (1992) p.62. For a detailed discussion of Article 27 see Elizondo (2001) p.59-72.

[96] See Elizondo (2001) p.54-83.

Figure 5.36: Expropriation Risk in Mexico 1982-1997

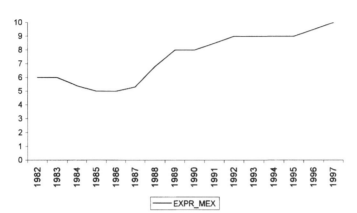

Source: Own figure and calculations using yearly data from PRS (1998) normalized to a 1-10 scale.

In other words, the signing of NAFTA was an important step towards a better institutional framework for foreign investors because it widely extended the protection of foreign owned property in Mexico against acts of direct and creeping expropriation.

For empirical evidence on the impact of expropriation risk on FDI in Mexico I calculated the statistical correlation of the index variables with FDI inflows and the FDI/GDP ratio respectively. The results are displayed in the two scatter-plots in Figure 5.37.

Figure 5.37: Correlation between Expropriation Risk and FDI

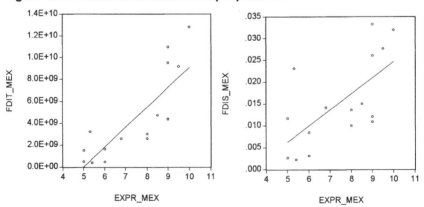

Source: Own figure using yearly averages of monthly data by PRS Group 2003 and yearly data of the World Bank (2002b).

An inspection of the Mexican data strongly suggests a positive impact of lower expropriation risk on FDI as both scatter-plots indicate a positive correlation. Moreover, additional empirical evidence for the panel of Latin American countries from Chapter 4 indicates that the reported correlation is not spurious as the risk indicator turns out to be positive, significant and robust.[97]

It has already been argued that private property rights are not only affected by outright expropriations but also by more subtle policies that do not imply a total loss of the title to private assets but that nevertheless seriously reduce their value. To give only a few examples foreign property may be affected by discriminatory taxation, restriction of operations, excessive labor legislation and costs, repatriation restrictions as well as governmental breach of contract and so on. Although the variety of potentially influential variables that determine the risk of creeping expropriation make the concept hard to quantify, the Investment Profile indicator of PRS Group is a suitable proxy variable. This indicator is "a measure of the government's attitude toward inward investment as determined by four components: the risk to operations, taxation, repatriation, and labor costs".[98]

Figure 5.38 which depicts the evolution of the investment profile in Mexico between 1984 and 2003 shows that in the aftermath of the Mexican debt crisis the investment profile of the Mexican economy was continuously declining.

Figure 5.38: Investment Profile in Mexico 1984-2003

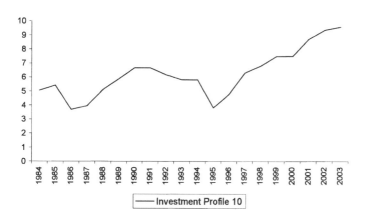

Source: Own figure and calculations using yearly averages of monthly data by PRS Group (2003) normalized to a 1-10 scale. Index values for 2003 are calculated using data for January and February.

The process of liberalizing and opening the economy however that begun thereafter entailed a steady improvement of the investment profile which

---

[97] The governance indicators GOVI and GOVII that contain the subindicator "Expropriation Risk" were found to be robust determinants of FDI. See Table 4.4 and 4.5 in Chapter 4.
[98] See PRS Group (2003).

reached its peak during the early 90s. Political turmoil and the financial crisis in 1994 implied a short fall of investment profile which thereafter shows a steady upward trend that is peaking in 2003. It has to be stressed that the signing of NAFTA considerably influenced the investment profile of Mexico in various ways. First, as already pointed out NAFTA property rights protection also covers actions of creeping expropriations. Although legal enforceability and security are still limited by difficulties to provide for clear evidence of acts of creeping expropriation by host governments, NAFTA clearly strengthens legal certainty of foreign investors. Second, NAFTA forbids transfer restriction on foreigners and the imposition of performance requirements which could both considerably dilute foreign property rights. Despite of these guarantees figure 5.38 shows that the amelioration of the investment profile did not start until 1995. However, the period when NAFTA came into effect was a period of crisis for the Mexican political system as well as for the economy. Therefore, the missing empirical evidence that NAFTA strengthened the investment profile in Mexico may be due to the fact that the amelioration of legal certainty may have been statistically outweighed and overcompensated by the deterioration of other sub-parts of the indicator.

To assess the influence of the investment profile on FDI to Mexico figure 5.39 depicts the correlation between the indicator and incoming FDI as well as the FDI/GDP ratio.

Figure 5.39: Correlation between Investment Profile and FDI

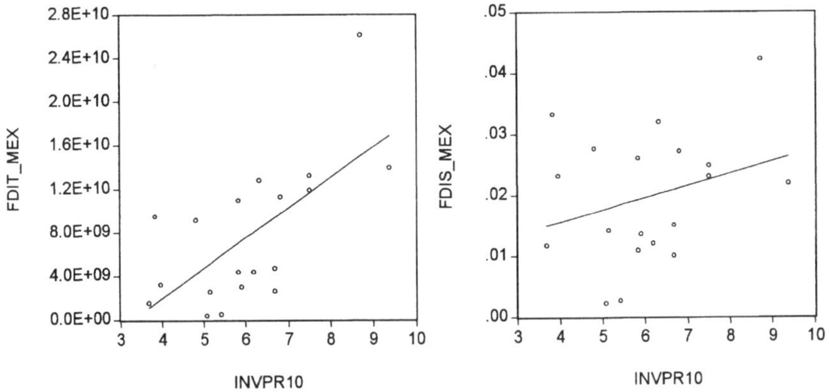

Source: Own figure using yearly averages of monthly data by PRS Group 2003 and yearly data of the World Bank (2002b).

The two scatter-plots permit the careful conclusion that investment profile has a positive impact on FDI in Mexico although the evidence for the FDI/GDP ratio is less striking. However, it is hard to decide if the empirical results suffer from the small data set bias as additional evidence from the panel analysis in

Chapter 4 is missing for this indicator.[99] Although the conclusion of this paragraph necessarily has to be careful, the empirical evidence from Mexican data suggests a positive impact of lower expropriation and creeping expropriation risk on FDI flows to Mexico.

5.3.4 Societal Factors of Risk
5.3.4.1 Overview
The following paragraphs are dedicated to analyzing the impact of societal political risk variables on FDI flows to Mexico. For the analysis I use the simple theoretical framework based on the concept of social capital that has been described in paragraph 3.1.2.4. evaluating the impact of socioeconomic variables on transaction costs and private investment incentives. All numerical statistical results are depicted in table A.2 in Annex II while the following paragraphs simply show scatter-plots illustrating the correlation. Although it has to be underlined that the interpretation of results has to be careful due to the lack of reliable data, the analysis indicates the impact of a given variable on FDI flows to Mexico. The following chapter starts with the evaluation of societal tensions due to religion, ethnic provenience or other internal factors.

5.3.4.2 Ethnic, Religious and other Internal Conflicts
Despite of many other problems, since the revolution Mexico did not experience greater societal instabilities or even political turmoil. With the exception of left wing guerrilla activity and student protests during the late 60s and early 70s that have been violently repressed by the government Mexico neither experienced violent manifestations of social unrest.[100] Instead, the well-established corporatist PRI rule ensured a degree of societal stability that is unusual for a Latin American country. As a legacy of the Spanish colonial rule the vast majority of the country is roman-catholic. The dominating ethnical group are the "mestizos", descendants of Spanish and indigenous people. Despite of these facts contemporary Mexico is still characterized by a vast ethnic, social and economic heterogeneity holding enormous potential for future conflict. In the south and the southeast of Mexico live large proportions of indigenous people, who largely only speak pre-hispanic languages and often live in poor economic conditions or poverty.[101] The economic reforms in the agrarian sector during the 80s and 90s that dismantled the old system of subsidies and transfers hardly hit rural small scale producers of coffee, maize and other crops.[102] In 1994 economic difficulties and problems of racial discrimination of ethnic minorities provoked an armed uprising in the southern federal state of Chiapas by the Ejército Zapatista de Liberación Nacional

---

[99] An empirical analysis of this indicator could not be performed because it was not available for all countries in the sample.

[100] See Philip (1992) for an analysis of the student movement and the guerilla groups. Mainwaring underlines that most of the left wing groups were never serious contenders for power. See Mainwaring (1999).

[101] See Otero (1996) p.3. Nine million of the eleven million indigenous people living in Mexico are considered as extremely poor. See PRS Group (2000) p.13.

[102] See Harvey (1996) p.191-199. For a detailed analysis of the agrarian reform see Gates (1996).

(EZLN). Although one central focus of the EZLN is the strengthening of minority rights, it is hard to decide if the uprising was essentially motivated by ethnic reasons or rather by the poor economic situation and extreme poverty in the south of Mexico as well as by a rejection of the liberal reforms implemented by the Mexican government.[103] Although actively promoting the strengthening of indigenous rights and basic autonomy for these groups, the *zapatista* movement is not characterized by exclusionary nationalism or secessionist motives.[104] A second group of rebels, the Popular Revolutionary Army (EPR) emerged in Oaxaca and Guerrero indicating that the problem of societal unrest is no longer limited to the state of Chiapas.[105]

To quantify political risk that originate in ethnical or religious differences I use indicators that are provided by PRS Group. The ethnic tension indicator is "a measure of the degree of tension attributable to racial, national, or language divisions". Lower ratings (higher risk) are given to those countries where tensions are high because the opposing ethnic groups are intolerant and unwilling to compromise with the government.[106] Classifying the EZLN in this manner is difficult as talks between the rebel leaders and the central government were initiated shortly after the conflict and are still underway. However, even if the national government initiated a constitutional amendment that guaranteed autonomy and the protection of indigenous rights in 1998, the negotiations have been difficult and were occasionally interrupted by large scale protest or even violent acts.[107]

Figure 5.40 depicts the evolution of the ethnic tensions indicator in Mexico between 1984 and 2003. As evidenced by the data levels of ethnic tensions remained unchanged at a low level during the 80s and 90s. Ratings began to deteriorate when the new government of president Fox did not manage to reach an agreement with the EZLN.[108] Despite of this problem and the deterioration of the rating it has to be underlined that the economic implications of the problems in Chiapas and in other southern states are only of minor importance for MNEs since foreign investors, whose installations are not situated in those regions are hardly affected by these local instabilities.[109]

---

[103] The fact that ethnic origin and economic conditions are often correlated suggests that both factors are relevant for the uprising. On the motives of the Chiapas rebellion see Rabasa/Arias (2002) and López y Rivas (2002).

[104] See Harvey (2001).

[105] The EPR engaged in several violent attacks in the period from 1996-1999. See PRS Group (2000) p.44.

[106] See PRS Group (2003).

[107] See Rabasa/Arias (2002). In December of 1997 45 Chiapas Indians were killed in the village Acteal by paramilitary forces apparently linked to the armed forces and the PRI. In the aftermath of the killings Zedillo replaced his interior minister and the governor of Chiapas resigned. See PRS Group (2000) p.39. In 1998 eight Zapatistas were killed in a firefight with the army. See PRS Group (1999) p.B11.

[108] For the reasons of the deterioration of the peace talks see López y Rivas (2002).

[109] FDI in Chiapas and other southern states is scarce due to the economic backwardness of the region. See table 5.8 in paragraph 5.1.2.3.

Figure 5.40: Ethnic Tensions in Mexico 1984-2003

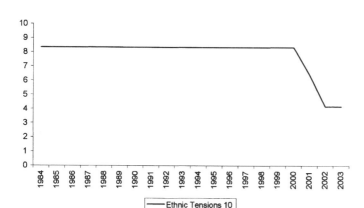

Source: Own figure and calculations using yearly averages of monthly data by PRS Group (2003) normalized to a 1-10 scale. Index values for 2003 are calculated using data for January and February.

However, since poor economic conditions of the indigenous population in rural areas are a problem that is not limited to the state of Chiapas, future conflicts may also arise in other poor and remote rural areas of the country as for example in Guerrero, Puebla, Oaxaca or Tamaulipas.[110] Despite of possible risks in the future the correlation between the ethnic tensions rating and the inflows of FDI and the FDI/GDP ratio respectively show no indication of a positive relationship between the two variables.[111]

The same result holds for an analysis of the influence of religious tensions on FDI. As already pointed out religious beliefs are homogenous in Mexico and dominated by the roman catholic confession.[112] Furthermore, the revolutionary heritage of Mexico implies that education and public life were not dominated by religious convictions implying that the potential risk of violent social conflicts due to religious divisions is limited. For the quantification of the variable I use an indicator that is provided by PRS group. This indicator is "a measure of religious tensions arising from the domination of society and/or governance by a single religious group, or a desire to dominate, in a way that replaces civil law by religious law, excludes other religions from the political/social processes, suppresses religious freedom or expressions of religious identity. The risks involved range from inexperienced people imposing inappropriate policies to civil dissent or civil war.[113]

---

[110] See López y Rivas (2002).

[111] As the relationship between the two variables was of no major importance the scatter-plot will not be displayed here. For the results of the statistical correlation see Appendix II.

[112] According to PRS Group (2000) 89% of Mexico's population is Roman Catholic and 6% protestant.

[113] See PRS Group (2003).

Figure 5.41: Religious Tensions in Mexico 1984-2003

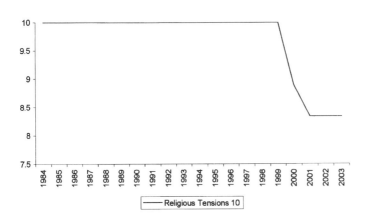

Source: Own figure and calculations using yearly averages of monthly data by PRS Group (2003) normalized to a 1-10 scale. Index values for 2003 are calculated using data for January and February.

The development of the rating which is depicted in figure 5.41 suggest that religious tensions have not been an influential risk factor in Mexico since for all the years prior to the 2000 rating the country attained the lowest possible level of risk. That is, the measure indicates the absence of political risks resulting out of religious conflicts.

Another suitable measure for the assessment of internal political conflicts is the indicator "Internal Conflict" that has been developed by PRS Group. Instead of focusing on societal risks that result from ethnic or religious tensions this indicator is "a measure of political violence and its actual or potential impact on governance, taking into consideration such factors as whether threats exist, whether they have political objective considering the size and strength of support, and the geographic nature of the conflict".[114]

Figure 5.42 depicts the evolution of this indicator between 1984 and 2003. The high indicator values suggest only a minor risk position for foreign investors. Nevertheless, the political difficulties of the late 80s and the mid 90s are clearly mirrored by the deteriorating development of the indicator values during this periods although risks originating in internal conflicts still remain on a moderate level. Despite of the severe economic crisis during the 80s public demonstrations caused little civil strife.

The severest problems of violence usually were related to drug trafficking. Between 1989 and 1995 reported terrorist attacks totaled 93 including 31 assassinations, 12 kidnappings and 22 bombings.[115] Between 1991 and 1997 Mexico registered 297 cases of terrorist attacks including 85 assassination, 54

---

[114] See PRS Group (2003).
[115] See PRS Group (1995).

kidnappings and 22 bombings. During 1996 Mexico City experienced more than 3000 protest marches and 1997 a large protest of teachers paralyzed the City. Despite of these events most serious violence remained largely confined to the Chiapas region and was not directed against foreign businesses.[116]

Figure 5.42: Internal Conflict in Mexico 1984-2003

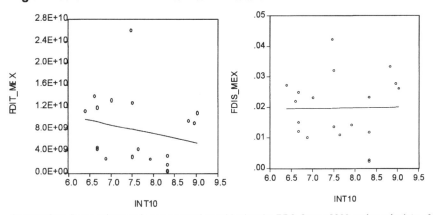

Source: Own figure and calculations using yearly averages of monthly data by PRS Group (2003) normalized to a 1-10 scale. Index values for 2003 are calculated using data for January and February.

Despite of the Zapatista conflict and growing societal resistance to liberalization policies and the opening of the economy, internal risk seems not to be among the most important risk factors for foreign investors.

Figure 5.43: Correlation between Internal Conflict and FDI

Source: Own figure using yearly averages of monthly data by PRS Group 2003 and yearly data of the World Bank (2002b).

---

[116] An exception was the kidnapping of a leading Japanese businessman in 1996 that spread fear among foreign executives. See PRS Group (1999) p.D2.

Figure 5.43 depicts the correlation between internal conflict and FDI flows and the FDI/GDP ratio respectively. The initial hypothesis that postulated a minor role of internal conflict for foreign investment decisions is confirmed by the inspection of the data which does not indicate a positive correlation between the measure of internal conflict and the inflows of FDI to Mexico. The analysis of internal conflicts confirms the general result that measures of societal conflict do not seem to be influential variables for FDI inflows to Mexico. This result is in line with the results of the panel analysis in Chapter 4 that likewise did not find a robust influence of societal risk variables on FDI inflows to Latin American countries.[117]

This additional empirical evidence concerning the impact of societal risk variables on FDI flows does not suggests that the results for the Mexican case are simply biased by the small data sample. One may therefore conclude that indicators of societal risk do not have a major impact on FDI flows to Mexico and that although reforms in this field may be socially desirable they are hardly an improvement of the institutional environment for foreign investors. Even the major upheavals and conflicts in Mexico, as the uprising in Chiapas, do not imply elevate risks for foreign companies as these conflicts are restricted to remote rural areas whereas foreign investors are usually concentrated in urban areas. In spite of these findings, it has to be underlined that these risks may become more influential in the future, if the government does not succeed in resolving these societal conflicts.

5.3.4.3 Governmental Legitimacy in Mexico
The importance of regime legitimacy for transaction costs has been underlined in Chapter 3, where it was argued that regimes with low levels of legitimacy may cause the risk of future civil strife when discontent of the population is growing over time.[118] Despite of its theoretical importance the empirical measurement of regime legitimacy is not straightforward. One approach is to assess the degree of confidence that people have in national institutions as low levels of legitimacy should coincide with low confidence and vice versa. The description of the current political system in Mexico already showed that the level of trust and confidence that Mexicans have in political institutions is rather low. Therefore, using societal level of confidence in governmental institutions as a proxy for regime legitimacy implies low ratings for the Mexican government.

Other important social strains in Mexico during the late 80s and the 90s are the rapidly increasing population, an inequitable income distribution, vast regional differences in development, as well as crime and corruption.[119] High population growth in Mexico is an important potential source of societal conflict since between 1967 and 1996 the Mexican population doubled leading to one million new workers every year entering the labor market without great

---

[117] See Table 4.3 in Chapter 4.
[118] See World Bank (2003).
[119] Problems of crime and public insecurity have already been discussed in paragraph 5.3.3.2.

chances to get a proper job.[120] Moreover, the liberal reforms of the 80s considerably lowered living standards that have been kept up artificially by high consumptive government spending. The decade witnessed a particular massive decline in real wages which nearly fell by 30% during the 80s which is shown in figure 5.44.

Figure 5.44: Real Wages in Mexico 1980-1990 (1981=1)

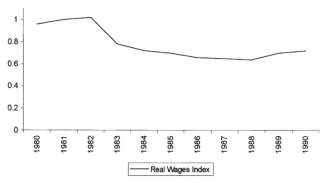

Source: Own figure with data from Krämer (1995).

In addition, a wave of bankruptcies hit those smaller companies which could not compete with the intensified competition of foreign companies. The 1994-95 financial crisis increased hardships as the economy passed into recession and many workers have been laid off.[121] As an immediate consequence of the crisis real wages fell by 25% in 1995.[122] In particular the southern states of Mexico have lagged export-oriented northern states have profited from the integration with the US.[123]

An empirical indicator of societal satisfaction containing these variables has been provided by PRS Group. The indicator Socioeconomic Conditions is an "estimate of the general public's satisfaction or dissatisfaction with the government's economic policies, covering a broad spectrum of factors ranging from infant mortality and medical provision to housing and interest rates. Different weights are applied in different societies, depending upon the relative political impact."[124] Hence, the indicator measures how the socioeconomic situation in a given country influences the satisfaction of the people with government policy. Although a proxy variable, it is reasonable to argue that low levels of public satisfaction with governmental institutions coincide with low levels of regime legitimacy and vice versa.

---

[120] See PRS Group (2000) p.14-15.
[121] In 1995 Mexican GDP fell by 6.2%.
[122] See PRS Group (1999) p.G3.
[123] Life Expectancy is 20 years higher in the North than in the South. Per capita consumption and average wages are five times higher in the North. See PRS Group (2000) p.15.
[124] See PRS Group (2003).

An inspection of the Mexican data shows that the indicator for socioeconomic conditions largely coincides with the evolution of the economic situation. This direct correlation between national economic performance and socioeconomic conditions stems from the fact that social benefits as unemployment insurance or public welfare are scarce in Mexico which implies that economic cycles have a direct effect on living standards of the population. As figure 5.45 indicates the socioeconomic situation ameliorates during the late 80s after the most serious effects of the debt crisis have been overcome.

Figure 5.45: Socioeconomic Conditions in Mexico 1984-2003

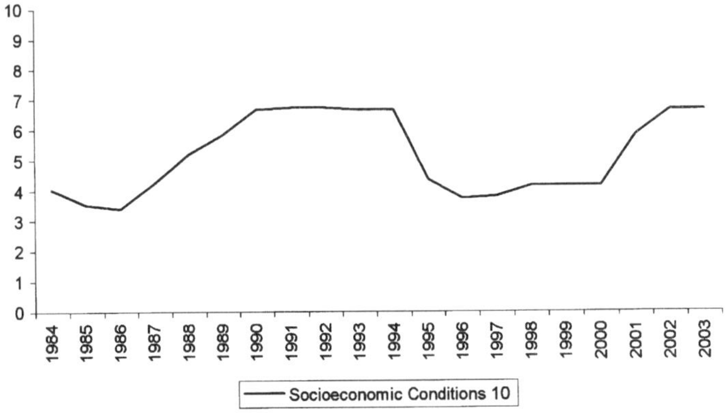

Socioeconomic Conditions 10

Source: Own figure and calculations using yearly averages of monthly data by PRS Group (2003) normalized to a 1-10 scale. Index values for 2003 are calculated using data for January and February.

Between the late 80s and the financial crisis in 1994 conditions kept stable. Following the financial crisis of 1994 and the resulting recession socioeconomic conditions quickly deteriorated reaching again the low levels of the post debt crisis years. As late as in 2000 the indicator shows the first signs of recovery reaching again mid 90s levels.

To analyze the impact of socioeconomic conditions on FDI flows to Mexico the two scatter-plots in figure 5.46 show the correlation between the indicator and FDI flows and the FDI/GDP ratio respectively. An inspection of the data does not reveal a clear pattern that would indicate the positive relationship between the two variables that would have been theoretically expected. As further empirical evidence from the panel analysis in Chapter 4 is not available for this indicator the analysis of the data does not permit a clear cut conclusion about the influence of regime legitimacy proxied by the socioeconomic conditions variable. One of the two depicted correlations rather suggest the counter-intuitive result that worsening socioeconomic conditions imply higher levels of FDI.

Figure 5.46: Correlation between Socioeconomic Conditions and FDI

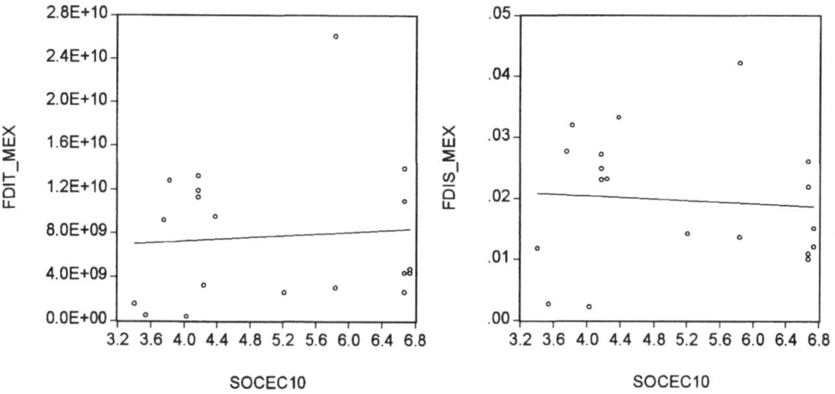

SOCEC10   SOCEC10

Source: Own figure using yearly averages of monthly data by PRS Group (2003) and yearly data of the World Bank (2002b).

Although it has to be underlined that this result may also be due to the size of the available data set, it has to be concluded that the empirical analysis of Mexican data does not permit the conclusion that societal risk factors have an influence on incoming FDI. This empirical evidence is supported by the results of the panel analysis in Chapter 4 that could not identify a robust relationship between societal indicators of risk and FDI inflows to Latin American countries. The joint findings of the two empirical studies suggest that the influence of variables that determine the level of societal transaction cost is not as important as the influence of governance related variables. The following paragraphs analyze the impact of aggregate political risk indicators on FDI flows to Mexico.

5.3.5 Aggregate Political Risk in Mexico

After reviewing the sub-indices of political risk this paragraph is dedicated to the analysis of aggregate political risk levels in Mexico. To do so three different aggregate risk indicators will be used and the evidence of preceding paragraphs will be briefly summarized. Up to now the empirical evidence highlights the importance of macroeconomic and governance related risk factors for FDI to Mexico. Economic and financial risk as well as democratic reliability, political constraints, expropriation risk and bureaucratic quality showed a positive correlation with incoming FDI. Other theoretically influential variables as the rule of law and corruption however, showed no evidence of a positive correlation contradicting the empirical evidence from Chapter 4. Despite of these findings it is most likely that these risk factors are nevertheless of particular importance in Mexico as evidenced by the study of qualitative empirical evidence on Mexico.[125]

---

[125] See the literature on corruption and rule of law that is cited in the paragraphs 5.3.3.2 and 5.3.3.3.

At the same time the empirical evidence on the influence of societal risk factors suggested that these variables play a minor role in determining Mexican FDI since religious, ethnic or other societal tensions did not turn out to be of major importance for FDI flows. Even the most severe societal instability in Mexico, the Chiapas conflict, does not seem to be a menace for foreign asset holders. Likewise this study did not find a positive correlation between socioeconomic conditions and FDI. Nevertheless, it has to be underlined that social conflicts in Mexico, although locally restricted at the moment, are a potential risk that may gain importance in the near future. High levels of poverty, violation of human rights and high distributive inequality in Mexico are all potential reasons for serious societal conflicts. This future threat is even more important as the process of political reform and democratization in Mexico weakens the power of the central government to violently repress social tensions.

In addition to these findings this paragraph assesses if aggregate political risk variables have an influence on FDI flows to Mexico. For this analysis three different aggregate risk indicators will be used. The first indicator that will be examined in this context is the Opacity Index that has been calculated by PWC for the year 2001. This Index that is based on global surveys of company officials, bankers, equity analysts, and in-country PWC consultants provides an estimate of the adverse effects of opacity on the cost and availability of capital in 35 countries. Opacity is defined as "the lack of clear, accurate, formal, easily discernible, and widely accepted practices". The Global Opacity Index offers a composite "O-Factor" ranking for each country, based on opacity data in the following five areas:

1) Corruption in government and the bureaucracy
2) Laws governing contracts or property rights
3) Economic policies (fiscal, monetary, and tax-related)
4) Accounting standards
5) Business regulations

Together, these create the acronym CLEAR (Corruption, Legal, Economic, Accounting, Regulatory). Opacity in any of these areas will raise the cost of doing business as well as curtail the availability of funds. Two unique measures result from the Index: the O-Factor, and rankings as well as measurements of the risk premium that is attributable to opacity when countries borrow through sovereign bond issuances in international or domestic capital markets. These multiple measures help demonstrate real-world costs associated with opacity where the O-Factor is the score of a country based on survey responses. High numbers indicate a high degree of opacity and low numbers indicate a low degree of opacity.[126] Due to its characteristics the opacity index is suitable as a proxy variable for aggregate political risk and may be used to calculate the amounts of foregone FDI flows due to opacity. Table 5.9 summarizes the results for Mexico. Opacity in the country has been estimated at a score of 48 with the benchmark score being

---

[126] See PWC (2001a), PWC (2001b).

13 in Singapore. The index values of the sub-categories illustrate that in particular legal certainty, economic policy and the regulatory environment are weak in Mexico, a result that with the exception of the economic policy environment is in line with the preceding analysis of political risk in Mexico. The tax equivalent shows the effect of opacity when it is interpreted as if it imposes a hidden tax on private corporations. The index score of 15 for Mexico indicates that the effects of opacity in the country are equivalent to levying an additional 15-percent corporate income tax.

Table 5.9: Effects of Opacity in Mexico

O-Factor	C	L	E	A	R	Tax-Equivalent (%)	Risk Premium (Basis Points)	Deterred FDI (% Lower Bound)	Deterred FDI (Mio US$ Lower Bound)	Deterred FDI (% Point est.)	Deterred FDI (Mio $) Point Est.
48	42	58	57	29	52	15%	308	53	6477	70	8554

Source: PWC (2001a), PWC (2001b)

The Risk Premium indicates the increased cost of borrowing faced by countries due to opacity, expressed in basis points (100 basis points = one percentage point) since on average, countries with higher opacity tend to have to pay higher interest rates on issued debt. The score of 308 for Mexico indicates that the country needs to pay international investors an extra 3,08 percent on sovereign debt due to opacity. The columns Deterred Investment show how incoming FDI flows would respond if the country managed to reduce its current level of opacity to that of the benchmark, that is, to the level of the average of the 4 countries with the lowest ratings. The results for Mexico show that the country could increase its inward FDI by 53 to 70% if it could reduce its opacity to the level of the benchmark group. In dollar terms this would represent an amount between 6477 to 8554 Mio. US$. Considering the scores of the sub-categories, in particular improvements in the fields of legal certainty, national economic policy and the regulatory environment show enormous potential of attracting higher inward FDI.[127] Unfortunately lacking data does not permit to analyze the evolution of the Opacity Index over time.

The aggregate political risk indicator that has been constructed by PRS Group is "a means of assessing the political stability of a country on a comparable basis with other countries by assessing risk points for each of the component factors of government stability, socioeconomic conditions, investment profile, internal conflict, external conflict, corruption, military in politics, religion in politics, law and order, ethnic tensions, democratic accountability, and bureaucracy quality. Risk ratings range from a high of 100 (least risk) to a low of 0 (highest risk), though lowest de facto ratings generally range in the 30s and 40s."[128] This indicators thus pools the information of the various sub-

---

[127] See PWC (2001b).
[128] See PRS Group (2003).

indicators and thereby constructs an overall measure of aggregate political risk in Mexico.

Figure 5.47 shows the evolution of this aggregate risk indicator for the time period 1984-2003.

Figure 5.47 Political Risk in Mexico 1984-2003

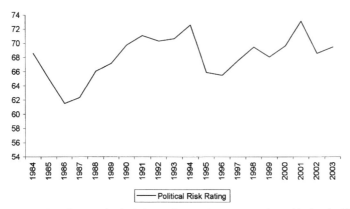

Source: Own figure and calculations using yearly averages of monthly data by PRS Group (2003). Index values for 2003 are calculated using data for January and February.

Again the mid 80s are marked by a serious deterioration of the risk index. Since the beginning of the economic and political reform period in the mid 80s however, the risk index shows a steadily growing pattern reaching its summit in the mid 90s indicating a success of the reforms implemented by the Mexican government. Following the financial crisis of 1994 the aggregate risk rating fell again showing a slow pace of recovery afterwards that with small variations extends to the present time.

To test for the statistical correlation of aggregate political risk and FDI figure 5.48 depicts two scatter-plots illustrating the correlation between political risk and yearly FDI inflows as well as the FDI/GDP ratio. The patterns of the scatter-plots and the statistical correlation between the two variables indicate a weak positive influence of aggregate political risk on FDI flows to Mexico. However, as additional empirical evidence from the panel analysis in Chapter 4 is missing these findings have to be interpreted with caution. The weak correlation is surprising as several sub-indicators of the aggregate political risk index turned out to be positively correlated with FDI inflows. A possible explanation for the weaker correlation of the aggregate risk index is that the index also contains societal risk variables that were not found to be positively correlated with FDI and produce a bias.

Figure 5.48: Correlation between Political Risk and FDI

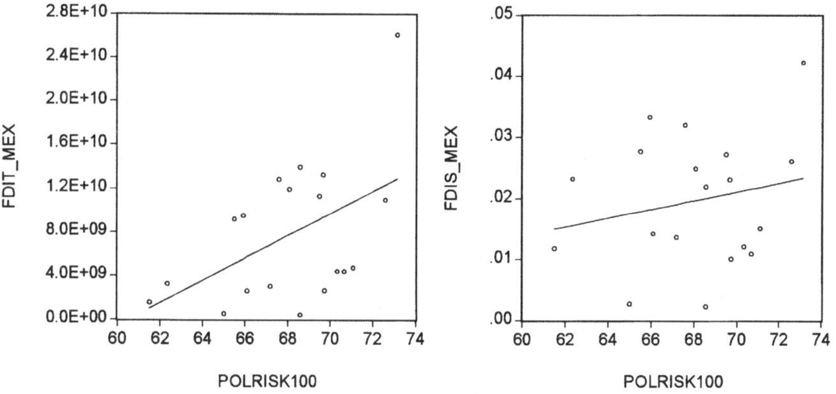

Source: Own figure using yearly averages of monthly data by PRS Group (2003) and yearly data of the World Bank (2002b). Index values for 2003 are calculated using data for January and February

Another PRS measure of aggregate risk is the so-called composite index that is constructed by using a weighted average of economic, financial and political risk.[129] Higher values of the index indicate lower risk and vice versa. Ratings range from 0–100 with values in the interval 0-49.5 characterizing a high risk environment and index values from 80-100 representing countries of low risk. Figure 5.49 shows the development of the indicator for the period 1984-2003. Similar to the aggregate political risk index the composite risk index reaches its all time low in the mid 80s reflecting the economic downturn of Latin American countries following the debt crisis.

Figure 5.49: Composite Risk in Mexico 1984-2003

Source: Own figure and calculations using yearly averages of monthly data by PRS Group (2003). Index values for 2003 are calculated using data for January and February.

---

[129] The exact formula for calculating the index is 0.5 (Political Risk + Financial Risk + Economic Risk).

After the implementation of liberal economic reforms the composite risk index experienced a long upward movement with the first decreases following the financial crisis in 1994. After the Tequila-crisis however, the index shows a rapid recovery and is since then oscillating around pre-crisis levels. Since an important subpart of the risk index focuses on macroeconomic risks this empirical observation is in line with theoretical considerations and highlights that the period of economic reform is accompanied by an important amelioration of composite risk.

To analyze the effects of composite risk on the inflows of FDI to Mexico figure 5.50 depicts the correlation between the risk index and FDI as well as the FDI/GDP ratio which suggest a positive influence of lower composite risk on FDI inflows and the FDI/GDP ratio.

Figure 5.50: Correlation between Composite Risk and FDI

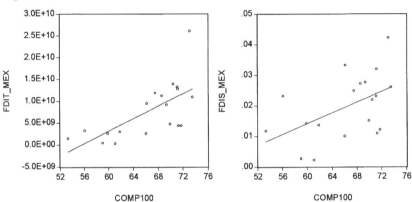

Source: Own figure using yearly averages of monthly data by PRS Group (2003) and yearly data of the World Bank (2002b).

Again there is no further econometric evidence from the panel analysis in Chapter 4 that could remove doubts concerning the small sample bias of the presented results implying that these findings have to be interpreted carefully. However, given the important role of economic and financial risk for the calculation of the index it is hardly surprising to see a positive correlation as the two sub-indices also showed a positive correlation with FDI flows to the country.

Summing up, one can conclude that both composite and political risk are positively correlated with inflows of FDI to the country suggesting a positive impact of lower risk ratings on Mexican FDI. In addition simulations based on the Opacitiy-Index suggest that political risk is an important obstacle for incoming FDI.

5.4 Risk Mitigation Strategies in Mexico
5.4.1 National Risk Mitigation Strategies
5.4.1.1 Investment Enhancement by Incentives

Since the outbreak of the debt crisis Mexico initiated a process of political and economic reform to restore its attractiveness for FDI. In Chapter 3 the establishment of investment incentives has been identified as a theoretical possibility to compensate international investors for high levels of political or country risk. It was argued that although the establishment of investment incentives may in the short run be a successful measure to attract foreign investors it is doubtful that it is the most efficient strategy since the granting of incentives is costly for host governments.[130]

Although since the mid 80s Mexico eagerly tried to attract FDI, the government never engaged in large programs of investment incentives.[131] This has been part of the general Mexican economic strategy not to accord foreign investors any more favorable treatment than their domestic counterparts.[132] Exceptions from this general practice of risk mitigation without the granting of incentives are governmental programs to foster the establishment of businesses that are located outside the metropolitan areas of Mexico City, Guadalajara and Monterrey. Some industries enjoyed tax incentives when they were considered to foster employment levels or to fulfill other beneficial societal tasks. Moreover, some of the state governments granted incentives to attract new industries in form of reduced prices for land or reductions in property taxes. However, there are no tax incentives that are specifically designed to attract FDI. The most extensive programs of incentives under the Mexican development plan are those that are provided to stimulate the exports of manufactured goods. But again also in export promotion programs there are no special measures that exclusively benefit foreign investors.[133]

The absence of large scale incentives programs may in part be explained by Mexico's attractiveness for FDI due to strong fundamentals. Mexico offers a large domestic market, a rich and diverse resource endowment, an urbanized, educated workforce and a developed infrastructure.[134] These advantages and liberal reforms of the outworn economic development strategy made international investors aware of the investment opportunities in Mexico. The successive liberalization of the foreign investment law and the opening of the economy to foreign trade implied a further growing attractiveness of Mexico as a destination for FDI. Comparatively low labor costs and the geographic proximity to the large US markets have all been contributing factors that rendered Mexico an attractive destination for FDI. The integration of the

---

[130] See paragraph 3.4.2.1.
[131] See OECD (2000). The big exception is the Maquiladora-program which grants several incentives to firms as for example exemptions from import duties.
[132] See PWC (1991).
[133] See PWC (1991).
[134] Whiting (1992) considers that these factors create an important advantage for Mexico's attractiveness for foreign investors if compared to other developing countries in the region and elsewhere. See Whiting (1992) p.27-30.

country into the North American market with the signing of NAFTA enforced Mexico's attractiveness to MNEs without the granting of special incentives programs. It is important to stress that the establishment of a large scale investment incentive program would not have tackled the main obstacles for FDI in Mexico. As pointed out in this chapter a major problem in Mexico was lacking credibility and efficiency of various governmental institutions, lacking rule of law and widespread political corruption. Investment incentives however, are no longer proper instrument to attract foreign investors when a minimum credibility of the national government is missing. This is essentially due to the fact that investors cannot be sure that promised incentives are really granted afterwards and that established contracts are honored in the long run. A lacking rule of law and inefficiency of the domestic judiciary aggravate this problem as MNEs do not have access to a credible organization of conflict resolution. Therefore, it seems reasonable that Mexico chose another strategy of risk mitigation without extensively relying on the potentially positive effects of investment incentives. The next paragraph discusses the Mexican strategy to foster international investments by reforms of the domestic institutional structure.

5.4.1.2 The Beauty Contest

Despite of the economic and political reforms in Mexico during the last years the previous chapters still identified impediments for a favorable investment climate in Mexico. Nevertheless, it is evident that Mexico made enormous progress in the amelioration of its domestic investment climate during the period 1982 to 2003. As already discussed in Chapter 3, the strategy of establishing domestic reforms to attract foreign capital is theoretically efficient but faces many problems of efficient implementation. The so called domestic "beauty contest" basically consists of reforming national institutions that have been turned out to be an impediment for private economic activity. Mexico's efforts in this field have been high and were not solely concentrated in the economic sphere but also consisted in promoting the process of political opening and democratization. Important political determinants of investment that have been identified in the previous paragraphs have been missing constraints on the executive branch, expropriation risk and bureaucratic quality. Although the empirical evidence for other potentially influential variables has not been convincing, other empirical findings and qualitative assessments suggested that also corruption and the rule of law are important institutional determinants of FDI flows.

Political constraints and democratic reliability of the government increased during the last years due to political reforms and democratization. The downfall of the one party state dominated by the PRI and the limitation of Mexican presidentialism by a better functioning system of opposition parties diminished the discretionary freedom of the Mexican government to freely conduct national policy. Although far from being complete, judicial reform and the strengthening of the legislative branch implied a better control of governmental decisions that ensured a higher degree of political continuity. At the same time abuses of public power and political corruption are more difficult to flourish in a political environment that establishes better mechanisms of control and societal checks and balances. A higher degree of rule of law permits creating an atmosphere of higher legal certainty and transparency that is favorable for private investments.

In economic policy the establishment of a stable macroeconomic environment and continued efforts to liberalize helped create a favorable investment climate in Mexico. Compared to the desastrous macroeconomic environment after the debt crisis Mexico achieved important goals by promoting fiscal discipline, limiting inflation and fostering international trade. Despite of its social consequences macroeconomic stabilization policy in Mexico has been a success story as evidenced by falling risk spreads on sovereign debt. Although the financial crisis in 1994 that was followed by a severe recession was a reminder of macroeconomic volatility and instability in the country, Mexico's bonds were rated as investment grade at the beginning of the new millennium.

Summing up, Mexico's efforts and results in the amelioration of national institutions and the maintenance of macroeconomic stability have been enormous. Nevertheless liberal economic policies are still rejected by a large part of the population and by leftist parties explaining the need to lock-in domestic policy reform. To do so, Mexico accompanied its domestic reform efforts with a strategy of international risk mitigation by signing various international agreements to promote the integration of the country into the world economy.

5.4.2 The International Risk Mitigation Strategy
As already pointed out above the idea of international risk mitigation strategies is integrating the country into a framework of international law and thereby limiting potential risks for foreign investors by increased international credibility. Although the objectives of Mexican foreign policy changed considerably during the 20th century, its scope has always been limited by the need to ensure the external capital flows on which the country depended.[135] After the outbreak of the debt crisis international credibility of Mexico reached an all time low and economic crisis affected the country more severely than ever before. For that reason Mexico's foreign policy of the post-debt-crisis years and in particular of the de la Madrid government is to a large extent dominated by economic goals and limitations.[136] WHITING even argues that the internationalization of the world economy and the outbreak of the Latin American debt crisis were the most important international constraints for the Mexican government that promoted the enactment of liberal economic reforms while avoiding a fallback to the economic nationalism of the pre-crisis years.[137] The de la Madrid administration managed to gain the support of international actors and to tackle the immense economic problems by reforming public

---

[135] See Heredia (2000).
[136] See Rico (2000) p.119-176.
[137] See Whiting (1992).

finances, liberalizing international trade and promoting macroeconomic stability. To lock-in these reforms against societal pressure and to gain further international credibility Mexico joined GATT in 1985 which has been the first important step of Mexico's international risk mitigation strategy.

De la Madrids successor Salinas continued on the path of economic reform and liberalization. During his administration the strategy of regaining international credibility that made it possible to attract FDI and technology has been the driving force behind the conduct of foreign policy. Salinas *sexenio* was thus characterized by an "economization" of foreign policy which culminated in the signing of NAFTA. Foreign policy and the presentation of Mexico on the international stage were means of demonstrating the capacity of Mexico to continue on the path of economic reform, to attract foreign investors, and to integrate the country into the world economy.[138]

To reach these objectives Mexico embarked on a strategy of an intensification and diversification of its international relations. Internationalization was realized on the multilateral level as well as on the bilateral level by various international agreements and memberships in free trade agreements. Despite various integration projects in Latin America and other regions of the world the major ambition of the Salinas administration was to achieve a deeper economic integration with the North American market and in particular with the USA. Moreover, Salinas sought to promote Mexico's integration with other developed nations by signing an cooperation agreement with the European Union in 1991 and joining OECD in 1994.[139] Since then Mexico signed various bilateral free trade agreements or bilateral investment treaties designed to increase the reciprocal protection of international investors.[140]

All these international agreements and treaties implied obligations for the Mexican government concerning the implemented economic policy as well as the reform of the political system. Besides adhering to basic investor protection, joining OECD also meant accepting and domestically promoting the values and principles of this organization as the protection of human rights, plural democracy and the establishment of a market economy.[141] Following the dramatic events in 1994 Mexico was subject to severe international criticisms for the lack of democracy, inequality, poverty and injustice with the most important criticism coming from sources inside the US that opposed the signing of NAFTA. Although Mexico initiated various efforts to evade the demands of international organizations, together with national efforts international pressure helped sustaining the process of political and economic reform. Thus, international obligations did not only help to lock-in reforms but were also in part responsible for further efforts of the Mexican government.

---

[138] See Heredia (2000) and Castro Rea et al. (1999).
[139] See Castro Rea et al. (1999).
[140] See Siqueiros (2001).
[141] For an overview of the FDI related rules of OECD see Fernandez (2002) p.269.

All Free Trade Agreements that have been signed by Mexico include investment chapters. These chapters contain provisions concerning the national treatment of international investors, on expropriation and compensation, on investment related transfers and on dispute settlement mechanisms.[142] However, the deepest credibility enhancing consequences for Mexican politics resulted out of the signing of NAFTA, in particular if one focuses on the credibility effects for international investors. Although NAFTA's explicit focus is on trade barrier reduction, the agreement had a powerful impact on decisions to locate production.[143] The treaty intensified the ties between Mexico and the North American market and contained many regulations that helped enhancing investor confidence. Given the preponderant role of US investment in Mexico it held enormous potential for the stimulation of further FDI flows. As already pointed out the reduction of trade barriers, the further opening of the economy for international investment and the higher legal security and protection of foreign investors were a major step towards a better institutional environment for foreign investors.[144] Even before NAFTA came into effect the mere possibility of such an agreement stimulated FDI flows to the country.[145] The empirical evidence for the positive effects of NAFTA on FDI inflows is overwhelming. After NAFTA negotiations were announced in 1990 FDI flows to Mexico already showed an important upward trend between 1991 and 1993.[146] After coming into effect in 1994 FDI flows to Mexico nearly tripled and sustained these high levels during the 90s despite of the detrimental impact of the financial crisis in late 1994. Likewise the FDI/GDP ratio reached new heights after the signing of the agreement by temporarily rising from around 1% in the pre-NAFTA-years to levels around 3% during the late 90s.[147]

But the effects of NAFTA also extend to the future since the treaty makes national policy reversals more costly. NAFTA is an instrument through which Mexican governments will be bound to their commitments and a political tool that increases investor confidence by locking in reforms and immunizing

---

[142] An Investment Chapter is also part of the negotiations of the Free Trade of the Americas (FTTA). See Fernandez (2002) p.268-272

[143] Peres (1990) argues that FDI promotion was a central motivation for the Mexican administration to negotiate NAFTA. See Peres-Nuñez (1990b).

[144] The Bank of Mexico writes: "The NAFTA removes significant investment barriers, ensures basic protection for NAFTA investors, and provides a mechanism for the settlement of disputes between NAFTA investors and NAFTA countries. The NAFTA requires each country to provide non-discriminatory treatment to investors and investments from other countries. Thus, each country will accord NAFTA investors "national treatment" (treatment no less favorable than that accorded to its own investors), as well as "most favored nation treatment" (treatment no less favorable that it accords to investors from other countries)." Banco de México (1994) p.192.

[145] Oman speaks of an announcement effect. See Oman (2000) p.104.

[146] See paragraph 5.2.2.2.

[147] In an analysis of the stimulating effects of NAFTA for FDI to the Mexican market Graham/Wada find that better investor protection and the access to the North American market were the most influential factors. See Graham/Wada (2000) p.786-789.

national politicians against populist pressure.[148] At the time of writing the lock-in-mechanism has turned out to be a success. Despite of extensive public pressure during the last years that has been particularly severe in the agrarian sector, up to now NAFTA contents have not been altered or renegotiated. Moreover, the Mexican experience with the dispute settlement mechanism highlights that the arbitrating body defended the principle ideas of the agreement to protect foreign investors.[149] In addition NAFTA was in part responsible for the lower country risk rating and lower interest rate spreads for Mexican sovereign debt. The fact that Mexico has recently been assigned an investment grade by international rating agencies was also related to the signing of the FTA.[150]

The success of the NAFTA investment chapter as a tool for fostering FDI flows even made it a raw model for other trade and investment negotiations, for example with the European Union. Therefore, it is to be expected that lower risk levels for European investors will likewise result in higher levels of FDI to Mexico by European companies. However, up to now there has been no substantial rise in the amount of European FDI to Mexico since the Free Trade Agreement between the two parties has been signed.[151] Thus, empirical

---

[148] See World Bank (1997) p.101, Munro (1995), Ramirez (2001) and Ramirez (2002). Perez-Nuñez argues that limiting the discretionary freedom of future Mexican governments to enhance investor confidence was one of the explicit goals of the Salinas administration. See Perez-Nuñez (1990b). Grosse writes: „This logic [increased foreign investment] has to do with the increased confidence that investors feel now that Mexico is tightly tied to the US market and the US policy framework. Investors are anticipating a much more stable and transparent policy framework for MNEs to deal with, thus encouraging them to include Mexico as a "safe" location for globally integrated production and distribution." Grosse (2003) p.664. The need for a lock in mechanism for economic reforms is demonstrated by the electoral success of PRI dissidents from the left wing Corriente Democrático in 1988. These politicians that should later found the left-center party PRD essentially wanted to revise "neo-liberal" economic reforms. See Langston (2002) p.74-79. After the Salinas administration a new wave of economic nationalism emerged led by PRI conservatives and members of the PRD. Part of the PRD's program is also a revision of NAFTA itself. Theses forces are also responsible for the failure of the Zedillo government's efforts to privatize and open the electricity sector for foreign participation. Probably the greatest resistance against free market reforms came from the EZLN which launched their upheaval in Chiapas on 1 January 1994 exactly the date when NAFTA came into effect. See PRS Group (2000). However, as the PRS Group's political risk report for 1999 argues that even if the PRD were to participate in government, it could not fully nullify trade and investment liberalization, as certain commitments given in the NAFTA treaty are irreversible. See PRS Group (1999) p.E4.

[149] See González de Cossio (2002) who reviews the Mexican experiences with the arbitration mechanism. The most prominent example of arbitration was the case of the US firm Metalclad that was awarded a compensation because necessary licenses for production have not been granted by the Mexican authorities.

[150] Blázquez/Santiso write: "The FTA (Nafta) served as a credibility anchor since it was perceived by the financial markets as a mechanism that could reduce adverse selection and eliminate a potential problem of time-inconsistency with respect to the Mexican reform process." Blázquez/Santiso (2003).

[151] See Secretería de Economía (2002).

evidence for the credibility enhancing effects of the European Free Trade Agreement is still missing.

Nevertheless the signing of NAFTA impressively illustrates the important role of international risk mitigation in the economic strategy of Mexico. While the results of domestic institutional reforms, except for the maintenance of macroeconomic stability, are still moderate, international integration succeeded in attracting immense FDI flows in short time. In addition Mexico's integration strategy placed the economy back on a growth path and diminished the probability of major economic shocks in the future.[152] This empirical evidence leads to the conclusion that Mexico's international risk mitigation strategy played an important role in regaining international investor confidence and in defending liberal economic reforms against populist domestic pressure. Nevertheless, most Mexican NAFTA critics tend to neglect these important dynamic effects of regional integration with the Northern American market.

5.5 Conclusion
The empirical investigation of political risk and the institutional environment for foreign investors revealed that the impact of political risk variables on FDI varies considerably with the sources of risk. In accordance with the empirical results of the panel analysis in Chapter 4 this chapter showed that the most influential political risk variables are those that are closely related to governmental action or the political system of Mexico. In particular expropriation risk, political constraints, bureaucratic quality and democratic reliability showed the theoretically expected positive correlation with incoming FDI. In contrast to the results of Chapter 4 I find that macroeconomic risk factors are influential political risk variables in Mexico since an index of macroeconomic stability has been found to be positively correlated with FDI flows to the country. The same holds for an indicator of financial risk that measures the government's ability to fulfill its financial obligations from official, commercial and trade obligations. Variables that measured socioeconomic phenomena in turn, did not indicate high risks or did not turn out to be correlated with FDI which is in line with the empirical results of the panel analysis in Chapter 4 that likewise finds a minor importance of societal risk factors as determinants of FDI flows. An index of aggregate political risk turned out to be weakly correlated with FDI while an indicator of composite political risk, that additionally comprises economic and financial risk showed a stronger positive correlation. Furthermore, the Opacity-Index permits an evaluation of deterred FDI due to political risk that indicates that FDI flows to Mexico could be increased by up to 70% when political risk in the form of opacity could be diminished to risk levels of a benchmark group. Summing up, despite of methodological deficiencies due to missing data the empirical evidence

---

[152] The successful integration of Mexico with the US economy led other Latin American Nations to seeking closer ties with the US. Ecuador recently adopted the US dollar as official currency linking itself to US monetary policy. Chile has been seeking to join NAFTA and now negotiated a bilateral treaty with the US. Members of the Caribbean Common market and the Central American Common market likewise have been pursuing efforts to link themselves with the US. See Grosse (2003) p.664 -666.

suggests a strong impact of government related risk factors and macroeconomic risk indicators. Faced with the dramatically high risk ratings as a consequence of the Latin American debt crisis Mexico embarked on a mixed strategy of risk mitigation based on domestic institutional reform and international risk mitigation via regional integration. It is argued that the signing of NAFTA played a crucial role for the increased investor confidence by improving market access, increasing investor protection, locking in domestic reforms and "importing" credibility from the northern neighbors.

5.6 Chapter Summary

Chapter 5.1 offers an analysis of the current political system of Mexico and its implications for the economy of the country which is restricted to those characteristics that are assumed to be influential for the investment decisions of foreign investors. It argues that the Mexican political system of the past was characterized by high levels of political discretion for the executive branch and low levels of checks and balances. A weak congress and national judiciary implied that the executive was not adequately controlled and individual constitutional guarantees were hard to enforce. Despite of reforms the national media remained partially controlled which further reduced the possibility to effectively control the government. Moreover, it is argued that the process of political reform and democratization only slowly changed this patterns of governance in Mexico.

Paragraph 5.2 presents some stylized facts of Mexican economic history and analyzes the historical development of the presence of foreign companies in Mexico. It is argued that Mexico has a long interventionist and nationalist tradition in its policy towards foreign investment that in part stems from the domination of foreign capital in the years preceding the revolution. With the example of NAFTA the chapter briefly describes the increased property rights protection and legal certainty that international treaties offer for foreigners willing to invest in the country. Furthermore, it describes the evolution of the structure of FDI flows to Mexico showing that the country succeeded in constantly upgrading incoming FDI from natural resource exploration to manufacturing and services.

Paragraph 5.3 is dedicated to the analysis of potential political risk factors and their impact on FDI to Mexico. The chapter analyzes the impact of macroeconomic risk factors, governance related risk factors and societal risk factors. Since more sophisticated econometric methods could not be applied due to data limitations, instead qualitative assessments and statistical correlations are used to evaluate the influence of political risk on FDI. I find that governance related risk factors have an important influence on FDI to Mexico, while the role of societal risk factors seems limited. In contrast to the findings in Chapter 4 however, also macroeconomic risk factors have turned out to be positively correlated with FDI flows to Mexico. With the exception of the influence of macroeconomic risk factors the results are in line with the results of the panel analysis in Chapter 4 which likewise indicate an important impact of governance related risk variables.

6 Conclusion and Outlook

This volume analyzed the influence of political risks and the institutional environment on the investment decisions of foreign investors in Latin American countries. The results shed some light on the initial questions of how political risk influences the investment decisions of MNEs and what are the sources of political risk. The theoretical analysis in Chapter 2 presents a macroeconomic and a microeconomic model of investment to analyze investment behavior under uncertainty. Both models permit to derive the result that higher degrees of uncertainty have a depressing impact on investment spending, if investments are assumed to be irreversible. By extending these basic results to FDI decisions the theoretical models suggest that higher uncertainty resulting from political events should depress investment flows and that increasing political risk in countries is, all other things equal, expected to result in lower inflows of FDI.

To facilitate the analysis the author used a simple theoretical framework that allows for the study of the impact of institutional factors on FDI flows to Latin American countries and to Mexico. The empirical impact of different risk factors is assessed by examining a panel of Latin American countries for the time period from 1982 to 1997 and a case study on Mexico for the years 1982-2003. The results of the empirical analysis confirm the central hypothesis of this work that political risk has an important influence on FDI flows to Latin America, although empirical results vary largely with different risk indicators. In the panel analysis aggregate measures of political risk did not turn out to have a robust impact on incoming FDI to Latin American countries. The same result holds for classical indices of country risk based on hard macroeconomic data for the assessment of country risk. Likewise I find that societal risk variables are not robust determinants of incoming FDI to Latin American countries. In turn, governance related risk factors were found to be significant and robust determinants of FDI.

While macroeconomic risk variables do not turn out to be of importance for FDI in the panel analysis for Latin American countries, the case study on Mexico suggests the opposite. The results concerning other risk factors are more straightforward to interpret since also in the case study on Mexico societal risk factors were not found to be influential determinants of incoming FDI. Governance-related risk factors showed a positive correlation with FDI indicating that they are influential for FDI flows to Mexico.

These results are in line with the author's hypothesis that societal political risk factors are not of major importance for FDI flows to Latin America. The empirical results suggest that societal characteristics as religious or ethnic tensions, socioeconomic conditions or internal conflicts are not influential determinants of FDI. Despite of the obvious societal need to solve these problems, social reforms are no viable way to promote FDI. These findings suggest that the insignificance of aggregate political risk variables for FDI flows that has been found in many older empirical studies stems from the fact that most risk indices contain a fraction of societal risk components with a large weight. Many of the indicators that have been used in earlier research even show a societal conflict bias that does not adequately mirror the current political and socioeconomic situation of Latin American countries. Therefore, the failure of many studies to find a significant relationship between political risk and FDI rather stems from methodological deficiencies than from the lack of relationship between the two variables.

In contrast, it is hardly surprising that the most significant and robust determinants of FDI are variables that measure political risk originating from governmental action or failure. The results of this work impressively highlight the importance of good, transparent and rules based governance in Latin America as a prerequisite for the attraction of more FDI. While the reforms of the 80s and 90s were partly successful in implementing an economic order based on the market and political systems that are now more open and democratic than ever before, a second generation of reforms that ameliorate the institutional environment for business activities in Latin America is still on the way. Although officially democratic, many countries still have characteristics of authoritarian rule and weak national institutions that often hinder a proper functioning of markets and that distort private investment incentives. The qualitative analysis of the Mexican case impressively highlights how inefficiencies in government, public administration, judiciary and high levels of corruption may create an unfavorable investment climate despite of strong fundamentals as macroeconomic stability, a large domestic market, low wages and easy access to the US market. It also underlines the difficulties of overcoming ideological resistance against foreign capital, which has a long tradition in post-revolutionary Mexico and in nearly all other Latin American countries. Thus, besides a further economic liberalization, Mexico, and surely most of the other Latin American countries as well, need an institutional reform that increases the quality of national institutions and permits to attract more FDI.

The study of the Mexican case additionally highlighted that although institutional reforms were initiated the results only materialize slowly which requires a short term strategy to complement domestic institutional reforms. It was shown that Mexico successfully chose a strategy of multilateral and bilateral economic integration to mitigate high political risks. Interpreted in this way integration efforts as the membership in NAFTA not only have the static effects that are described in the theory of regional integration. Instead, integration is a valuable tool for locking in reforms against populist pressure and gaining credibility on the international stage. Furthermore integration efforts were crucial to improve the legal certainty of investors and the protection of property rights against predatory government interventions which have a long tradition in Mexican economic policy. The impressive increase of FDI to Mexico following its membership in NAFTA highlights the importance of this credibility effect for the Mexican economy.

While reaping the short-term credibility effects stemming from international economic integration Mexico simultaneously embarked on a strategy of national institutional reform. The case study shows that the internal process of political reform and democratization is interwoven with the project of economic liberalization. The growing importance of opposition parties and growing citizen participation had important implications for the institutional environment of doing business in Mexico. Better control and higher checks and balances in the Mexican political system reduce the potential for the abuse of public power and the scope of nepotism that dominated in Mexico during the PRI governance. Reform of the judiciary allows for better contract enforcement and bureaucratic reform permits a more efficient provision of basic public services. A freer press and more societal controls will limit the blatantly high levels of corruption. Although still on a low level, the protection of individual citizens and businessmen against arbitrary and predatory government intervention increased. Hence, the dismantling of the semi-authoritarian PRI government did not only have political consequences but also positively influenced the business environment and investment incentives of national and international investors. Therefore, it may be argued that in Mexico the processes of democratization, institutional and economic reform are interdependent in the sense that progresses in either of these policy fields also have positive side effects on the other processes.

Despite of these initial successes, as theory predicts, the process of institutional reform is lengthy and results take a long time to materialize. For Mexico and other Latin American countries the results of this analysis highlight the importance of an institutional reform that allows for better governance and public administration. Second generation reforms that aim at strengthening the institutional environment would allow for completely reaping the benefits from better functioning markets while simultaneously attracting more foreign capital. Thus, Mexico as well as other Latin American countries, have to continue the process of reform by focusing on the amelioration of national institutions that permit a better functioning of markets. However, recent events in Latin America are not provoking a particularly optimistic outlook for the years to come. The serious economic and political crisis in Argentina, the populist Chavez regime in Venezuela, civil strife in Bolivia and the stagnating process of political reform in Mexico due to the deadlock in government indicate that still important societal resistance has to be overcome to successfully implement institutional reforms.

Annex I

A: Formula for the transfer of hard macroeconomic data to a 1-10 scale (based on the Methodology used by World Economic Forum (2002)[1]

$$9 \times \frac{(CountryValue - SampleMinimum)}{(SampleMaximum - SampleMinimum)} + 1$$

B: Table A.1: Variables Used for the Panel Analysis

Group	Variable	Full Name	Description	Type	Source	Expected Sign
Dep.	FDIT	Total net FDI	Net inflows of investment to acquire a lasting management interest (10 percent or more of voting stock) in an enterprise operating in an economy other than that of the investor	Continuous values	World Bank: World Development Indicators 2002	
Dep.	FDIS	Total net FDI divided by GDP	Same as FDIT but divided by GDP	Continuous values	World Bank: World Development Indicators 2002, Own calculations	
Dep.	FDIP	Total net FDI divided by population size	Same as FDIT but divided by Population Size	Continuous values	World Bank: World Development Indicators 2002, Own calculations	
X	OPEN	Openness	Sum of exports and imports divided by GDP	Continuous values	World Bank: World Development Indicators 2002	Positive
X	TELE	Telephone lines	Number of telephone lines per 1000 people	Continuous values	World Bank: World Development Indicators 2002	Positive
I	AGRISK	Aggregate Risk	Aggregate Political Risk, constructed by aggregating MACRO I, GOVII, SOCII	Discrete Values		Positive
I	BUDG	Budget Deficit	Public Budget deficits as percentage of GDP, used for the construction of MACROI	Continuous values	World Bank: World Development Indicators	Negative

---

[1] See World Economic Forum (2002) p.48-51.

I	BURE	Quality of Bureaucracy	High scores indicate an established mechanism for recruitment and training, autonomy from political pressure, and strength and expertise to govern without drastic changes in policy or interruptions in government services when governments change	Discrete values ranging from 0-6, with 6 implying the best value (high quality)	ICRG IRIS 3 Dataset	Positive
I	BURE10	Quality of Bureaucracy	Same as BURE	ranging from 0-10, with 10 implying the best value (high quality)	ICRG IRIS 3 Dataset	Positive
I	CORRU	Corruption in Government	Lower scores indicate that high government officials are likely to demand special payments" and that "illegal payments are generally expected throughout lower levels of government" in the form of "bribes connected with import and export licenses, exchange controls, tax assessment, police protection, or loans	Discrete, values ranging from 0-6, with 6 implying the best value (lower corruption)	ICRG IRIS 3 Dataset	Positive
I	CORRU10	Corruption in Government	Same as CORR	Same as CORRU but values reaching from 0-10	ICRG IRIS 3 Dataset	Positive
I	CURR	Current Account Deficit	Current Account Deficit as percentage of GDP	Continuous	World Bank: World Development Indicators	Negative
I	ETHN	Ethnic Tensions	Measures the degree of tension within a country attributable to racial, nationality, or language divisions. Lower ratings are given to countries where racial and nationality tensions are high because opposing groups are intolerant and unwilling to compromise. Higher ratings are given to countries where tensions are minimal, even though such differences may still exist.	Discrete, values ranging from 0-6, with 6 implying the best value (low ethnic tensions)	ICRG IRIS 3 Dataset	Positive

I	ETHN10	Ethnic Tensions	Same as ETHN	Discrete, values ranging from 0-10, with 10 implying the best value (low ethnic tensions)	ICRG IRIS 3 Dataset	Positive
I	EXPR	Expropriation Risk	This variables evaluates the risk "outright confiscation and forced nationalization" of property. Lower ratings "are given to countries where expropriation of FDI is likely	Discrete, values ranging from 0-10, with 10 implying the best value (lowest risk of expropriation)	ICRG IRIS 3 Dataset	Positive
I	GOVI	Governance I	Measures political risk resulting out of government behavior, constructed by aggregating EXPR, REPU, CORRU10 and BURE10	Discrete, values ranging from 0-10, with 10 implying the best value (lowest risk of harm to investor by national government)	ICRG IRIS 3 Dataset, Own calculations	Positive
I	GOVII	Governance II	Measures political risk resulting out of government behavior, constructed by aggregating EXPR, REPU, CORRU10 and BURE10 and POLIII	Discrete, values ranging from 0-10, with 10 implying the best value (lowest risk of harm to investor by national government)	ICRG IRIS 3 Dataset, POLCON, Own calculations	Positive
I	INF	Inflation Rate	Yearly inflation rate as measured by the consumer price index, used for the construction of MACROI	Continuous values in percentages	World Bank, World Development Indicators 2002	Negative
I	ISPRE	Interest Rate Spread	Spread over LIBOR (London Interbank Offer Rate) is the interest rate charged by banks on loans to prime customers minus LIBOR, used for the construction of MACROI	Continuous values in percentage	World Bank, Global Development Finance 2002	Negative
I	MACROI	Macro Economic Environment	Measures political risk resulting out of the Macroeconomic Environment, constructed by aggregating INF, ISPRE, BUDG, RESDEB, SHORT	Discrete Values between 1-10 with one being the lowest (risky macro-economic environment)	World Bank, Global Development Finance, World Development Indicators 2002, own calculations	Positive

I	POLCIII	POLCON Indicator	Measures the degree to which governmental discretion is subject to external constraints	Continuous values between 0-1 with 1 signifying maximal constraints	Henisz (2002), Henisz (2000).	Positive
I	POLCV	POLCON Indicator	Same as POLCIII but includes two additional veto points (the judiciary and sub_federal entities)	Continuous values between 0-1 with 1 signifying maximal constraints	Henisz (2002), Henisz (2000).	Positive
I	REPU	Repudiation of government contracts	Addresses the possibility that foreign businesses, contractors, and consultants face the risk of a modification in a contract taking the form of a repudiation, postponement, or scaling down" due to "an income drop, budget cutbacks, indigenization pressure, a change in government, or a change in government economic and social priorities.	Discrete values from 0-10 with lower scores signifying a greater likelihood that a country will modify or repudiate a contract with a foreign business	ICRG IRIS 3 Dataset	Positive
I	RESDEB	Reserves debt ratio	Ratio of international reserves and total external debt, used for the construction of MACROI	Continuous values	World Bank, Global Development Finance 2002	Positive
I	RULE	Rule of Law Tradition	reflects the degree to which the citizens of a country are willing to accept the established institutions to make and implement laws and adjudicate disputes. Higher scores indicate: sound political institutions, a strong court system, and provisions for an orderly succession of power. Lower scores indicate a tradition of depending on physical force or illegal means to settle claims. New leaders may be less likely to accept the obligations of the previous regime.	Discrete values from 0-6 with lower scores signifying a weak rule of law tradition in the society	ICRG IRIS 3 Dataset	Positive

I	RULE10	Rule of Law Tradition	Same as RULE	Discrete values from 0-10 with lower scores signifying a weak rule of law tradition in the society	ICRG IRIS 3 Dataset, own calculations	Positive
I	SHORT	Fraction of Short Term Debt in Total Debt	Fraction of short term external debt in total external debt, used for the construction of MACRO I	Continuous	World Bank: World Development Indicators	Negative
I	SOCII	Societal Risk I	Measures political risk resulting in government behavior, constructed by aggregating RULE10, ETH10.	Discrete values from 0-10 with lower scores referring to higher societal risks	ICRG IRIS 3 Dataset, own calculations	Positive
Z	BART	Barriers to Trade	Measure of trade barriers, proxied by taxes on international trade including import duties, export duties, profits of export or import monopolies, exchange profits, and exchange taxes as a percentage of current government revenue	Continuous Values	World Bank, World Development Indicators 2002	Positive
Z	EXCH	Exchange Rate	Exchange Rate of Local currency with US Dollar	Continuous Values	International Financial Statistics (IMF)	Negative
Z	GROW	Economic Growth Rate	Yearly growth rates of GDP	Continuous values in percentages	World Bank, World Development Indicators	Positive
Z	TAXP	Taxes on profits	Measures a country´s tax burden proxied by taxes on income, profits, and capital gains are levied on wages, salaries, tips, fees, commissions and other compensation for labor services; interest, dividends, rent, and royalties; capital gains and losses; and profits of businesses, estates, and trusts as a percentage of current revenue	Continuous values in percentages	World Bank, World Development Indicators	Negative

Source: Own table

Annex II

Table A.2: Correlation of Political Risk Indicators with FDI Flows to Mexico

RISK INDICATOR	DEPENDENT VARIABLE	
	FDIT (FLOWS)	FDIS (FDI/GDP RATIO)
ECRISK50		
COEFFICIENT	1.37E+09***	0.001655***
P-VALUE	(0.0000)	(0.0045)
R^2	0.721117	0.385625
FINRISK50		
COEFFICIENT	4.77E+08**	0.000720*
P-VALUE	(0.0327)	(0.0531)
R^2	0.241399	0.202709
GOVSTAB 10		
COEFFICIENT	2.06E+09*	0.001007
P-VALUE	(0.0695)	(0.6059)
R^2	0.180838	0.015993
POLCIII02		
COEFFICIENT	4.02E+10***	0.075638***
P-VALUE	(0.0000)	(0.0000)
R^2	0.782131	0.637421
DEMOC10		
COEFFICIENT	3.18E+09***	0.004467***
P-VALUE	(0.0000)	(0.0004)
R^2	0.724987	0.528631
MILI10		
COEFFICIENT	-2.62E+09***	-0.003246***
P-VALUE	(0.0000)	(0.0045)
R^2	0.682934	0.387018
LAW10		
COEFFICIENT	-5.67E+09***	-0.007232***
P-VALUE	(0.0002)	(0.0094)
R^2	0.560018	0.335473
BUREII10		
COEFFICIENT	3.22E+09***	0.003624**
P-VALUE	(0.0001)	(0.0222)
R^2	0.583158	0.271433
CORRUII10		
COEFFICIENT	-1.88E+09	-0.002464
P-VALUE	(0.4697)	(0.5674)
R^2	0.031163	0.019620
EXPR		
COEFFICIENT	1.82E+09***	0.003675***
P-VALUE	(0.0001)	(0.0068)
R^2	0.664380	0.418304

Table A.2: Continued

	DEPENDENT VARIABLE	
RISK INDICATOR	FDIT (FLOWS)	FDIS (FDI/GDP RATIO)
INVPR10		
COEFFICIENT	2.77E+09***	0.001989***
P-VALUE	(0.0021)	(0.2321)
R^2	0.434773	0.082834
ETHNII10		
COEFFICIENT	-3.22E+09**	-0.002776
P-VALUE	(0.0239)	(0.2648)
R^2	0.265740	0.072555
RELIG10		
COEFFICIENT	-8.22E+09***	-0.007858**
P-VALUE	(0.0005)	(0.0753)
R^2	0.518070	0.174367
INT10		
COEFFICIENT	-1.63E+09	0.000180
P-VALUE	(0.3669)	(0.9524)
R^2	0.048123	0.000216
SOCEC10		
COEFFICIENT	4.02E+08	-0.000650
P-VALUE	(0.7433)	(0.7480)
R^2	0.006478	0.006236
POLRISK100		
COEFFICIENT	1.02E+09	0.000716
P-VALUE	(0.0310)**	(0.3861)
R^2	0.245421	0.044477
COMP100		
COEFFICIENT	7.13E+08	0.000875
P-VALUE	(0.0017)***	(0.0298)**
R^2	0.447646	0.248496

Source: Own table, p-values are in parentheses, *estimator significant at the 10% level, **estimator significant at the 5% level, ***estimator significant at the 1% level.

Table A.3: Restrictions on FDI in Mexico:

RESTRICTIONS ON FOREIGN INVESTMENT IN MEXICO

RESERVED ACTIVITIES FOR THE STATE (ARTICLE 5)	ACTIVITIES RESERVED TO MEXICANS OR MEXICAN COMPANIES WITH FOREIGNERS EXCLUSION CLAUSE: (ARTICLE 6)	ACTIVITIES AND ACQUISITIONS UNDER SPECIFIC REGULATIONS (ARTICLE 7)	ECONOMIC ACTIVITIES REQUIRING A FAVORABLE RESOLUTION BY THE CNI TO PARTICIPATE IN A PERCENTAGE HIGHER THAN 49% (ARTICLE 8)
I. Petroleum and other hydrocarbons; II. Basic petrochemicals; III. Electricity; IV. Generation of nuclear energy; V. Radioactive minerals; VI. Repealed by an Order published in the Official Gazette of the Federation on June 7, 1995. VII. Telegraph; VIII. Radiotelegraphy; IX. Postal service; X. Repealed by an Order published in the Official Gazette of the Federation on May 12, 1995. XI. Bank note issuing; XII. Minting of coins; XIII. Control, supervision and surveillance of ports, airports and heliports; and XIV. Others as expressly provided by applicable legal provisions.	I. Domestic land transportation for passengers, tourism and freight, not including messenger or courier services; II. Gasoline retail sales and distribution of liquefied petroleum gas; III. Radio broadcasting services and other radio and television services, other than cable television; IV. Credit unions; V. Development banking institutions, under the terms of the law governing the matter; and VI. Rendering of professional and technical services set forth expressly by applicable legal provisions.	I. Up to 10% in: Cooperative companies for production; II. Up to 25% in: a) Domestic air transportation; b) Air taxi transportation; and c) Specialized air transportation; III. Up to 49% in: a) Repealed by an Order published in the Official Gazette of the Federation on January 19, 1999. b) Repealed by an Order published in the Official Gazette of the Federation on January 19, 1999. c) Repealed by an Order published in the Official Gazette of the Federation on January 19, 1999. d) Repealed by an Order published in the Official Gazette of the Federation on January 19, 1999. e) Insurance companies. f) Bonding companies. g) Currency exchange houses; h) Bonded warehouses; i) Financial leasing companies; j) Factoring companies; k) Limited scope financial institutions; l) Companies to which article 12 Bis of the Securities Market Law refers; m) Repealed by an Order published in the Official Gazette of the Federation on June 4, 2001; n) Repealed by an Order published in the Official Gazette of the Federation on June 4, 2001; o) Retirement funds management companies; p) Manufacture and commercialization of explosives, firearms, cartridges, ammunitions and fireworks, not including acquisition and use of explosives for industrial and extraction activities nor the preparation of explosive compounds for use in said activities; q) Printing and publication of newspapers for circulation solely throughout Mexico; r) Series "T" shares in companies owning agricultural, ranching, and forestry lands; s) Fresh water, coastal, and exclusive economic zone fishing not including fisheries; t) Integral port administration; u) Port pilot services for inland navigation under the terms of the law governing the matter; ipping companies engaged in commercial exploitation of ships for inland and coastal navigation, excluding tourism cruises and exploitation of marine dredges and devices for port construction, conservation and operation; w) Supply of fuel and lubricants for ships, airplanes, and railway equipment.	I. Port services in order to allow ships to conduct inland navigation operation, such as towing, mooring and barging. II. Shipping companies engaged in the exploitation of ships solely for high-seas traffic; III. Concessionaire or permissionaire companies of air fields for public service; IV. Private education services of pre-school, elementary, middle school, high school, college or any combination; V. Legal services; VI. Credit information companies; VII. Securities rating institutions; VIII. Insurance agents; IX. Cellular telephony; X. Construction of pipelines for the transportation of petroleum and products derived therefrom; XI. Drilling of petroleum and gas wells; and XII. Construction, operation and exploitation of general railways, and public services of railway transportation.

References

ABEL, Andrew B. / EBERLY, Janice C. (1994):
A Unified Model of Investment under Uncertainty, American Economic Review, 84, 5, 1369-1384.

ABRAMOVICH, Ivan Baron (2001):
Die Wachstumsdiktatur: ein seltenes institutionelles Arrangement, List Forum für Wirtschafts- unf Finanzpolitik, 27, 2, 139-157.

ADAM, Dietrich (1994):
Investitionscontrolling, München.

ADAM, Dietrich (1996):
Planung und Entscheidung: Modelle-Ziele-Fallstudien, 4.Auflage, Wiesbaden.

AHARONI, Yair (1966):
The Foreign Investment Decision Process, Boston.

AKERLOF, George A. (1970):
The Market for "Lemons": Quality Uncertainty and the Market Mechanism, The Quarterly Journal of Economics, 84, 3, 488-500.

ALCHIAN, Armen A. / DEMSETZ, Harold (1973):
The Property Right Paradigm, The Journal of Economic History, 33, 1, 16-27.

ALEXANDER, Dean C. (1995):
Mexico´s Foreign Investment Law of 1993, Amendments to the Maquila Decree, and an Overview of Maquiladoras, in: Rubin, Seymour J. (ed.): Nafta and Investment, The Hague, 65-83.

ALVARADO, Arturo / DAVIS, Diane (2001):
Cambio político, inseguridad pública y deterioro de estado de derecho en México: Algunas hipótesis en torno del proceso actual, in: Alvarado, Arturo / Arzt, Sigrid (eds.): El desafío democrático de México: Seguridad y estado de derecho, México D.F., 115-143.

AYALA ESPINO, José (2002):
Fundamentos institucionales del mercado, Mexico D.F.

BALTAGI, Badi H. (2002)
Econometric Analysis of Panel Data, 2nd edition, Chichester, New York, Weinheim.

BANCO DE MEXICO (1993):
The Mexican Economy, Mexico D.F.

BANCO DE MEXICO (1994):
The Mexican Economy, Mexico D.F.

BARRO, Robert J. / SALA-I-MARTIN, Xavier (1995):
Economic growth, New York, St. Louis, San Francisco.

BARRO, Robert J. (1996):
Democracy and Growth, Journal of Economic Growth, 1, 1, 1-27.

BARZEL, Yoram (2000):
Property rights and the evolution of the state, Economics of governance, 1, 25-51.

BASI, Raghbir S. (1963):
Determinants of U.S. Private Direct Investment in Foreign Countries, Kent.

BBVA (2003):
Latinfocus, diverse volumes.

BEKKER, Gina / PATRICK, Robert (1998):
Workshop on the Rule of Law and the Underprivileged in Latin America: A Rapporteurs´ Report, Hellen Kellogg Institute for International Studies, Working Paper 246, Notre Dame.

BELEJACK, Barbara (1997):
Sound Bites and Soap Operas: How Mexican Television Reported the 1994 Presidential Elections, in: Orme, William A. (ed.): A Culture of Collusion: An inside look to the Mexican Press, Boulder, 51-58.

BENMANSUR, Hacène / VADCAR, Corinne (1995):
Le Risque Politique dans le Nouveau Contexte International , Paris.

BERNARDINI, Piero (2001):
Investment Protection under Bilateral Investment Treaties and Investment Contracts, Journal of World Investment: Law, Economics and Politics, 2, 2, 235-247.

BILLET, Bret L. (1991):
Investment Behavior of Multinational Corporations in Developing Areas, New Brunswick.

BILLINGTON, Nicholas (1999):
The Location of Foreign Direct Investment: An Empirical Analysis, Applied Economics, 31, 1, 65-76.

BLÁZQUEZ, Jorge / SANTISO, Javier (2003):
Mexico: Is it an emerging market ?, BBVA Working Papers 3/03, Bilbao.

BLOMSTRÖM, Magnus / PERSSON, Hoakan (1983):
Foreign Investment and Spillover Efficiency in an Underdeveloped Economy:
Evidence from the Mexican Manufacturing Industry, Stockholm.

BLOMSTRÖM, Magnus / WOLFF, Edward N. (1994):
Mutlinational Corporations and Productivity Convergence in Mexico, in
Baumol, William J. et al. (eds.): Convergence of Prodcutivity: Cross-National
Studies and Historical Evidence, Oxford.

BLOMSTRÖM, Magnus / KOKKO, Ari (2003):
The Economics of Foreign Direct Investment Incentives, NBER Working Paper
9489, Cambridge.

BLONIGEN, Bruce A. / FEENSTRA, Robert C. (1997):
Protectionist Threats and Foreign Direct Investment, in: Feenstra, Robert C.:
(ed.): The Effects of US Trade Protection and Promotion Policies, Chicago, 55-
80.

BOLAÑOS GUERRA, Bernardo (1994):
Presidencialismo y posmodernidad, in: Córdova Vianello, Lorenzo et al. (eds.):
Esayos sobre presidencialismo mexicano, Mexico D.F., 93-134.

BRUNETTI, Aymo / KISUNKO, Gregory / WEDER, Beatrice (1997):
Institutional Obstacles for Doing Business: Data Description and Methodology
of a Worldwide Private Sector Survey, Survey conducted for the World
Development Report 1997, Washington D.C.

BUBNOVA, Nina B. (2000):
Governance Impact on Private Investment: Evidence from the International
Patterns of Infrastructure Bond Risk Pricing, World Bank Technical Paper
No.488, Washington D.C.

BUCKLEY, Peter J. (1987):
The Theory of the Multinational Enterprise, Stockholm.

BUCKLEY, Peter J. / CASSON, Mark (1976): The Future of the Multinational
Enterprise, London.

BURGER, Bettina (1998):
Ausländische Direktinvestitionen, technologische Spillover-Effekte und
industrielle Entwicklung, dargestellt am Beispiel Mexikos, Baden-Baden.

BUSCAGLIA, Edgardo / DAKOLIAS, Maria / RATLIFF, William (1995):
Judicial Reform in Latin America: A Framework for National Development,
Hoover Institution, Stanford.

CALDERÓN, Alvaro / MORTIMORE, Michael / PERES, Wilson (1995):
Mexico´s Incorporation into the New Industrial Order: Foreign Investment as a
Source of International Competitiveness, ECLAC Desarollo Productivo N.21,
Santiago de Chile.

CAMP, Roderic Ai (2003):
Politics in Mexico: The Democratic Transformation, 4th edition, New York.

CARBONELL Y SÁNCHEZ, Miguel (1994):
Presidencialismo y creación legislativa, in: Córdova Vianello, Lorenzo et al.
(eds.): Esayos sobre presidencialismo mexicano, Mexico D.F., 135-187.

CARREÑO CARLÓN, José / VILLANUEVA, Ernesto (1998):
Derecho de la información en Mexico, in: Carreno Carlón, José / Villanueva,
Ernesto (eds): Temas fundamentales de derecho de información en
Iberoamérica, Mexico D.F., 141-158.

CÁRDENAS, Enrique (2000a):
The Great Depression and Industrialization: The Case of Mexico, in:
Cardenas, Enrique; Ocampo, José Antonio; Thorp, Rosemary (eds.): An
Economic History of Twentieth-Century Latin America, Volume 2: Latin
America in the 1930, Houndmills, Basingstoke, Hampshire, 195-211.

CÁRDENAS, Enrique (2000b):
The Process of Accelerated Industrialization in Mexico, 1929-1982, in:
Cardenas, Enrique; Ocampo, José Antonio; Thorp, Rosemary (eds.): An
Economic History of Twentieth-Century Latin America, Volume 3:
Industrialization and the State in Latin America: The Postwar Years,
Houndmills, Basingstoke, Hampshire, 176-204.

CASSON, Mark (1979):
Alternatives to the Multinational Enterprise, London.

CASSOU, Steven P. (1997):
The Link Between Tax Rates and Foreign Direct Investment, Applied
Economics, 29, 10, 1295-1301.

CASTAÑEDA, Jorge G. (1997):
Limits to Apertura: Prospects for Press Freedom in the New Free-Market
Mexico, in: Orme, William A. (ed.): A Culture of Collusion: An inside look to the
Mexican Press, Boulder, 131-140.

CASTRO, Juventino V. (2000):
Hacia el sistema judicial mexicano del XXI, Mexico D.F.

CASTRO REA, Julián et al. (1999):
La política exterior de América del Norte en los noventa: confluencia en el pragmatismo económico, in: Castro Rea, Julián, /Jackson, Robert J./ Mahler, Gregory S. (eds.): Los sistemas políticos de América del Norte en los años noventa, Mexico D.F.

CAVES, Richard Earl (1974):
International Trade, International Investment and Imperfect Markets, Princeton.

CEPAL (2000):
Foreign Investment in Latin America and the Caribbean, Santiago.

CFI (1997):
Inversión Extranjera Directa, Washington D.C.

CHAKRABARTI, Avik (2001):
The Determinants of Foreign Direct Investment: Sensitivity Analysis of Cross-Country Regressions, Kyklos, 54, 89-114.

CHAND, Vikram K. (2001):
Mexico´s Political Awakening, Notre Dame.

CHIRINKO, Robert S. (1993):
Business Fixed Investment: Modeling Strategies, Empirical Results, and Policy Implications, Journal of Economic Literature, 31, 1875-1911.

CLAQUE, Christopher et al. (1996):
Property and Contract Rights in Autocracies and Democracies, Journal of Economic Growth, 1, 2, 243-276.

CLARK, J. Maurice (1917):
Business Acceleration and the Law of Demand: A Technical Factor in Economic Cycles, The Journal of Political Economy, 25, 3, 217-235.

COASE, Ronald (1937):
The Nature of the Firm, Economica, 4, 386-405.

COLE, Harold L. / ENGLISH, William B. (1991):
Expropriation and Direct Investment, Journal of International Economics, 30, 3/4, 201-227.

CONGER, Lucy (1997):
From Intimidation to Assassination: Silencing the Press, in: Orme, William A. (ed.): A Culture of Collusion: An inside look to the Mexican Press, Boulder, 99-107.

CONSULADO GENERAL DE MÉXICO (2001):
Freihandelsabkommen zwischen Mexiko und der Europäischen Union,
Hamburg.

CÓRDOVA VIANELLO, Lorenzo (1994):
El sistema presidencial en México: Orígenes y Razones, in: Córdova Vianello,
Lorenzo et al. (eds.): Esayos sobre presidencialismo mexicano, Mexico D.F.,
1-64.

CORNELIUS, Wayne A. (1996):
Mexican Politics in Transition: The Breakdown of a One-Party-Dominant
Regime, San Diego.

COVARRUBIAS VELASCO, Ana (2000):
El problema de los derechos humanos y los cambios en la política exterior, in:
Lajous, Roberta / Torres, Blanca (eds.): México y el mundo: Historia de sus
relaciones internacionales, Tomo IX: La política exterior de México en la
década de los noventa, Mexico D.F., 49-72.

CULEM, Claudy G. (1988):
The Locational Determinants of Direct Investments Among Industrialized
Countries, European Economic Review, 32, 4, 885-904.

DAHL, Robert (1998):
On Democracy, Yale.

DEININGER, Klaus / SQUIRE, Lyn (1996)
A New Data Set Measuring Income Inequality, The World Bank Economic
Review, 10, 3, 565-591.

DEMSETZ, Harold (1967):
Toward a Theory of Property Rights, American Economic Review, 57, 2, 347-
359.

DIRECIÓN GENERAL DE INVERSIÓN EXTRANJERA (2003):
http://www.economia.gob.mx/?P=1156.

DIXIT, Avinash K. / PINDYCK, Robert S. (1994):
Investment under Uncertainty, New Jersey.

DOLLAR, David / KRAAY, Aart (2001):
Growth is Good for the Poor, Policy Research Working Paper 2587,
Washington.

DOMINGO, Pilar (1999):
Judicial Independence and Judicial Reform in Latin America, in: Schedler, Andreas / Diamond, Larry / Plattner, Marc F. (eds.): The Self Restraining State: Power and Accountability in New Democracies, Boulder, London, 151-175.

DOWNS, Anthony (1957):
An Economic Theory of Democracy, New York.

DRABEK, Zdenek / PAYNE, Warren (2001):
The Impact of Transparency on Foreign Direct Investment, WTO Staff Working Paper ERAD-99-02, Washington D.C.

DUNNING, John H. (1981):
International Production and the Multinational Enterprise, London.

DUNNING, John H. (1993):
Multinational Enterprises and the Global Economy, Wokingham.

DURHAM, J. Benson (1999):
Economic Growth and Policy Regimes, in: Journal of Economic Growth, 4, 1, 81-111.

EATON, Jonathan / GERSOVITZ, Mark (1983):
Country Risk: Economic Aspects, in: Herring, Richard J. (ed.) Managing International Risk, Cambridge, 75-99.

EATON, Jonathan / GERSOVITZ, Mark / STIGLITZ, Joseph E. (1986):
The Pure Theory of Country Risk, NBER Working Papers 1894, Cambridge.

EDWARDS, Sebastian (1990):
Capital Flows, Foreign Direct Investment, and Debt-Equity Swaps in Developing Countries, National Bureau of Economic Research, Working Paper 3497, Cambridge.

EGGERTSSON, Thrainn (1990):
Economic Behavior and Institutions, Cambridge.

ELIZONDO, Carlos (1987):
La silla embrujada: Historia del corrupción en México, Mexico D.F.

ELIZONDO, Carlos (1999):
Mexico: Foreign Investment and Democracy, in: Armijo, Leslie Elliot (ed.) Financial Globalization and Democracy in Emerging Markets, Basingstoke, 133-150.

ELIZONDO, Carlos (2001):
La importancia de las reglas: Gobierno y empresario depués de la
nacionalización bancaria, Méxcio D.F.

ERB, Claude B. et al. (1996):
The Influence of Political, Economic, and Financial Risk on Expected Fixed-
Income Returns, The Journal of Fixed Income, 6, 1, 7-30.

ERLEI, Mathias / LESCHKE, Martin / SAUERLAND, Dirk (1999):
Neue Institutionenökonomik, Stuttgart.

FARRAR, Donald Eugene (1963):
The Investment Decision under Uncertainty, New York.

FATEHI, Kamal / SAFIZADEH, M. Hossein (1994):
The Effect of Sociopolitical Instability on the Flow of Different Types of Foreign
Direct Investment, Journal of Business Research 31, 65-73.

FAYERWEATHER, John (1973):
Nationalism and the Multinational Firm, in: Kapoor, Ashok / Grub, Phillip D.
(eds.): The Multinational Enterprise in Transition: Selected Readings and
Essays, Princeton.

FERNANDEZ, Carlos Garcia (2002):
International Investment Agreements and Instruments, in: OECD, New
Horizons for Foreign Direct Investment, Paris, 265-277.

FERNÁNDEZ-ARIAS, Eduardo (2001):
A Comment on the paper of Charles P. Oman, in: OECD, Foreign Direct
Investment Versus other Flows to Latin America, Paris, 89-91

FISCHER, Anton (1999):
Direktinvestitionen, Exportmotor oder –bremse ?, Bern.

FISHER, Irving (1997):
The Theory of Interest, London, First published 1930.

FITZGERALD, E. V. K. (2000):
Restructuring through the Depression: Mexico 1925-1940, in: Cardenas,
Enrique; Ocampo, José Antonio; Thorp, Rosemary (eds.): An Economic
History of Twentieth-Century Latin America, Volume 2: Latin America in the
1930, Houndmills, Basingstoke, Hampshire.

FFRENCH-DAVIS, Ricardo (2000):
Reforming the Reforms in LA, Houndmills, Basingstoke

FREEDOM HOUSE (2003):
Country Ratings, http://www.freedomhouse.org/ratings/.

FREEMAN, Richard B. / OOSTENDORP, Remco H. (2000):
Wages around the World: Pay across Occupations and Countries, NBER
Working Paper 8058, Cambridge.

FREY, Bruno (1984):
International Political Economics, New York.

FRÖBEL, Folker / HEINRICHS, Jürgen / KREYE, Otto (1981):
The New International Division of Labor: Structural Unemployment in
Industrialized Countries and Indutrialization in Developing Countries,
Cambridge.

FROOT, Kenneth A. / STEIN, Jermey C. (1991):
Exchange Rates and Foreign Direct Investment: An Imperfect Capital Markets
Approach, Quarterly Journal of Economics, 106, 4, 1191-1217.

FRÜHLING EHRLICH, Hugo (2001):
Las reformas policiales y la consolidación democrática en América Latina, in
Alvarado, Arturo / Arzt, Sigrid (eds.): El desafío democrático de México:
Seguridad y estado de derecho, México D.F., 37-66.

FUKUYAMA, Francis (1995):
Trust, New York.

FUKUYAMA, Francis (2001):
Social Capital, Civil Society and Development, Third World Quarterly, 22, 1, 7-
20.

GARIBALDI, Jose Alberto (2001):
Political and Administrative Corruption: A Comparative View of their
Organization and Development, International Society for New Institutional
Economics Conference 2001.

GATES, Marilyn (1996):
The Debt Crisis and Economic Restructuring: Prospects for Mexican
Agriculture, in: Otero, Gerardo (ed.): Neo-Liberalism Revisited: Economic
Restructuring and Mexico's Political Future, Boulder, 43-62.

GILESPIE, Kate / MCBRIDE, J. Brad (1996):
Smuggling in Emerging Markets: Global Implications, Columbia Journal of
World Business, 31, 40-54.

GÖTZE, Uwe / BLOECH, Jürgen (1993):
Investitionsrechnung, Berlin, Heidelberg.

GÓMEZ TAGLE, Silvia (1999):
Los partidos mexicanos en la transición mexicana, in: Castro Rea, Julián,
/Jackson, Robert J./ Mahler, Gregory S. (eds.): Los sistemas políticos de
América del Norte en los años noventa, Mexico D.F., 247-271.

GONZÁLEZ DE COSSIO, Francisco (2002):
The Mexican Experience with Investment Arbitration: A Comment, The Journal
of World Investment, 3, 3, 473-486.

GONZÁLEZ GÓMEZ, Javier (2001):
The Culture of Illegality and Economic Development in Mexico, Paper
presented during the 2nd Summer School on Social Justice in Market
Economies at the Ibero America Institute Göttingen, mimeo.

GORDON, Wendell C. (1975):
The Expropriation of Foreign-Owned Property in Mexico, Westport.

GRAHAM, Edward M. / WADA, Erika (2000):
Domestic Reform, Trade and Investment Liberalization, Financial Crisis, and
Foreign Direct Investment into Mexico, World Economy, 23, 6, 777-797.

GRIFFITH-JONES, Stephany (2000):
International Capital Flows to Latin America, Institute of Development Studies,
University of Sussex.

GROSSE, Robert (1989):
Multinationals in Latin America, London.

GROSSE, Robert (2001):
Intra- and Extraregional Foreign Direct Investment in Latin America, in:
Franco, Andrés (ed.): Financing for Development in Latin America and the
Caribbean, Tokyo, 119-143.

GROSSE, Robert (2003a):
The Eclectic Theory in Latin America, in: Gray, H. Peter (ed.): Extending the
Eclectic Paradigm in International Business, Cheltenham, 55-68.

GROSSE, Robert (2003b):
International Business in Latin America, in: Oxford Handbook on International
Business, 652-680.

GUDOFSKY, Jason L. (2000):
Shedding light on Article 1110 of the NAFTA Concerning Expropriations: An Environmental Case Study, Northwestern Journal of International Law and Business, 21,1, 243-315.

GUISINGER, Stephen E. (1986):
Do Performance Requirements and Investment Incentives Work?, Word Economy, 9, 1, 79-96.

HABER, Stephen et al. (1999):
Political Instability, Credible Commitment, and Economic Growth: Evidence from Revolutionary Mexico, ISNIE Working Paper, Prepared for the annual meeting 1999 in Washington D.C.

HARMS, Philipp (2000):
International Investment, Political Risk and Growth, Boston.

HARMS, Philipp / URSPRUNG, Heinrich W. (2002):
Do Civil and Political Repression Really Boost Foreign Direct Investments ?, Economic Inquiry, 40, 4, 651-663.

HARVEY, Neil (1996):
Rural Reforms and the Zapatista Rebellion: Chiapas 1988-1995, in: Otero, Gerardo (ed.): Neo-Liberalism Revisited: Economic Restructuring and Mexico´s Political Future, Boulder, 187-208.

HARVEY, Neil (2001):
Globalisation and Resistance in Post Cold War Mexico: Difference, Citizenship and Biodiversity Conflicts in Chiapas, Third World Quarterly, 22, 6, 1045-1061.

HASHMI, Anaam / GUVENLI, Turgut (1992):
Importance of Political Risk Assessment Functions in U.S. Multinational Corporations, Global Finance Journal, 3, 2, 137-144.

HATEM, Fabrice (1997):
International Investment: Towards the Year 2001, United Nations, Geneva.

HATEM, Fabrice (1998):
International Investment: Towards the Year 2002, United Nations, Geneva.

HECKSCHER, Eli (1950):
The effects of foreign trade on the Distribution of Income, in: Ellis, H.S. / Metzler, L.A. (eds.): Readings in the Theory of International Trade, London.

HENISZ, Witold J./ ZELNER, Bennet A. (1999):
Political Risk and Infrastructure Investment, Paper prepared for the World
Bank Conference in Rome, September 8-10, Washington.

HENISZ, Witold J. (2000a):
The Institutional Environment for Multinational Investment, Journal of Law,
Economics & Organization, 16, 2, 334-364.

HENISZ, Witold J. (2000b):
The Institutional Environment for Economic Growth, Economics and Politics,
Volume 12, No. 1,1-31.

HENISZ, Witold J. (2002a):
Politics and International Investment: Measuring Risk and Protecting Profits,
Cheltenham.

HENISZ, Witold J. (2002b):
The Institutional Environment for Infrastructure Investment, Industrial and
Corporate Change, 11, 2, 355-389.

HENISZ, Witold J./ ZELNER, Bennet A. (2003a):
Political Risk Management: A Strategic Perspective, in: Moran, Theodore (ed.)
International Political Risk Management: The Brave New World. Washington
D.C., forthcoming.

HENISZ, Witold J./ ZELNER, Bennet A. (2003b):
Managing to Keep the Lights On (and the Profits Flowing): Political Risk
Identification, Mitigation and Analysis in Electricity Generation, Working Paper,
Wharton School, Pennsylvania.

HEREDIA, Blanca (2000):
El dilemma entre crecimiento y autonomía: reforma económica y
reestructuración de la politica exterior en México, in: Lajous, Roberta / Torres,
Blanca (eds.): México y el mundo: Historia de sus relaciones internacionales,
Tomo IX: La política exterior de México en la década de los noventa, Mexico
D.F., 29-48.

HOBBES, Thomas (1966):
Leviathan, Oxford.

HOLLAND, Kenneth M. (1999):
Los sistemas judiciales de América del Norte, in: Castro Rea, Julián, /Jackson,
Robert J./ Mahler, Gregory S. (eds.): Los sistemas políticos de América del
Norte en los años noventa, Mexico D.F., 181-212.

HOWELL, Llewellyn D. / CHADDICK, Brad (1994):
Models of Political Risk for Foreign Investment and Trade: An Assessment of three approaches, in: The Columbia Journal of World Business, 29, 70-91.

HOWELL, Llewellyn D. (ed.) (1998):
The Handbook of Country and Political Risk Analysis, 2nd edition, New York.

HOWELL, Llewellyn D. (ed.) (2001a):
The Handbook of Country and Political Risk Analysis, 3rd edition, New York.

HOWELL, Llewellyn D. (2001b):
Defining and Operationalizing Political Risk, in: Howell, Llewellyn D. (ed.): Political Risk Assessment: Concept, Method and Management, New York.

HUBBARD, R. Glenn (1994):
Investment under Uncertainty: Keeping One's Options Open, Journal of Economic Literature, 32, 4, 1816-1831.

HUNTINGTON, Samuel P. (1989):
Modernization and Corruption, Reprint from 1968 in Heidenheimer, A. / Johnston, M. / Le Vine, V. (eds.): Political Corruption: A Handbook, New Brunswick, 377-388.

HYMER, Stephen H. (1976):
The International Operations of National Firms: A Study of Direct Foreign Investment, Cambridge.

HYMER, Stephen H. (1990):
The Large Multinational Corporation: An Analysis of Some Motives for the International Integration of Business, translated from Revue Economique, 19, 6, 1968, in: Casson, Mark (ed.): Multinational Corporations, Great Yarmouth, 3-31.

IADB (2000):
Development Beyond Economics, Economic and Social Progress in Latin America 2000 Report, Washington.

IADB (2001):
Competitiveness: The Business of Growth: Economic and Social Progress in Latin America, Washington.

INEGI (2003):
Información estadística, http://www.inegi.gob.mx.

ISHAM, Jonathan et al. (1995):
Governance and Returns on Investment: an Empirical Investigation, World Bank Policy Research Paper 1550, Washington D.C.

JACKSON, Sharon / MARKOWSKI, Stefan (1995):
The Attractiveness of Countries to Foreign Direct Investment: Implications for the Asia-Pacific Region, Journal of World Trade: Law, Economics, Public Policy, 29, 5, 159-179.

JAIN, Arvind K. (2001):
Corruption: a Review, Journal of Economic Surveys, 15, 1, 71-121.

JANEBA, Eckhard (2001):
Attracting FDI in a Politically Risky World, NBER Working Paper No. 8400, Cambridge.

JORGENSON, Dale W. (1963):
Capital Theory and Investment Behaviour, American Economic Review, 53, Issue 2, Papers and Proceedings of the 75th Annual Meeting of the American Economic Association, 247-259.

JORGENSON, Dale W. (1971):
Econometric Studies of Investment Behavior: A Survey, Journal of Economic Literature, 9, No. 4, 1111-1147.

JOST, Thomas / NUNNENKAMP, Peter (2002):
Bestimmungsgründe deutscher Direktinvestitionen in Entwicklungs- und Reformländern: hat sich wirklich etwas verändert ?, Institut für Weltwirtschaft Kiel, Arbeitspapier 1124, Kiel.

JUNG, Kwang W. / SINGH, Harinder (1996):
The Determinants of Foreign Direct Investment in Developing Countries, in: Transnational Corporations, 5, 2, 67-105.

KAO, C. (1999)
Spurious Regression and Residual-based Test for Cointegration in Panel Data, Journal of Econometrics, 90, 1-44.

KATZ, Alfred (1999):
Staatsrecht: Grundkurs im öffentlichen Recht, 14. Auflage, Heidelberg.

KEENAN, Joe (1997):
La Gacetilla: How Advertising Masquerades as News, in: Orme, William A. (ed.): A Culture of Collusion: An inside look to the Mexican Press, Boulder, 41-48.

KEMSLEY, Deen (1998):
The Effect of Taxes on Production Location, in: Journal of Accounting Research, 36, 321-341.

KENNEDY, Charles R. (1991):
Managing the International Business Environment: Cases in Political and Country Risk, New Jersey.

KEYNES, John M. (1989):
The General Theory of Employment, Interest, and Money, Amherst, first published in 1936.

KINDLEBERGER, Charles P. (1969):
American Business Abroad: Six Lectures on Direct Investment, New Haven.

KLAPPER, Leora F. / LOVE, Inessa (2002):
Corporate Governance, Investor Protection, and Performance in Emerging Markets, World Bank Policy Research Working Paper 2818, Washington D.C.

KNACK, Stephen / KEEFER, Philipp (1995):
Instiutions and Economic Performance: Cross-Country Test Using Alternative Institutional Measures, Economics and Politics, 7, 3, 207-227.

KNACK, Stephen / ZAK, Paul J. (2003):
Building Trust: Public Policy, Interpersonal Trust, and Economic Development, The Rule of Law, Freedom, and Prosperity, 10, 91-107.

KNICKERBOCKER, Frederic T. (1973):
Oligopolistic Reaction and Multinational Enterprise, Boston.

KNIGHT, Alan (1988):
The Politics of Expropriation: The Mexican Petroleum Nationalization, Austin.

KNIGHT, Alan (2000):
Export-led Growth in Mexico,c.1900-1930, in: Cardenas, Enrique; Ocampo, José Antonio; Thorp, Rosemary (eds.): An Economic History of Twentieth-Century Latin America, Volume 1: The Export Age, Houndmills, Basingstoke, Hampshire.

KOJIMA, Kiyoshi (1973):
A Macroeconomic Approach to Foreign Direct Investment, Hitotshobashi Journal of Economics, 14, 1, 1-21.

KOJIMA, Kiyoshi (1977):
Direct Foreign Investment between Advanced Industrialized Countries, Reprint from Hitotshobashi Journal of Economics, 18, 1, Tokyo.

KONRAD, Kai A. (2001):
Repeated Expropriation Contests and Foreign Direct Investment, Centre for
Economic Policy Research Discussion Paper 2695, London.

KRÄMER, Moritz (1995a):
Stabilization and Poverty in Latin America, in: Sautter, Hermann (ed.):
Indebtedness, Economic Reforms, and Poverty, Frankfurt a. M., 75-122.

KRÄMER, Moritz (1995b):
Programa Nacional de Solidaridad: Poverty and Power Politics in Mexico, in:
Sautter, Hermann (ed.): Indebtedness, Economic Reforms, and Poverty,
Frankfurt a. M., 123-168.

KRÄMER, Moritz (1997):
Politische Ökonomie von Wirtschaftsreformen: Mexico 1982-1994, Frankfurt a.
M.

KRAVIS, Irving B. / LIPSEY, Robert E. (1982):
The Location of Overseas Production and Production for Exports by U.S.
Multinational Firms, Journal of International Economics, 12, 3/4, 201-223.

KURZMAN, Charles / WERUM, Regina / BURKHART, Ross E. (2002):
Democracy´s Effect on Economic Growth: A Pooled Time-Series Analysis,
1951-1980, Studies in Comparative International Development, 37, 1, 3-33.

KWON, Yung-Chul (2002):
Korean Multinationals´Foreign Direct Investment Projects: Variability in the
Micro- and Macro-Level Determinants, The International Trade Journal, 16, 2,
203-229.

LAFFONT, Jean-Jacques / TIROLE, Jean (1994):
A theory of incentives in procurement and regulation, Second Printing,
Cambridge.

LALL, Sanjaya (2002):
FDI and Development: Research Issues in the Emerging Context, in Bora, Bijit
(ed.): Foreign Direct Investment: Research Issues, London, 325-345.

LAMBSDORFF, Johann (2001):
How Corruption in Government Affects Public Welfare: a Review of Theories,
Zentrum für Globalisierung und Europäisierung der Wirtschaft, Discussion
Paper 9, Göttingen.

LANGSTON, Joy (2002):
Breaking Out is hard to Do: Exit, Voice, and Loyalty in Mexico´s One-Party
Hegemonic Regime, Latin American Politics and Society, 44, 3, 61-88.

LEAMER, Edward E. (1983)
Let´s Take the Con out of Econometrics, American Economic Review, Volume 73, Issue 3, 31-43.

LEAMER, Edward E. (1985)
Sensitivity Analysis Would Help, American Economic Review, Volume 75, Issue 3, 308-313.

LEDERMAN et al. (2001):
Mexico – Five Years after the Crisis, in: World Bank (edt.): Annual World Bank Conference on Development Economics, Washington, 263-282.

LEE, Woojin (2003):
Is Democracy More Expropriative than Dictatorship ? Tocquevillian Wisdom Revisited, Journal of Development Economics, 71, 155-198.

LESSARD, Donald R. (1993):
Country Risk and the Structure of International Finance Intermediation, in: Das, Dilip K. (ed.) International Finance: Contemporary Issues, London, New York, 451-470.

LEVINE, Ross / RENELT, David (1992):
A Sensitivity Analysis of Cross-Country Growth Regressions, American Economic Review, 82, 4, 942-963.

LEVY, Haim (1998):
Stochastic Dominance: Investment Decision Making under Uncertainty, Boston.

LEVI, Margaret (1988):
Of Rule and Revenue, Berkeley.

LIN, Nan (2001):
Social Capital: Theory and Research, New York.

LINZ, Juan J. / VALENZUELA, Arturo (1994):
Presidential or Parliamentary Democracy: Does it make a difference ?, Baltimore.

LIPSEY, Robert E. (1999):
The Role of Foreign Direct Investment in International Capital Flows, NBER Working Paper No. 7094, Cambridge.

LIPSEY, Robert E. (2001a):
Foreign Direct Investors in Three Financial Crises, NBER Working Paper No. 8084, Cambridge.

LIPSEY, Robert E. (2001b):
Foreign Direct Investment and the Operations of Multinational Firms:
Concepts, History, and Data, NBER Working Paper No. 8665, Cambridge.

LOMNITZ, Claudio (2000):
Lomnitz, Claudio (ed.) Vicios públicos, virtudes privados: la corrupción en
México, Mexico D.F.

LÓPEZ, Bruno (1997):
Balancing Act: Surviving as a Television Reporter in Mexico, in: Orme, William
A. (ed.): A Culture of Collusion: An inside look to the Mexican Press, Boulder,
89-96.

LÓPEZ PRESA, José Octavio et al. (1998):
Corrupción y cambio, Mexico D.F.

LÓPEZ PORTILLO VARGAS, Ernesto (2001):
Seguridad pública y democracia: hacia la seguridad ciudadana – relativizar al
poder frente a la libertad, in: Alvarado, Arturo / Arzt, Sigrid (eds.): El desafío
democrático de México: seguridad y Estado de derecho, México D.F., 67-79.

LÓPEZ Y RIVAS, Gilberto (2002):
Deterioro del proceso de paz en Chiapas, in: Salinas, Mario / Oswald Spring,
Úrsula (eds.): Culturas de paz: Seguridad v democracia en América Latina,
Centro Regional de Investigaciones Multidisciplibarias UNAM, Mexico D.F.,
291-304.

LOREE, David W. / GUISINGER, Stephen E. (1995):
Policy and Non-Policy Determinants of U.S. Equity Foreign Direct Investment,
Journal of International Business Studies, 26, 281-299.

LUCAS, Robert E. (1993):
On the Determinants of Foreign Direct Investment, Evidence from East and
South Asia, World Development, 21, 391-406.

LUJAMBIO, Alonso (1998):
Mexican Parties and Congressional Politics in the 90s, in: Serrano, Mónica
(ed.): Governing Mexico: Political Parties and Elections, London, 170-184.

LUNN, John (1980):
Determinants of U.S. Foreign Direct Investment in the EEC: Further Evidence,
European Economic Review, 13, 93-101.

LUSTIG, Nora Claudia; ROS, Jaime (1999):
Economic Reforms, Stabilization Policies, and the Mexican Desease, in:
Taylor, Lance (ed.): After Neoliberalism: What Next for Latin America,
Michigan.

MACHIAVELLI, Niccolo (1997):
The Prince, New Haven.

MADDALA, G. S. / WU, Shaowen (1999):
A Comparative Study of Unit-Root Tests with Panel Data and a New Simple
Test, Oxford Bulletin of Economics and Statistics, 61, 4, 631-652.

MAINWARING, Scott / SHUGART, Matthew S. (1997):
Presidentialism and Democracy in Latin America, Cambridge, New York.

MAINWARING, Scott (1999):
Democratic Survivability in Latin America, The Helen Kellogg Institute for
International Studies, Working Paper 267, Notre Dame.

MARKWICK, Sandy (2001):
Customizing Risk Analysis as a Tool for Strategic Management, in: Howell,
Llewellyn D. (edt.) (2001): Political Risk Assessment: Concept, Method and
Management, New York.

MASSICOTTE, Louis (1999):
Las legislaturas de los tres países de TLC: una evaluación comparativa, in:
Castro Rea, Julián, /Jackson, Robert J./ Mahler, Gregory S. (eds.): Los
sistemas políticos de América del Norte en los años noventa, Mexico D.F., 75-
105.

MAURO, Paolo (1995):
Corruption and Growth, Quarterly Journal of Economics, 60, 3, 681-712.

MAXFIELD, Sylvia (1990):
Governing Capital: International Finance and Mexican Politics, Ithaca, London.

MCGUIRE, Martin C. / OLSON, Mancur (1996):
The Economics of Autocracy and Majority Rule: The Invesible Hand and the
Use of Force, Journal of Economic Literature, 34, 1, 72-96.

MCILROY, James (2002):
NAFTA´s Investment Chapter: An Isolated Experiment or a Precedent for a
Multilateral Investment Treaty?, The Journal of World Investment: Law,
Economics, politics, 3, 1, 127-146.

MCKINSEY&COMPANY (2002):
Global Investor Opinion Survey, London.

MERKEL, Wolfgang (1999):
Systemtransformation: Eine Einführung in die Theorie und Empirie der
Transformationsforschung, Augsburg.

MIGA (2002):
Foreign Direct Investment Survey, Washington D.C.

MILLER, Marjorie / DARLING, Juanita (1997):
The Eye of the Tiger: Emilio Azcárraga and the Televisa Empire in: Orme,
William A. (ed.): A Culture of Collusion: An inside look to the Mexican Press,
Boulder, 59-70.

MOHENO, Roberto Blanco (1979):
La corrupción en México, Mexico D.F.

MOLANO, Walter (2001):
Approaches to Political Risk Analysis, in: Howell, Llewellyn D. (ed.) (2001):
Political Risk Assessment: Concept, Method and Management, New York, 17-
35.

MONTESQUIEU, Charles (1979):
De l´esprit des lois, first published in 1748, Paris.

MORAN, Theodore H. (1998):
Foreign Direct Investment and Development: The New Policy Agenda for
Developing Coutries and Economies in Transition, Washington D.C.

MORENO, Alejandro (1998): Party Competition and the Issue of Democracy:
Ideological Space in Mexican Elections, in: Serrano, Mónica (ed.): Governing
Mexico: Political Parties and Elections, London, 38-57.

MORENO OCAMPO, Luis (1993):
En defensa propria, 3rd edition, Buenos Aires.

MORISET, Jacques / PIRNIA, Nedia (2002):
The Impact of Tax Policy and Incentives on FDI, in: Bora, Bijit (ed.): Foreign
Direct Investment: Research Issues, London, 273-291.

MORRIS, Stephen D. (1991):
Corruption and Politics in Contemporary Mexico, Tuscaloosa, London.

MORRIS, Stephen D. (2000):
"La politica acostumbrada" o "política insólita" ? El problema de la corrupción
en el México contemporáneo, in: Lomnitz, Claudio (ed.) Vicios públicos,
virtudes privados: la corrupción en México, Mexico D.F., 221-237.

MOYNIHAN, Mary C. (1997):
Mexican News and American Diplomacy: U.S. State Department Monitoring of
Press Freedom Violations in Mexico, in: Orme, William A. (ed.): A Culture of
Collusion: An inside look to the Mexican Press, Boulder, 109-120.

MUNRO, Debra L. (1995):
From Nationalism to Nation State Building: A Time Series Analysis of Foreign Direct Investment in Mexico, Ann Arbor.

NACIF, Benito (2003):
Policy Making under Divided Government in Mexico, Hellen Kellogg Institute for International Studies, Working Paper 305, Notre Dame.

NEWFARMER, Richard (2002):
Foreign Direct Investment: Policies and Institutions for Growth, in: OECD, New Horizons for Foreign Direct Investment, Paris, 248-264.

NG, Linda F. Y. Ng / TUAN, Chyau (2002):
Building a Favorable Investment Environment : Evidence for the Facilitation of FDI In China, The world economy, 25, 8, 1095-1114.

NIGH, Douglas (1988):
The of Political Events on United States Direct Foreign Investment: A pooled Time-Series Cross Sectional Analysis, in: Journal of International Business Studies, 16, 1-17.

NORTH, Douglas C. / THOMAS, Robert Paul (1973):
The Rise of the Western World: A new economic history, Cambridge.

NORTH, Douglas C. (1986):
The New Institutional Economics, Journal of Institutional and Theoretical Economics, 142, 230-237.

NORTH, Douglas C. (1990):
Institutions, Institutional Change and Economic Performance, Cambridge.

NORTH, Douglas C. (1991):
Institutions, in: The Journal of Economic Perspectives, 5, 1, 97-112.

NYE, John V. C. (1997):
Thinking about the State: Property Rights, Trade, and Changing Contractual Arrangements in a World with Coercion, in: Drobak, John N. / Nye, John V. C. (eds.): The Frontiers of New Institutional Economics, San Diego, 121-142.

OBSTFELD, Maurice (1995):
International Capital Mobility in the 90s, in: Kennen, Peter (ed.): Understanding Interdependence, 201-261.

O'DONNELL, Guillermo (1998):
Polyarchies and the (Un)rule of Law in Latin America, The Helen Kellog
Institute for International Studies, Working Paper 254, Notre Dame.

OECD (1992):
OECD Economic Surveys: Mexico 1991/1992, Paris.

OECD(1994):
Assessing Investment Opportunities in Economies in Transition, Paris.

OECD (1996a):
Trade Liberalization Policies in Mexico, Paris.

OECD(1996b):
OECD Benchmark Definition of Foreign Direct Investment, 3rd edition, Paris.

OECD (2000):
OECD Economic Surveys: Mexico 2000, Paris.

OECD (2001):
Citicens as Partners: information, consultation and public participation in
policy-making, Paris.

OETZEL, Jennifer / BETTIS, Richard A. / ZENNER, Marc (2001):
Country Risk Measures: How Risky are They ?, Journal of World Business, 36,
2, 128-145.

OHLIN, Bertil (1933):
Interregional and International Trade, Cambridge.

OLSON, Mancur (1982):
The Rise and Decline of Nations: Economic Growth, Stagflation, and Social
Rigidities, New Haven.

OLSON, Mancur (1993):
Dictatorship, Democracy, and Development, American Political Science
Review, 87, 3, 567-576.

OMAN, Charles P. (2000):
Policy Competition for Foreign Direct Investment: A Study of Competition
Among Governments to Attract FDI, OECD Development Center Studies,
Paris.

OMAN, Charles P. (2001):
The Perils of Competition for Foreign Direct Investment, in: OECD, Foreign
Direct Investment Versus Other Flows to Latin America, Paris, 63-84.

ORME, William A. (1997):
Overview: From Collusion to Confrontation, in: Orme, William A. (ed.): A Culture of Collusion: An inside look to the Mexican Press, Boulder, 1-17.

ORTIZ, Edgar (1994):
NAFTA and Foreign Investment in Mexico, in: in: Rugman, Alan M. (edt.): Foreign Investment and NAFTA, Columbia, 155-179.

OSEGHALE, Braimoh D. (1993):
Political Instability, Interstate Conflict, Adverse Changes in Host Government Policies and Foreign Direct Investment: A Sensitivity Analysis, New York.

OTERO, Gerardo (1996):
Neoliberal Reforms and Politics in Mexico: An Overview, in: Otero, Gerardo (ed.): Neo-Liberalism Revisited: Economic Restructuring and Mexico´s Political Future, Boulder, 1-25.

PEELER, John (1998):
Building Democracy in Latin America, Boulder.

PENNER, Ann E. (1999):
Las constituciones y el federalismo, in: Castro Rea, Julián, /Jackson, Robert J./ Mahler, Gregory S. (eds.): Los sistemas políticos de América del Norte en los años noventa, Mexico D.F., 29-73.

PERES-NUÑEZ, Wilson (1990a):
Foreign Direct Investment and Industrial Development in Mexico, OECD Development Centre Studies, Paris.

PERES-NUÑEZ, Wilson (1990b):
From Globalization to Regionalization: The Mexican Case, OECD Development Center, Technical Paper 24, Paris.

PERRIDON, Louis / STEINER, Manfred (1995):
Finanzwirtschaft der Unternehmung, 8. überarbeitete Auflage, München.

PESCADOR CASTAÑEDA, Fernando (1971):
Breves antecedentes historicos sobre las inversiones extranjeras directas, in: Vázquez Tercero, Héctor (ed.): Inversiones Extranjeras Privadas en Mexico, Mexico D.F. , 69-104.

PETERS, Enrique Dussel (2000):
La inversión extranjera en México, CEPAL Publication Series „Desarollo Productivo" 80, Santiago de Chile.

PETERS, Enrique Dussel (2001):
Globalisierung auf Mexikanisch, Journal für Entwicklungspolitik, 17, 3, 4, 223-240.

PHILIP, George (1992):
The Presidency in Mexican Politics, New York.

PHILIPS, Peter C. B. / MOON, Hyungsik R. (1999)
Linear Regression Limit Theory for Non-Stationary Panel Data, Econometrica, 67, 5, 1057-1111.

PHILIPS, Peter C. B. / MOON, Hyungsik R. (2000)
Non-Stationary Panel Data Analysis: An Overview of some Recent Developments, Econometric Reviews, 19, 3, 263-286.

PINDYCK, Robert S. (1991):
Irreversibility, Uncertainty and Investment, Journal of Economic Literature, 29, 3, 1110-1148.

PINDYCK, Robert S. / RUBINFELD, Daniel L. (1991)
Econometric Models and Economic Forecasts, 3rd edition, New York, St. Louis, San Francisco.

PRILLAMAN, William C. (2000):
The Judiciary and Democratic Decay in Latin America: Declining Confidence in the Rule of Law, Westport.

PRITZL, Rupert F. J. (1997):
Korruption und Rent-Seeking in Lateinamerika: Zur politischen Ökonomie autoritärer politischer Systeme, zugl. Dissertation Universität Freiburg, Baden-Baden.

PRS Group (1995):
Political Risk Yearbook 1995, Mexico, East Syracuse.

PRS Group (1998):
IRIS III Dataset, East Syracuse.

PRS Group (1999):
Political Risk Yearbook 1999, Mexico, East Syracuse.

PRS Group (2000):
Political Risk Yearbook 2000, Mexico, East Syracuse.

PRS Group (2003):
Political Risk Data, East Syracuse.

PRUD´HOME, Jean Francois (1998):
The Instituto Federal Electoral (IFE): Building an Impartial Electoral Authority, in: Serrano, Mónica (ed.): Governing Mexico: Political Parties and Elections, London, 139-155.

PRZEWORSKI, Adam / LIMONGI, Fernando (1993):
Political Regimes and Growth, The Journal of Economic Perspectives, 7, Issue 3, 51-69.

PRZEWORSKI, Adam et al. (2000):
Democracy and Development: Political Institutions and Well-Being in the World 1950-1990, Cambridge.

PUTNAM, Robert (1993):
Making Democracy Work: Civic Traditions in Modern Italy, Princeton.

PWC (1991):
Doing business in Mexico, Mexico D.F.

PWC (2001a):
The Opacity Index.

PWC (2001b):
Investigating the cost of opacity: Deterred Foreign Direct Investment.

RABASA, Emilio / ARIAS, Alán (2002):
La política del estado mexicano ante la insureección dek EZLN, in: Salinas, Mario / Oswald Spring, Úrsula (eds.): Culturas de paz: Seguridad v democracia en América Latina, Centro Regional de Investigaciones Multidisciplibarias UNAM, Mexico D.F. , 277-290.

RAMIREZ, Miguel D. (2000):
Foreign Direct Investment in Mexico: A Cointegration Analysis, Journal of Development Studies, 37, 1, 138-162.

RAMIREZ, Miguel D. (2001):
Foreign Direct Investment in Mexico and Chile: A Critical Appraisal, in: Baer, Werner / Miles, William R. (eds.): Foreign Direct Investment in Latin America: Ist Changing Nature at the Turn of the Century, Binghampton, 55-82.

RAMIREZ, Miguel D. (2002):
Foreign Direct Investment in Mexico during the 1990s: An Empirical Assessment, Eastern Economic Journal, 28, 3, 409-423.

RAWLS, John (1971):
A Theory of Justice, Cambridge.

RAZ, Joseph (1977):
The Rule of Law and Its Virtue, The Law Quarterly Review, 93, 195-211.

RICHTER, Rudolf / FURUBOTN, Eirik (1999):
Neue Institutionenökonomik, 2. Auflage,Tübingen.

RICO, Carlos (2000):
México y el mundo: Historia de sus relaciones exteriores, Tomo VIII: Hacia la globalización, Mexico D.F.

RIVA PALACIO, Raymundo (1997):
A Culture of Collusion: The Ties that Bind the Press and the PRI, in: Orme, William A. (ed.): A Culture of Collusion: An inside look to the Mexican Press, Boulder, 21-32.

ROBERTSON, David (2002):
Multilateral Investment Rules, in: Bora, Bijit (ed.): Foreign Direct Investment: Research Issues, London, 310-323.

RODRÍGUEZ, Francisco (2000):
The Political Economy of Latin American Growth, Paper prepared for the World Bank´s Global Development Network Research Project, Washington D.C.

RODRÍGUEZ, Rogelio Hernández (1998a):
Parliamentary Elites and the Polarisation of the Party System in Mexico, in: Serrano, Mónica (ed.): Governing Mexico: Political Parties and Elections, London, 58-68.

RODRÍGUEZ, Rogelio Hernández (1998b):
The Partido Revolucionario Institutional, in: Serrano, Mónica (ed.): Governing Mexico: Political Parties and Elections, London, 71-94.

RODRÍGUEZ, Rogelio Hernández (1999):
El presidencialsimo Mexicano: Cuanto es indispensable limitarlo ?, in: Migallón, Fernando Serrano (ed.): Homenaje a Rafael Segoria, Mexico D.F.

RODRIK, Dani (2001):
Why is there so much economic insecurity in Latin America ?, CEPAL Review, No.73, 7-30.

ROLFE, Robert J. et al. (1993):
Determinants of FDI Incentive Preferences of MNEs, Journal of International Business Studies, 24, 335-355.

ROMER, David (2001):
Advanced Macroeconomics, 2nd edition, New York.

ROOT, Franklin R. (1968):
Attitude of American Executives Towards Foreign Government and Investment Opportunities, Economic and Business Bulletin, 2.

ROOT, Franklin R. (1973):
Analyzing Political Risks in International Business, in: Kapoor, Ashok / Grub, Phillip D. (eds.): The Multinational Enterprise in Transition: Selected Readings and Essays, Princeton, 354-365.

ROOT, Franklin R. (1994):
International Trade and Investment, 7th edition, Cincinnati.

ROS, Jaime (1993):
Mexico´s Trade and Industialization Experience since 1960: A Reconsideration of Past Policies and Assessment of Current Reforms, Kellogg Institute, Working Paper 186, Notre Dame.

RUBIO, Luis et al. (1994):
A la puerta de la ley: El estado de derecho en México, México D.F.

RUGMAN, Alan M. (1981):
Inside the Multinationals: The Economics of Internal Markets, London.

RUGMAN, Alan M. / GESTRIN, Michael (1994):
NAFTA´s Treatment of Foreign Direct Investment, in: Rugman, Alan M. (edt.): Foreign Investment and NAFTA, Columbia, 47-79.

SACERDOTI, Giorgio (2000):
The Admission and treatment of Foreign Investment under Recent Bilateral and Regional Treaties, Journal of World Investment: Law, Economics and Politics, 1, 1, 105-126.

SADER, Frank. (1993):
Privatization and Foreign Investment in the Developing World: 1988-1992, World Bank Policy Research Working Paper 1202, Washington D.C.

SÁNCHEZ, Manuel et al. (1993):
The Privatization Process in Mexico: Five Case Studies, in: Sánchez, Manuel; Corona, Rossana (eds.): Privatization in Latin America, Inter-American Development Bank, Washington D.C.

SÁNCHEZ-GAMPER, Philipe Alphonse (1989):
Del Coflicto al Consenso: Los empresarios y la politica de inversiones extranjeras en Mexico 1944-1970, Mexico D.F.

SANDRINO, Gloria L. (1994): The Nafta Investment Chapter and Foreign Investment in Mexico: A Third World Perspective, Vanderbilt Journal of Transnational Law, 27, 4, 259-327.

SARMIENTO, Sergio (1997):
Trial by Fire: The Chiapas Revolt, the Colossio Assassination, and the Mexican Press in 1994, in: Orme, William A. (ed.): A Culture of Collusion: An inside look to the Mexican Press, Boulder, 33-39.

SARRE, Miguel (2001):
Seguridad ciudadana y justicia penal frente a la democracia, la division de poderes y el federalismo, in: El desafío democrático de México: Seguridad y estado de derecho, México D.F., 83-114.

SCHIFFER, Mirjam / WEDER, Beatrice (2000):
Catastrophic Political Risk versus Creeping Expropriation: What determines Private Infrastructure Investment in Less Developed Countries, ISNIE Working Paper, Prepared for the annual meeting 2000.

SCHINKE, Rolf (1993):
Debt-Equity Swaps: Cost and Benefits, in: Sautter, Hermann (ed.): Economic Reforms in Latin America, Göttinger Studien zur Entwicklungsökonomik, Frankfurt a. M., 97-130.

SCHMIDT, Manfred G. (2000):
Demokratietheorien, 3. Auflage, Augsburg.

SCHMITZ, Andrew / BIERI, Jurg (1972):
EEC tariffs and U.S. Direct Investments, in: European Economic Review, 3, 259-270.

SCHNEIDER, Friedrich / FREY, Bruno S. (1985):
Economic and Political Determinants of Foreign Direct Investment, World Development, 13,161-175.

SCHÖLLHAMMER, Hans (1978):
Identification, Evaluation and Prediction of Political Risks From an International Business Perspective, in: Gehrtman, Michel / Leontiades, James (eds.): European Research in International Business, Amsterdam, 91-109.

SCHUMPETER, Joseph A. (1993):
Capitalism, Socialism and Democracy, London.

SECRETARÍA DE ECONOMÍA (2002):
Inversión de la Union Europea en Mexico, Mexico D.F.

SECRETARÍA DEL TRABAJO Y PREVISIÓN SOCIAL (1994):
Inversión extranjera y empleo en México, Mexico D.F.

SEMO, Ilán (1996):
The Mexican Political Pretransition in Comparative Perspective, in: Otero,
Gerardo (ed.): Neo-Liberalism Revisited: Economic Restructuring and
Mexico´s Political Future, Boulder, 107-126.

SEPÚLVEDA, Bernardo / CHUMACERO, Antonio (1973):
La inversion extranjera en México, Mexico D.F.

SHAMSUDDIN, Abul F. M. (1994):
Economic Determinants of Foreign Direct Investment in Less Developed
Countries, The Pakistan Development Review, 33, 41-51.

SHEPSLE, Kenneth A. (1991):
Discretion, Institutions, and the Problem of Government Commitment, in:
Bourdieu, Pierre; Coleman, James S. (eds.): Social Theory for a Changing
Society, Boulder, 245-266.

SHERWOOD, Robert M. et al. (1994):
Judicial Systems and Economic Performance, World Bank, Washington D.C.

SIMON, Jeffrey D. (1982):
Political Risk Assessment: Past Trends and Future Prospects, in: Columbia
Journal
of World Business,17, 62-71.

SIQUEIROS, José Luis (2001):
An Overview of Arbitration Mechnisms Between States and Investors: The
Mexican Experience, Journal of World Investment: Law, Economics and
Politics, 2, 2, 249-257.

SMITH, Adam (1976):
Inquiry into the Nature and Causes of the Wealth of Nations, Chicago.

SMITH, Clifford Neil (1971):
Predicting the Political Environment of International Business, Long Range
Planning, 4, 7-14.

SOLOMON, Joel (1997):
The Measure of Violence: Problems in Documentation, in: Orme, William A.
(ed.): A Culture of Collusion: An inside look to the Mexican Press, Boulder,
121-129.

STEIN, Ernesto / DAUDE, Christian (2002):
Institutions, Integration and the Location of Foreign Direct Investment, in:
OECD, New Horizons for FDI, Paris, 101-128.

SUN, Qian / TONG, Wilson / YU, Qiao (2002):
Determinants of Foreign Direct Investment across China, in: Journal of
International Money and Finance, 21, 79-113.

SUTHERLAND, Sharon (1999): El poder ejecutivo y la adminitración pública en
Estados Unidos, Canadá y México, in: Castro Rea, Julián, /Jackson, Robert J./
Mahler, Gregory S. (eds.): Los sistemas políticos de América del Norte en los
años noventa, Mexico D.F., 107-179.

SWAN, Mony de / MARTORELLI, Paola / MOLINAR HORCASITAS, Juan (1998):
Public Financing of Political Parties and Electoral Expenditures in Mexico, in:
Serrano, Mónica (ed.): Governing Mexico: Political Parties and Elections,
London, 139-155.

SWEDENBORG, Brigitta (1979):
The Multinational Operations of Swedish Firms: An Analysis of Determinants
and Effects, Industrial Institute of Economic and Social Research, Stockholm.

SWENSON, Deborah L. (1994):
The Impact of U.S. Tax Reform on Foreign Direct Investment in United States,
Journal of Public Economics, 54, 243-266.

TAMAYO Y SALMORÁN, Rolando (1989):
Introducción al estudio de la constitución, Mexico D.F.

TAVARES, José / WACZIARG, Romain (2001):
How Democracy Affects Growth, European Economic Review, 45, 1341-1378.

THEOBALD, Christian (1999):
Zur Ökonomik des Staates: Good Governance und die Perzeption der
Weltbank, Baden-Baden.

TOBIN James (1969):
A General Equilibrium Approach To Monetary Theory, in: Journal of Money,
Credit and Banking, 1, Issue 1,15-29.

TRANSPARENCY INTERNATIONAL (2001):
National Survey on Corruption and Governance (NSCG) / Encuestra nacional
de Corrupcion y Buen Gobierno, Mexico D.F.

TRANSPARENCY INTERNATIONAL (2003):
Corruption Perceptions Index 2003, (and older Volumes),
http://wwwuser.gwdg.de/~uwvw/corruption.cpi_2003.html.

TSAI, Pan-long (1994):
Determinants of Foreign Direct Investment and Its Impact on Economic
Growth, Journal of Economic Development, 19, 1, 137-163.

TSEBELIS, George (1995):
Decision Making in Political Systems: Veto Players in Presidentialism,
Parliamentarism, Multicameralism and Multipartism, British Journal of Political
Science, 25, 289-325.

TU, Jenn-Hwa / SCHIVE, Chi (1995):
Determinants of Foreign Direct Investment in Taiwan Province of China: A
New Approach and Findings, Transnational Corporations, 4, 2, 93-103.

TULLOCK, Gordon (2002a):
Undemocratic Governments, Kyklos, 55, 2, 247-264.

TULLOCK, Gordon (2002b):
The Theory of Public Choice, in: Tullock, Gordon / Seldon, Arthur / Brady
Gordon L. (eds.): Government Failure: A Primer in Public Choice, Washington,
3-79.

TUMAN, John P. / EMMERT, Craiq F. (1999):
Explaining Japanese Foreign Direct Investment Latin America 1979-1992,
Social Science Quarterly, 80, 539-555.

UN (1992):
The Determinants of Foreign Direct Investment: A Survey of the Evidence,
New York.

UNCTAD (1994):
World Investment Report 1994: Transnational Corporations, Employment and
the Workplace, New York, Geneva.

UNCTAD (1999a):
Lessons from the MAI, New York, Geneva.

UNCTAD (1999b):
World Investment Report 1999: Foreign Direct Investment and the Challenge
of Development, New York, Geneva.

UNCTAD (2000):
World Investment Report 2000: Cross-border Mergers and Acquisitions and
Development, New York, Geneva.

UNCTC (1992):
FDI and Industrial Restructuring in Mexico, New York.

UNDP (2000):
World Income Inequality Database, New York.

UNGAR, Mark (2002):
Elusive Reform: Democracy and the Rule of Law in Latin America, Boulder.

VÁZQUEZ TERCERO, Héctor (1971):
La politica mexicana sobre inversiones extranjeras, in: Vázquez Tercero,
Héctor (ed.): Inversiones Extranjeras Privadas en Mexico, Mexico D.F.

VERNON, Raymond (1963):
The Dilemma of Mexico´s Development: The Roles of the Private and Public
Sectors, Cambridge.

VERNON, Raymond (1966a):
An Interpretation of the Mexican View, in: Vernon, Raymond (ed.): How Latin
America Views the U.S. Investor, New York, 95-117.

VERNON, Raymond (1966b):
International Investment and Trade in the Product Cycle, The Quarterly
Journal of Economics, 80, Issue 2, 190-207.

WEI, Shang-Jin (2000):
How Taxing is Corruption on International Investors ?, The Review of
Economics and Statistics, 82, 1, 1-11.

WEILER, Todd (2001):
Metalclad v. Mexico: A play in three parts, Journal of World Investment: Law,
Economics and Politics, 2, 4, 685-711.

WEIMER, David L. (1997):
The Political Economy of Property Rights, in: Weimer, David L. (ed.): The
Political Economy of Property Rights: Institutional Change and Credibility in
the Reform of Centrally Planned Economies, Cambridge, 1-19.

WELDON, Jeffrey (1997):
The Logic of Presidencialismo in Mexico, in: Mainwaring, Scott / Shugart,
Matthew S. (eds.): Presidentialism and Democracy in Latin America,
Cambridge, New York, 225-258.

WELLS, Louis T. et al. (2001):
Using Tax Incentives to Compete for Foreign Investment: Are they Worth the Cost ?, FIAS Occasional Paper 15, Washington D.C.

WEST, Gerald T. (2001):
Managing Project Political Risk, in: Howell, Llewellyn D. (edt.) (2001): Political Risk Assessment: Concept, Method and Management, New York, 47-58.

WEST, Gerald T. / MARTIN, Keith (2001a):
The Resurgence of Political Risk Insurance, in: Howell, Llewellyn D. (edt.) (2001): Political Risk Assessment: Concept, Method and Management, New York, 139-162.

WEST, Gerald T. / MARTIN, Keith (2001b):
The Political Risk Insurance: The Renaissance Revisited, in: Moran, Theodore H. (ed.): International Political Risk Management: Exploring New Frontiers, Washington D.C., 207-230.

WHEELER, David / MODY, Ashok (1992):
International Investment Location decision: The Case of U.S. firms, Journal of International Economics, 33,1/2, 57-76.

WHITE, Halbert (1980):
A Heteroskedasticity-Consistent Covariance Matrix Estimator and a Direct Test Heteroskedasticity, Econometrica, 48, 817-838.

WHITING, Susan H. (1998):
The Mobilization of Private Investment as a Problem of Trust in Local Governance Structures, in: Braithwaite, Valerie / Levi, Margaret (eds.): Trust and Governance, New York, 167-193.

WHITING, Van R. (1992):
The Political Economy of Foreign Investment in Mexico: Nationalism, Liberalism, and Constraints on Choice, Baltimore.

WILLIAMSON, John (2001):
Issues Regarding the Composition of Capital Flows, Development Policy Review, 19, 1, 12-29.

WILLIAMSON, Oliver E. (1985):
The Economic Institutions of Capitalism: Firms, Markets, Relational Contracting, New York.

WILLIAMSON, Oliver E. (1991):
Comparative Economic Organization: The Analysis of Discrete Structural Alternatives, Administrative Science Quarterly, 36, 2, 269-296.

WINTROBE, Ronald (1998):
Lessons of Democracy from a Study of Dictatorship, in: Borner, Silvio /
Paldam, Martin (eds.): The Political Dimension of Economic Growth,
Basingstoke, Hampshire, 20-37.

WINTROBE, Ronald (2001):
How to Understand, and Deal with Dictatorship: an economist´s view,
Economics of Governance, 2, 1, 35-58.

WIONCZEK, Miguel S. (1966):
A Latin American View, in: Vernon, Raymond (ed.): How Latin America Views
the U.S. Investor, New York, 3-48.

WOODWARD, Douglas P. / ROLFE, Robert J. (1993):
The Location of Export-oriented Foreign Direct Investment in the Caribbean
Basin, Journal of international business studies 24, 121-144.

WOOLCOCK (2002):
Social Capital in Theory and Practice: where do we stand ?, in: Isham,
Jonathan et al. (eds.): Social Capital and Economic Development: Well Being
in Developing Countries, Cheltenham, 18-39.

WOOLDRIDGE, Jeffrey M. (2002)
Econometric Analysis of Cross Section and Panel Data, Cambridge, London.

WORLD BANK (1994):
Governance: The World Bank's Experience, Washington D.C.

WORLD BANK (1997):
The State in a Changing World, World Development Report 1997, Washington
D.C.

WORLD BANK (1998):
Beyond the Washington Consensus: Institutions Matter, Washington D C.

WORLD BANK (2000):
Anticorruption in Transition: A Contribution to the Policy Debate, Washington
D.C.

WORLD BANK (2002a):
Global Development Finance, Washington D.C.

WORLD BANK (2002b):
World Development Indicators, Washington D.C.

WORLD BANK (2003):
Sustainable Development in a Dynamic World: Transforming Institutions,
Growth, and Quality of Life, World Development Report 2003, Washington.

WORLD ECONOMIC FORUM (2002):
The Global Competitiveness Report 2001/2002, New York, Oxford.

WRIGHT, Harry K. (1971):
Foreign enterprise in Mexico: Laws and Policies, Chapel Hill.

WTO (2003):
World Trade Report 2003, Geneva.

ZELNER, Bennet A. / HENISZ, Witold J. (1999):
Political Risk and Infrastructure Investment, Paper prepared for the World
Bank Conference in Rome, September 8-10, Washington.

Göttinger Studien zur Entwicklungsökonomik
Göttingen Studies in Development Economics

Herausgegeben von / Edited by Hermann Sautter

Die Bände 1-8 sind über die Vervuert Verlagsgesellschaft (Frankfurt/M.) zu beziehen.

Bd./Vol. 9   Hermann Sautter / Rolf Schinke (eds.): Social Justice in a Market Economy. 2001.

Bd./Vol.10   Philipp Albert Theodor Kircher: Poverty Reduction Strategies. A comparative study applied to empirical research. 2002.

Bd./Vol.11   Matthias Blum: Weltmarktintegration, Wachstum und Innovationsverhalten in Schwellen ländern. Eine theoretische Diskussion mit einer Fallstudie über „Argentinien 1990-1999". 2003.

Bd./Vol.12   Jan Müller-Scheeßel: Die Privatisierung und Regulierung des Wassersektors. Das Beispiel Buenos Aires/Argentinien. 2003.

Bd./Vol.13   Ludger J. Löning: Economic Growth, Biodiversity Conservation, and the Formation of Human Capital in a Developing Country. 2004.

Bd./Vol.14   Silke Woltermann: Transitions in Segmented Labor Markets. The Case of Brazil. 2004.

Bd./Vol.15   Jörg Stosberg: Political Risk and the Institutional Environment for Foreign Direct Investment in Latin America. An Empirical Analysis with a Case Study on Mexico. 2005.

www.peterlang.de

Ralph Leonhardt

Foreign Direct Investment, Ownership, and the Transfer of Technology

Frankfurt am Main, Berlin, Bern, Bruxelles, New York, Oxford, Wien, 2004.
164 pp., num. tab.
European University Studies: Series 5, Economics and Management.
Vol. 3085
ISBN 3-631-52558-3 / US-ISBN 0-8204-7302-2 · pb. € 34.–*

Using a survey of more than 1000 German investment projects in Central and Eastern Europe, this study analyses the strategies of international joint ventures. Their risks and, in particular, their innovative potential is investigated. As a statistical tool for the analysis of share equations the conditional Tobit model is introduced. The theoretical base is a continuous time, full information model of a joint venture. Surprisingly, sufficient and necessary conditions for joint venture instability and technology transfer can be derived. The survey is used to apply the introduced concepts and to demonstrate the validity of the approach empirically.

Contents: The Econometrics of Ownership Shares · Conditional Tobit Estimation · International Technology Transfer and the Joint Venture Lifecycle · Spillover and Joint Venture Instability · The Value of Transferred Knowlege · Policy Recommendations · Appendix

Frankfurt am Main · Berlin · Bern · Bruxelles · New York · Oxford · Wien
Distribution: Verlag Peter Lang AG
Moosstr. 1, CH-2542 Pieterlen
Telefax 00 41 (0) 32 / 376 17 27

*The €-price includes German tax rate
Prices are subject to change without notice
Homepage http://www.peterlang.de

Peter Lang · Europäischer Verlag der Wissenschaften